HOUSING IN ZIMBABWE: STEWARDSHIP AND PERI-URBANITY IN CONTEMPORARY AFRICA

INNOCENT CHIRISA

HOUSING IN ZIMBABWE: STEWARDSHIP AND PERI-URBANITY IN CONTEMPORARY AFRICA

INNOCENT CHIRISA

ACADEMICA PRESS
WASHINGTON – LONDON

Library of Congress Cataloging-in-Publication Data

Names: Chirisa, Innocent, author.
Title: Housing in Zimbabwe : stewardship and peri-urbanity in contemporary Africa / Innocent Chirisa.
Description: Washington : Academica Press, 2020. | Includes bibliographical
references and index. | Summary: "This book is a study of peri-urban housing development planning in Africa"-- Provided by publisher.
Identifiers: LCCN 2019036016 | ISBN 9781680531978 (hardcover)
Subjects: LCSH: Urbanization--Environmental aspects--Zimbabwe. | Housing--Environmental aspects--Zimbabwe. | City planning--Zimbabwe. |
Environmental management--Zimbabwe.
Classification: LCC HT384.Z55 C55 2019 | DDC 307.76096891--dc23
LC record available at https://lccn.loc.gov/2019036016

Contents

CHAPTER 1
HOUSING, ENVIRONMENT AND PERI-URBANITY: AN OVERVIEW

Overall, the concepts of housing, stewardship, peri-urbanisation and peri-urbanity are complex. It is asserted that suburbanisation or peri-urbanisation "…has always been with us" and are synonymous with urban sprawl[1]. Peri-urbanisation (also referred to as peri-urban growth or "suburban expansion" is typified by housing development[2]. The physical house (shelter) and accompanying infrastructure make up a habitat. Housing is, thus, a collection of many elements that include aspects of transport and circulation and health and sanitation[3]. It also entails the

---

[1] Day. B, "The Quality of Sprawl" *Tom Mckenna Memorial Lecture*, pp2 <URL:http://www.greataustraliandream.net.au >, *Accessed on 6 March 2007*.(2005)

[2] Torres.H. et.al., São Paulo Peri-Urban Dynamics: Some Social Causes and Environmental Consequences (2008:3)

[3] Bourne, "The Geography of Housing," *V H Winston and Sons Ltd:* London. (1981); Ozaki. R,Uršic.M, "What makes "urban" urban and "suburban" suburban? Urbanity and patterns of consumption in everyday life," *Paper presented at the Sociology of Consumption Research Network, the ESA 2005 Conference, Toruń, Poland, 9-12 September 2005*. <URL: http://www.sifo.no/files/Ozaki_Ursic.pdf,> *Accessed on 27 June 2011*. (2005); Hardoy et al., "The Poor Die Young: Housing and Health in Third World Cities," *Earthscan Publications Ltd*: London.(1990); McElfish J.M, "Commentary: Ten Things Wrong with Sprawl," <URL: http://www.emagazine.com /view/?3641,> *Accessed on 22 April 2008.* (2008); Light.I, "Immigration and Ethnic Economies in Giant Cities, in Crowley, John (ed.)" *International Social Science Journal Issue 181*, Blackwell Publishing/UNESCO: Paris. (2004); Walt. G, "Health Policy – an introduction to process and power," *Zed Books. London*.(1994); Marshall. F, "What does peri-urban sustainability mean in the context of Delhi?" <URL: http: //stepscentre-thecrossing.blogspot.com / 2008 / 12/ what-does-peri-urban-sustainability.html:>, *Accessed on 2April 2009*.(4 December 2008); Siyeni.Y.M, "Expanding Water Service Delivery through Partnership between Water Utility and Small Scale Water Providers in Lusaka, Zambia" *A Case of Lusaka"s Peri-Urban Areas.* University essay from Linköpings universitet/Tema vatten i natur och samhälle<. URL: http://www.essays. se/essay/4d116540c8/,> *Accessed on 14 August 2010*. (2008)

development of social classification and administration and governance structures and processes[4].

This chapter seeks to review literature in light of the following four objectives of this study on housing and peri-urban stewardship: identifying and classifying stakeholders in housing delivery in the peri-urban zones with the view of explaining policy and practical bearings by each over time, explanation on differential processes and trends in the transformation and quality of the physical provision of shelter (stocks) in peri-urban settlements, relating global and regional efforts in the housing and stewardship debate and practices regarding peri-urban settlements, and, proposing practical and policy alternatives in tackling peri-urban housing and stewardship matters at different levels of analysis (local and regional). In light of these objectives, the chapter therefore, diagnoses the following topics: sustainability in peri-urban human settlements, theories and approaches to stewardship, instruments and mechanisms for peri-urban sustainability[5]. The other topics are stewardship and collaboration of actors, classification of actors in the shaping of peri-urban settlements, processes in peri-urban housing, global and regional practices in peri-urban housing and stewardship and continuity and change – urban and peri-urban settlement policies in Zimbabwe. The overall aim of the chapter is to answer theoretically the questions: How, and by what standards, is stewardship a sustainability factor in housing and environmental processes of peri-urban habitats? Who and by what instruments do actors demonstrate this stewardship of place?

---

[4] Duany et al.. "Suburban Nation," *The Rise of Sprawl and the Decline of the American Dream,* North Point Press: New York. (2003); Kamete. A. Y, et.al,, "Managing the interface between urban councils and the surrounding rural districts councils" *The case of Bulawayo City Council and Umguza Rural District Council.* Municipal Development Programme for Eastern and Southern Africa (MDP-ESA): Harare.(2001); Kamete,"Governance for sustainability? Balancing social and environmental concerns in Harare," *Chr.Michelsen Institute. <URL: www.cmi.no.>* (2002a).

[5] Mobile Lives Forum, "Sustainbale mobilities in peri-urban areas," *Which lifestyles in the alter-urbain, suburban rural/citta diffusa/Zwischenstadt? Brochure for The 2nd International Meeting of Mobile Lives Forum on January the 24th and 25th,* 2013 at the Maison Rouge, Paris 12 (2012)

Human settlements, in general, portray certain critical patterns that reveal that communities not only depend on their environments[6]. In the process, resources are exploited sometimes to the effect of degrading the environment, leaving huge scars and eyesores on it. Certainly, there is profound dependency on the natural environment by the peri-urban dwellers and such is an issue in *usus, habitatio* and *usufruct* in land law[7]. Usus means the legal right one has to use the other's property; habitation refers to the right to occupy a dwelling; and, usufruct is the right to enjoy the fruits that result within the space and domain or space that one has access to[8]. In place stewardship, it is critical to see the link between rights, access and use to space and what it provides to inhabitants[9].

Most peri-urban dwellers operate on the off-plot space around them for different purposes: farming, extractions, dumping, to name these three[10]. As the study shall demonstrate, the two settlements under study – Ruwa and Epworth, public common spaces have become the new places of work especially by the poor households. Overall, the common spaces are important elements as natural and physical capital in space. Place stewardship and housing are critical in endeavours to understand peri-urban development. In Zimbabwe, generally, urban sprawl, explained by

---

[6] Huby. M, "Social Policy and the Environment," Open University Press: Buckingham; HUCHZERMEYER M., "The new instrument for upgrading informal settlements in South Africa: Contributions and Constraints, " *UCT Press*, Cape Town. (2006).

[7] Urimah (2010)

[8] Green. C, "An Analysis of the Use Of Limited Real Rights in Tax Planning." *Unpublished MBA Thesis, Faculty of Business and Economic Sciences,* Nelson Mandela Metropolitan University. <URL:http://dspace.nmmu.ac.za:8080/jspui/bitstream/10948/809/1/Consolidated%20thesis%20document%20_V3_%203_.pdf,> *Accessed on 01 May 2013.* (2008)

[9] Mobile Lives Forum, "Sustainbale mobilities in peri-urban areas," *Which lifestyles in the alter-urbain, suburban rural/citta diffusa/Zwischenstadt? Brochure for The 2nd International Meeting of Mobile Lives Forum on January the 24th and 25th,* 2013 at the Maison Rouge, Paris 12 (2012)

[10] Allen, "Environmental planning and management of the peri-urban interface: perspectives on an emerging field." *Environment & Urbanisation* 15(1) (2003) pp. 135-147; Mobile Lives Forum, "Sustainbale mobilities in peri-urban areas," *Which lifestyles in the alter-urbain, suburban rural/citta diffusa/Zwischenstadt? Brochure for The 2nd International Meeting of Mobile Lives Forum on January the 24th and 25th,* 2013 at the Maison Rouge, Paris 12 (2012)

massive shelter developments on the horizontal plane, is a cause of concern in urban environmental management debates and circles[11]. Place stewardship implies stakeholders being in the forefront of determining their own destiny[12]. Thus, the notion has generational implications. Failure to acknowledge the views, aspirations, interests and values by various peri-urban stakeholders means futility towards the creation of sustainable peri-urban human settlements.

Peri-urban areas being zones of transition imply that their sustainable management is a concern for many groups including planners and the people staying there. Spatially, the dwelling conditions especially for the poor and low-income, the peri-urban produce complex realities for example regarding issues of transactions in land, land degradation and sanitary living. Sustainable development of peri-urban settlements is difficult and complex given an array of factors militating against it; largely it tends to happen in a haphazard manner[13]. The environment is a key component to the production, consumption and recreational patterns governing housing and place stewardship[14]. Overall, the subject of sustainability is not only about continuity but, also about dialogue and the creation of forums and contracts that shape places and the people that dwell there. Sustainability of 'precarious' places like the peri-urban is

---

[11] Mutanga. B, "Housing Shortages because of Legislation, Policy and Attitude," *National Housing Convention Report (Public Private Partnership) Victoria Falls Nov. 1997,* National Housing Convention (1997), pp 106-108; McElfish, "Commentary: Ten Things Wrong with Sprawl," <URL: http://www.emagazine. com/view /?3641>,*Accessed on 22 April 2008*. (2008)

[12] McKinney et al., "Working across Boundaries: A Framework for Regional Collaboration, in LeRoyer Ann ed. Land Lines 16(3)," *Lincoln Institute of Land Policy*, Cambridge (USA). (2004)

[13] Oram.N, "Towns in Africa," *Oxford University Press*: London,(1965); Irurah.D, "Urbanisation and Housing Challenges: Cities in Africa Conference." *Parallel sessions on urban land management – Rapporteur"s Report;* December 8, 2003. (2003); Muzvidziwa. V.N, "Informal Settlement Dwellers and Environmental Problems." *UNISWA Research Journal of Agriculture, Science and Technology (Special Volume No. 1)*(2005) pp 25-37. ; Chirisa. I, "Population Growth and Rapid Urbanisation in Africa: Implications for Sustainability." *Journal of Sustainable Development in Africa 10(2),*(2008) pg.364-391.

[14] BHP,BHP Billiton Sustainability Report. <URL:http://www. bhpbilliton. com / home/ investors / reports / Documents / 2006SummarySustainabilityReport.pdf, > *Accessed on 7 November 2007.*(2006).

complicated by the fact that the areas are fluid and unstable. In this view, it is acknowledged that

> this space is in fact much more complex and diverse, giving rise to a number of concepts to better grasp it: alter-urban, suburban, rings, *périurbain, citta diffusa, Zwischenstadt*, etc. This could be another way for modern societies to spatialise themselves, not necessarily in conflict with compact cities but in coexistence and complementarity.[15]

Stewardship revolves around finding solutions of better management and environmental sustainability[16]. Apparently, environmental sustainability is essentially about striking a balance between three factors: economy (market), ecology and equity (society)[17]. These factors are the three concerns of prosperity, planet and people, respectively[18]. It is therefore imperative to try to dissect between the conceptual and operational meanings of terms discussed in this book as to infer appropriate understanding to the gist of the matters at hand.

In most developing countries, many major cities are 'spilling-over' their populations into the adjacent smaller settlements whose populations also continue to grow by leaps and bounce[19]. Thus, behind the

---

[15] Mobile Lives Forum,"Sustainbale mobilities in peri-urban areas," *Which lifestyles in the alter-urbain, suburban rural/citta diffusa/Zwischenstadt? Brochure for The 2nd International Meeting of Mobile Lives Forum on January the 24th and 25th,* 2013 at the Maison Rouge, Paris 12pg 1, (2012)

[16] Conforth, 2004; Pastoriza.D; Arino.A, "When Agents Become Stewards: Introducing Learning in the Stewardship Theory." <URL: http://www.iese.edu/en/files/6_40618.pdf,> *Accessed on 21 June 2008.(*2008)

[17] Habitat Platform, "Treasures in your neighbourhood: International exchange at neighbourhood level." *VNG Uitgeverij: The Hague.*(2002); Nnkya.T. J, "Why planning does not work? Land-use planning and residents rights in Tanzania," *Mkuki na Nyota Publishers*: Dar es Salaam. (2008); Beatley. T, "Biophilic Cities: Integrating Nature into Urban Design and Planning," *Island Press,* Washington. (2011)

[18] Ansell. N; van Blerk. L, "Where we stayed was very bad…"-migrant children"s perspectives on life in informal rented accommodation in two southern African cities. *Environment and Planning 37*: pp423-440. (2004); Kamete. A,Y, "Governance for sustainability? Balancing social and environmental concerns in Harare," *Chr.Michelsen Institute.* <URL: www.cmi.no.>(2002); Savory.A, "Holistic Resource Management," *Gilmour Publishing*. Harare, (1988)

[19] Briggs.J; Mwamfupe.D, "Peri-urban development in an era of Structural Adjustment in Africa," *The City of Dar es Salaam,* Tanzania. *Urban Studies 37(4,*

whole process of peri-urbanisation is urbanisation itself (see Figure 2.1). Symptomatic with this peri-urbanisation is the increasing number of housing units in areas found at the city-edge[20]. This has led to a novel kind of 'housing question," given the wide array of challenges associated with it in this rather 'fragile zone." Among the challenges noted regarding peri-urban dwelling units is their immodest character in terms of the construction technologies employed. In addition, incremental modes of delivery are applied; over time, they tend to produce a mosaic of discordant townscapes. Furthermore, insecurity with regard to the tenure status of the citizens is a critical factor of concern[21]. There is general over-reliance by the builders on the immediate biophysical environment as a source of building materials leading sometimes to intense land degradation. Inadequacies in water and sanitation delivery[22] are rife. Above all, the general inconsistencies in the policy regarding peri-urban areas make pose difficulties in finding lasting solutions to the management of this environment and the human habitats themselves.

In the ensuing paragraphs, the author attempts to define concepts central to this study. In the nomenclature are terms including peri-urban area, housing, peri-urban housing, stewardship, environmental stewardship, stewardship and community building. The processes begin with rapid urbanisation that has become phenomenal in the recent times in

---

(2000) pp797-809; Briggs. J ;Yeboah.I, "Structural Adjustment and the Contemporary Sub-Saharan African City." *Area 33(1):* pp18-26. (2001)

[20] Johnson.J.H,"Urbanisation (Second Edition)," *Thomas Nelson and Sons Ltd,* South Melbourne. (1990); Allen.A, "Environmental planning and management of the peri-urban interface: perspectives on an emerging field." *Environment & Urbanisation* 15(1). (2003)pp. 135-147.

[21] MacAuslan, 2002

[22] Mukuka.L, "Factors affecting delivery of social and infrastructure services in municipalities – A case study of housing, water supply and sanitation in Bwacha Compound, Kabwe, in Municipal Development Program – MDP, undated," *Addressing poverty in the context of decentralisation in Eastern and Southern Africa – Case studies in Malawi, Uganda, Zambia and Zimbabwe: MDP Working Paper 3,* Municipal Development Programme for Sub-Saharan Africa.(2001) Harare, pp 105-128; Shah. F, "Local Financing for Rural and Peri-Urban Water Supply and Sanitation." <URL: www.protos.be/protosh2o/copy_of_Links-metbestanden/Local FinRurPeriUrbWATSAN.pdf,> *24 June 2011.(*2007)

Africa and the developing world, at large.[23] At the centre of focus becomes the peri-urban interface as it works for both the environmental resources and space for housing in most cases leading to the increase in ecological footprint[24]. Place stewardship and planning are the critical panacea to correct the ills of and tendency towards degradation and moving towards sustainability in human settlements.

Peri-urban interfaces are also defined as areas outside formal urban boundaries and urban jurisdictions that are in a process of urbanisation.[25] They progressively assume many of the characteristics of urban areas and sometimes they are also defined as suburban. A suburb is defined as "...the outer or peripheral, mainly residential, parts of a town or city largely dependent upon services and employment concentrated in its central business district."[26] The process has demographic insinuations. Originally the word suburb meant, "...the territory immediately outside the walls of a town or city (often occupied by craftsmen seeking to escape guild regulations)".[27] A peri-urban area is'"...not only a zone of direct impact experiencing the immediate impacts of land demands from urban growth and pollution, but is also a wider market-related zone of influence that is recognisable in terms of the handling of agricultural and natural resource products ...."[28]. Explicitly, there are strong ties between the centre and the periphery, especially the most immediate and proximity, in

[23] Shildo.G, "Housing Policy in Developing Countries," *Routledge*, London. (1990)
[24] Mobile Lives Forum, "Sustainbale mobilities in peri-urban areas," *Which lifestyles in the alter-urbain, suburban rural/citta diffusa/Zwischenstadt? Brochure for The 2nd International Meeting of Mobile Lives Forum on January the 24th and 25th,* 2013 at the Maison Rouge, Paris 12pg 1, (2012).
[25] Government of Swaziland, "The Draft Peri-urban Growth Policy." Available: www.ecs.co.sz/periurban/pup_periurban_policy.htm (1997); Douglas.I, "Peri-urban ecosystems and societies: Transitional zones and contrasting values. McGregor, D., Simon, D. and Thompson, D. (eds) *The Peri-Urban Interface*, Earthscan, London,"pg 18-27.(2006)
[26] Small J;Witherick.M, "A Modern Dictionary of Geography," *Third Edition, Arnold*: London.pg 23(1986)
[27] Small J; Witherick.M, "A Modern Dictionary of Geography," *Third Edition, Arnold*: London.pg 23(1986)
[28] PU-GEC (Peri-urbanisation and Global Environmental Change) (2009)., Peri-urban Area, URL: <http://web.ntpu.edu.tw/~shuli/PUGEC_02Peri-urban.htm,> *Accessed on 27 June 2011*.pg 1(2009)

terms of location, the peri-urban zone. Beyond the peri-urban zone is the 'exurban zone' which, is largely rural.[29]

In this study, a peri-urban area is taken to mean the area immediately behind the de facto boundaries of the city, and, is often treated as either suburban or 'pre-urban'[30]. It is prudent to see how others have conceptualised the peri-urban. A peri-urban zone (also referred to as the 'urban margin'), "...begins just beyond the contiguous built-up urban area and sometimes extends as far as 150 km from the core city, or as in the Chinese case as far as 300 km. It is marked by changing mosaic of both traditional and modern land-use."[31]. It is observed that the peri-urban region is a "contested ground" where "processes of urban growth and development intersect with the pressures for rural preservation"[32]. Peri-urban housing is a major contributor to environmental degradation[33].

Managing peri-urban areas has administrative overtones given the financial stress and inadequate staffing for peri-urban research and development characterising most developing countries[34]. Consequently,

---

[29] Fishman.R. A; Gechter. K. I, "Smart Growth: An Overview and Issues." *Paper prepared for American College of Real Estate Lawyers Conference, March 18-21, 2004, Orlando,* Florida (2004); Stoian, 2003; CLARK. J., "Peri-Urban Agglomerations in Southeast Asia - Exurban Change Project White Paper," <URL: http://exurban.osu.edu/papers/periurban_se_aggl.pdf>, *Accessed on 22 April 2008.* (2006).

[30] Mobile Lives Forum, Sustainbale mobilities in peri-urban areas," *Which lifestyles in the alter-urbain, suburban rural/citta diffusa/Zwischenstadt? Brochure for The 2nd International Meeting of Mobile Lives Forum on January the 24th and 25th,* 2013 at the Maison Rouge, Paris 12pg 1, (2012).

[31] Webster. D, "On the Edge: Shaping the Future of Peri-urban East Asia," *Asia/Pacific Research Center,* <URL: http://APARC.stanford.edu>, *Accessed on 22 April 2008*.pg 6(2002)

[32] Bourne et al., "Contested Ground, The Dynamics of Peri-Urban Growth in the Toronto Region." *Canadian Journal of Regional SciencelRevue canadienne des sciences régionales, XXV 1: 2&3 (Surnmer-Autumn Été-autonme 2003)*: pp251 (2003) ; Bourne.L. S,, "The Geography of Housing," *V H Winston and Sons Ltd,* London. (1981);

[33] Huby.M, "Social Policy and the Environment," *Open University Press,*Buckingham. (1998); Nkambwe.M, "Problems of Data Acquisition and Information Management for Planning Peri-Urban Settlements in Botswana." *The International Archives of the Photogrammetry, Remote Sensing and Spatial Information Sciences, Vol. XXXIV, Part 6/W6*: pp 144-146. (2006)

[34] Nkambwe.M, "Problems of Data Acquisition and Information Management for Planning Peri-Urban Settlements in Botswana." *The International Archives of the*

most peri-urban habitats are in a state of flux hence unsustainable development. Most peri-urban dwellers have 'a wait and see approach' as they lack in full information of what is happening to them[35].

The peri-urban zone is synonymous with land use conflicts and uncertainty[36]. Thus, living in the peri-urban is largely precarious especially for the low-income groups of society[37]. There are different actors in the peri-urban that are identified as: the *seekers* who are defined by their lifestyle including religious communities and those seeking alternative life styles, the *survivors* who include do-it-yourself (DIY) home builders and those keeping horses thriving on an adaptive life, the *speculators*, "including farm stays and retreats, the pet industry, boutique farmers, recreational providers, landscape suppliers, the equine industry

---

Photogrammetry, Remote Sensing and Spatial Information Sciences, Vol. XXXIV, Part 6/W6: pp 144-146. (2006); Allen, Allen.A, "Environmental planning and management of the peri-urban interface: perspectives on an emerging field." *Environment & Urbanisation* 15(1). (2003)pp. 135-147; UNFPA, "State of World Population 2007."*Unleashing the Potential of Urban Growth.* UNFPA: New York. (2007); Home.R, "Eating farmland, growing houses": *Peri-urban settlements and customary land tenure in Botswana, Southern Africa,* <URL: http://www.n-aerus.net/web/ sat /workshops/2001/papers/home.pdf>(2001); Nguyen M. I,"Analyzing the encroachment process of informal settlements in the periurban of Ho Chi Minh City, Vietnam," *unpublished Master"s thesis*, Lund University: Lund(2006)

[35] Murowe. S; Chirisa. I, "Sally Mugabe Heights: The tale of an incidental Zimbabwean peri-urban housing scheme seeking legitimation," *Zambezia XXXIII (i/ii)*: pp71-89 (2006).

[36] Butterworth.J et al., "Peri-Urban Water Conflicts - Supporting dialogue and negotiation," *Technical Paper Series 50*, IRC international Water and Sanitation Centre: Delft, the Netherlands. (2007). ; Dube.C, "Housing coops frustrated over land," *Zimbabwe Independent.* <URL: http://www.thezimbabweindependent.com/business/14311.html>, *Accessed on 22 April 2008.*(2004); Jenkins. P,"African Cities: Competing claims on urban land," *News for the Nordic Africa Institute no. 3*: Nordic Africa Institute: Uppsala.(2006) ; Larsson. A; Schylter.A, "Changing gender and housing conflicts," Chapter 14 in Sithole-Fundire S.A. Zhou, A. Larsson & A. Schlyter (1995)., "*Gender Research on Urbanisation, Planning and Everyday Life,*" Zimbabwe Women"s Resource Centre Network: Harare. (1995).

[37] Hansen. T,"Housing standards and health, welfare, policy and planning," *Paper presented to the ENHR Conference on Sustainable Urban Areas, 25-28 June 2007, Rotterdam*, <URL www.enhr2007rotterdam.nl, Accessed on 2 August 2007.> (2007); Chirisa. I, "Peri-urban Dynamics and regional planning in Africa: Implications for building healthy cities," *Journal of Africa Studies and Development 2 (2)* (2010) pp. 015-026.

and developers and real estate agents," and, the *strugglers*, "characterised by the 'holding-on' farmers."[38]

Such taxonomy is critical in the identification of the processes and patterns of development in the peri-urban some of which, in effect, define the lifestyles by the peri-urban dwellers[39]. Though these actors are acting at a much-localised level, it must be borne in mind that there is a whole range of 'hidden' and as well 'distant' actors who sporadically cause changes in the local place. A good number of the actors identified live in precariousness, being uncertain yet how they act or react to impending urban development leave a long-term imprint on the environment[40]. Most peri-urban dwellers live informally; they are not formally recognised by the authorities[41]. In certain circumstances, they are with a 'rural footing' yet striving to lead 'urban lives'[42] . It is pointed out to the symbiotic relationship between the city and the countryside, especially in the rural-urban fringe and mentions that,

> "Big cities and the countryside can get along well together. Big cities need real countryside close by. And a countryside – from man's point of view – need big cities with all their diverse opportunities and productivity so human beings can be in a position to appreciate the rest of the natural world instead of cursing it."[43]

---

[38] Choy. D.L et al. "Change and Continuity in Peri-Urban Australia,": *Peri-Urban Futures and Sustainable Development,* <URL: http://periurban.org.au/references/monograph4.pdf.>, *Accessed on 29 April, 2013.* (2008:5)

[39] Mobile Lives Forum, "Sustainbale mobilities in peri-urban areas," *Which lifestyles in the alter-urbain, suburban rural/citta diffusa/Zwischenstadt? Brochure for The 2nd International Meeting of Mobile Lives Forum on January the 24th and 25th,* 2013 at the Maison Rouge, Paris 12pg 1, (2012)

[40] Choy. D.L et al. "Change and Continuity in Peri-Urban Australia,": *Peri-Urban Futures and Sustainable Development,* <URL: http://periurban.org.au/references/monograph4.pdf.>, *Accessed on 29 April, 2013.* (2008)

[41] Murowe.S; Chirisa.I, "Sally Mugabe Heights: The tale of an incidental Zimbabwean peri-urban housing scheme seeking legitimation," *Zambezia XXXIII (i/ii)*: pp71-89.(2006)

[42] Grant.M. R, "Rental Shelter as a Coping Mechanism in Gweru, Zimbabwe," *PHD Thesis, Queen"s University*, Ontario, Canada.(1991)

[43] Jacobs. J, "The death and life of great American cities – The failure of town *planning," Penguin Books*, New York. (1965:461).

Most of the peri-urban settlements enjoy "... relatively lower population densities, mixed land-uses and rapid land-use change, land speculation and uncertain land tenure, fast-growing population and infrastructure requirements, mix of newcomers and long-established dwellers, heterogeneous and changing social and economic structures, diversified livelihood strategies, and a fragmented institutional landscape, made worse by rapid change and unclear boundaries, jurisdictions and competencies."[44] They are not exactly uniform in their typologies. The typologies of peri-urban and their habitats demonstrate their non-uniformity.[45]

There are different types of peri-urbanisation: displaced-urbanisation, ex-urbanisation, anti-urbanisation and hidden-urbanisation. These include Ex-urbanisation which is characterised by wealthy urbanites moving into the countryside, Displaced-urbanisation that happens in response to factors of employment, living costs and housing availability, Anti-urbanisation that is associated with a self-sufficient lifestyle with preference to smaller communities, amenity-driven retirement migration and Hidden urbanisation by extension, is characterised by the engagement by households and communities in non-agricultural activities; farmsteads are converted to accommodate these. Households commute to access other land-use zones. Each variant of urbanisation is associated with a different type of impact. As noted, peri-urbanisation is "...both as a driver and an effecter of global environmental changes"[46]. It is a clear indicator of the urbanisation trend[47]. By checking on land-use and land cover change over time, one can conclude the effects of the peri-urbanisation process. One major and obvious impact of peri-urbanisation is that it transforms the environmental character of a place. The major manifestation is that the

---

[44] Sanchez-Cuenca, 2011:1

[45] Iaquinta. D; Drescher.W,"Peri-urban Typology Defined, Defining Peri-urban: Understanding Rural-Urban Linkages and Their Connection to Institutional Contexts." *Paper presented at the Tenth World Congress, IRSA,* Rio: August 1, 2000.(2000)

[46] PU-GEC (Peri-urbanisation and Global Environmental Change) (2009)., Peri-urban Area, URL: <http://web.ntpu.edu.tw/~shuli/PUGEC_02Peri-urban.htm,> *Accessed on 27 June 2011*.pg 1(2009)

[47] Castells. M, "The Urban Question, *MIT Press" Cambridge*, Massachusetts. (1978).

natural environment will be displaced and replaced by a built environment[48]

Five different types of peri-urban areas are identified and these are influenced by the relationship that the peri-urban areas share with the urban areas[49]. The first type is what is called the *village peri-urban*, which is countryside that is non-proximate to the city either geographically or in travel time[50]. It derives from circulation and migration and embodies a network-induced institutional context wherein change is effected through diffusion or induction while institutions remain stable and traditional in orientation[51]. This scenario has led to a 'chaotic urbanisation' process in Malawi, for example, chiefs in some peri-urban areas continue to dish out land regardless of any planning principles hence the perpetration of a chaotic urbanisation[52]. The second type is the diffuse peri-urban, which is a geographically urban fringe that derives from a multiple-source point in-migration. It embodies an amalgamated institutional context where there is a high demand for negotiating novel institutional forms to address conflicting traditions and world urban views.

---

[48] Stren.R.E, "An Urban Problematique: The Challenge of Urbanisation for Development Assistance," *Centre for Urban and Community Studies*, Toronto. (1992); McElfish J.M, "Commentary: Ten Things Wrong with Sprawl," <URL:http://www.emagazine.com/view/?3641,> *Accessed on 22 April 2008.* (2008); Gordon. P ; Richardson.H.W, "Are compact cities a desirable planning goal?"*Journal of the American Planning Association 63(1)*: pp95-117 (1997)

[49] Iaquinta. D; Drescher.W,"Peri-urban Typology Defined, Defining Peri-urban: Understanding Rural-Urban Linkages and Their Connection to Institutional Contexts." *Paper presented at the Tenth World Congress, IRSA,* Rio: August 1, 2000.(2000)

[50] Ibid.

[51] Benjamin. S, "Presenting Two in Contesting Spatialities: Do Everyday Institutional contestations erode the neo-liberal Urban Reforms Agenda?" <URL: http://igs.cla.umn.edu/pdf/BenjaminPaper.pdf>, *Accessed on 21 November 2008.* (2008)

[52] Kawonga.A. J.C, "Access to land for low-income housing in Malawi: The case of Zomba Municipality, in Municipal Development Program – MDP, undated," *Addressing poverty in the context of decentralisation in Eastern and Southern Africa – Case studies in Malawi, Uganda, Zambia and Zimbabwe: MDP Working Paper 3,* Municipal Development Programme for Sub-Saharan Africa: Harare, pp 65-81.(1996); Chikhwenda.E.J.W, "Sustainability of Shelter Provision in Malawi"s Urban Centers: the Case of Blantyre City," *in Journal of Sustainable Development in Africa 4(1),* pp 25-35. (2002)

The third type is called the *chain peri-urban.*, which is also a geographically urban fringe but, derives primarily from chain migration. Traditions and institutions are transplanted with some modification from donors who come in with institutional needs, analyse the situation and may offer some capacity building programmes[53]. Fourthly, there is *place peri-urban area*, which is geographically close to the city urban fringe and derives from in-place urbanisation, natural increase and migration[54]. The fifth one is the *absorbed peri-urban*, which geographically is within the city, having been absorbed and derived from displacement of traditional structures. The roots of social arrangements lie in the traditions of a previously resident culture group. The traditions are then maintained through 'ritualism."

It is important to note that the taxonomy of peri-urban is largely spatial and perhaps does not tell much about the physical products and artefacts, specifically housing types, associated with each typology[55].Seven typologies of self-help or self-managed housing developments in the peri-urban interface have been identified and these include; classic border *colonias*, non-border peri-urban informal subdivisions, semi-urban or rural housing subdivisions, recreational subdivisions, retirement subdivisions, mobile home communities and trailer parks[56].

- The classic border *colonias* are located "…mostly in the border region, almost always beyond the city limits and buried in the rural hinterland"[57]. The very low-income Mexican or

---

[53] Iaquinta. D; Drescher.W,"Peri-urban Typology Defined, Defining Peri-urban: Understanding Rural-Urban Linkages and Their Connection to Institutional Contexts." *Paper presented at the Tenth World Congress, IRSA,* Rio: August 1, 2000.(2000))

[54] Thornton.A, "Beyond the Metropolis: Small Town Case Studies of Urban and Peri-urban Agriculture in South Africa,". *Urban Forum 19(3)*: pp 243-262. (2008)

[55] Iaquinta. D; Drescher.W,"Peri-urban Typology Defined, Defining Peri-urban: Understanding Rural-Urban Linkages and Their Connection to Institutional Contexts." *Paper presented at the Tenth World Congress, IRSA,* Rio: August 1, 2000.(2000)

[56] Ward.P. M; Peters.P. A, "Self-help housing and informal homesteading in peri-urban America: Settlement identification using digital imagery and GIS,." *Habitat International 31(2)*, pp205-218 (2007:16)

[57] Ibid, pg16.

Mexican origin populations occupy the classic border *colonias*.

- The non-border peri-urban informal subdivisions are, "…low density, larger individual lots, idiosyncratic dwelling arrangements and placement on lots, unpaved streets, and, when seen from above, from the numerous
- 'lozenge'-shaped trailer home roofs." Occupiers are of "mixed ethnicity"[58].
- Semi-urban or rural housing subdivisions are the third typology and are marked by low-density in extensity. The settlements have similar physical dwelling structures with severe servicing deficiencies and the occupants are mainly widows or widowers.
- The fourth type, coming in various shapes, sizes and types are recreational subdivisions. These are the most preferred by the better-off working class "whose hobbies or preferences are for outdoor life (keeping horses for example), as well as those wishing to have an affordable second home residence for weekends and vacations even if this is a trailer or mobile home-type unit"[59]. Levels of servicing are very low.
- The fifth typology is, retirement subdivisions. In physical outlook they resemble the recreation subdivisions yet providing "relatively low-cost options to so-called downsizers - parents whose children have left home and who are now living on modest or limited savings and pensions"[60]. Provision of amenities to residents is minimal.
- The other category comprises of, "manufactured homes not involving self-help and which are located in formal subdivisions, usually within city jurisdictions rather than in the peri-urban (rural) area." These are the mobile home communities and trailer parks. The former is an alternative for those who cannot access conventional mortgage finance or

---

[58] Roth. A, "After the bubble, ghost towns across America," *The Wall Street Journal*, <URL: http://www.galesburg.com/business/x223022858/After-the-bubble-ghost-towns-across-America>(2008)

[59] Ward.P. M; Peters.P. A, "Self-help housing and informal homesteading in peri-urban America: Settlement identification using digital imagery and GIS,." *Habitat International 31(2)*, pp205-218 (2007:16)

[60] Ibid.

state insured housing[61] . The houses are built within the code yet occupy low-cost peripheral locations. They are in the form of modular homes and the occupiers are usually homeowners.

- The trailer parks, on the other hand, are located within city limits or what Ward and Peters refer to as 'extra territorial jurisdiction (ETJ)'[62].

The foregoing conceptualisations of the peri-urban show the complexity of issues ridden in this environment especially with respect to urban development. The suburban zone is a place that offers a better appreciation of rural and urban interactions (rural-urban linkages) including the aspect of urbanism whereby peri-urban dwellers assume urban living styles and fashions[63].

This study adopts the broader definition of housing as 'many aspects at one go." This coincides with the definition of housing which considers it as, "…a bundle of services such as neighbourhood services (parks, schools); a location (accessibility to jobs and amenities) and proximity of certain types of neighbours (a social environment). It embraces more than shelter or lodging for human habitation."[64] Housing is thus a process, an experience, basic need, a human right, a commodity of value, an investment, and shelter plus habitat, to name but these few,

---

[61] Roth. A, "After the bubble, ghost towns across America," *The Wall Street Journal*, <URL:http://www.galesburg.com/business/x223022858/After-the-bubble-ghost-towns-across -America>(2008)

[62] Ward.P. M; Peters.P. A, "Self-help housing and informal homesteading in peri-urban America: Settlement identification using digital imagery and GIS,." *Habitat International 31(2)*, pp205-218 (2007:16)

[63] Kamete.A.Y.et.al, "Managing the interface between urban councils and the surrounding rural districts councils: The case of Bulawayo City Council and Umguza Rural District Council,. *Municipal Development Programme for Eastern and Southern* Africa (MDP-ESA): Harare., (2001); Cavailhès. J et al., "The peri-urban city, why to live between the suburbs and the countryside" *Regional Science and Urban Economics 34(6)*, pp681-703 (2004); Ruby. J, "When is a Suburb not a suburb? When it is Oak Park," *A Paper presented at the 2002 American Anthropological Association Meetings: A Work in Progress, Circulated from comments, criticisms and suggestions*, Accessed on 27 June 2011.(2002)

[64] Gbadeyan. R. A, "Private Sector"s Contributions to the Development of the Nigerian Housing Market," *Current Research Journal of Social Sciences 3(2)*: pp.104-113. (2011:105)

and is noted as a process[65]. A process is an activity that "…takes place over time and which has a precise aim regarding the result to be achieved"[66]. It is hierarchical, meaning that it [process] may consist of a partially ordered set of sub-processes.

A process is usually seen as an abstracted way of working. It can be characterised by "... attributes of purpose (what is to be achieved and why); structure (how will the goal be achieved); rationale (what is the reasoning behind this process); roles (which roles are present, which responsibilities are associated, which incentives are present and what are the criteria for these roles); and, ordering (which phasing or sequence is applied)"[67]. A process is thus a collection of purpose, structure, rationale, structure, roles and ordering. All these aspects are entailed in 'housing as a process' includes. It is asserted that;

> "…a house is not just a shell for habitation; it is also an unfolding of our experience. A house is not an act or a series of acts; it is not an object but an experience; it is not a commodity to be bought and sold but an activity essential to life. Instead of being the unfolding of our existence and the expression of our freedom, our houses have become the imprisonment of our existence, the denial of our lives."[68]

---

[65] Kamete. A.Y,"Continuity with change: a review of Zimbabwe" public sector urban low income housing production system," in *Development Southern Africa 15(1) Autumn*: pp13-28(1998), "The quest for affordable urban housing: a study of approaches and results in Harare, Zimbabwe," *Development Southern Africa*, 18(2): 31–44.(2001a); "Civil society, housing and urban governance, the case of urban housing cooperatives in Zimbabwe,". In A. Tostensen, I. Tvedten and M. Vaa (Eds.), *Associational Life in African Cities: Popular responses to the urban crisis*, pp. 162–179. Uppsala: The Nordic Africa Institute.(2001c); Munzwa. K.M, "Housing development project financing in Zimbabwe with special focus on housing co-operatives" in Brown A and C Davidson eds. Responsive design and plan implementation, *Department of City and Regional Planning, Cardiff University*, Cardiff. (1999)

[66] Muller.G, "What is a Process? Embedded Systems Institute," *Eindhoven, The Netherlands*, <URL: http://www.gaudisite.nl/WhatIsAProcessPaper.pdf>, *Accessed on 27 June 2011*.pg.1(2008)

[67] Ibid,(2008:1)

[68] Alexander. C et al. "The grass roots housing process," <URL: http://www.livingneighborhoods.org/library/grassroots.htm>, *Accessed on 22 April 2008.*(1973)

Part of a process is the experience. This interesting dimension is housing development whereby the process of housing is observed to be wide and complex, partly due to the complexity of procedures and stakeholders involved. The chief mechanism through which new units of housing are created from the existing stock, or the size of existing units altered in the short-involved processes of subdivision and consolidation (merger)[69]. The housing production and consumption formula, stands out as follows[70]:

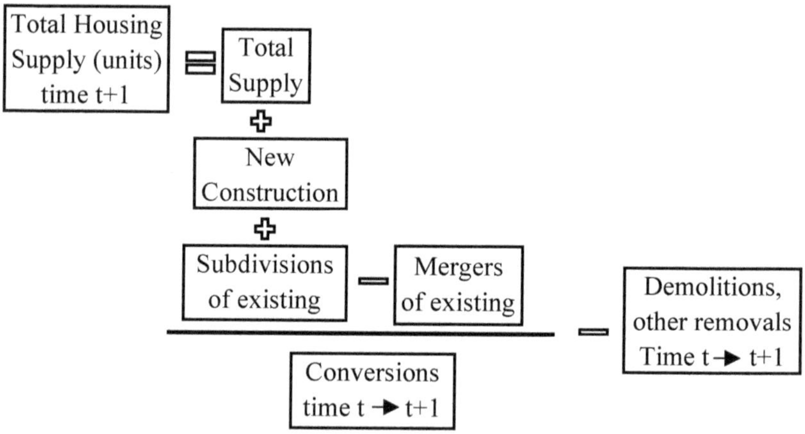

Symbolically, this is:

$H_{t+1} = H_t + NC_{t,t+1} + Cnet_{t,t+1} - D_{t,t+1}$

Where,

H_{t+1} is the Total Housing Units over time

H_t is the Total Supply of Housing through time

C is New Construction

D is Demolitions

[69] GoZ, "Regional, Town and Country Planning Act: Chapter 29:12," *Government Printers*:,Harare. (1996);Jenkins. P,"African Cities: Competing claims on urban land," *News for the Nordic Africa Institute no. 3*: Nordic Africa Institute: Uppsala.(2006) ; Seyama.S.S, "Chapter 8: Urban Planning and Development, Problems and Prospects for the Future, in Muzvidziwa Victor N and Agostino M Zamberia (eds.)" *Urbanisation and Development in Swaziland*, Department of Sociology, University of Swaziland, JAN Publishing Centre Ltd (JANPC): Manzini. (2006)

[70] Bourne.L. S,)., "The Geography of Housing," *V H Winston and Sons Ltd*, London. (1981);

Release of housing units of different quality, from the existing stock, hinges on the filtering process[71]. In Africa, most of the times, the rate of housing production is far less than the expected. In Ghana, for example, it is shown that of the required 113,000 urban housing units, only 36,000 are provided annually[72]. This mismatch triggers households to look for own modes of housing provision[73]. As a commodity, housing offers financial security and social status[74]. As land prices continue to soar, a growing number of households are unable to develop their parcels on their own. Funds for housing can be raised through incremental savings, informal loans from family members, and the sale of remaining assets are no longer sufficient to develop a parcel within a meaningful period. To structure financial cooperation between partners in the valorisation of real estate, a variety of joint ownership agreements and tenancy arrangements have emerged.

---

[71] Grigsby, 1963 quoted in Bourne.L. S, , "The Geography of Housing," *V H Winston and Sons Ltd*, London. (1981); ; Mbiba.B ; Ndubiwa.M, "Decent construction and the role of local authorities: the case of Bulawayo city, Zimbabwe,". *Research Report for the Urban and Peri-Urban Research Network (Peri-NET), [S.I.],* <URL: http://eprints.lse.ac.uk/3015/1/Bulawayo_report.pdf>, *Accessed on 22 April 2008.(*2006)

[72] Awotona. A,, "A review of housing research in West Africa," *Third World Planning Review 18(1)*: pp45-58. (1996)

[73] Butcher. C, "The Potentials and Possible Roles of Housing Co-operatives in Meeting the Shelter Needs of Low Income Urban Households" *A paper prepared for the Zimbabwe Institute of Regional & Urban Planners" Annual School (4-6 July, 1990):*,Harare. (1990); Chirisa. I;Munzwa. K.M, "Collective Collateralisation, Group Democracy and the Urban Marginalised Communities in Zimbabwe," A Case of Tashinga Housing Co-operative in Harare, *Local Governance Development Journal 2(1)*: pp31-46.(2008)

[74] CUDS, "Housing Microfinance Initiatives – Synthesis And Regional Summary: Asia, Latin America and Sub-Saharan Africa with Selected Case Studies," *Center for Urban Development Studies, Harvard University Graduate School of Design*, Development Alternatives Inc. (Dai), Maryland(2000);Bourne.L. S,, "The Geography of Housing," *V H Winston and Sons Ltd*, London. (1981); ; Kamete.A.Y, Urban governance, poverty and urban housing," In O. Musandu-Nyamayaro and T. Mubvami, (Eds.), Urban Governance Outreach Research, pp. 13–27. Harare, *Department of Rural and Urban Planning and the Ford Foundation.* (1997); AlsayedA.H, "Housing Management Systems," *Theoretical Approach. Paper presented to the ENHR Conference on Sustainable Urban Areas, 25-28 June 2007*, Rotterdam. <URL: www.enhr2007rotterdam.nl, Accessed on 2 August 2007>.(2007)

Housing stock or the standing stock of housing is, "...the inventory of residential structures or individual dwelling units currently occupied or available for occupancy"[75]. This pattern changes over time in response to the net balance of adjustments in the different components of supply summaries in the formula given above. The total housing inventory is therefore the inherited stock or supply from previous periods plus (or minus) the net balance of new construction and conversions less removals. The different methods through which housing units can be added to the housing inventory are summarised as new units built on previously undeveloped land, through modifications in the form and usage of existing stock or by replacement of existing units with new construction[76]. Each of these processes can also take different forms depending on the location (as extensions to the built area or infilling), the scale and the nature of development (in price, occupancy, tenure, size and design), and in the origin of the investment decisions involved (public or private).

As a basic need, housing ensures decency and privacy to the users. As an investment, households usually allocate 10% to 15% of their earnings to shelter and inhabit whatever product this amount will buy (tent, hut, shack, or discarded automobile body. In this aspect, it is perceived as an investment because it offers prospects of lucrative returns. The property is used to generate revenues while it appreciates over time[77]. Households generate additional income by renting out space in their building for residential accommodations and commercial micro-enterprises [78].

---

[75] Bourne.L. S, "The Geography of Housing," *V H Winston and Sons Ltd*, London. (1981); pg.26

[76] Bourne.L. S, "The Geography of Housing," *V H Winston and Sons Ltd*, London. (1981)

[77] CUDS, "Housing Microfinance Initiatives – Synthesis And Regional Summary: Asia, Latin America and Sub-Saharan Africa with Selected Case Studies," *Center for Urban Development Studies, Harvard University Graduate School of Design*, Development Alternatives Inc. (Dai), Maryland(2000)

[78] Macwan"gi. M, "Social and physical conditions of nannies in high cost residential areas of Lusaka, Zambia," Chapter 12 in Sithole-Fundire S.A. Zhou, A. Larsson & A. Schlyter, 1995: Gender Research on Urbanisation, Planning and Everyday Life, *Zimbabwe Women"s Resource Centre Network*. Harare.(2005); Tevera.D.S ;Chimhowu.A.O, "Urban Growth, Poverty and Backyard Shanties in Harare,

Households can locate where they can (pavement, cliff side, ravine, garbage dump, drainage channel) as long as the site is marginal enough to deter displacement and close enough to transportation so as to permit access to employment opportunities. This is the general definition of housing as shelter.

Nevertheless, shelter is more than a roof over one's head. It is underscored that, because one's living environment (call that habitat):

> "... involves more than simply a roof over your head ... the city-wide approach [has been introduced]. The strategy is to work with local partners on quality of life and to support city links. A good living environment embraces decent housing and access to education, health care, work and social provision, and so a range of partners is involved. The citywide approach brings together those partners, from the police service to housing associations, and from welfare organisations to schools – and safeguards the continuity of cooperative ties. The principal role is played by local people. They are the experts when it comes to their neighbourhood or city. They are entitled to a liveable environment. Habitat initiatives come from the grassroots."[79]

Despite the call for citywide and strategic approaches to habitat and environmental issues, in most developing countries, approaches by players remain piecemeal, departmentalised hence lacking in efficacy. In most peri-urban environments in Africa, actors are working as individuals, households or individual cooperatives yet the impacts they produce over time are cumulative and pose threat to the commons. In this aspect, the theory of tragedy of the commons tends to hold to the assault and degradation of the common environmental assets.

A study of life on the edge, looking at residential property values in the urban-rural interface, estimated the contribution of both urban-rural fringe location and lake proximity on residential property values in three upstate counties of South Carolina (United States) through estimation of

---

Zimbabwe," in *Geographical Journal of Zimbabwe Number 31, Geographical Association of Zimbabwe*. Harare.(1998); Tevera. D.S;Chikanda. A, "Urban Poverty, Livelihood Strategies and Policy Responses in Harare, Zimbabwe, The Case of Ward Three in Mbare High-density Suburb," *Geographical Journal of Zimbabwe Number 31, Geographical Association of Zimbabwe*, Harare.(2000)

[79] Habitat Platform, "Treasures in your neighbourhood: International exchange at neighbourhood level." *VNG Uitgeverij: The Hague.* (2002)

spatial hedonic housing price models. It observed that location in the urban fringe and the urban-rural interface are found to have a positive impact on residential housing values relative to either urban or more rural locations[80]. The lakes in the upstate contributed positively to housing values to the extent that the house had a view of a lake, lake access or Lake Frontage =[81]. This is evidence to show how natural features found in the peri-urban zone can enhance the value of housing estates. The foregoing description typifies the 'suburban' types of peri-urban housing by the well-to-do classes.

On the contrary, in sub-Saharan Africa, peri-urban human settlements are often characterised by a mosaic of quality in terms of materials used by the builders or developers in putting up the structures[82]. Remarked has been that, "...often...what distinguishes the poor from the non-poor is substandard housing.... dangerous housing is a concern for the poor. The most frequent problems include leaking roofs, cracked and mouldy walls, broken windows, rotting floors, blocked toilets and rusted pipes."[83] In this case, a house becomes more of a liability than an asset especially as maintenance costs "...drain resources" which a family or household could have used for other purposes and needs[84]. In this respect, thatched mud huts are more expensive to maintain than those houses built of conventionally accepted building materials like common and face bricks under tiles or corrugated iron or asbestos sheets.

Peri-urban and informal sector settlements tend to be treated as synonymous with labels like "...squatter settlements, marginal

---

[80] Espey et al ., "Living on the edge, Residential Property Values in the Urban Rural Interface," *Journal of Agricultural and Applied Economics (December 2007)*, pp 19-34.(2007)

[81] Kahn.M.E, "The Environmental Impact of Suburbanisation," *Journal of Policy Analysis and Management 19(4)*, pp569-586.(2000); Harvey. D, "Urban Land Economics. The Economics of Real property," *Basing stoke*, Macmillan(1991); Cadman. I.,"Property development, 3rd edition," *Chapman and Hall Publishers*, London (1978)

[82] Oram.N, "Towns in Africa," *Oxford University Press*: London,(1965); Bourne.L. S, "The Geography of Housing," *V H Winston and Sons Ltd*, London. (1981)

[83] World Bank, "Voices of the Poor: Can anyone hear us?," *Oxford University Press*: New York. (2000:51)

[84] Ibid., (2000)

settlements, shanty towns, urban slums, or illegal settlements"[85] . Peri-urban areas or the urban fringes are described as having a mix of urban and rural enclaves. These areas are transitional zones that are neither town nor country. Nevertheless, they are largely linked functionally to the urban areas. Some of their conspicuously noted characteristics include; lower prices of land relative to urbanized centres, fewer controls and restrictions on development, *de facto* subdivisions[86]. These subdivisions are based on inheritance of land by those who settled before these areas were incorporated into urban local authority areas, and an array of housing structures, from simple pole and dagga huts to highly sophisticated brick under tile modern urban houses[87]. Peri-urban housing is, in this study, taken to refer to the processes of subdivisions leading to the development of shelter and attendant services as well as housing stocks found on the edges of established urban centres[88]. This contrasts inner-city housing whereby at the peak of new building moves further from the centre, a smaller wave of rebuilding emerges near the centre[89].

The notion of stewardship has connotations of 'looking after," being vigilant and watchful with caring responsibility regarding a specified object or subject. stewardship has been loosely defined as, "...the careful and responsible management of something entrusted to our care."[90]

---

[85] Hogrewe. W.et. al,"The Unique Challenges of Improving Peri-Urban Sanitation," *WASH Technical Report No. 86., Report prepared for the Office of Health, Bureau for Research and Development*, U.S. Agency for International Development, under WASH Task No. 339, U.S. Agency for International Development: Washington, DCpg.9(1993)

[86] GoZ, "Study and Review of the Current Minimum High-density Housing Standards," *Government Printers*, Harare.(2001)

[87] Muzvidziwa.V.N, "Urbanisation and Development in Swaziland," *JAN Publishing Centre*, Manzini.(2006)

[88] Phelps, 1998;Muzvidziwa. V.N, "Informal Settlement Dwellers and Environmental Problems." *UNISWA Research Journal of Agriculture, Science and Technology (Special Volume No. 1)*(2005) pp 25-37. ; Kovats.R; Akhtar.S, "Climate, climate change and human health in Asian cities," *Environment and Urbanisation 20(1):* pp165-176.(2008).

[89] Tevera.D.S ;Chimhowu.A.O, "Urban Growth, Poverty and Backyard Shanties in Harare, Zimbabwe," in *Geographical Journal of Zimbabwe Number 31, Geographical Association of Zimbabwe*. Harare.(1998)

[90] ARS, "Regional Stewardship: A commitment to Place," *Monograph Series. ARS*, California. (2000:4)

It is further stated that, the notion when applied to a place, combines 'citizenship' with 'stewardship of place." Stewardship is the commitment to place; at the same time, commitment is more than just attachment. It is explained that in relation to land that stewardship involves "…the way land is looked after, for whose benefit, and with what legitimacy and authority the 'steward' acts on behalf of others"[91]. However, it is argued that stewardship happens in a context of competing interests because there are many actors who have diverse and most of the times divergent interests. Thus, "…in terms of practical management of land, [they] are clearly contested"[92]. Fundamental disagreements on issues of land ownership and land-use often arise. For instance, landowners may justify their position as care for the land and its people. On the other hand, the state bureaucracy presumes to exercise that role in the name of the eminent domain and representative democracy. Communitarian groups, using their closeness to the inhabitants of an area, assert their priority over the other two. As well, indigenous activists may invoke an ancient clan democracy as cultural precedent for decentralised control of the land[93]). Such is the extent to which conflicts arises and is defined in space.

Spatially, stewardship can be understood to take place at various levels of intervention including the plot, ward, district, city, region, nation, supranational region or globe. Describing regional stewardship, regional stewards have been described as "... leaders who are committed to the long-term well-being of places".[94] Such leaders are, thus "...integrators who cross boundaries of jurisdiction, sector, and discipline to address complex issues such as sprawl, equity, education and economic development... leaders who combine 360-degree vision with the ability to mobilise diverse coalitions of action". From the citation it can be noted that the value of stewardship is embraced in the philosophy of, "...the

---

[91] Bryden. J ; Hart.K, "Land reform, planning and people: an issue of stewardship" <URL:http://www.caledonia.org.uk/land/documents/Land%20Reform%20&%20Stewardship.pdf> *Accessed on 27 August 2010.* (2006:6)

[92] Ibid., pg.77

[93] Ibid., (2000)

[94] ARS, "Regional Stewardship: A commitment to Place," *Monograph Series. ARS*, California. (2000:3)

careful and responsible management of the things entrusted to our care"[95]. Or, as simply put by some other scholars, stewardship is the notion of "responsible care"[96]. However, to think that all regional stewards care responsibly may be an overstatement. Sometimes there are issues to do with personality, charisma, resource availability and regional politics that may hinder the smooth flow of the expected outcomes of careful responsibility.

At least as a principle, stewardship calls on all those involved in the product life cycle to share responsibility for minimising the environmental and human impacts that result from the production, use and disposal of the product.[97] Like housing, stewardship is both a process and a value with certain expected outputs all being defined by specific approaches. It is observed that definitions of stewardship are quite inconsistent and contextual.[98] In particular, the following types of stewardship have been identified in practice:

- *"Material stewardship* (for instance, inputs like consumables, energy, water, explosives and equipment),
- *Resource stewardship* (for example, optimising use of resources for both current and future generations),

---

[95] Albemarle County, "Embracing Our Value of Stewardship," <URL: http://www.albemarle.org/upload/images/forms_center/departments/budget/forms/FY09_Budget_Overview.pdf> *Accessed on 27 August 2010.* Pg.4(2008)

[96] Bryden. J ; Hart.K, "Land reform, planning and people: an issue of stewardship" <URL:http://www.caledonia.org.uk/land/documents/Land%20Reform%20&%20Stewardship.pdf> *Accessed on 27 August 2010.* (2006:5)

[97] Taylor.J, "Declining Life Support Systems: An NGO Response,". *WESSA, Wildlife and Environment Society of South Africa – A Celebration of 85 Years of Caring for the Earth:* pp18-20. (2011); BHP, BHP Billiton Sustainability Report. <URL:http://www.bhpbilliton.com/home/investors/reports/Documents/2006SummarySustainabilityReport.pdf, > *Accessed on 7 November 2007.(*2006).

[98] Young.C, "True Stewardship, Brownfields," *AG News for America.* <URL: www.brownfieldagnews.com/>, *Accessed on 4 August 2007.*(2007); Schnug.E. et al. "Organic farming – stewardship for food security, food quality, environment and nature conservation," in Aspects of Applied Biology *79*: pp 57-62.(2006); Smith.K, "Stewardship of Land and Resources," *The Housing Journal (2005)*: pp10-11. (2005);BHP, BHP Billiton Sustainability Report. <URL:http://www.bhpbilliton.com/home/ investors / reports / Documents/2006SummarySustainabilityReport.pdf,> *Accessed on 7 November 2007.(*2006); New Brunswick, "Private land stewardship: a guide for landowners," *New Brunswick,* Canada(undated).

- *Product stewardship*, which is the shared responsibility with others in the life cycle of products or commodities so that harm of the environment is minimised due to those resources' exposure to the environment, and
- *Process stewardship*, which refers to the different processes applied to a product as it moves through its life cycle including extraction and smelting. Potentially produced outputs include emissions, leakages, wastes and greenhouse gases. Process stewardship is pinned on the ability of the involved actors (producers and consumers) understanding these processes (or outputs) in order to minimise harm to people and the environment."[99]

It is asserted that stewardship represents a complex but increasingly necessary constituent of long-term environmental management. It is thus noted that, the U.S. Department of Energy (DOE) characterises stewardship as all activities required to protect human health and the environment from the residual hazards posed by nuclear and/or chemical materials, waste, and any contamination remaining after clean-up is completed[100]. They also affirm that effective stewardship requires collective participation and cooperation of various levels of government, industry, and the public at large. Such participation and cooperation rely heavily upon governments' and industry's ability and willingness to understand the views of the public[101]. As a programmatic philosophy, stewardship represents a fundamental shift in incremental or 'quick-fix' mentality of managing processes. Furthermore, they argue that stewardship centres on the development and the continual evaluation of long-term clean-up solutions. Overall, though, is that stewardship is a

---

[99] BHP, BHP Billiton Sustainability Report. <URL:http://www.bhpbilliton.com / home/investors/reports/Documents/2006SummarySustainabilityReport.pdf,> *Accessed on 7 November 2007pg 1.(*2006).

[100] Williams.B.L;Magsumbol.M.S, "Perceptions toward Stewardship among Residents Living Near U.S. Department of Energy Nuclear Facilities,". *Environment, Development and Sustainability:* pp 49-78. (2006)

[101] AASCU, "Stepping Forward As Stewards of Place - A Guide for Leading Public Engagement at State Colleges and Universities," *American Association of State Colleges and Universities*, New York. (2002)

messy reality. True stewardship is rooted in understanding rights and obligations in any context[102]

Ecological footprint can be a menace to the natural environment[103]. Green building is one way towards the appreciation of environmental stewardship. One presenter, at the National Housing Convention in Zimbabwe pointed out clearly that,

"In all instances, it must be remembered that the natural environment is the primary source of satisfaction of our basic human needs. It is thus most important that the built environment is treated as an affordable amelioration of the natural environment and not as a strong competitor, whose success spells inevitable doom to the natural environment."[104]

The characteristics (or practices and behaviours) of sound environmental stewardship entail three basic ethics, namely: protecting the natural systems and using of natural resources effectively and efficiently, making environment a key part of internal priorities, values and ethics, leading by example and holding oneself accountable [105]. This coincides with one conceptualisation of stewardship.[106] It is a moral obligation to care for the environment and the actions undertaken to provide that care,

---

[102] Aristizabal. N; Gomez.A.O, "Chapter 6: Are services more important than titles in Bogotá?" In PAYNE GEOFFREY (ed.) (2002)., *Land, Rights and Innovation – Improving tenure security for the urban poor*, ITDG Publishing: London. (2002); ; Armitage.L, "Customary Land Tenure in Papua New Guinea," *Status and Prospects.*< URL: http://dlc.dlib.indiana.edu/archive/00001043/00/armitage.pdf,> *Accessed on 22 April 2008.*(2000) , Arnott.R, "Housing Policy in Developing Countries," *The Importance of the Informal Economy (Working Paper No. 13),* <URL: http://www.growthcommission.org/storage/cgdev/documents/gc-wp-013_web.pdf>, *Accessed on 2 November 2008(*2008)

[103] Holden.E., "Ecological footprints and sustainable urban form,".*Journal of Housing and the Built Environment 19*: pp91–109 (2004)

[104] Gurney.E.T, "Definition and Standards in Housing," National Housing Convention Report (Public Private Partnership) Victoria Falls Nov. 1997, National Housing Convention: pp 50-56 (1997:54)

[105] EPAESSC, "Everyday Choices: Opportunities for Environmental Stewardship (Technical Report)," <URL: http://www.epa.gov/innovation/pdf/techrpt.pdf>, *Accessed on27 August 2010.* (2005:9)

[106] Powers and PEER Associates (2009:2)

and an ethic of personal responsibility, an ethic of behaviour based on reverence for the Earth and a sense of obligation to future generations[107].

Effective care for the environment hinges on individuals using resources wisely and efficiently, in part by placing self-imposed limits on personal consumption and altering personal expectations, habits and values[108]. To them appropriate use of natural resources within the stewardship ethic involves taking actions that respect the integrity of natural systems.[109] One scholar, applying the stewardship principle to housing has underscored that, stewardship

> "...is an aspect of Habitat II goal of sustainable development. Housing co-op members try to conserve and recycle resources; we house ourselves modestly, in the context of our societies; we plan and maintain our buildings to pass them own to the next generation."[110]

Despite these concerns, it must be noted that, what normally defines how people in a given local behave is a function of their aspirations, desires, context of operation and access to resources to achieve what they want to achieve. In most cases, in Africa, the low-income groups who dwell in the peri-urban are often at the mess of the diktats of the political environment and those who are in power (the elite). While there may be need for 'stewardship education," there are more constraints than incentives to achieve this, especially in the developing countries.

Stewardship education is defined as, "... a process designed to develop an internalized stewardship ethic and the skills necessary to make considered choices and take environmentally responsible actions."[111] To this end, most successful, stewardship education programmes should be designed to influence beliefs, values, intentions, action skills, and

---

[107] Dixon et al. "Stewardship of the Great Lakes environment, A review of literature," *HDRU Publication No. 95-5, Dept. of Natural Resour., N.Y.S. Coll. Agric. and Life Sci.*, Cornell Univ., Ithaca, N.Y.(1995)

[108] Ibid.(1995)

[109] ibid(1995)

[110] Trodin. R, "Statement by the International Co-operative Alliance" <URL:http://www.un.org/Conference/habitat/eng-stat/7/ica7.txt>, *Accessed on 23 July 2008* (2007:1),

[111] Siemer"s (2001) in Powers and PEER Associates (2009:4)

behaviours related to specific environmental issues. In this aspect, programmes ought to address the entry-level, ownership level and empowerment level, variables that have to be correlated with behaviour change. These variables include: environmental sensitivity, knowledge about ecology, in-depth understanding of environmental issues, a sense of personal investment in specific environmental issues, knowledge of environmental action strategies, skills in using environmental action strategies, an internal locus of control, and intentions to take action. Siemer advocates that stewardship education should be viewed as a set of sequential learning experiences that take place over an extensive period, in a combination of formal and non-formal settings, within the context of a supportive social environment[112]. Though this framework has been developed with schoolchildren in mind, the same principles and philosophies are equally applicable with respect to adults in different communities.

Stewardship education could be in the form of inculcating within the citizens a stewardship culture whereby they begin to see the place in which they live, not as a second, transient and unimportant home but rather as a permanent place to live and invest in. This means making citizens, in the first place, to relate to their place, which is wholly owned by them, supposedly 'defend' it against all woes and vagaries including the risks and disasters associated with climate change. Citizens will, in turn, make appropriate choices for building materials that are not only durable but amenable to the challenges of say, climate change. They can also organise themselves to manage the microenvironments they occupy. The whole idea is to have an approach that is integrative, holistic and collaborative and one that allows for strategic communal visioning and practical action[113].

[112] Powers and PEER Associates, 2009:2

[113] Hopkins.L. ;Zapata.M.A, "Engaging the Future: Forecasts, Scenarios, Plans, and Projects edited," *Journal of Regional Science,(*2008); Stoll.L, "Regional Collaboration: A framework for solving complex planning problems." *The Land Tracker 6(2):* pp 1-4. (2006)

The role of households in peri-urban governance should not be ignored[114]. Households (individuals and families) act at a local micro-scale yet the impact they make on a wider scale is huge. Researchers have put across reasons for moderating the negative impacts by adopting a governance approach in which the micro-scale actors are made aware of the impacts of their actions. Perhaps this is the *modus vivendi* of what stewardship is about. Describing the level of civic awareness in peri-urban Zambian settlements, it is said that the level of ignorance "... is high because civic awareness is low. The knowledge of what is expected of a good responsible citizen is often absent. This is usually revealed by the [high] levels of vandalism of public property, pollution and careless waste dumping along roadways."[115] Justifying the need for civic awareness and the creation of a stewardship sense in inner-city housing projects, is has been argued, "It is not a matter of poverty or wealth but of social services provision, socialisation (for example learning how to flash a toilet and improving their way of living. People must be taught of how to live in certain environments. If you do not tame them and allow a *laissez faire* approach, then there will be anarchy. People will make what is available in their environments if they are exposed...."[116] Civic awareness, inculcating a stewardship sense and regulating and facilitating actions, is the responsibility of defined actors.

Researches, especially in American studies have concentrated on the generic aspects of the subject of rural landscape, industrial pollution

---

[114] Cortemiglia. A., "Involving informally housed communities in shaping local government policies aimed at poverty alleviation," *A South African perspective*, *A thesis for the Doctor of Literature and Philosophy in Development Studies*, University of South Africa. (2006).

[115] Mwanamakondo.B.Y, "The state of resettlement areas in Zambia," *A paper presented at the Swedish Cooperative Centre (SCC) at the Chrismar Hotel, 27-28 February 2007*, Lusaka.pg3. (2007)

[116] Rubin. M, "Inner-city redevelopment programmes and its impact on housing and evictions. Presentation made at Refresher Course on Urbanising Africa," *the city centre revisited at Witwatersrand University, Johannesburg: 16-27 August 2010* (2010:1)

and institutional analysis of stewardship.[117] Looked into widely have been urban stewardship and the role civil society is organised towards promotion of environmental stewardship. It is important to see environmental stewardship education as part of the broader human rights education or the rights-based approach to development in which citizens' consciousness is raised so that they are better positioned to manage affairs affecting them in everyday life. The worst threatened variable ever since the creation of human productivity on Earth is the natural environment. As the built environment grows and expands, it threatens this natural environment. Much of the development and assault happens in the peri-urban areas[118]. There is no doubt whatsoever that environmental education, like any other form of 'enlightenment' and conscious raising, is critical for community building and hence resilience.

Continuous community engagement "... is a cornerstone of heritage recognition, value and value-based conservation. The overriding goal is to manage urban continuity and change to retain tangible and intangible value".[119] This implies that meaningful place stewardship can

---

[117] Dixon et al. "Stewardship of the Great Lakes environment, A review of literature," *HDRU Publication No. 95-5, Dept. of Natural Resour., N.Y.S. Coll. Agric. and Life Sci.*, Cornell Univ., Ithaca, N.Y.(1995)5; AASCU, "Stepping Forward As Stewards of Place - A Guide for Leading Public Engagement at State Colleges and Universities," *American Association of State Colleges and Universities*, New York. (2002); TheobaldD.M, "Landscape patterns of exurban growth in the USA from 1980 to 2020,". *Ecology and Society* 10(1): 32. <URL: http://www.ecologyandsociety.org/vol10/iss1/art32/,>, *Accessed on 27 July 2008* 2005;Williams.B.L;Magsumbol.M.S, "Perceptions toward Stewardship among Residents Living Near U.S. Department of Energy Nuclear Facilities,". *Environment, Development and Sustainability:* pp 49-78. (2006); Zorich. D.M, "Defining stewardship in the digital age, in First Monday 12(7)" <URL: http://firstmonday.org/issues/issue_7/zorich/index.html>, *Accessed on 2 August 2007.* (2007);Young.C, "True Stewardship, Brownfields," *AG News for America.* <URL: www.brownfieldagnews.com/>, *Accessed on 4 August 2007.*(2007); Powers Andrew and PEER Associates, (2009); WhiteA.L, "Who speaks for future generations?," *Business for Social Responsibility* (BSR),< URL: www.bsr.org>(2007)

[118] Svendsen.E; Campbell.L, " Urban Ecological Stewardship, Understanding the Structure, Function and Network of Community-based Urban Land Management," *City and the Environment1 (1)*: pp 1-31. (2008)

[119] O"Donnell.P.M, "Preservation of the Spirit of Place," <URL:http ://www.international.icomos.org/quebec2008/cd/toindex/77_pdf/77-hFCw-13.pdf>, *Accessed on 27 June 2011.pg8.* (2008)

be achieved by community participation that often calls for community visioning. These dimensions are part of community building. Community building is "… a process whereby various community capitals are brought together to build a community of experience and interaction"[120]. This capacity inventory is simply a questionnaire designed to identify a person's skills; areas of knowledge and experience, commitments; and the willingness to be involved in community building or economic development activities. Community building implies combining interests in diversity linking place stewardship to the concept of community building as has been asserted "...embraces, in its ambit, the conditioned actions of humanity in the production of outputs and outcomes as they radiate from the latent and natural capacities and aptitudes of people. Community building is an activity aimed at the modification of the environment by exploiting the 'unity-in-diversity' philosophy and channelling of the unified forces of humanity and sociality in the production of [sustainable] habitats."[121]

For community building to happen successfully, a paraphernalia of success factors ought to be considered. With reference to geographical space like that of peri-urban, these are better examined through the tenets and components of the sustainable livelihoods framework (SLF). The need for the instrumentation of a capacity inventory of the actors or stakeholders is suggested and it goes beyond the human capital involved in local development. Thus, it includes certain key assets or capitals enshrined in the sustainable livelihoods' framework. These key assets include natural

---

[120] Amirahmadi. H, "Toward a Theory of Community Capital," *Paper presented at the Sixth Sharjah Urban Planning Symposium, Sharjah, The United Arab Emirates.* <URL: http://www.caspianassociates.com/towards.doc, > *Accessed on 22 April 2008.*(2003:6)

[121] Novicevic. M.M et al. "Communities of Creative Practice, Follett"s Seminal Conceptualisation," *International Journal of Public Administration 30(4):* pp367-385(2007);[121] Ziller. A, "The role of planning in community building," *Unpublished Doctor of Philosophy Degree Thesis*, *Faculty of Architecture*, University of Sydney: Sydney, (2004)., , MIT, "Just Jerusalem Competition, Jerusalem 2050," Cambridge,(2007) <http://web.mit.edu.justjerusalem/> *Accessed on 23 August 2007.* (2007), Chirisa. I, "Prospects for the asset-based community development approach in Epworth and Ruwa, Zimbabwe," A housing and environmental perspective. *African Journal of History and Culture 1(2):* pp028-035. (2009:30)

capital (the natural endowment as rainfall, enjoyed in a particular place), social capital (assets of social relationships and networks in place), and human capital (including health, knowledge and skills by the local people). They also entail physical capital (including the hard infrastructure – roads, dams, buildings, in place), financial capital (including lines of credit and institutions for lending in place), political capital (including the ability of the citizens in place to freely engage in democratic dialogue and the ability of the leadership to grant political will to issues of local progression)[122]. Moreover, the list is also spiritual capital (including the capability by the local leaders to motivate and inspire the local citizens into progressive action for local development)[123]. Spirituality is more than religion though the two are mutually reinforcing. It is plain that, at the beginning of most peri-urban housing projects, mutual support by beneficiaries (in most cases organised by a trust, consortium, federation or cooperative) is a critical factor.[124] In some cases, members have 'educated' their groups on how to manage their affairs including caring for the resources that they share, the environment or habitat space included. Following is an outline theoretical framework for the study.

---

[122] Kretzmann. J.P, "Building Communities from the Inside Out.". <URL: http://www.thecommunityconnection.org/CC_aboutpubs/14_Bldg_Comms_InsideOut.doc>, *Accessed on 22 April 2008,* (1995)

[123] Chirisa. I, "Prospects for the asset-based community development approach in Epworth and Ruwa, Zimbabwe," A housing and environmental perspective. *African Journal of History and Culture 1(2):* pp028-035. (2009:30); Johnson.A.J, "Mary Parker Follett: Laying the Foundations for Spirituality in the Workplace," *International Journal of Public Administration 30(4)*: pp425-440. (2007); Neefjes, "Environments and Livelihoods for Sustainability," *OXFAM GB*, London.(2000); Nhema. F, "Speech By The Minister Of Environment And Natural Resources Management Hon. Francis Nhema (MP) At The National Housing Convention at Victoria Falls, 28 October 2009." (2009); Pasteur. K, "Tools for Sustainable Livelihoods: Policy Analysis," *Institute of Development Studies*, Brighton(2001)

[124] Johnson.A.J, "Mary Parker Follett: Laying the Foundations for Spirituality in the Workplace," *International Journal of Public Administration 30(4)*: pp425-440. (2007)

CHAPTER 2
THEORIES IN STEWARDSHIP AND HOUSING

The study focuses on the processes and outcomes of housing and stewardship in peri-urban settlements in Zimbabwe. There are essentially two types of peri-urban settlements in Zimbabwe, namely, the suburban type and the informal hence semi-rural. The first, called 'suburban type' caters for those households and families that are relatively wealthy and can afford surplus income to build, maintain and afford spacious apartments away from the city centre. They enjoy motorable distances from, 25 to 40 kilometres from the centre. For the Harare Metropolitan area, this 'suburban type' is typified by such areas like Beatrice, south of Harare, Seke and Chihota to the south-east, Juru, north-east, Christon Bank (about 40 kilometres from Harare City Centre) and Ruwa (25 kilometres from Harare City Centre).

The study hinges on two critical concepts of stewardship and housing both of which have a set of theories that explain them. Peri-urban is taken as a place and location in which the processes of stewardship and housing are expressed. There are a number of theories linked to stewardship, for example, the Agency Theory, Stewardship Theory, Resource Dependency Theory, Stakeholder Theory and the Managerial Hegemony Theory[125]. These theories are largely from the business world.

---

[125] BESG, 2003; Ferguson.B, "Process, Policy, and Public-Private Partnerships in Housing in Developing Countries, What Can the United States Learn?," <URL: http://www.huduser.org/Publications/pdf/brd/07Ferguson.pdf>, *Accessed on 22 April 2008.*(2007); Corteiglia. A, "Involving informally housed communities in shaping local government policies aimed at poverty alleviation," *A South African perspective*, A thesis for the Doctor of Literature and Philosophy in Development Studies, University of South Africa. (2006); Cornforth.C.J,The goveramce of social enterprises: a paradox perspective. *Annals of Public and Cooperative Economics*

Specifically, I examine the Stewardship Theory (also known as the Partnership Model)[126]. Stewardship is largely a qualitative aspect[127]. Use of clear and precise qualitative indicators assists in establishing a measurement of the qualitative aspect[128]. The key features of the stewardship or partnership model that, in a way advance the notion and practice of sustainability as advocated for by this study and contributors identify the key features as:

a) Recognition of regions and actors as collaborative partners for a common good[129],
b) Existence and exercise of political capital and will in support of collaborative initiatives;
c) Support of community, neighbourhood and regional networks,
d) Promotion o 'bottom-up' initiatives to the raising of people's standards of living;
e) The ending of the top-down stovepipe model hence the promotion of both vertical and lateral coordination of housing and environmental management initiatives and practices,

---

75(1): 11-32. (2004); Donaldson.L ;Davis. J.H; "CEO governance and shareholder returns, Agency theory or stewardship theory,". *Paper presented at the annual meeting of the Academy of Management*, Washington, DC. (1989); "Stewardship theory or agency theory, CEO governance and shareholder returns," *Australian Journal of Management 16*: pp 49-64.(1991)

126 Cornforth.C.J,The goveramce of social enterprises: a paradox perspective. *Annals of Public and Cooperative Economics 75(1)*: 11-32. (2004); Pastoriza.D; Arino.A, "When Agents Become Stewards: Introducing Learning in the Stewardship Theory." <URL: http://www.iese.edu/en/files/6_40618.pdf,> *Accessed on 21 June 2008.(*2008), Lurccort.R, "Regional Visioning Public Participation - Best Practices," *Report prepared for Sustainable Pittsburgh.*< URL: http://www.sustainable pittsburgh.org/pdf/Regional_ Visioning_Jan_05.pdf,> *Accessed on 22 April 2008.* (2005)

127 Bryden. J ; Hart.K, "Land reform, planning and people: an issue of stewardship" <URL:http://www.caledonia.org.uk/land/documents/Land%20Reform%20&%20Stewardship.pdf> *Accessed on 27 August 2010.* (2006:6); ARS, "Regional Stewardship: A commitment to Place," *Monograph Series. ARS*, California. (2000:4); Powers and Peer Associates; 2009; Young.C, "True Stewardship, Brownfields," *AG News for America*. <URL: www.brownfieldagnews.com/>, *Accessed on 4 August 2007.*(2007)

128 Mulwa.F.M, "Participatory Monitoring and Evaluation of Community Projects," *Paulines Publications Africa*, Nairobi.(2008)

129 Anstein.S.R., "A Ladder of Citizen Participation,". *Journal of American Institute of Planners 35(4)*: pp216-224.(1969)

f) Creation and promotion of policy and legislative instrument that build capacity and recognition of local planning initiatives,
g) Community visioning through such techniques and models and scenario and strategic planning,
h) Formulation and enhancement of tools that inculcate a sense of responsibility among the different players in place and space, and,
i) General awareness of environmental and place processes like climate change[130].

All these factors, frameworks and tools are instruments for achieving place stewardship, which creates environmental sustainability.[131]. In other words, they are the keys to achieving sustainable development, as it ought to be. Without unbundling sustainable development, is just another concept, fuzzy and lofty[132]. Five basic paradigms are useful in understanding stewardship. There are; the biblical Judeo - Christian tradition[133], the traditionalist

---

[130] Mukamuri.B, "Indigenous knowledge, perceptions and management of climate change in South Central Zimbabwe,". *Presentation in the Earth in Transition (EIT) Proceedings for the Society for Ecological Restoration International, Zaragosa, Spain on September 12, 2005,* <URL: http://www.ser.org/iprn/proceedings.asp>, *Accessed on 13 October 2011.*(2005); Mukuka.L, "Factors affecting delivery of social and infrastructure services in municipalities – A case study of housing, water supply and sanitation in Bwacha Compound, Kabwe, in Municipal Development Program – MDP, undated," *Addressing poverty in the context of decentralisation in Eastern and Southern Africa – Case studies in Malawi, Uganda, Zambia and Zimbabwe: MDP Working Paper 3,* Municipal Development Programme for Sub-Saharan Africa,,Harare, pp 105-128.(2001); [130] Ziller. A, "The role of planning in community building," *Unpublished Doctor of Philosophy Degree Thesis, Faculty of Architecture,* University of Sydney: Sydney, (2004); Zorich. D.M, "Defining stewardship in the digital age, in First Monday 12(7)" <URL: http://firstmonday.org/issues/issue_7/zorich/index.html>, *Accessed on 2 August 2007.* (2007)

[131] Girardet.H., "Creating Sustainable Cities (Schumacher Briefings 2,": *Greenbooks for the Schumacher Society*:,Bristol. (1999).

[132] Manjengwa.J, "Linking environment and development, easier said than done," learning from the Zimbabwean experience, *Development Southern Africa 24(2):* pp 225-240. (2007)

[133] UNDP, "Human Development Report 2007/2008 – Fighting climate change: human solidarity in a divided world," *Palgrave Macmillan*: New York.(2007)

vernacular[134], the business management[135]and the ecological environment[136]. Specific in each are the concepts of serving and service. Emphasis is placed on the steward or caretaker[137]. Such has been highlighted by scholars[138]. Other scholars, on the same

---

134 du Toit.F., "Musha: The Shona Concept of Home: Aspects of Zimbabwe Architecture Monograph 1," *Zimbabwe Publishing House*, Harare. (1981); Highlands. D., "What"s Indigenous? An Essay on Building" in Turan, M. (ed.) "Vernacular Architecture: Paradigms of Environmental Response," *Aldershot, Avebury*, 31-62. (1990); Gilbert. A ,Ward.P.M, "Land for the rich and land for the poor," Gugler J (ed.)., "The Urbanisation of the Third World," *Oxford University Press*, London. (1990);Huby.M, "Social Policy and the Environment," *Open University Press*,Buckingham. (1998); ; Kumar.A., "Housing Report - Rural mud house with pitched roof," *World Housing Encyclopedia*. <URL: http://www.world-housing.net/whereport1view.php?id=100056>, *Accessed on 22 April 2008(*2005)

135 Merill, (2007)

136 Girardet.H., "Creating Sustainable Cities (Schumacher Briefings 2,": *Greenbooks for the Schumacher Society*:,Bristol. (1999), ;Lannas. J; Turpie.J. K, "Valuing the Provisioning Services of Wetlands, Contrasting a Rural Wetland in Lesotho with a Peri-Urban Wetland in South Africa," *Ecology and Society 14(2)*: 18. <[Online] URL: http://www.ecologyandsociety.org/vol14/iss2/art18/>, *Accessed on 2 October 2010.* (2009:22); Lawrence. R. J, "Housing and health: Beyond Disciplinary Confinement," *Journal of Urban Health 83(3):* pp540-549(2006); Merill,(2007); Marshall. F, What does peri-urban sustainability mean in the context of Delhi? <URL: http://stepscentre-thecrossing.blogspot.com/2008/12/what-does-peri-urban-sustainability.html:>, *Accessed on 2April 2009*.(4 December 2008); and the place-based community approach ; Marshall.F et al. "*On the Edge of Sustainability:* Perspectives on Peri-urban Dynamics," STEPS Working Paper 35, STEPS, Centre Brighton. (2009); Mwanamakondo.B.Y, "The state of resettlement areas in Zambia," *A paper presented at the Swedish Cooperative Centre (SCC) at the Chrismar Hotel, 27-28 February 2007*, Lusaka.pg3. (2007), Myers.G.A, "Social Construction of Peri-Urban Places and Alternative Planning in Zanzibar," *African Affairs 109* (437): pp575-595.(2010)

137 Arthurson.K, "Social mix and social interaction: do residents living in different housing tenures mix?," *Paper presented to the ENHR Conference on Sustainable Urban Areas, 25-28 June 2007, Rotterdam.*< URL: www.enhr2007rotterdam.nl>, *Accessed on 13 July 2008.* (2007)

138 de Vries.J.R, "Trust as a central concept in planning research and practice," *Paper presented at the 23rd Congress of the Association of European Schools of Planning, 15th – 18th July 2009*, Liverpool, UK (2009), Saltman ; Ferroussier-Davis, "The concept of stewardship in health policy," *Bulletin of the World Health Organisation, 2000*, 78 (6): pp 732-739. (2000), Davis J.H et al. "Toward a stewardship theory of management," *Academy of Management Review* 22: pp20-47. (1997), Arthurs; Busenitz, "The Boundaries and Limitations of Agency Theory and Stewardship Theory in the Venture Capitalist/Entrepreneur Relationship," *Entrepreneurship*

train[139]. Specifically, on housing development and processes, grassroots models of housing have been spoken of[140]. The same has been stressed by different scholars and institutions who have highlighted the notion of 'vernacular architecture'[141]. Vernacular architecture is the major

---

Theory and Practice (Winter): pp 145-162. (2003), Svendsen.E; Campbell.L, " Urban Ecological Stewardship, Understanding the Structure, Function and Network of Community-based Urban Land Management," *City and the Environment1 (1)*: pp 1-31. (2008).

139 Thomas. D., Architecture and the urban environment – a vision for the new age, *Architectural Press: London* (2002), Mulenga, et al. "Building Links for Improved Sanitation in Poor Urban Settlements," *Recommendations from Research in Southern Africa, Institute of Irrigation and Development Studies*, Southampton. (2004); Hogrewe. W.et. al,"The Unique Challenges of Improving Peri-Urban Sanitation," *WASH Technical Report No. 86., Report prepared for the Office of Health, Bureau for Research and Development*, U.S. Agency for International Development, under WASH Task No. 339, U.S. Agency for International Development: Washington, DCpg.9(1993)), Ben-Ami. D ; Ramp.D, "Modelling the effect of roads and other disturbances on wildlife populations in the peri-urban environment to facilitate long-term viability," Road Ecology Center eScholarship Repository, John Muir Institute of the Environment, *University of California*, Davis. <URL: http://repositories.cdlib.org/jmie/roadeco/Ben-Ami2005a> *Accessed on 22 April 2008*. (2005)

140 Schilderman. T, "Putting people at the centre of reconstruction,". Chapter 1 in Lyons Michal and Theo Schilderman with Camillo Boano eds. "Building Back Better - Delivering people-centred housing reconstruction at scale," *Practical Action Publishing Ltd/ Schumacher Centre for Technology and Development*, Warwickshire, <URL: www.practicalactionpublishing.org>, *Accessed on 27 June 2011.(*2010), Gilbert. A,, "Forms and Effectiveness of Community Participation in Squatter Settlements," *Regional Development Dialogue 8(4)*: pp 56-85; (1987); "Land and Shelter in Mega-Cities," Some Critical Issues, in Fuchs Roland J., Ellen Brennan. Joseph Chaimie. Fu-chen Lo, and Juha Uitto (eds.), "Mega-City Growth and the Future," *United Nations University*, Tokyo.(1994), High et al. "Understanding informal institutions," Networks and communities in rural development. <URL: http://econ.core.hu/doc/konf/High2005.pdf>, *Accessed on 22 April 2008.* (2005), Turner. A. G, "Sampling frames and master samples," <URL: unstats.un.org/unsd /demographic/meetings/egm/Sampling.../no_3.pdf>, *Accessed on 12 March 2013.* (1976), Hamdi (1995); [140] Alexander. C et al. "The grass roots housing process," <URL:http://www.livingneighborhoods.org/library/grassroots. htm>, *Accessed on 22 April 2008.*(1973))

141 Gough.K, "From Bamboo to Bricks: Self-Help Housing and the Building Materials Industry in Urban Colombia," PhD thesis, University College London. (1992); Kellett "Constructing Home: Production and Consumption of Popular Housing in Northern Colombia," PhD thesis, University of Newcastle upon Tyne. (1995), "The Construction of Home in the Informal City," in F. Hernández, M. Millington, and I.

explanation for peri-urban housing informality as which largely defines Epworth in Zimbabwe.

The stewardship of the environment is a multifarious and value-laden reality amid growing urban expanding largely due to increasing urbanisation. Its meaning is distorted as one tries to put together the pieces that define human settlements and the actors that contribute to their making. human settlements have been defined to "…mean the totality of the human community – whether city, town or village – with all the social, material, organisational, spiritual and cultural elements that sustain it."[142] Unpacking the totality as stressed here becomes a complex reality especially if communities are settling on 'fluid' territories called the peri-urban. Housing as a major land consumer is a critical issue of concern in the biophysical environment.[143] It is associated with increased sand extractions, rock blasting (quarrying) and exploitation of natural resources for livelihood support. Housing and its effect on the natural physical environment have a bearing on environmental politics and it has thus been opined that housing development "... has effects on the environment in terms of land-use, loss of amenity and waste production, and these are felt unevenly by different sectors of the society. But the construction of housing, whether sophisticated homes for the affluent or the makeshift structures of wood, iron-zinc plates and asbestos roofing which are typical of shanty areas in many developing countries, in itself has environmental impacts. The building of homes and offices is estimated to consume

---

Borden (eds.), Transculturation: Cities, Space and Architecture in Latin America. *Amsterdam and New York*, Rodopi, pp 22-42(2005), "Contemporary Vernaculars: Informal housing processes and vernacular theory," *Journal of the International Society for the Study of Vernacular Settlements - ISVS e-journal 2(1)*: pp 1-12. 2001),Kellet ; Nappier "Squatter Architecture: a Critical Examination of Vernacular Theory and Spontaneous Settlement with Reference to South America and South Africa," *Traditional Dwellings and Settlements Review 6(2) May 1995*: pp 7-24. (1995), Rudofsky (1964) Lawrence (1987, 1990) Rapoport (1988), Stea and Turan (1990; 1993) Oliver (1990; 2006) ; UNDP, "Human Development Report 2007/2008 – Fighting climate change: human solidarity in a divided world," *Palgrave Macmillan*: New York.(2007)

[142] The Vancouver Declaration on Human Settlements, (1976)

[143] Savory.A, "Holistic Resource Management," *Gilmour Publishing*. Harare, (1988); Alberti.M, "Advances in Urban Ecology, *Integrating Humans and Ecological Processes in Urban Ecosystems,*" *Springer,* New York., (2009)

between one sixth and one half of the world's physical resources, wood, minerals, energy and water"[144].

Property or stand-owners or tenants in 'suburban' peri-urban areas are highly structured and formalised at least in the notion that they can hold their municipal government accountable because they contribute in most, if not all, matters that go with the improvement of their larger space. The next category of peri-urban, typically informal and semi-rural, has evolved organically, sometimes from being rural into becoming urban. Most dwellers have accessed their land illegally[145]. They tend to build very poor structures. This is a major handicap for them; they have a 'restrained' and limited voice to make local government structures work for them. As well, they lack the capacity to improve their general livelihood and living conditions. Overall, this has a bearing on their housing and habitat environments. For the poor household, living in a peri-urban area, which is poorly serviced with the dwellings and their vicinities poorly constructed, made and maintained, is what constitutes the notion of "urban penalty"[146].

In the early years of establishment, peri-urban areas are under immense environmental 'assault." Years after the constructions, by some resilient capacities, they are expected to renew themselves. A number of elements are there to support community resilience, namely, adaptation, social learning, nurturing diversity and flexibility, and creating opportunities for self-organisation). A thesis of "building communities from the inside out" puts resilience into context. Resilience is an endogenous virtue in community members[147]. In light of resilience, the

---

[144] Huby.M, "Social Policy and the Environment," *Open University Press*, Buckingham. Pg67(1998);

[145] Rodgerson, 1997

[146] UNCHS, "*The state of the world"s cities 200,"* United Nations Centre for Human Settlements (Habitat), Nairobi(2001); Sverdlik. F, "Ill-health and poverty: a literature review on health in informal settlements," *Environment and Urbanisation 23(1)*: pp 123-155. (2011); Kessides.C, *The Urban Transition in Sub-Saharan Africa: Implications for Economic Growth and Poverty Reduction*, The Cities Alliance: Washington D. C. (2006)

[147] Kretzmann. J.P, "Building Communities from the Inside Out.". <URL: http://www.thecommunityconnection.org/CC_aboutpubs/14_Bldg_Comms_InsideO

stewardship of place becomes a direct response of a community to its real or perceived common challenges. Despite different interests that individual or organisations serve, they are most likely to collaborate on issues that affect them as a community – the common challenges[148]. Partnership and stewardship acknowledge the existence of differences among group members or even the partners.

With spatial references to places, different groups therein will always hold different opinions and views. The respect of these differences helps in shaping the future of these groups by an integrationist manner to create a difference. In the same vein, it is argued, "Imagining cities as profoundly ecological and natural, and working to further strengthen connections of urbanites with nature, also requires leaders – elected officials, community activists, and design professionals, among others – to step forward and to advance and advocate for often bold ideas and ambitious green agendas."[149] Progressive development comes by appropriately handling differences. This has been advanced regarding participatory budgeting in Brazil[150]. Contentious politics applied by groups in certain cities and towns tended to get biased towards liveliness and competitiveness in the process of planning and delivery of services hence progress as opposed to those succumbing to co-optation. This means that debate and strong argumentation by groups are healthier to policy formulation and implementation than passivity and tendencies towards co-optation. What is important is to embrace all views and formulate a much stronger position.

---

ut.doc>, *Accessed on 22 April 2008,* (1995) BESC, "Partnerships for better living: An introductory guide to Habitable Environments Partnerships," *Built Environment Support Group*, Pietermaritzburg. (2003)

148 ARS, "Regional Stewardship: A commitment to Place," *Monograph Series. ARS*, California. (2000:4); de Vries.J.R, "Trust as a central concept in planning research and practice," *Paper presented at the 23rd Congress of the Association of European Schools of Planning, 15th – 18th July 2009*, Liverpool, UK (2009),

149 Beatley. T, "Biophilic Cities: Integrating Nature into Urban Design and Planning," *Island Press*, Washington.pg 148 (2011)

150 Wampler.B, "Participatory Budgeting in Brazil: Contestation, Cooperation and Accountability," *Pennsylvania University Press*,Pennsylvania.(2007);World Bank , Brazil: "Toward a More Inclusive and Participatory Budget in Porto Allegre Volume 1: Main Report," *World Bank*, Washington DC., (2008)

This study is partly informed by the stewardship theory or partnership model. The theory is part of the broader collective theory in which actors collaborate to solve common problems[151].in commemorating "Follett's model of unified pluralism"[152] it is asserted that communities, in practice, learn and adapt to manage problems embedded in (or brought about by) the different interests they wield. Unified pluralism requires social trust and tolerance. It is a way of conflict resolution and interests' integration[153]. Integration has been described as "a way of handling complexity" in diversity[154]. It is argued, regarding diversity that, "this diversity of interests does not imply that they should oppose each other; rather they may only confront each other. The confronting of interests assumes the preservation of interests of diverse individual interests and, therefore, should result in integration rather than compromise."[155] It is observed that "Compromising with the old ways, or even combining old ways, keeps us always old"[156].

Stewardship is integral to policy formulation, implementation and reform. Policy reform ought to negate some old practices because they tend to work against innovation. The way communities respond to government action (policy) is a matter of two basic internal forces:

---

[151] Ferguson.B, "Process, Policy, and Public-Private Partnerships in Housing in Developing Countries, What Can the United States Learn?," <URL: http://www.huduser.org/Publications/pdf/brd/07Ferguson.pdf>, *Accessed on 22 April 2008.*(2007); Taylor.J, "Declining Life Support Systems: An NGO Response,". *WESSA, Wildlife and Environment Society of South Africa – A Celebration of 85 Years of Caring for the Earth:* pp18-20. (2011); BHP, BHP Billiton Sustainability Report.

[152] Novicevic. M.M et al. "Communities of Creative Practice, Follett"s Seminal Conceptualisation," *International Journal of Public Administration 30(4):* pp367-385(2007))

[153] Gehan.R; Gehani. R, "Mary Parker Follett"s Constructive Conflict: A "Psychological Foundation of Business Administration" for Innovative Enterprises," *International Journal of Public Administration 30(4)*: pp387-404.(2007).

[154] De Kort.A.I, "Designing a Strategic Plan Development Approach for Integrated Area Development Projects" *Published PHD Thesis, University of Twente*, The Netherlands. (2009:9)

[155] Novicevic. M.M et al. "Communities of Creative Practice, Follett"s Seminal Conceptualisation," *International Journal of Public Administration 30(4):* pp377 (2007)

[156] Ibid, (2007)

resilience and capacity[157]. The Theory of Civic Capacity argues that communities respond to government enforcement according to individual capacities[158]. Three components of civic capacity have been identified as civic capital, civic competency and civic enterprise [159]. In stewardship, different interests are represented. An integrationist approach ought to be creative enough not to overlook or undermine community and individual capacities, defined as "civic capacity".

Box 2.1: Three Components of Civic Capacity[160]

- *Civic capital:* is the network of social and cultural institutions.
- *Civic competency*: is the set of knowledge, skills and capabilities collectively possessed by the community.
- *Civic enterprise*: refers to the shared history of the community and their tradition of joint action. It also includes an expectation that the same individuals will work together on the same and other problems again in the future.

However, it is observed that "a common error in the analysis of human systems is the oversimplification of treating groups as if they behave as one individual: "the government has decided…" and "…it is the will of the people that…. As far as decision-making is concerned, policy analysis, therefore, has to take into account that policies, programmes and

[157] Svendsen. L, "Cultivating Resilience, Urban Stewardship as a Means to Improving Health and Well-being Campbell, Lindsay; Wiesen, Anne, eds," . *Restorative commons: creating health and well-being through urban landscapes. Gen. Tech Rep. NRS-P-39.* U.S. Department of Agriculture, Forest Service, Northern Research Station: pp58-87.(2009)

[158] Shinn. C. W, "Theory, Research and Practice," *Administrative Theory and Praxis 21*: 103-119. (1999)

[159] Box 2.1; Shipley. R;Newkirk. R, Vision and visioning in planning: what do these terms really mean? *Environment and Planning: Planning and Design 2*: pp 573-579(1999); Shinn (1998) cited by Dent, "Civic capacity and community response to government action, Endangered Species Act and state law in the Methow and Walla Walla in the Pacific Northwest," *International Journal of Public Administration 31(3)*: pp262-276.(2008:270

[160] Dent, "Civic capacity and community response to government action, Endangered Species Act and state law in the Methow and Walla Walla in the Pacific Northwest," *International Journal of Public Administration 31(3)*: pp262-276.(2008:270)

projects are shaped partly by the overall institution by which they are formulated, partly by the composition of parts and partly be the influence of particular individuals.... In other words, a policy is shaped by the nature of the problem that it is supposed to tackle."[161] Thus, integral to civic capacity, as already stated, is resilience. resilience is described as a concept of ecological origins. In resilience there is an emphasis on the multiple ways, "...a system can respond to hazard occurrence, including its ability to absorb hazard impacts, to learn from, adapt to and recover from them, and to reorganise after impacts. In other words, a resilient system is able to absorb impacts without changing its fundamental functions; at the same time, it is able to renew, reorganise and adapt when hazard impacts significantly"[162].

Stewardship as the foundation of collective responsibility is pinned on the individuals' capacity to apprehend the situation at hand[163]. Place context-based knowledge, experiential-based wisdom, religiosity and income-level are at the centre-stage of place stewardship[164]. Peri-urban settlements are normally examined from a broader regional view that, at times, includes huge metropolitan developments. the three goals of regional collaboration, in the framework of stewardship, are outlined as

---

[161] de Valk. P, "An Analysis of Planning Policy in Zimbabwe (Unpublished Paper)," *Department of Rural and Urban Planning, University of Zimbabwe*, Harare. (1986:5-6)

[162] Lopez-Marrero. T ; Tschakert.P, "From theory to practice: building more resilient communities in flood prone," *Environment and Urbanisation 23(1):* pp229-249. (2011:6)

[163] De Kort.A.I, "Designing a Strategic Plan Development Approach for Integrated Area Development Projects" *Published PHD Thesis, University of Twente*, The Netherlands. (2009:9)

[164] Mukamuri.B, "Indigenous knowledge, perceptions and management of climate change in South Central Zimbabwe,". *Presentation in the Earth in Transition (EIT) Proceedings for the Society for Ecological Restoration International, Zaragosa, Spain on September 12, 2005,* <URL: http://www.ser.org/iprn/proceedings.asp>, *Accessed on 13 October 2011.*(2005);Girardet.H., "Creating Sustainable Cities (Schumacher Briefings 2,": *Greenbooks for the Schumacher Society*:,Bristol. (1999), ; Ozaki. R,Uršic.M, "What makes "urban" urban and "suburban" suburban? Urbanity and patterns of consumption in everyday life," *Paper presented at the Sociology of Consumption Research Network, the ESA 2005 Conference, Toruń, Poland, 9-12 September 2005.* <URL: http://www.sifo.no/files/Ozaki_Ursic.pdf,> *Accessed on 27 June 2011.* (2005);

liveable community (involving the preservation and creation of places to live and work), healthy environment (encapsulating aspects to do with maintenance and restoration of the natural infrastructure) and vibrant economy (shaped by preparing people and places to succeed)[165]. Speaking of regional stewards, their calibre and approaches, it is underscored that, regional stewards,

> "... share power and mobilise people, ideas.... tend to be *committed to the long-term well-being of a particular place.* They apply the same *entrepreneurial spirit* and persistence to solving regional challenges that business entrepreneurs apply in building a business; they are civic entrepreneurs. They see the need for more connected regional approaches to address social, economic and environmental issues; *they are integrators.* They build support from leaders, citizens, interest groups and policy makers toward a shared vision; *they are coalition builders.* [They] hold themselves and each other accountable to achieve tangible results and sustained outcomes.... Regardless of their background or station in life, they share a common belief in the need *to work across boundaries* to accomplish the goals of stewardship."[166]

At the heart of the stewardship philosophy is the idea that with careful planning, infrastructure development and management, and, protection of ecosystems, it is possible to talk of sustainable development. It is suggested that "stewardship-based economics," contrasted to "ownership-based economics" be equated to a market economy[167]. According to the supporters of ideas, stewardship-based economics entitles all individuals the right to live and share and enjoy the earth's resources (social equity). In this arrangement, there is a balance between

---

[165] Parr, J et al. "The practice of stewardship," *Developing leadership for regional action. Denver,* CO: Alliance for Regional Stewardship: March. (2002) ; Mckinney et al. Working across Boundaries: A Framework for Regional Collaboration, in LeRoyer Ann ed. *Land Lines 16(3),* Lincoln Institute of Land Policy: Cambridge (USA).(2004)

[166] Mckinney et al. Working across Boundaries: A Framework for Regional Collaboration, in LeRoyer Ann ed. *Land Lines 16(3),* Lincoln Institute of Land Policy: Cambridge (USA).(2004)

[167] Kao. R, "Stewardship-based economics," *World Scientific Publishing Co.* (2007)

private and public interest[168]. Central to economic-led stewardship are the concepts of discounting and the net present value.

According to the Endogenous Human Capital Model, an individual can shape his or her future by incurring the costs today with the expectation of reaping benefits in future[169]. Such a philosophy is important when one looks at behaviour, obligations and the sense of duty by people residing in a place towards the upkeep of the place. Because peri-urban spaces are always 'shifting," the dynamics behind this shift are inevitably critical for sustainable development processes, putting generational equity in perspective. Thus, in examining peri-urban settlements in light of stewardship, there are many processes that happen here, which, without a sense of sustainable development will be difficult to handle including managing erosion, deforestation, siltation of water bodies, land conflicts, to name these few. These aspects are discussed in both empirical and theoretical chapters of this book. Besides theories of stewardship, there are also housing theories.

There are many theories that explain the behaviour, aspirations, modalities and strategies defining how households and families try to provide or relate to their housing needs. These theories relate to various facets of housing in terms of its location, for example, the classical theories of location and structure of cities by theorists like Von Thunen, Alonso, Burgess, Ullman and Harris, to mention these few. Other related theories have to do with aspects including homeownership and rental housing and

---

[168] Young.C, "True Stewardship, Brownfields," *AG News for America.* <URL: www.brownfieldagnews.com/>, *Accessed on 4 August 2007.*(2007); WhiteA.L, "Who speaks for future generations?," *Business for Social Responsibility* (BSR),< URL: www.bsr.org>(2007); ; Manjengwa.J, "Linking environment and development, easier said than done," learning from the Zimbabwean experience, *Development Southern Africa 24(2):* pp 225-240. (2007);Gordon. P ; Richardson.H.W, "Are compact cities a desirable planning goal?"*Journal of the American Planning Association 63(1)*: pp95-117 (1997)

[169] McCann. P, "Urban and regional economics," *Oxford University Press* Oxford.(2001); Hogan P.H., "Human Capital and the Theory of Life-Cycle Investing." *American Association of Individual Investors (AAII) Journal*, pp 18-19.(2008) <URL: http:// www. hoganfinancial.com / publications/2008-05%20AAII % 20Human%20 Capital.pdf, Accessed on 22 April 2008.>;

the political economy[170]. Others explain how people in poverty try to find a way out of their plight or to adapt to their poor living conditions.

Urban poverty is typologised in relation to policy prescriptions and their outcomes some of which are related to the structure of the city like segregation and discrimination and social relations including social networking[171]. In this study, while the author acknowledges the multifarious nature of theories, the Theory of Housing Adjustment[172], the Anarchist Theory of Housing (championed by Pierre-Joseph Proudhon), the Marxist Theory of Housing put across by Friedrich Engels and the Housing Common(s) Theory, are singled out.[173] These theories are applied in the study because they relate to stewardship as applied in the study, that is, stewardship as care and stewardship as a partnership. In other words, in applying these theories the question on ways in which households build, maintain or relate to the shelter and housing practices that define them and their habitat at large. Housing is thus, not only physical structures but involves various/ a number of players;

a) Theory of Housing Adjustment

The Housing Adjustment Theory[174] explains the behaviour of households in society regarding the manner in which they seek to improve and adapt the dwellings and shelter if they consider the structures to be substandard[175]. Households and families are believed to assume respect of self or others by improving the type of dwelling in which they live in. There are two principal processes to this, namely "housing adjustment and

---

[170] Clarke.S ; Ginsburg.N, "The Political Economy of Housing." <URL: http://home pages.warwick.ac.uk/~syrbe/pubs/ClarkeGinsburg.pdf, Accessed on 31 March 2013. (1975)>

[171] Curley. A.M, "Theories of Urban Poverty and Implications for Public Housing Policy," *Journal of Sociology and Social Welfare 32(2)*: pp. 97-119. (2005)

[172] Morris. E ; Winter. M, "Housing, Family and Society." *John Wiley and Sons*, New York. (1978)

[173] Hodkinson .P. H, "The return of the housing question" *Ephemera - Theory & Politics in Organization, 12(4)*: pp. 427 (2012)

[174] Morris. E ; Winter. M, "Housing, Family and Society." *John Wiley and Sons*, New York. (1978)

[175] Steggell.C. D et al., "The role of theory in the study of housing,". *Housing and Society 28(1&2)*: pp.87-100.(1); "Exploring theories of human behaviour in housing research," . *Housing and Society 30(1)*: pp.3-32(2003)

housing adaptation" Adjustment involves altering the current structure or moving to another one deemed better than the current one. Adaptation, on the other hand, has to do with changing the 'contents' of the house. It involves making changes to the household itself, by sending away some members of bringing in some or changing the arrangement of the physical or material things in the house, for example shifting furniture around to create more space or bringing in new items to make the house look better. Overall, the theory has been widely used in housing research to explain dynamics including residential mobility and household structures and solidarity[176].

b) The Anarchist Theory of Housing (Pierre-Joseph Proudhon)

After observing the rampancy of exploitative private landlordism, Pierre-Joseph Proudhon advocated for its outlawing and for rentals paid by tenants to be converted into purchase payments on their dwellings.[177]. The idea was thus such conversions would then transform the property less tenants into property owners over time. Ownership of the property was opined as critical into improving the morality and behaviour of the working class whose plight had been considered by social reformers as the explanation behind the poor housing conditions of the working class. Anarchists are not comfortable with what they regard as "...the harmful role of the State and other large-scale, bureaucratic forms of [housing] provision"[178]. They yearn for people holding real property but without the state and private corporate organisations in control. They are anti-bureaucratic.

c) The Marxist Theory of Housing

In his study of housing in 1844, Friedrich Engels noted the plight of the working class with respect to the type of shelters that their capitalist employers built for them which were characterised by unsanitary

---

[176] Steggell et al. "The role of theory in the study of housing,". *Housing and Society 28(1&2)*: pp.87-100.(2001); "Exploring theories of human behaviour in housing research," . *Housing and Society 30(1)*: pp.3-32 (2003)

[177] Hodkinson.P. H, "The return of the housing question" *Ephemera - Theory & Politics in Organization, 12(4)*: pp. 427 (2012)

[178] ibid, pg.432

conditions and squalor[179]. Engels disagreed with the notion of the housing crisis but "...only a crisis of capitalism in which housing conditions formed just 'one of the innumerable smaller, secondary evils' caused by the exploitation of workers by capital"[180]. To him, as long as there were different business cycles through time, these business cycles would produce different housing questions hence a perennial challenge on shelter provision and maintenance. citing the global financial crisis 2007-2009, which saw mortgage finance at the market crumbling leading to great problems in the supply of both housing finance and housing stocks this is justified[181]. According to Engels, the bourgeoisie's panacea to the housing problem was what he called the 'Haussmann' in which they would revitalise inner cities and try constructing new houses whose ultimate push was of the working classes out to the periphery. This is described as gentrification and to Engels, this was not a sustainable and more precise solution to the poor working classes. Rather, the solution, he saw it in the working classes hence tenants themselves to change the capitalist society by way of a revolution and expropriation of private property.

It is asserted that "Marxists and socialists see the housing question as inseparable from capitalist social relations...."[182] In Zimbabwe, at independence, as in Britain in the 1970s, there was mass privatisation of council housing into homeownership schemes. I must also highlight that in the Marxist approach to housing falls also Fabianism. This Fabianism was development in the post-1945 era in the United Kingdom, "... as an attempt to apply a rigorous approach to the study of social problems. The application of empirically testable methods was seen as crucial to the validity of the research. The ultimate objectives were to influence policy makers and to encourage government agencies to take action....

---

[179] Clarke.S ; Ginsburg.N, "The Political Economy of Housing." <URL: http://homepages.warwick.ac.uk/~syrbe/pubs/ClarkeGinsburg.pdf, Accessed on 31 March 2013. (1975)>; Tabb.W.K, "Marxism, Crisis Theory and the Crisis of the Early 21st Century.," <URL: http://www.networkideas.org/featart/mar2011/William Tabb. pdf,> *Accessed on 31 March 2013*.(2011)

[180] Hodkinson.P. H, "The return of the housing question" *Ephemera - Theory & Politics in Organization, 12(4)*: pp. 427 (2012)

[181] Ibid, (2012)

[182] Ibid, pg432)

Researchers based at institutions such as the London School of Economics have been able to influence the policy agendas of a number of post-war administrations"[183]. In recent times, the agenda against social exclusion and seclusion in policy matters has heightened.

d) The Housing Common(s) Theory

The theory stresses the idea of shared resources deriving for such terms as natural commons (e.g. land, forests, water resources, air), customary and common law, public or social commons (like roads, knowledge, skills). There is also the notion of relational commons, which is "...embodied with the value practices of cooperation, mutual aid, solidarity, horizontality, non-hierarchy and equality"[184]. The final typology of commons is the anti-capitalist commons, which are "... those compositions of people and projects defined and organised along with the value practices of being-in-common, defending natural commons and/or producing social commons as a conscious act of creating limits to capital"[185].

Three ethical coordinates of commoning to guide political activism around housing, namely, prefigurative commoning, strategic commoning, and hegemonic communing are argued for[186]. Prefigurative commoning which is about "living-in-common" denotes trying to "…meet our housing needs and desires through the creation of non-hierarchical, small-scale, directly democratic, egalitarian and collective forms of housing in our everyday lives, what we might think of as the essential value-practices…"[187]. The utility of land is decided together as a community while space within walls is decided to the discretion of the household or family.

---

[183] Jacobs. K ;Manzi.T, "Evaluating the Social Constructionist Paradigm in Housing Research,". *Housing, Theory and Society 17*: pp.35–42.(2000:36)
[184] Hodkinson.P. H, "The return of the housing question" *Ephemera - Theory & Politics in Organization, 12(4)*: pp. 437 (2012)
[185] Hodkinson.P. H, "The return of the housing question" *Ephemera - Theory & Politics in Organization, 12(4)*: pp. 437 (2012)
[186] Ibid.
[187] Ibid, pg:438

Strategic communing is about "housing-as-commons". It does not treat a housing unit as a standalone artefact. Rather, this artefact is located within a neighbourhood and links up to other housing units. The neighbourhood is treated as a 'conglomeration of households organising themselves as a community and working in solidarity. Protection of a household hinges on the solidarity and number of ties it has established with other households within the neighbourhood. The ethic assumes "... re-privatisation of public housing, forcing more and more people out of a quasi-secure housing space that constrained the exploitative power of capital through its mix of low rents and legal protections, and into the private housing market where, through fear of mortgage defaults or evictions, people are more susceptible to capitalist"[188]. It is argued that strategic communing "... defends everyone's 'right to stay put' regardless of tenure, whether against privatisation, demolition, repossession, eviction, commodification or displacement" [189].

Hegemonic commoning or "circulating the housing commons" argues that tenant control "... enables people to create community social relationships among people in a building and often in the surrounding neighbourhood as well. It enables people to use non-market means of maintaining and repairing their building... Producing housing commons, therefore, takes place at the apex of resistance and creation"[190]. Power to resist or to create is the recipe for success among the underclass or tenants to determine their stay in a place. It is argued that there is "a need for a balance between control which enables and control which inhibits. On housing supply grounds alone, African cities have much to gain from encouraging transformations."[191] In light of this observation, I critically examine the significant processes and issues in peri-urban housing and stewardship with the view highlight why informal settlements tend to dominate the African urban space and how certain enclaves of orderly settlements are created.

---

[188] Ibid.

[189] Ibid.,pg439

[190] Hodkinson.P. H, "The return of the housing question" *Ephemera - Theory & Politics in Organization, 12(4)*: pp. 439 (2012).

[191] Tipple, (2004:20)

The growth of any settlement is explained by a number of factors. Mostly, these have to do with location, accessibility and availability of opportunities[192]. A close look at most metropolitan regions around the world reveals the disjointed nature of core-urban centres with the smaller and satellite towns that draw their 'life' from that core. The interdependence between the core and the peripheral satellites is revealed in the space exchanges and interchanges of the labour, commodity and service markets[193]. Housing is a major aspect of the service market that characterises metropolitan regions. In spatial physical terms, usually, the core regions and the satellites are separated by green and brown fields. In this 'grey' zone, activities including farming, forestry and waste dumping are practised[194]. Yet, peri-urban housing is also a major developmental aspect characterising this space.

Peri-urbanisation, today, is a major challenge including in developed countries like the United States of America[195]. Besides, interregional conflicts are rampant in which case the peri-urban zones are mainly ridden with these challenges. A systems approach is critical in studying the "...complex interactions between urban land-use,

---

[192] Malpezzi. S, "Economic Analysis Of Housing Markets in Developing and Transition Economies," Chapter 44 Mill E.S and P. Cheshire eds. "Handbook of Regional and Urban Economics," *Elsevier Science B. V*(1999); Snoxell. S, "Formalisation of Urban Markets and Street Trading – Research Project. Presentation in Peri-NET (Urban and Peri-urban Research Network) (2002).," Contentious Development: Urban and Peri-urban Transformations and Livelihoods in Africa. *Report of a Peri-NET Workshop, East and Southern Africa held at Fairview Hotel, Nairobi, Kenya, 7-9 October 2002.* (2002); Kuriakose.B, "An alternative approach to housing Tsunami reconstruction project by SIFFS"< www.preventionweb.net>, *Accessed on 22 April 2008.*(2006)

[193] Douglas.I, "Peri-urban ecosystems and societies: Transitional zones and contrasting values. McGregor, D., Simon, D. and Thompson, D. (eds) *The Peri-Urban Interface*, Earthscan, London,"pg 18-27.(2006)

[194] Murray.S," Managing forest influences in urban and peri-urban areas,".< URL: http://www.fao.org/docrep/w0312E/w0312e08.htm,> *Accessed on 27 June 2011.(*2008)

[195] Allen.A, "Environmental planning and management of the peri-urban interface: perspectives on an emerging field." *Environment & Urbanisation* 15(1). (2003)pp. 135-147; Ward.P. M; Peters.P. A, "Self-help housing and informal homesteading in peri-urban America: Settlement identification using digital imagery and GIS,." *Habitat International 31(2)*, pp205-218 (2007:16)

environmental change, and socioeconomic system on peri-urban area".[196] Peri-urban ecosystems provide a significant service to cities. This study adopts the definition of peri-urbanisation as a process triggered by urbanisation where excess urban populations find themselves located at the city-edge zones so that both demographic swelling and changes in the environment are experienced. The environment sees the replacement of the natural environments by increasing built environmental features (buildings, roads and related aspects). With increasing urbanisation, the peri-urban areas stand out as areas in which challenges of environmental sustainability and infrastructure provision are critical.

Urbanisation is an emergent phenomenon affecting the economic, social, environmental, administrative and planning aspects of the peri-urban zone of any urban centre[197]. At a more localised level, it has been singled out that there are three distinct but operationally contradictory processes of sustainable development[198]. First is the *development imperative*, favouring market expansion and the externalisation of costs and sustained profits. Second is the *community imperative* in which the meeting basic human needs (food and housing included) is central to the social equity agenda of which increasing economic development is said to

---

[196] PU-GEC (Peri-urbanisation and Global Environmental Change) (2009)., Peri-urban Area, URL: <http://web.ntpu.edu.tw/~shuli/PUGEC_02Peri-urban.htm,> *Accessed on 27 June 2011*.pg 1(2009)

[197] Block. C, "Informal Housing Sector Strategies," *A paper prepared for the Zimbabwe Institute of Regional & Urban Planners" Annual School (4-6 July, 1990)*, Harare. (1990); Wekwete.K.H, "New Directions for Urban Development and Management in Zimbabwe in Rapidly Urbanising Countries," The Case of Zimbabwe. *Habitat International 16(2)* pp53-63(1992);Gordon. P ; Richardson.H.W, "Are compact cities a desirable planning goal?"*Journal of the American Planning Association 63(1)*: pp95-117 (1997);Muzvidziwa. V.N, "Informal Settlement Dwellers and Environmental Problems." *UNISWA Research Journal of Agriculture, Science and Technology (Special Volume No. 1)*(2005) pp 25-37. ; Muzvidziwa.V.N, "Urbanisation and Development in Swaziland," *JAN Publishing Centre*, Manzini.(2006); Hardoy et al., "The Poor Die Young: Housing and Health in Third World Cities," *Earthscan Publications Ltd*: London.(1990); ; Iaquinta. D; Drescher.W,"Peri-urban Typology Defined, Defining Peri-urban: Understanding Rural-Urban Linkages and Their Connection to Institutional Contexts." *Paper presented at the Tenth World Congress, IRSA,* Rio: August 1, 2000.(2000)

[198] Masser. I, "Managing our future," An *International Journal of Applied Earth Observation and Geo-information 3(4)*,(2000);

buttress the creation of community reliance. Third, and lastly, is the *ecological imperative*, which stresses the importance of biotic and abiotic factors as they interact and try to produce balanced ecosystems[199].

One scholar has argued that, "... instead of asking how emergent patterns of human settlements and activities affect ecological processes, the question we should ask is how humans, interacting with their biophysical environment, generate emergent phenomena in urbanising ecosystems. How do these patterns selectively amplify or dampen ecological processes and functions? Cities are... human-natural systems in which people are the dominant agents..."[200]. Indeed, sustainability, as a concept, "... has been largely neglected in the theorisation of the peri-urban."[201] In most developing countries, urban informality[202] and haphazardness is a by-product of chaotic urbanisation[203]. In the colonial

---

199 Masser. I, "Managing our future," An *International Journal of Applied Earth Observation and Geo-information 3(4)*,(2000); Douglas.I, "Peri-urban ecosystems and societies: Transitional zones and contrasting values. McGregor, D., Simon, D. and Thompson, D. (eds) *The Peri-Urban Interface*, Earthscan, London,"pg 18-27.(2006)

200 Alberti.M, "Advances in Urban Ecology, *Integrating Humans and Ecological Processes in Urban Ecosystems," Springer,* New York., (2009)

201 Marshal et al *"On the Edge of Sustainability:* Perspectives on Peri-urban Dynamics," STEPS Working Paper 35, STEPS, Centre Brighton. (2009:13)

202 Marshall. F, "What does peri-urban sustainability mean in the context of Delhi?" <URL: http://stepscentre-thecrossing.blogspot.com/2008/12/what-does-peri-urban-sustainability.html:>, *Accessed on 2April 2009.*(4 December 2008 Siyeni.Y.M, "Expanding Water Service Delivery through Partnership between Water Utility and Small Scale Water Providers in Lusaka, Zambia" *A Case of Lusaka"s Peri-Urban Areas.* University essay from Linköpings universitet/Tema vatten i natur och samhälle<. URL: http://www.essays.se/essay/4d116540c8/,> *Accessed on 14 August 2010.* (2008); Gilbert. A ,Ward.P.M, "Land for the rich and land for the poor," Gugler J (ed.)., "The Urbanisation of the Third World," *Oxford University Press*, London. (1990); Hardoy ; Sattertwaite, "Squatter Citizen: Life in the Urban Third World," *Earthscan Publications*, London.(1995); Mapira.J, An Historical Perspective of the Problem of Housing and Some Attempted Solutions in the City of Mutare (1890-2002). *Zambezia* XXXI (i/ii), University of Zimbabwe, Harare: pp 80-103 (2004)

203 Akroffi.E.O., "Urbanisation and the Urban Poor in Africa,". *Paper presented at the Promoting Land Administration and Good Governance, 5th FIG Regional Conference, Accra, Ghana, March 8-11, 2006*
(2006); Madayi.Z, "Land Transactions and Rent Appropriation in Peri-Urban Areas of Dar es Salaam. PowerPoint presentation for the NORAD Fellowship Network Conference held in Kampala 25th – 27th February," <URL: http://siu.no/vev.nsf/d

days, peri-urbanisation was largely driven by the policy objective of separate development[204]. Divergent interests, if not well harmonised, tend to work against sustainability[205].

While the colonial set-up separated people along racial lines, the post-colonial set-up is largely along income lines[206]. Low-income earners'

48a0ecf27ae054dc1256f630063e8d7/708a7443a9fa2900c125700e003d93bd/$FILE/Workshop%20A%20PRESENTATION%20ON%20LAND%20TRANSACTIONS%20IN%20PERI-URBAN.ppt>, *Accessed on 22 April 2008*. (2005); UNFPA, "State of World Population 2007."*Unleashing the Potential of Urban Growth.* UNFPA: New York. (2007)

204 Kamete.A.Y,"Government, Building Societies and Civil Society," Exploring the Interface in the Context of Urban Low-income Housing in Zimbabwe, in *African Review on Money Finance and Banking*, Felice Tambussi: Milan: pp 77-98.; "Government, building societies and civil society, exploring the interface in the context of urban low-income housing in Zimbabwe,. *Savings and Development*: pp77–98. http://www.fgda.org/pubblicazioni_schedarivista.php?Id=461, Accessed on 22 April 2008.(1999b); "Restrictive control of urban high-density housing in Zimbabwe, deregulation and challenges for urban design," *Housing, Theory and Society,* 16(3): 136–151. (1999c); Yeboah. I.E, "Housing the Urban Poor in Twenty-First Century Sub-Saharan Africa," Policy Mismatch and a Way Forward for Ghana, in *GeoJournal 62(1-2)*: pp 147-161 (2005); Chikanza, (2002).

205 Oram.N, "Towns in Africa," *Oxford University Press*: London,(1965); World Bank, "Voices of the Poor: Can anyone hear us?" *Oxford University Press:* New York.(2000); Hardoy et al., "The Poor Die Young: Housing and Health in Third World Cities," *Earthscan Publications Ltd*: London.(1990); ;Small J;Witherick.M, "A Modern Dictionary of Geography," *Third Edition, Arnold*: London.pg 23(1986); Edwards. M. M, "Community Guide to Development Impact Analysis," Wisconsin Land-use Research Program, Program on Agricultural Technology Studies, *University of Wisconsin–Madison*, Madison. <URL: www.cherry.gatech.edu/6602/ 2002-archive/PUBP6602-2002.pdf >(2000)

206 UNHABITAT, "*The state of African cities 2008: A framework for addressing urban challenges in Africa,*" UNHABITAT: Nairobi.(2008); UNHABITAT,"Global report on human settlements 2009," *Planning sustainable cities*: UNHABITAT, Earthscan (2009); TibaijukaA. K, "Report of the Fact-Finding Mission to Zimbabwe to assess the Scope and Impact of Operation Murambatsvina," *UN Habitat*, Nairobi. (2005); Tibaijuka A.K, "Building Prosperity – Housing and Economic Development Earthscan" London. (2009); Myers.G.A, "Peri-Urban Land Reform, Political-Economic Reform, and Urban Political Ecology in Zanzibar,". *Urban Geography*, 29 (3), pp. 264–288. <URL:http://spot.colorado.edu/~hunterlm/EnvSocReadings/Wk3MoreTheory/MyersPoliticalEcologyZanzibar.pdf,> *Accessed on 2 April 2008*. (2008); Stein. A ;Vance.I, "The role of housing finance in addressing the needs of the urban poor: Lessons from Central America," *Environment and Urbanisation 20(1)*: pp13-30. (2008); Solo.T.V, "Financial exclusion in Latin America – or the social costs of not banking the poor," *Environment and Urbanisation 20(1)*: pp89-108.(2008)

living is synonymous with squalor. High-income earners, on the other hand, are in a position to manage well, not only their household affairs, but also even the affairs to do with their neighbourhoods. Thirdly, and linked to the second point, the advocacy in the planning of ‘mixed development,” that is breaking down the ideologically and physically set boundaries along racial and income lines, the better-off households often resist living close to the poor and squalid[207].

It is argued that poor communities “...often live in the most hazardous and unhealthy environments in urban areas. Most build their homes and grow their food on river floodplains in towns and cities. Others construct their shelters on steep, unstable hillsides, or along the foreshore on former mangrove swamps or tidal flats. People suffering these poor conditions may find difficulties compounded by the consequences of climate change.”[208] The well-to-do classes often shun low-income classes in society. This happens in the framework called Not-In-My-Backyard-ISM (NIMBYISM)[209]. Where social factors are the dividing factor, the collaboration will prove very difficult to attain. Fourthly, peri-urban settlements, being in the interface of urban and rural areas, often experience conflicts in such aspects as land tenure, livelihood strategies

---

[207] Malpezzi. S, “Economic Analysis Of Housing Markets in Developing and Transition Economies,” Chapter 44 Mill E.S and P. Cheshire eds. “Handbook of Regional and Urban Economics,” *Elsevier Science B. V*(1999); ;Ball.M,” Improving Housing Markets, RICS Leading Edge Series,”<URL: www.rics.org/NR/rdonlyres/6D4B2A3B-A598-4C4B-9868-7B0A18C7090A/>, *Accessed on 22 April 2008. (*2003); Schylyter, 2003; Cormarck. I, “Towards Self-Reliance – Urban Social Development in Zimbabwe,” *Mambo Press,* Gweru. (1983)

[208] Douglas et al in Satterthwaite ed. (2008:187)

[209] Hardoy et al., “The Poor Die Young: Housing and Health in Third World Cities,” *Earthscan Publications Ltd*: London.(1990); ,Small J; Witherick.M, “A Modern Dictionary of Geography,*” Third Edition, Arnold*: London.pg 23(1986);Edwards. M. M, “Community Guide to Development Impact Analysis,” Wisconsin Land-use Research Program, Program on Agricultural Technology Studies, *University of Wisconsin–Madison*, Madison. <URL: www.cherry.gatech.edu/6602/2002-archive/PUBP6602-2002.pdf >(2000);UNHABITAT,”Global report on human settlements 2009,*” Planning sustainable cities*: UNHABITAT, Earthscan (2009); Tibaijuka A.K, “Building Prosperity – Housing and Economic Development Earthscan” London. (2009)

and land management practices[210]. These in themselves are militating factors against the management of sustainable human settlements. Fifthly, the fragility in the management of peri-urban settlements is a factor in the development of undesirable outcomes including proneness to the contraction of communicable diseases such as cholera, dysentery, typhoid and related diseases[211]. Because of this, peri-urban settlements are better seen as areas of 'civic sympathy' as there are many humanitarian organisations attracted to working here[212].

---

210 Kombe.W.J,)., "Land-use dynamics in peri-urban areas and their implications on the urban growth and form: the case of Dar es Salaam, Tanzania,". *Habitat International 29(1)*: pp 113-135 (2005); Matovu.G, "Upgrading Urban Low-Income Settlements in Africa," *Constraints, Potentials and Policy Options. Paper presented at the Regional Roundtable on Upgrading Low-Income Settlements, Johannesburg, South Africa: October 3-5 2000.*< URL: http://www.worldbank.org/urban/ upgrading/afrnd/docs/mdp_low_income_upgrading_paper_2000_final_doc.pdf, > *Accessed on 22 April 2008.(* 2000); Seyama.S.S, "Chapter 8: Urban Planning and Development, Problems and Prospects for the Future, in Muzvidziwa Victor N and Agostino M Zamberia (eds.)" *Urbanisation and Development in Swaziland,* Department of Sociology, University of Swaziland, JAN Publishing Centre Ltd (JANPC): Manzini. (2006); Glennon.M ; Kretser.K, "Impacts to wildlife from low density, exurban Development -Information and Considerations for the Adirondack Park," *Adirondack Communities & Conservation Program - Technical Paper No. 3. Available:* <http://www.wcs.org/adirondacks,> *Accessed on 22 April 2008.*(2005);Williams.B.L;Magsumbol.M.S, "Perceptions toward Stewardship among Residents Living Near U.S. Department of Energy Nuclear Facilities,". *Environment, Development and Sustainability:* pp 49-78. (2006), Dube.C, "Housing coops frustrated over land," *Zimbabwe Independent*. <URL: http://www.thezimbabwe independent.com/business/14311.html>, *Accessed on 22 April 2008.*(2004); Jenkins. P,"African Cities: Competing claims on urban land," *News for the Nordic Africa Institute no. 3*: Nordic Africa Institute: Uppsala.(2006)

211 Malizia.E.E, "City and Regional Planning: A Primer for Public Health Officials," *The Art of Health Promotion*, May/June 2005: pp 1-12.(2005); IDRC, "Catastrophe or New Society? A Latin American World Model, International Development Research Centre," Ottawa. *Catastrophe or New Society? A Latin American World Model, International Development Research Centre: Ottawa*. (1976)

212 Sigauke.N, "Improving Urban Livelihoods: Epworth Sustainable Livelihoods Benchmark Study," <URL: http://practicalaction.org/docs/region_southern_africa/ Epworth_Benchmark_Study.pdf>, *Accessed on 27 June 2011*.(2002:20); "Knowledge and Information Systems (KIS) In Epworth - ITDG Southern Africa Report.,"< URL: http: // practicalaction.org / docs/region_southern_africa/kis.pdf, 27 June 2011.> (2002b), Chikanza, (2001)

In most cases, peri-urban settlements are places of 'wants. They are often left out in the provision of basic urban services including meeting energy needs like electricity. Settlers are often left to their own means of survival[213]. Some of the practices are unsustainable for example deforestation as they destroy existing forests to harness firewood[214]. They also dig shallow wells or depend on streams and rivers for water[215]. Peri-urban settlements become defined zones from which the ecological footprint impact is felt[216]. The building materials and construction technologies used in peri-urban settlements as 'transition zones' are

---

[213] Musekiwa.A, "Low-income housing development in Harare: a historical perspective," Chapter 5 in ZINYAMA L, D TEVERA AND S CUMMING (eds.) 1993: *Harare: The Growth and Problems of the City*, *University of Zimbabwe,* Harare. (1993); Aarland,K ; Nordvik.V, "Low-income households and the dynamics of housing demand," *Paper presented to the ENHR Conference on Sustainable Urban Areas, 25-28 June 2007, Rotterdam.* URL: www.enhr2007rotterdam.nl, *Accessed on 2 August 2007*.(2007)

[214] Intsiful, George. W.K, "Housing and urban development initiatives as means towards the alleviation of poverty," in *RICS Foundation Our Common Estate Paper Series*. <URL: www.rics-foundation.org>(2004) ; Dirwai.D, "Demographic Study of a holding camp: The case of Hatcliffe Extension, Zimbabwe,". *Unpublished MSc thesis, Centre for Population Studies, University of Zimbabwe*: Harare. (2000); Gandidzanwa.P, "Attitudes and practices towards water supply and sanitation facilities: the case study of the Epworth upgrading programme," *Unpublished M.Sc. thesis, University of Zimbabwe*, Harare. (2003); Jack, 2008;Kahn.M.E, "The Environmental Impact of Suburbanisation," *Journal of Policy Analysis and Management 19(4)*, pp569-586.(2000); Mwesigwa.D, "Water and Sanitation in peri-urban settlements," *Paper presented at the 21st WEDC Conference with the theme:* Sustainability of Water and Sanitation Systems, held in Kampala: Uganda.(1995); Knuth. L, "Legal and institutional aspects of urban, peri-urban forestry and greening," *A working paper for discussion, FAO Legal Papers Online #48.* <URL: http://www.fao.org/legal/prs-ol/paper-e.htm,> *Accessed on 22 April 2008.* (2005)

[215] Muniz ; Garlindo, (2005)

[216] Hasse.J ;Lathrop.R, "Land resource impact indicators of urban sprawl," *Applied Geography 23*: pp159–175 (2003);Home.R, "Eating farmland, growing houses": *Peri-urban settlements and customary land tenure in Botswana, Southern Africa,* <URL:http://www.naerus.net/web/sat/workshops/2001/papers/home.pdf>(2001); "Negotiating security of tenure for peri-urban settlement: traveller gypsies and the planning system in the United Kingdom," in *Habitat International 26(3):* pp 335-346. (2002). Dzemydiene. D, "Preface to Sustainable Development Problems in the Issue." *Baltic Journal on Sustainability 14(1)*, (2008) pp 8-10; Wackernagel.M ;William.R, "Our Ecological Footprint,," *New Society Publishers*, Gabriola Island, BC.(1996)

important in the sustainability debate[217]. Appropriate technology is thus a critical subject of discussion in peri-urban stewardship.

For some scholars, sustainability is attainable by respecting eight basic principles in development, namely, partnerships and accountability, participation and transparency, systemic approach, concern for the future, equity and justice, ecological limits, local-global interdependence and local relevance[218]. These are the pillars for place, process, product and material stewardship, all important raw materials to the understanding of stewardship, which is the one pillar among three upon which this study is built upon. It is argued thus, "The adoption of goals for sustainable urban development requires an assessment of the effect of development on both the natural and human environment. This suggests integrated approaches to urban development, which combine social, economic, and environmental considerations, to give equitable access to resources both within and between generations." [219]Nevertheless, to achieve this one has to understand the interplay of politics taking place. In Zimbabwe, for example, one has to bear in mind why certain processes and developments like the adoption of the fast-track land reform programme in 2000 and Operation Murambatsvina have adversely affected the formally business-

---

[217] Alexander. C et al. "The grass roots housing process," <URL: http://www. livingneighborhoods.org/library/grassroots.htm>, *Accessed on 22 April 2008.*(1973); Spaling,H ; Wood,J, "Greed, need or creed? Farmland ethics in rural-urban fringe," *Land-use Policy 15(2)*:pp105-118.(1998);Savory.A, "Holistic Resource Management," *Gilmour Publishing*. Harare, (1988);Anstein.S.R., "A Ladder of Citizen Participation,". *Journal of American Institute of Planners 35(4)*: pp216-224.(1969);;Nnkya, "Why planning does not work? Land-use planning and residents rights in Tanzania," *Mkuki na Nyota Publishers*: Dar es Salaam (2008); Hetch, 1996; Chambers, 1997; UNHABITAT, "*The state of African cities 2008: A framework for addressing urban challenges in Africa,*" UNHABITAT: Nairobi.(2008);; UNHABITAT,"Global report on human settlements 2009*," Planning sustainable cities*: UNHABITAT, Earthscan (2009); 2010

[218] Masser. I, "Managing our future," An *International Journal of Applied Earth Observation and Geo-information 3(4)*,(2000)

[219] Brown.A.C, "Cities for the urban poor in Zimbabwe: urban space as a resource for sustainable development," Westerdoff David and Deborah Eade ed. Development and Cities (A Development in Practice Reader): Essays from Development Practice, *OXFAM GB/UNSRID*, Oxford: pp263-281 (2002:265)

as-usual processes in land acquisition and building of houses, respectively.[220]

It is argued that, an "…alternative way of seeing sustainability is to recognise that it may be better understood as a capacity to change in accordance with a changing world. What do communities need? They need the confidence to manage, the capacity to analyse, the experience to act well."[221] Local communities have a critical role to play in defining their destinies. Nevertheless, in most African cities, the role of these communities is sometimes undermined by the fact that they lack essential knowledge in defining what they need, who they are and who they need to collaborate with. Thus, community sustainability is undermined due to the fact the local communities remain peripheral in planning and management of the affairs of the places and spaces of interaction and development. Both historical and institutional factors are important in explaining why this is so. Matters of historicity include colonialism and racial separatist ideologies. Institutional factors include the fact the despite having a multiplicity of laws governing affairs in space, arbitrary breach of the provisions of such laws sometimes due to political interferences and non-enforcement the course events resemble anarchy and wily disregard of the rules.

Peri-urban areas remain a major focal point of analysis in terms of processes, patterns of development and management practices. Stewardship, in this context of study, is about how the peri-urban areas are shaped through policy, actions and perceptions of the peri-urban dwellers and the agents and other forces[222]. Moreover, the centrality of habitable urban centres and sustainable shelter provision to human development has

---

[220] Marongwe.N, "The Fast Track Resettlement and Urban Development Nexus: the case for Harare," Paper Presented at the Symposium on Delivering Land and securing Rural Livelihoods: Post Independence Land Reform and Resettlement in Zimbabwe, Mont Clair, Nyanga, 26-28 March 2003. <URL: http://www.sarpn. org.za/documents/ d0000617/P624-nelson.pdf>, *Accessed on 22 April 2008*.(2003); Toriro.P.," The Urban Housing Question in the Context of Operation Murambatsvina and Operation Garikai/Hlalani Kuhle," *Policy Brief prepared on behalf of the African Institute for Agrarian Studies*, Harare.(2006)

[221] Mitlin. D,, "Sustaining markets or poverty reduction?," *Environment and Urbanisation 14(1):* pp 173-177.(2002)

[222] "When we accept ownership…, we also accept stewardship." <URL:http://www. blixxhorses.org/pdf/stewardship.pdf>, *Accessed on 15 May 2012.*

been noted with multifarious declarations and resolutions at different conferences and forums in the last twenty years or so[223]. Housing is a complex process involving a multiplicity of actors, factors and outcomes. It becomes even more complex when it is in the rural-urban interface where the interests and expectations regarding land management, ownership and use are diverse. These actors and factors explain the philosophy and practice of stewardship. Stewardship is a term whose roots are clearly religious; whose practice is evident in many societies and whose application and reference to peri-urban areas has not been fully explored but whose essence is justified by the emphasis today of the considerations of environmental sustainability[224]. What distinguishes a steward from an agent is perhaps the level of accountability and oversight involved. There seems to be more oversight, power of discretion and accountability involved in stewardship than in agency.

Rapid urbanisation, hence the demand for urban infrastructure in peri-urban areas, is rampant in the developing world. It is estimated that "...up to 45% of the 1.4 billion people who will join the world urban population by 2020 will live in peri-urban areas" which will exert insurmountable pressure "...on the already deteriorating infrastructure in these areas and on the pace of its development"[225]. Since most of the peri-urban land is in customary hands, modalities to acquire it for urban development will need to be worked out[226]. Despite the challenges

---

[223] for example, the Vancouver, 1976; Rio de Janeiro, 1992; Instabul, 1996; Recife, 1996; Florence, 1997; Johannesburg, 2002

[224] Muzvidziwa. V.N, "Informal Settlement Dwellers and Environmental Problems." *UNISWA Research Journal of Agriculture, Science and Technology (Special Volume No. 1)*(2005) pp 25-37. Kamete. A,Y, "Governance for sustainability? Balancing social and environmental concerns in Harare," *Chr.Michelsen Institute.* <URL: www.cmi.no.>(2002a); Dzemydiene. D, "Preface to Sustainable Development Problems in the Issue." *Baltic Journal on Sustainability 14(1)*, (2008) pp 8-10

[225] Akrofi. E.O ; Whittal.J, "Land for Peri-urban Infrastructure in Customary Areas: A case study of Kumasi, Ghana. Land for Peri-urban Infrastructure in Customary Areas," *A Case Study of Kumasi, Ghana, FIG Working Week 2011: Bridging the Gap between Cultures, Marrakech, Morocco, 18-22 May 2011* (2011)

[226] Nsama.N, "Gender Dimensions of Land Customary Inheritance under Customary Tenure in Zambia," Paper presented at the Shaping the Change XXIII FIG Congress, Munich, Germany, October 8-13, 2006. <URL: http://www.fig.net/pub/ fig2006/

associated with peri-urban areas, their significance of these areas to urban economies cannot be underestimated. First, they provide alternative housing for different groups as already outlined even in one study[227].

Peri-urban areas are "… the initial point of access into the urban environment of incoming people because of their relatively low financial cost."[228] in South Africa, land alienation, migrant labour policies, apartheid spatial planning and violence are the four predominant forces that have formed and removed informal settlements over the years[229]. However, these factors may also provide us with a basis to argue for collaborative action managing the housing and spatial planning challenges affecting the country as well as others in sub-Saharan Africa, especially where peri-urbanisation related metropolitan growth is rampant. Peri-urbanisation or suburbanisation is defined as "…the decentralisation of people, employment and services from the inner and central areas of a town and city and their relocation towards the margins of the built-up area, a process leading to the accretion of suburbs."[230] peri-urbanisation is also "… a process of the physical expansion of settlement areas but also socio-economic transformation ... A major spatial development beyond the urban fringes."[231].

---

papers/ps07/ps07_04_nsama_0731.pdf,> *Accessed on 27 June 2011.*(2006); Laleye. O.M ; Ayeni. V, "Two Issues for Contemporary Africa: Political Boundaries and Traditional Rulers," *International Journal of Politics, Culture, and Society 6(4)*: pp 555-571 (2005).

[227] Ward.P. M; Peters.P. A, "Self-help housing and informal homesteading in peri-urban America: Settlement identification using digital imagery and GIS,." *Habitat International 31(2)*, pp205-218 (2007:16)

[228] Akrofi. E.O ; Whittal.J, "Land for Peri-urban Infrastructure in Customary Areas: A case study of Kumasi, Ghana. Land for Peri-urban Infrastructure in Customary Areas," *A Case Study of Kumasi, Ghana, FIG Working Week 2011: Bridging the Gap between Cultures, Marrakech, Morocco, 18-22 May 2011* (2011)

[229] Marx.C ; Charlton.S, "Urban Slums Reports: The case of Durban, South Africa," *Unpublished Report*. (2003)

[230] Small J;Witherick.M, "A Modern Dictionary of Geography," *Third Edition, Arnold*: London.pg 23(1986)

[231] Zasada, Fertner, Piorr and Nielsen, (2011:59)

CHAPTER 3
PROCESSES AND CONTEXTS IN PERI-URBAN HOUSING AND STEWARDSHIP

Environmental management and land allocation are the cause of concern in peri-urban areas[232]. Overall, health risks, poor environmental care, insecurity and weak urban governance are characteristic of peri-urban areas. By and large, peri-urban housing is an involving process and, on the whole, includes sub-processes including sometimes migration of households from the core cities into the immediate hinterland, planning and regularisation (in the case of informal settlements), acquisition of land and materials, production and construction. Other processes have negative overtones and include erosion, pollution by households[233].

There is a close correlation between the informal economy and informal settlements[234]. describing the situation in Pakistan, it is concluded "...the informal sector provides land at an affordable cost to the poor with immediate possession and with no paperwork. It arranges for curtailing speculation and adjusts its standards according to the paying capacity of the client, something state agencies have failed. Although

---

[232] Knuth. L, "Legal and institutional aspects of urban, peri-urban forestry and greening," *A working paper for discussion, FAO Legal Papers Online #48.* <URL: http://www.fao.org/legal/prs-ol/paper-e.htm,> *Accessed on 22 April 2008.* (2005)

[233] Edusa.S; Simon. D, "Land-use and land allocation in Kumasi peri-urban villages, in McGregor Duncan and James Quashie-Sam eds. CEDAR/IRNR Paper 9 <URL:http://www.gg.rhul.ac.uk/kumasi/Project_Related_Papers/Cedar_IRNR/Paper_9_9tml>, *Accessed on 13 October 2011.*(2001); Briggs.J; Mwamfupe.D, "Peri-urban development in an era of Structural Adjustment in Africa," *The City of Dar es Salaam,* Tanzania. *Urban Studies 37(4,* (2000) pp797-809

[234] Sietchiping. R, "Prospective Slum Policies: Conceptualization and Implementation of a Proposed Informal Settlement Growth Model," *Paper presented at the Third Urban Research Symposium on "Land Development, Urban Policy and Poverty Reduction," 4-6 April 2005, Brasilia, Df, Brazil:* <URL: http://citeseerx.ist.psu.edu /viewdoc / download?doi=10.1.1.124.6877&rep=rep1&type=pdf, 10 June 2010.> (2005)

technical advice for house building provided by the sector is substandard, without it housing conditions in low-income conditions would be much worse."[235] The proliferation of slums is partly explained by the rigidity of urban planning regulations associated with other factors such as poor governance, corruption and nepotism[236].

Slums can be divided into "slums of hope" and "slums of despair"[237]. The first are settlements on an upward trend, largely made up of newer, usually self-built structures, and those are in or have recently been through a process of development, consolidation and improvement. The other category comprises "declining" neighbourhoods in which environmental conditions and services are in a process of seemingly inevitable decay. Epworth could be just a slum of hope. A slum is an area that combines to various extents the following characteristics: inadequate access to safe water, inadequate access to sanitation and other infrastructure, poor structural quality of housing, overcrowding and insecure residential status[238]. These characteristics are in tandem with efforts to measure the Millennium Development Goals (MDG) specifically Goal 1, 'Eradicate extreme poverty and hunger' and Goal 7, 'Ensure environmental sustainability' all of which are linked to managing housing poverty and enhancing environmental stewardship,

---

[235] Hassan. A, "The unplanned revolution – Observations on the processes of socio-economic change in Pakistan," *Oxford University Press*, Oxford. (2008: 195-6)

[236] Sietchiping. R, "Prospective Slum Policies: Conceptualization and Implementation of a Proposed Informal Settlement Growth Model," *Paper presented at the Third Urban Research Symposium on "Land Development, Urban Policy and Poverty Reduction," 4-6 April 2005, Brasilia, Df, Brazil:* <URL: http://citeseerx.ist.psu.edu/viewdoc/download?doi=10.1.1.124.6877&rep=rep1&type=pdf, 10 June 2010.> (2005)

[237] Thomas.S, "Urbanisation as a driver of change," *The Arup Journal 1/2008*: pp58-66.(2008)

[238] UNHABITAT, "Situation Analysis of Informal Settlements in Addis Ababa, Cities without Slums Sub-Regional Programme for Eastern and Southern Africa," *Addis Ababa Slum Upgrading Programme, United Nations Human Settlements Programme (UNHABITAT)*, Nairobi. <URL: www.unhabitat.org>(2007a)

UNHABITAT , "What are slums and why do they exist?" (Secretary General"s visit to Kibera, Nairobi 30-31 January, 2007), <URL: http://www.unhabitat.org /downloads/docs/Press_SG_visit_Kibera07/SG%2013.pdf>, *Accessed on 22 April 2008 (2007b);* Thomas.S, "Urbanisation as a driver of change," *The Arup Journal 1/2008*: pp58-66.(2008)

respectively[239]. Overall, governmental attitudes, responses and policies towards slums have changed since the 1950s from centralised control of housing to neo-liberal approach to the emerging preventative approach.

- the laissez-faire attitudes in the 1950s and 1960s,
- sites and services programmes in the 1970s,
- slum upgrading in the 1980s [240](, and,
- the enabling strategies and security of tenure in the 1990s and Cities without Slums action plan in the 2000s[241].

In most cases, peri-urban processes in most African cities are nothing but 'contentious development' especially with respect to urban and peri-urban transformations and livelihoods. examines the dynamics associated with Kampala City of Uganda, those of the City of Nairobi, Kenya, Manzini, Swaziland, Harare, Zimbabwe, the City of Lusaka, Zambia. In all these studies, the rampancy and the rise of the urban informal sector activities (street trading and exploitation of the natural endowments) by the peri-urban dwellers are noted. Subdivisions of land for housing are also revealed[242]. Synonymous with each of these activities

---

[239] Tibaijuka A.K, "Building Prosperity – Housing and Economic Development Earthscan" London. (2009)9

[240] Gulyani.S; Connors.G,)., "Urban upgrading in Africa: a summary of rapid assessments in ten countries," *World Bank,* Washington DC. URL: http://www.worldbank.org/urban/upgrading/docs/afr-assess/countrysummary.pdf>, *Accessed on 22 April 2008.(*2002)

[241] UNHABITAT, "Situation Analysis of Informal Settlements in Addis Ababa, Cities without Slums Sub-Regional Programme for Eastern and Southern Africa," *Addis Ababa Slum Upgrading Programme, United Nations Human Settlements Programme (UNHABITAT),* Nairobi. <URL: www.unhabitat.org>(2007a)
UNHABITAT , "What are slums and why do they exist?" (Secretary General"s visit to Kibera, Nairobi 30-31 January, 2007), <URL: http://www.unhabitat .org/downloads/docs/Press_SG_visit_Kibera07/SG%2013.pdf>, *Accessed on 22 April 2008 (2007b).* ; Tibaijuka A.K, "Building Prosperity – Housing and Economic Development Earthscan" London. (2009)

[242] Asiama.S, Land for housing the Urban Poor in Africa – Some Policy Options, in Amis P and P Lloyd, *Housing Africa"s Urban Poor,* Manchester University Press: UK. (1990); Peri-NET, "Contentious Development: Urban and Peri-urban Transformations and Livelihoods in Africa. Report of a Peri-NET Workshop," *East and Southern Africa held at Fairview Hotel,* Nairobi, Kenya, 7-9 October 2002. (2002); Nuwagaba.A, Kampala city, "Contentious Development: Urban and Peri-urban Transformations and Livelihoods in Africa." *Report of a Peri-NET Workshop,*

are numerous conflicts, given the multiplicity of players with different interests[243]. Formalising urban markets and street trading are noted as a justified action to reduce the contention associated with some of the processes in peri-urban development as highlighted[244].

Moreover, the processes of land, materials' acquisition and construction are critical in the peri-urban analysis as they influence the overall product of the houses there. It is argued that squatters are "... less worried about what they will build than where they will build it and less concerned about initial standards than about initial layout. Secure possession of properly located land, where they can live now, is far more important than the promise of a modern house that may never materialise. Given the land and the right circumstances – that is, adequately located, properly planned, and with the secure title – experience has shown that development to contemporary standards will surely take place, even if

East and Southern Africa held at Fairview Hotel, Nairobi, Kenya, 7-9 October 2002.(2002); Kinyungu.N.A, The city of Nairobi, Kenya, "Contentious Development: Urban and Peri-urban Transformations and Livelihoods in Africa." *Report of a Peri-NET Workshop, East and Southern Africa held at Fairview Hotel,* Nairobi, Kenya, 7-9 October 2002.(2002); Sihlongonyane.F, the city of Manzini, "Contentious Development: Urban and Peri-urban Transformations and Livelihoods in Africa." *Report of a Peri-NET Workshop, East and Southern Africa held at Fairview Hotel,* Nairobi, Kenya, 7-9 October 2002.(2002); Chimhanda.D, The city of Harare, , "Contentious Development: Urban and Peri-urban Transformations and Livelihoods in Africa." *Report of a Peri-NET Workshop, East and Southern Africa held at Fairview Hotel,* Nairobi, Kenya, 7-9 October 2002.(2002); Muziamba. M, The City of Lusaka, Zambia, "Contentious Development: Urban and Peri-urban Transformations and Livelihoods in Africa." *Report of a Peri-NET Workshop, East and Southern Africa held at Fairview Hotel,* Nairobi, Kenya, 7-9 October 2002.(2002); Rakodi.C, "Land for Housing in African Cities: Are Informal Delivery Systems Institutionally Robust and Pro-Poor?," In *Global Urban Development Magazine 3(1),* Global Urban Development (GUD): London. <URL: http://www. globalurban.org,> *Accessed on 27 June 2011.* (2007)

[243] Spaling,H ; Wood,J, "Greed, need or creed? Farmland ethics in rural-urban fringe," *Land-use Policy 15(2)*:pp105-118.(1998)

[244] Snoxell. S, "Formalisation of Urban Markets and Street Trading – Research Project. Presentation in Peri-NET (Urban and Peri-urban Research Network) (2002).," Contentious Development: Urban and Peri-urban Transformations and Livelihoods in Africa. *Report of a Peri-NET Workshop, East and Southern Africa held at Fairview Hotel, Nairobi, Kenya, 7-9 October 2002.* (2002)

slowly."[245] Usually, the poor depend most on their immediate natural environment for livelihoods, materials for housing construction and deposition of waste. For livelihoods, peri-urban agriculture is a major venture by the peri-urban dwellers. Erosion and pollution are major threats to peri-urban development. the Maqalika catchment on the periphery of Maseru was studied and it was noted of serious erosion explained by the rapid and ill-planned urban development in the area since the 1970s[246].

As previously highlighted, peri-urbanisation in a number of contexts is characterised with is the phenomenon known as the ecological footprint[247]. The ecological footprint *problematique* in Zimbabwe manifests itself in and around the small settlements in many forms. Chief among these characteristics is the decrease in woodland resources as residents poach firewood, destruction by housing developers of forests[248]. There is also increasing siltation of water bodies, non-collection of household garbage due to local authority constraints in finances and equipment, decreased capacity of local authorities to cut grasses during the rainy season. In addition, the loss of farming land due to various development schemes is a critical challenge. Households often indulge in actions that are marked by a host of environmental reversals that in turn, triggered a host of natural negative developments. These actions can be termed community and household actions, engineered in the demand-side philosophy of utilitarianism. Deforestation in response to the energy crisis in the country, illicit sand extractions and quarrying (in a bid to provide cheap raw materials for housing construction in urban and peri-urban

---

[245] Charles Abrams (1964) cited by Noero.J, "Four reasons why housing problem cannot be solved. Buchanan Chris ed." *Planning – Architectural and Planning Review for Southern Africa 135*. (1994) pp 87

[246] Rowntree et al. "Changing Patterns of Erosion In A Peri-urban Catchment, Maseru, Lesotho, Sediment and Stream Water Quality in a Changing Environment," *Trends and Explanation (Proceedings of the Vienna Symposium, August 1991) IAHS Publ. no. 203, 1991*. (1991)

[247] Marshall.F et al. "On the Edge of Sustainability: Perspectives on Peri-urban Dynamics," *STEPS Working Paper 35, STEPS, Centre Brighton.* (2009)

[248] Mapedza.E, "Forestry policy in colonial and postcolonial Zimbabwe: continuity and change," *Journal of Historical Geography 33(4)*:pp 833-851 (2007)

areas), over-fishing of the small rivers and streams in a bid to address food insecurity issues in households, pollution of land, water and air[249].

The quality of a settlement depends, largely, in most cases, on the origins and history of the settlement. It also depends on the availability or non-availability of attendant services (roads, water and sanitation, etc), knowledge, attitudes, perceptions and practices of the households in the place[250], times and seasons in the year, and whether or not there are interest or special groups in improving the habitat. In addition, the selection of appropriate technology for managing drainage flows from low-cost peri-urban settlements has been a major issue in South Africa[251]. This is explained by the inadequacy in drainage in dense peri-urban of the country. Largely, the quality of houses in peri-urban settlements, as everywhere, is a function of different factors. Given the incapacity of the state and the private sector in sub-Saharan African countries to cater for the influx of people due to urbanisation, "...peri-urban areas with their associated informal mechanisms meet the land needs for the majority of the poor and urbanising people"[252]. the impoverishment of city dweller is attributed to inadequate and decaying quality of housing[253]. The low

---

[249] Zingoni et al., "Effects of a semi-formal urban settlement on groundwater quality: Epworth (Zimbabwe)," Case study and groundwater quality zoning. *Physics and Chemistry of the Earth, Parts A/B/C 30 (11-16),* pp 680-688 (2005); Munhenga. C, "Board Fines Firm for Dumping Chemicals," The Herald, Zimpapers, Harare. (2011)

[250] Williams.B.L;Magsumbol.M.S, "Perceptions toward Stewardship among Residents Living Near U.S. Department of Energy Nuclear Facilities,". *Environment, Development and Sustainability:* pp 49-78. (2006)

[251] Kisembo. C, "Appropriate Technology Options for Managing Drainage Flows From Low-Cost Peri Urban Settlements In South Africa," *Unpublished Masters of Science Thesis, Faculty of Engineering and the Built Environment, University of Witwatersrand*, Johannesburg.(2004); SWH, "How do we select systems in peri-urban areas?" *Workshop on water and sanitation in peri-urban areas on the 12th of December at 10.00-15.00* (2006)

[252] Akrofi. E.O ; Whittal.J, "Land for Peri-urban Infrastructure in Customary Areas: A case study of Kumasi, Ghana. Land for Peri-urban Infrastructure in Customary Areas," *A Case Study of Kumasi, Ghana, FIG Working Week 2011: Bridging the Gap between Cultures, Marrakech, Morocco, 18-22 May 2011* (2011)

[253] Sietchiping. R, "Prospective Slum Policies: Conceptualization and Implementation of a Proposed Informal Settlement Growth Model," *Paper presented at the Third Urban Research Symposium on "Land Development, Urban Policy and Poverty*

standard of housing (which translates to urban and peri-urban informality) is the primary indicator of the deterioration of living conditions in cities in developing countries.

Globally and regionally, the peri-urban question is a critical issue of concern[254]. Homelessness in the city pushes low-income citizens to the periphery[255]. Quite differently, nineteenth-century Europe and America suburbs were predominantly havens of the wealthy and middle-class families[256]. It was the transport revolution then (railway and tram network extensions), that permitted the sub-urbanites to live greater distances away from the city centres.

The aftermath of the Second World War saw in London, the Greater London Plan recommending for the establishment of ten satellite towns to meet the housing shortage. In 1945, the New Towns Committee acquired land to establish the new towns. The British New Towns Act 1946 provided the government with the power to implement these plans. Overall, the twentieth century experienced a vast proliferation of suburbs hence 'flight from the city' by the well-to-do classes. Increased affluence - characterised by increased car ownership - as well as, the general thrust by local authorities of building housing estates in the rural-urban fringe

---

Reduction," 4-6 April 2005, Brasilia, Df, Brazil: <URL: http://citeseerx.ist.psu.edu/viewdoc/download?doi=10.1.1.124.6877&rep=rep1&type=pdf,10June2010.> (2005)

254 Kyessi, (2005), Mara ;Alabaster, (2008);Chirisa. I, "Peri-urban Dynamics and regional planning in Africa: Implications for building healthy cities," *Journal of Africa Studies and Development 2 (2)* (2010) pp. 015-026; Sanchez-Cuenca, (2011);Allen.A, "Environmental planning and management of the peri-urban interface: perspectives on an emerging field." *Environment & Urbanisation* 15(1). (2003) pp. 135-147;Home.R, "Eating farmland, growing houses": *Peri-urban settlements and customary land tenure in Botswana, Southern Africa,* <URL: http://www.n-aerus.net/web/sat/workshops/2001/papers/home.pdf>(2001); (2002)

255 UNFPA, "State of World Population 2007."*Unleashing the Potential of Urban Growth.* UNFPA: New York. (2007)

256 Engels. F, "The Housing Question. Karl Marx and Frederick Engels," *Selected Works in Two Volumes*, Lawrence and Wishart Ltd: London.(1887); Smith.M, "A Guide to Housing," *Housing Centre Trust*, London. (1981); Small J; Witherick. M, "A Modern Dictionary of Geography," *Third Edition, Arnold*: London.pg 23(1986)

paved way for sub-urbanisation[257].

The author examines particular examples from North America, South Asia, Latin America, and East Asia. It is estimated that approximately 200 million people over the next twenty-five years will account for 40 per cent of urban population growth in peri-urban areas in East Asia[258]. In China, it is expected that peri-urbanisation will account for at least 40 per cent of future urban population growth in service-oriented extended urban regions such as Beijing, Shanghai, and Hangzhou, and over 60 per cent of future urban population growth in more industrial cities such as Chongqing, Chengdu, and Ningbo[259]. Coordinated development approaches involving various sectors and actors are advocated for as a way to manage the impending crisis[260]. Peri-urban expansion in South East Queensland, Australia is largely a result of farmland conversion, where formerly productive agricultural land is sub-divided for residential or rural-residential purposes[261]. This has altered the nature and identity of rural communities by increasing the social complexity and the potential for social conflict among landholders who manage rural properties.

It is observed that the USA housing production in the peri-urban, contrasts strongly that in Latin America (which could also be extended to Asian and African examples) where cities begin as "illegal occupations of

---

[257] Gordon. P; Richardson.H.W, "Are compact cities a desirable planning goal?" *Journal of the American Planning Association 63(1)*: pp95-117 (1997);); Cavailhès. J et al., "The peri-urban city, why to live between the suburbs and the countryside" *Regional Science and Urban Economics 34(6)*, pp681-703 (2004)

[258] Webster. D, "On the Edge: Shaping the Future of Peri-urban East Asia," *Asia/Pacific Research Center*, <URL: http://APARC.stanford.edu>, *Accessed on 22 April 2008*.pg 6(2002)

[259] Webster. D, "On the Edge: Shaping the Future of Peri-urban East Asia," *Asia/Pacific Research Center*, <URL: http://APARC.stanford.edu>, *Accessed on 22 April 2008*.pg 6(2002); Cai et al. "Emerging Third Stage Peri-Urbanisation," *Functional Specialisation in the Hangzhou Peri-Urban Region.*< URL: http://iis-db.stanford.edu/pubs/20294/webster_hangzhou_2003.pdf>, *Accessed on 22 April 2008*.(2003)

[260] Webster. D, "On the Edge: Shaping the Future of Peri-urban East Asia," *Asia/Pacific Research Center*, <URL: http://APARC.stanford.edu>, *Accessed on 22 April 2008*.pg 6(2002)

[261] NHT, (1997)

totally un-serviced lots). The gravity of the growing informal housing phenomenon (*Colonia*)[262]. It is pointed out to the following facts, that in Texas alone "... there are estimated to be over 400,000 people living in some 1600 or more *colonias*, and if one extends the definition to areas outside of the border, the numbers rise still further. In New Mexico and Arizona, the numbers are lower than Texas, but are nevertheless substantial: In Arizona, the 1990 Census suggested that approximately 162,000 people lived in 77 so-called ''*colonia* designated areas,'' while in New Mexico, it indicated that 70,000 lived in 141 settlements."

It is interesting to note that, the process of peri-urban challenges is a global rather than a mere localised problem[263]. What may be different is the extent to which the developed countries manage and monitor development that comes with peri-urbanisation. Good stewardship means constantly monitoring the developments with sustainability being the focus[264].

Theorisation and contextualisation of peri-urbanisation in Africa cannot be examined outside the framework of colonialism, structural adjustment, wars, political independence and cessation of conflict, liberalisation, and global politics[265]. For example, in southeast Nigeria, indigenous households, who claim a common ancestor, hold land under customary tenure [266]. In this arrangement, migrants to the area are

---

262 Ward.P. M; Peters.P. A, "Self-help housing and informal homesteading in peri-urban America: Settlement identification using digital imagery and GIS,." *Habitat International 31(2)*, pp205-218 (2007)

263 Wissen-Hayek et al. "Measuring and assessing urban sprawl: What are the remaining options for future settlement development in Switzerland for 2030?" – *Applied Spatial Analysis and Policy 4(4)*(2011) pp 249-279.(2011)

264 Vukovic. H, "Concepts of quality urban environment and sustainability," in Brown Alison and Celia Davison, eds. Responsive Design and Plan Implementation in Zimbabwe, *Workshop Proceedings 29 March to 1st of April 1999, Department of Rural and Urban Planning, University of Zimbabwe and Department of City and Regional Planning*, Cardiff University (1999); WhiteA.L, "Who speaks for future generations?," *Business for Social Responsibility* (BSR),< URL: www.bsr. org>(2007)

265 Marshall.F et al. "On the Edge of Sustainability: Perspectives on Peri-urban Dynamics," *STEPS Working Paper 35, STEPS, Centre Brighton.* (2009)

266 Tacoli. C, "Changing rural-urban interactions in sub-Saharan Africa and their impact on livelihoods," a summary, *Working Paper Series on Rural-Urban Interactions and Livelihood Strategies (Working Paper 7), International Institute for Environment and Development (IIED)*, London.(2002)

excluded from permanent rights to land. This typifies much of West Africa where rural to urban migration is on the increase[267]. Urban expansion 'eats away' agricultural land[268]. In the process, the farmer is impelled to look out for alternative livelihoods in the peri-urban zone[269].

With reference to Botswana, Malawi and South Africa, "legal pluralism" is spoken of[270]. This phenomenon makes it very difficult in the design of alternative tenure and administration systems in the peri-urban areas. In the same three countries, it is explained that the fate of "... slow and bureaucratic land allocation procedures resulting in long waiting lists in urban and peri-urban areas, slow land servicing, lack of transparency and accountability, corruption and self-allocation of land (e.g., by Land Board officials, cabinet ministers, chiefs, ward heads, and their families); and inadequate land allocation policies and guidelines."[271] Indeed, all these challenges make the management of peri-urban areas difficult amid demand for land in the zone[272].

---

[267] Laleye.O.M ; Ayeni. V, "Two Issues for Contemporary Africa: Political Boundaries and Traditional Rulers," *International Journal of Politics, Culture, and Society 6(4)*: pp 555-571 (2005).

[268] Home.R, "Eating farmland, growing houses": *Peri-urban settlements and customary land tenure in Botswana, Southern Africa,* <URL: http://www.n-aerus.net/web/sat/workshops/2001/papers/home.pdf>(2001); Nguyen M. I," Analyzing the encroachment process of informal settlements in the periurban of Ho Chi Minh City, Vietnam," *unpublished Master"s thesis*, Lund University: Lund(2006)

[269] Tacoli. C, "Changing rural-urban interactions in sub-Saharan Africa and their impact on livelihoods," a summary, *Working Paper Series on Rural-Urban Interactions and Livelihood Strategies (Working Paper 7), International Institute for Environment and Development (IIED*), London.(2002); Home.R, "Eating farmland, growing houses": *Peri-urban settlements and customary land tenure in Botswana, Southern Africa,* <URL: http://www.n-aerus.net/web/sat/workshops/2001/papers/ home .pdf>(2001);

[270] Nkwae. B, "Conceptual Framework for Modelling and Analysing Peri-urban Land Problems in Southern Africa. Ph.D. dissertation," *Department of Geodesy and Geomatics Engineering, Technical Report No. 235, University of New Brunswick, Fredericton, New Brunswick*, Canada, 363 pp.(2006:108)

[271] Nkwae. B, "Conceptual Framework for Modelling and Analysing Peri-urban Land Problems in Southern Africa. Ph.D. dissertation," *Department of Geodesy and Geomatics Engineering, Technical Report No. 235, University of New Brunswick, Fredericton, New Brunswick*, Canada, 363 pp.(2006:108)

[272] Thornton.A, "Beyond the Metropolis: Small Town Case Studies of Urban and Peri-urban Agriculture in South Africa,". *Urban Forum 19(3*): pp 243-262. (2008)

Land and hydrological surfaces heavily alter due to the conversion of land from rural to urban use. This is common in most developing countries where planning controls are not in place. Unplanned roads, drains and high-density of footpaths tend to promote erosion and sediment movement in these areas. On the outskirts of Maseru, the capital of Lesotho, it is observed shifting patterns of erosion in a small catchment experiencing rapid and ill-planned urban residential development. the Maqalika Reservoir was completed in 1983 and acts as a trap for sediment originating from the catchment which has an area of 11.04km^2 and a relief ranging from 1500 to 1820m above sea level (ASL)[273]. It is characterised by unplanned residential development. The unauthorised and arbitrary building is common in the area and only a few roads are tarred with the majority being unplanned earth roads that have developed from farm tracks. The stormwater drains and road ditches are mostly badly designed and unlined. In addition, footpaths dominate the area with some being found along roads and others across unfenced areas and around public amenities such as communal taps and boreholes. Quarrying, sandstone crushing and borrow pits for brick making are the major activities in the extraction of raw materials for building. These disturb the land surface and lead to serious sedimentation. The forthcoming paragraphs show how these processes have been described and explained in the literature.

In 1979, Lesotho promulgated the Land Act to create orderly urbanisation. However, it failed to garner support from the local chiefs who actually ignored it, having lost, then, powers to allocate land. This resulted in both illegal and unregulated development. In 1980, the government enacted the Town and Country Planning Act. This did not achieve the intended goals due to lack of resources, skilled workforce, finances, and the non-existence of local authorities to prepare and enforce the plans. it is observed that both medium and high-density housing were associated with severe erosion in 1979 while in 1985 low-density housing became critical as high-density housing no longer contributed as much. To

[273] Rowntree et al. "Changing Patterns of Erosion In A Peri-urban Catchment, Maseru, Lesotho, Sediment and Stream Water Quality in a Changing Environment," *Trends and Explanation (Proceedings of the Vienna Symposium, August 1991) IAHS Publ. no. 203, 1991.* (1991)

them, construction activity probably induced the severe erosion. They attribute rills and gullies to unpaved roads and poorly designed road drains with pronounced erosion being on duplex soils whose sub-strata are vulnerable to undercutting. Erosion has a negative effect on land values and development costs. As such, severely eroded land requires methods of reclamation in the form of land levelling and re-vegetation. The net effect of this is that road maintenance costs are significantly increased[274]. This case is interesting. It has not been seriously considered as a peri-urbanisation.

In Botswana, the land is held under three different tenure arrangements, namely, freehold/leasehold (6%), state land (formerly Crown Lands) (23%) and tribal land (71%). In the colonial days, within tribal land, three land tenure types existed namely residential plots in the village/urban areas, 'masimo' (ploughing fields around the village, although they could be up to 30 miles away), and 'moraka' (cattle post), with hunting areas beyond.[275] 'Tribesmen' were guaranteed an allocation. Masimo was intended for open access outside the ploughing season. New types of leases were introduced after independence. These are common law leases (99 or 50 years, pledgable) and residential leases. Residential leases are obtained on application at the land board by tribal members. The normal type of customary lease had unlimited duration but was not pledgable as collateral.

Today, tensions between customary and individual land tenure systems have increased due to the pressures of rapid urbanisation in the country. Gaborone, in particular, has experienced great pressure for land due to the shortage and high price of house-plots. The situation has been compounded by the tough anti-squatting policy within the city boundaries. People have turned to the adjacent tribal land board area for plots newly

---

[274] Rowntree et al. "Changing Patterns of Erosion In A Peri-urban Catchment, Maseru, Lesotho, Sediment and Stream Water Quality in a Changing Environment," *Trends and Explanation (Proceedings of the Vienna Symposium, August 1991) IAHS Publ. no. 203, 1991.* (1991)

[275] Home.R, "Eating farmland, growing houses": *Peri-urban settlements and customary land tenure in Botswana, Southern Africa,* <URL: http://www.n-aerus.net/web/sat/workshops/2001/papers/home.pdf>(2001);

created around existing villages[276]. They believe that they are exercising their birth right. There has been the propagation of illicit land transactions and uncontrolled house building. In 1991, in response, the Government set up a '*Presidential Commission of Inquiry to look into the Land Problems of Mogoditshane and Other Peri-Urban Villages*." The Commission toured the villages, held public meetings and interviewed some four hundred individuals. It noted that at least eight hundred illegally created plots. Further, the Commission established that there had been the utter collapse of the legal land allocation system. This case typifies the experiences in Epworth where households from Harare city continue to flock to this area[277].

In Ghana, and in particular, peri-urban Kumasi is characterised by chronic and serious water shortages. Formal supplies have lacked in capacity to provide safe water in peri-urban settlement hence individual and informal suppliers have devised their own ways of managing the water problem[278]. In the Asante region, the ownership of all customary land is vested in the Golden Stool[279]. This means it cannot be acquired or sold. What is transferred, rather, are the usufruct rights. But there are a number of ways in which acquiring the use of land for water and sanitation infrastructure in peri-urban Kumasi can be done. There is a consensus

---

[276] Zindoga.S, "Need For More Urban Housing In Southern Africa," *Southern African News Features.* (1999)URL: <http://www.sardc.net/Editorial/sanf/1999/ 10/15-10-1999-nf3.htm,> *Accessed on 22 April 2008*.(1999));World Bank, "In Search Of Land and Housing in the New South Africa," *The Case of Ethembalethu* <URL: www.worldbank.org/southafrica>(2004); Yeboah. I.E, "Housing the Urban Poor in Twenty-First Century Sub-Saharan Africa," Policy Mismatch and a Way Forward for Ghana, in *GeoJournal 62(1-2)*: pp 147-161 (2005);

[277] Chenga, Murambatsvina II hovers over Epworth, The Financial Gazette: URL:http://www.financialgazette.co.zw/national-report/3011-murambatsvina-ii-hovers-over-epworth.html, Accessed on 5 August 2010.(2010)

[278] Akrofi. E.O ; Whittal.J, "Land for Peri-urban Infrastructure in Customary Areas: A case study of Kumasi, Ghana. Land for Peri-urban Infrastructure in Customary Areas," *A Case Study of Kumasi, Ghana, FIG Working Week 2011: Bridging the Gap between Cultures, Marrakech, Morocco, 18-22 May 2011* (2011)

[279] Mends. T.M ; de Meijere.J, "A Study of the Institution of the Customary Land Tenure System in the Supply of Property Rights for Urban - An Example of Accra, Ghana," *Paper presented at the 5th FIG Regional Conference, Accra, Ghana: March 8-11, 2006.* <URL: www.fig.net/pub/accra/papers/ts03/ts03_01_mends _demeijere. pdf,> *Accessed on 22 April 2008.* (2006)

among communities in the Asante Region that conversion of land for farming into urban use or the parcelling of such land generates proceeds that are then shared equitably by the community. Community land must always be availed from this process. Self-help projects by the community have been noted as sustainable as it is knowledge enhancing among the actors[280]. Sometimes compulsory acquisition of land makes it easier for customary landholders to give up the land that is in their hands hence pave way for the installation of the requisite services and infrastructure[281].

There are six prominent metropolitan municipalities in South Africa namely Cape Town, eThekwini (Durban), Ekurhueleni (East Rand), Johannesburg, Tshwane (Pretoria) and Nelson Mandela Metropole (Port Elizabeth). these cities comprise 31% of the country's total population and contribute, in total, 55% of South Africa's GDP[282]. Widespread in most low-income settlements in South Africa are congestion, high densities and intensive site developments. These low-income settlements lack in space availability for facilities for example in Mfuleni Wetlands in the Western Cape[283]. In 1990, people fleeing violence in parts of the city and elsewhere established their squatter housing in this environmentally sensitive area.

---

[280] Magigi. W ; Majani.B.B.K, "Housing themselves in Informal Settlements: A Challenge to Community Growth Processes, Land Vulnerability and Poverty Reduction in Tanzania," *Paper presented at the 5th FIG Regional Conference, Accra, Ghana*, March 8-11, 2006 (2006);

[281] Akrofi. E.O ; Whittal.J, "Land for Peri-urban Infrastructure in Customary Areas: A case study of Kumasi, Ghana. Land for Peri-urban Infrastructure in Customary Areas," *A Case Study of Kumasi, Ghana, FIG Working Week 2011: Bridging the Gap between Cultures, Marrakech, Morocco, 18-22 May 2011* (2011)

[282] Roux. N, "Migration and Urbanisation, Towards a 10-Year Review of the Population Policy Implementation in South Africa (1998-2008)," *Department of Social Development*, Pretoria. (2009:13)

[283] Kisembo. C, "Appropriate Technology Options for Managing Drainage Flows From Low-Cost Peri Urban Settlements In South Africa," *Unpublished Masters of Science Thesis, Faculty of Engineering and the Built Environment, University of Witwatersrand*, Johannesburg.(2004); ; Lannas. J; Turpie.J. K, "Valuing the Provisioning Services of Wetlands, Contrasting a Rural Wetland in Lesotho with a Peri-Urban Wetland in South Africa," *Ecology and Society 14(2)*: 18. <[Online] URL: http://www.ecologyandsociety.org/vol14/iss2/art18/>, *Accessed on 2 October 2010*. (2009: 22)

It is observed that, in 2001, "Mfuleni had a population of about 22,885, 57% of whom were unemployed, and 79% of the population earned less than U.S. $230/month. After floods in 2001, more than 4000 people were resettled on open areas in Mfuleni. There are 7517 households in Mfuleni, of which 1117 are in informal settlements. Informal settlement dwellers are the main users of the wetland areas."[284] This case shows the extent to which desperate members of society will always seek to live at the edge of a city where they think they perceive to live quietly and harmoniously. But as they do so, they also plunge into disturbing certain environmental functions. Uneven development, landlessness, and structural unemployment, and historical systems of labour migration persist in the South African spatial economic sphere[285]. In this picture, the interconnectedness of rural, urban and peri-urban areas is evidently strong.

Millions of black South Africans live in peri-urban areas[286]. There has been a general failure by the supply has driven government programmes, development planning and environmental regulations, and the current land and housing markets to support the realisation of the peri-urban dwellers' aspirations to become home owners on sites of their choice in these peri-urban areas. Basing on the Ethembalethu case study, the reforms have been suggested on the following policy and programme areas: overcoming reluctance and resistance by municipalities and prospective neighbours to low-income settlements, making land-use planning in municipalities explicitly pro-poor, restructuring the land market, realigning planning processes; designing a land and housing programme targeted to peri-urban areas, reengineering programme

---

[284] Lannas. J; Turpie.J. K, "Valuing the Provisioning Services of Wetlands, Contrasting a Rural Wetland in Lesotho with a Peri-Urban Wetland in South Africa," *Ecology and Society 14(2)*: 18. <[Online] URL: http://www.ecologyandsociety.org/vol14/iss2/art18/>, *Accessed on 2 October 2010*. (2009: 22)

[285] Weiner. D ; Harris.T, "Community-integrated GIS for Land Reform in South Africa," *URISA Journal 15*: pp 62-73. (2003); Thornton.A, "Beyond the Metropolis: Small Town Case Studies of Urban and Peri-urban Agriculture in South Africa,". *Urban Forum 19(3)*: pp 243-262. (2008)

[286] World Bank, "In Search Of Land and Housing in the New South Africa," *The Case of Ethembalethu* <URL: www.worldbank.org/southafrica>(2004)

implementations and freeing up and building capacity[287]. Buttressing this, the institution proposes the establishment of a national task force to ensure appropriate follow up of the matters in this conundrum.

Relative to most African countries, urbanisation rates in Malawi have always been very low[288]. For a long time, the country has been the labour source market for Southern Africa and as such experienced low development in the industrial sector that could have triggered migration processes. Most of "... the Malawian urbanisation actually took place outside the country"[289]. Approximately 40 percent of the able-bodied men migrated annually into Zimbabwe, Zambia and South Africa. It was under the Kamuzu Hastings Banda's autocratic rule (1961 to 1994) that rural development was so esteemed higher above the urban development hence low urbanisation. In light of this, 80 percent of the Malawian population thrive on the rural sector for employment.

In 1975, Lilongwe was assigned the capital of Malawi. The growth of this centre has not been attributed to many people coming to the city but rather to the city shifting its boundaries outwards, especially between 1975 and 1980. Concisely, it is underscored that most of the villages "...were situated at the edges of town, where, over the years, parallel structures of governance and, living developed. This was all the more the case as these villages increasingly filled with inner-urban migrants who due to the decreasing number of so-called 'Planned Traditional Housing Areas' and cramped living conditions 'illegally' began to settle in and around these villages."[290]

---

287 World Bank, "In Search Of Land and Housing in the New South Africa," *The Case of Ethembalethu* <URL: www.worldbank.org/southafrica>(2004); Musandu-Nyamayaro.O," Housing Design Standards for Urban Low-income People," *Third World Review 15(4),* Liverpool University Press (1993)

288 Kalipeni.E, "Contained Urban Growth in Post-Independence Malawi," *East African Geographical Review 19(2),* pp. 49-66.(1997)

289 Rohregger.B, "Shifting boundaries of support, Renegotiating distance and proximity in trans-local support relations in an urban fringe area in Lilongwe City," Malawi. *Ethnic and Racial Studies, 29(6)*: pp 1153-1168. (2006:1155)

290 Rohregger.B, "Shifting boundaries of support, Renegotiating distance and proximity in trans-local support relations in an urban fringe area in Lilongwe City," Malawi. *Ethnic and Racial Studies, 29(6)*: pp 1153-1168. (2006:1155)

During the Banda regime (1961 to 1994), illegal lands were usually cleared by force with houses demolished. The Lilongwe City Council, in the early 1990s, changed its policy into one of 'upgrading." Invaded areas were simply legalised and incorporated into the city. Nevertheless, the lack of financial resources constrained the 'sites and services' initiatives. The result was residents starting on self-help schemes in infrastructure and services provisioning. Today, in most countries, Zimbabwe included, self-help housing is the modality most employed in low-income housing[291].

The other case is of Zambia where the plight of peri-urban settlements is quite evident. Environmental sustainability is a major issue of concern with regard to peri-urban housing in the country[292]. Describing the general state of peri-urban resettlement areas in Zambia has underscored where most of these settlements are located. They are found in areas "...which are totally unsuitable for housing developments because this is usually the portions of land that the well-to-do would avoid, such as *dambos*, near or next to sewer ponds, in the windward direction of factory fumes. [They are also found] next to quarries, areas with bad underground rock formation like Kanyama where water comes out of the ground instead of sinking down... These areas are generally filthy, particularly during the

---

[291] Cormarck. I, "Towards Self-Reliance – Urban Social Development in Zimbabwe," *Mambo Press,* Gweru. (1983); Dube.C, "Housing coops frustrated over land," *Zimbabwe Independent.* <URL: http://www.thezimbabweindependent.com/ business/ 14311.html>, *Accessed on 22 April 2008.*(2004); Fernandes. E, "Chapter 12: Combining tenure policies, urban planning and city management in Brazil, in PAYNE GEOFFREY (ed.), 2000," Land, Rights and Innovation – Improving tenure security for the urban poor, *ITDG Publishing*, London (2002); Gandidzanwa.P, "Attitudes and practices towards water supply and sanitation facilities: the case study of the Epworth upgrading programme," *Unpublished M.Sc. thesis, University of Zimbabwe*, Harare. (2003)Cortemiglia. A., "Involving informally housed communities in shaping local government policies aimed at poverty alleviation," *A South African perspective, A thesis for the Doctor of Literature and Philosophy in Development Studies*, University of South Africa. (2006); Garau et al. "A Home in the City: Urban Millennium Project Report on Improving the Lives of Slum Dwellers,". *Global Urban Development Magazine 2(1)*, Global Urban Development (GUD): London. URL: http://www. globalurban.org, Accessed on 22 April 2008.(2006).

[292] Heath et al., "Impact of climate change on peri-urban areas in Lusaka," *Report prepared by Cranfield University, Water Supply for the Urban Poor (WSUP),* London.(2010)

rains with heaps of uncollected garbage, spilling over latrines, shallow wells where you can almost scoop out water, stagnant stinking water posing all sorts of health risks. No wonder we now have perennial problems of cholera and other diseases associated with dirt..."[293] Like Malawi, the issue of traditional housing areas (THAs) is an issue here. These pose a health menace to peri-urban dwellers. Land conflicts at the city edge are rampant as well given the asymmetry between modern and traditional institutions in managing land[294].

In Mozambique and Angola, densification and expansion of peri-urban areas have doubled in Maputo and Luanda, respectively. It is reported that"...in the last two decades of the last millennium [in these two cities, there has been] the saturation and deterioration of existing social infrastructure [hence] its shortage."[295] The other challenges in the peri-urban areas of the two capital cities include inappropriate constructions, rampancy and escalation of erosion and flooding cases, marked inadequacies in infrastructure and service provision, increased deterioration in the environmental conditions of the areas, accentuation in social and spatial inequality and differentiation. The urban cores and the peri-urban areas signify great contrast. Outward migration of households and families from the urban cores into the peri-urban areas is rife. In Maputo, over 70% of the urban dwellers are residing in informal and low-income settlements[296]. This peri-urbanisation is typical of Epworth in Zimbabwe.

---

[293] Mwanamakondo.B.Y, "The state of resettlement areas in Zambia," *A paper presented at the Swedish Cooperative Centre (SCC) at the Chrismar Hotel, 27-28 February 2007*, Lusaka.pg2-3. (2007)

[294] Benjamin. S, "Presenting Two in Contesting Spatialities: Do Everyday Institutional contestations erode the neo-liberal Urban Reforms Agenda?" <URL: http://igs.cla.umn.edu/pdf/BenjaminPaper.pdf>, *Accessed on 21 November 2008.*(2008)

[295] Raposo.I, "Urban planning and management instruments and institutions versus socio spatial cohesion in Maputo and Luanda: resettlement or upgrading and rehabilitation of the informal peri-urban areas (land and housing issues)," "I*nformality and Access to Services in Cities of Africa" Workshop in Johannesburg, School of Architecture and Planning at Wits University, South Africa,* 3-4 July 2008.(2008:3)

[296] Jorgen. A, "Meanings and perceptions of the built environment in peri-urban areas of Maputo, Mozambique," *African Perspectives 2009, The African Inner City*(2009)

In Tanzania, peri-urban developments in Dar-es-Salaam were triggered by the conditions of the structural adjustment programme in Tanzania in the 1980s. It is noted that, many households,

> "... bought land and moved to the edge of the urban area from the city itself, primarily in response to a need to produce their own food to survive the growing economic crisis... The land vendors...frequently moved further out to buy land at a lower price, to farm in the long-term but with the longer-term hope that land prices will rise as Dar-es-Salaam expands spatially, and then the whole process will be repeated. ...In the early 1990s, the processes were becoming rather different as new conditions emerged because of structural adjustment. People did no longer have to respond to a crisis by using the peri-urban zone as a zone of survival, rather they were starting to use it as a zone of investment. Increasingly, it was developed for permanent housing and for the expansion of commercial agriculture supplying the city, and especially with products such as fresh milk, vegetables... oranges and other fruit."[297]

The Tanzanian experience shows the effect of the structural adjustment programmes (SAP) in Africa. Quite positively, SAPs triggered investments in infrastructure, agriculture and housing development for some households. In Zimbabwe, the impact of the same (structural adjustments) can still be felt two decades later, though they were 'discontinued'[298]. Summarised in Table 3.1 are the processes at each level (global, regional, national and local) and the implications these have on peri-urban housing and development.

The point is that relating these processes at different levels does not provide symmetry of solution given the differences in ideologies and policies pursued by different governments in different countries,

---

[297] Briggs.J; Mwamfupe.D, "Peri-urban development in an era of Structural Adjustment in Africa," *The City of Dar es Salaam,* Tanzania. *Urban Studies 37(4,* (2000) pp804

[298] Maphosa et al. "Zimbabwe"s Development Experiences since 1980: Challenges and Prospects for the Future," OSSREA, Addis Ababa(2007); Torres Haroldo Da Gama., Social and Environmental Aspects of Peri-Urban Growth in Latin American Megacities. *Paper presented at the United Nations Expert Group Meeting on Population Distribution, Urbanisation, Internal Migration and Development, Population Division, Department of Economic and Social Affairs, United Nations Secretariat*, New York, 21-23 January 2008

differences in approaches and the amount of detail on each. Context is a differentiating and defining factor in most cases. The policy nuances explain why, in certain cases, there have been continuities, discontinuities or even transformations in practices and experiences over the years. This has a strong bearing on planning and stewardship of the places in question. From these noted processes and developments regarding peri-urban housing development, a number of lessons can be drawn for conclusion.

Table 3.1: Processes at Global, Regional and Local Levels and Implications on Peri-urban Housing and Stewardship

Level	Process	Implications
Global	• The nineteenth century European and American suburbanisation and transport revolution and increased car ownership. • The 1944 the Greater London Plan recommending the establishment of ten satellite towns to meet the housing shortage. The 1945 the New Towns Committee that created government-sponsored corporations financed by the Exchequer • Increased population growth and peri-urbanisation in Asia as well as North and Latin America. • Aiding of peri-urban studies by sophisticated technologies including the applications of remote sensing or aerial photographs and techniques in geographic	• Zimbabwe was a colony of Britain. British spatial planning policies have shaped most settlements in the country. • Satellite towns have emerged around Harare (Harare, 1992), the capital of Zimbabwe in mimicry of the British stylized planning. • Colonially rural population influx into urban centres was controlled but post-independence developments • Use of sophisticated technologies for monitoring peri-urban development lags behind. • Rampancy in peri-urban subdivision through the process of land transfer is said to be very slow and inhibitive to housing development.

	information systems (GIS). • Increased peri-urban informal subdivisions • Metropolitanisation and regionalisation of urban processes • Peri-urban farming and forestry [299].	• Infrastructure provisioning in peri-urban settlements lagging behind. Meanwhile, areas designated for housing development continue undeveloped or have been temporarily allocated peri-urban agriculture.
Regional	• Colonialism - land alienation, migrant labour policies, apartheid spatial planning and violence • Structural adjustment for instance studies in Tanzania • Wars and post-war conflicts for example in Angola and Mozambique • Political independence and population influx in urban centres • Liberalisation and the open up of peri-urban land markets and housing development • Haphazard subdivisions – slum creation and expansion. congestion, high densities and intensive site developments • Increase urban primacy	• Most of these aspects have had a strong bearing on housing and peri-urban development in Zimbabwe. The effects that they have on the peri-urban scape have been so described in this study. Those whose analysis has been thin means further research and consideration for policy alternatives is necessary. Such areas include: - Urban expansion on tribal land in the context of livelihoods. - Peri-urban land development and speculation. - Stewardship, right to the city and housing rights.

[299] Murray.S," Managing forest influences in urban and peri-urban areas,".< URL: http://www.fao.org/docrep/w0312E/w0312e08.htm,> *Accessed on 27 June 2011.(*2008)

	• Metropolitanisation and the growth of urban regions • Increased contentions in peri-urban development • Increased land degradation and ecological footprint (deforestation, soil erosion, siltation, pollution and related environmental processes)[300]. • Urban spill over processes hence peri-urbanisation • Legal pluralism in the management of peri-urban land • Proliferation of the voluntary sector in peri-urban housing and infrastructure provision and advocacy • Selection and implementation of appropriate technology [301]. • Peri-urban studies in Botswana – the 1991	- Self-help housing and 'appropriate technology' - 'Researching with them (the peri-urban dwellers)' and the vernacular and grassroots approach. - Strategic (peri-) urban spatial planning (SUSP) and its dimensions in peri-urban stewardship? - Computing the quantum and extensity of damage resulting from peri-urban constructions towards evidence-based policy.[302] - Climate change, vernacular architecture and the peri-urban - Peri-urban housing versus Peri-urban farming[303]. These aspects show the gaps worth exploring and explaining as stemming from

---

[300] Holden.E., "Ecological footprints and sustainable urban form,".*Journal of Housing and the Built Environment 19*: pp91–109 (2004)

[301] SWH, "How do we select systems in peri-urban areas?" *Workshop on water and sanitation in peri-urban areas on the 12th of December at 10.00-15.00* (2006)

[302] Wissen-Hayek et al. "Measuring and assessing urban sprawl: What are the remaining options for future settlement development in Switzerland for 2030?" – *Applied Spatial Analysis and Policy 4(4)*(2011) pp 249-279.(2011)

[303] Branom-Zwick, "Food vs. Shelter: The Planning Debate," *Sightline Daily*. <URL: http://daily.sightline.org/daily_score/archive/2006/01/30/food_vs_shelter,> *Accessed on 22 April 2008.* (30 January 2006)

	'Presidential Commission of Inquiry to look into the Land Problems of Mogoditshane and Other Peri-Urban Villages' • Managing communicable diseases like cholera in Zambia • Climate change adaptation and mitigation • Water and sanitation provision • Peri-urban farming	this study. The regional examples cited show some semblance of some efforts done yet not in greater detail. The question is on how these fit in the context of Zimbabwe. At this level it is possible to make comparisons given similarities in certain experiences unlike some global cases which are so divorced from the African context that they are difficult to infer.
National	• Colonial processes and the resultant apartheid city; blacks as rural dwellers. • War and peri-urban squatting • Post-independence policies giving way to increased urbanisation. • Socio-economic policies • Structural adjustment: poverty and investment • Fast-track land resettlement programme and peri-urban housing projects by cooperatives and consortia • The emergence of peri-urban layout planning • Urban clean-up programme – Operation Murambatsvina • Public-sector housing programme – state provision and its failure	• The national experiences provide an immediate context to how settlements have been shaped over the years. Both the colonial and post-colonial experiences have paid a great role in shaping human settlements across the towns and cities and their peri-urban environs in the country. But some have also given identity to certain of the places. For instance, that Epworth survived demolitions during Operation Murambatsvina indicates how policy can be selective due to ideas and processes embedded in the

	– case of Operation Garikayi/Hlahlani Kuhle.	development of such places. Stewardship is shaped by ideology, politics and macro-economic processes in space.
Local	• Declaration of Growth points in Zimbabwe and the emergence of Ruwa as one • Slum upgrading in Epworth • 'Democratisation of local boards.." • Advocacy by NGOs – e.g. the Municipal Development Partnership for Eastern and Southern Africa (MDP-ESA) advocating for Participatory Budgeting in Ruwa and the Demonstration house by Practical Action in Epworth • Public Private Partnerships in Ruwa • Community Public Partnerships in Epworth	• Local processes are the immediate determinant of place-making. Stewardship is about the values, objectives, visions, dreams, aspirations and priorities by the local communities as they are shaped by the people themselves and institutions working with them. In studying sustainable development these local processes and initiatives are very critical. Planning, visioning and stewardship go hand-in-glove.

This chapter has shed light on the understanding of the concepts, theories and patterns of peri-urban housing and stewardship. It has provided a framework to understand the various approaches and debates that describe the complexity of the issues and in the subject of housing and stewardship in peri-urban settlements. It has been noted how three concepts defining this study – peri-urban, stewardship and housing – are very complex and loaded. Although there are theories and conceptual frameworks to try and explain the substantive and process issues associated with the terms, the realities and practices across the globe show some definitional and practice challenges to the clarity of the issues on the ground. Overall, the concepts are fraught with many ambiguities and difficult-to-reconcile debates. However, the foregoing analysis has provided some basis to the understanding the realities of peri-urban housing and stewardship, the following chapters are devoted to the realities in Zimbabwe in general and then the specifics that define the study areas of Ruwa and Epworth. The chapter to follow focuses on the local context of Zimbabwe in relation to the subject at hand and in keeping with the set objectives as described in Chapter 1.

CHAPTER 4
THE HISTORICAL CONTEXT OF HOUSING AND PERI-URBANITY IN ZIMBABWE

It is argued that the handling of "... the peri-urban squatter situation by the Zimbabwean authorities is symptomatic of the poor response at a policy level, to the challenges of rapid urbanisation.... Squatters' actions highlight their refusal to be condemned by the state as 'outcasts," and as they argue, they are normal citizens with rights to be respected by authorities. The location of peri-urban squatter settlements on land which both the national government and the local authority can conveniently disown has made it easier for both parties to deny that addressing the squatter situation is their responsibility." [304] In this chapter, I examine the context of housing, peri-urbanity and the stewardship through the lens of the observation, it is to see how the low-income peri-urban dwellers are usually in a state of flux and precariousness[305]. The question we are trying to understand here is: What are the historical, political, administrative and cultural contexts that define housing in Zimbabwe in general and peri-urban housing, in particular, and how the same factors echo the principles and practices of stewardship? As to be explained in the ensuing paragraphs, the continuity in the British planning practices and institutions, administrative conflicts, political contestations and cultural practices have tended to favour rigidity in practices rather than flexibility. This rigidity has produced a composite context in

---

[304] Mpofu.B, "Perpetual "Outcasts"? Squatters in peri-urban Bulawayo, Zimbabwe," *Afrika Focus 25(2)*: pp.61(2012:61)
[305] Ibid, pp61

which the delivery of housing is highly inelastic albeit increasing urbanisation.

Zimbabwe's colonial and post-colonial policies have been useful in shaping urban and peri-urban environments. Peri-urban development in Zimbabwe is linked to colonial housing policy. In the colonial days, black Africans were regarded as 'temporary citizens' in urban centres[306]. A number of legislations were passed to enforce the separatist ideology[307]. Such legislations include the Native Locations Ordinance Act (No 4 of 1906) which put employment as the chief determinant of one's tenure in town. In addition, was the Land Apportionment Act (No 30 of 1930, re-enacted in 1941). This statute technically put all urban land in the monopoly of the whites and made the government provide housing for blacks. It also saw the establishment of National Railways and other statutory commissions and the management townships for African workers. Besides the Land Apportionment Act were also the Native Registration Act of 1936 and the Native Passes Act of 1937.This restricted movement to and within urban centres. In the same vein, the African Urban Areas Accommodation and Registration Act of 1946 t further tightened the legal exclusion of blacks in urban areas. In 1969, the Land Tenure Act was promulgated leading to the proscription of the Land Apportionment Act. In keeping with the Land Tenure Act, the country was divided into two equal parts with 44.9 million acres being allocated to each race. The inequity was that the black to white ratio then was twenty to one[308]. Such an unfair distribution of land was to be the basis for the

---

[306] Mafico. C.J,C, "Urban low-income housing in Zimbabwe," *Averbury:Aldershot.(* 1991); Peck.A.J.A, *"Agora," Kingstons Limited*, Salisbury (Rhodesia). (1970), Mubvami, (2001);TibaijukaA. K, "Report of the Fact-Finding Mission to Zimbabwe to assess the Scope and Impact of Operation Murambatsvina," *UN Habitat*, Nairobi. (2005); Chaeruka. J ; Munzwa. K, "Assessing Regulatory Framework Bottlenecks for Low-cost Housing in Zimbabwe, Final Draft Report," *UNHABITAT and the Government of Zimbabwe*, Harare.(2009)

[307] Patel.D, "Some Issues of Urbanisation and Development in Zimbabwe," *Journal of Social Development in Africa 3(2)* :pp17-31 (1988); Mafico. C.J,C, "Urban low-income housing in Zimbabwe," *Averbury:Aldershot.(* 1991)

[308]Patel.D, "Some Issues of Urbanisation and Development in Zimbabwe," *Journal of Social Development in Africa 3(2)* :pp17-31 (1988); ,Mafico. C.J,C, "Urban low-

nemesis which saw blacks fighting hard to repulse whites from governing the land. It must be noted that by 1969, Rhodesia was already in a war, the Second Chimurenga that lasted for sixteen years, 1966 to 1979 and saw the country attaining the rule by the black majority in 1980.

In the Rhodesian economy, there was a lack of opportunities for black workers and businesspersons to obtain land on a freehold basis. This was "... the primary reason for the development of urban slums and the lack of commercial and industrial growth in black areas"[309]. Homeownership for blacks, in urban areas, was highly restricted. For this reason, the post Second World War saw the mass production of rental housing for blacks in the country[310]. In Salisbury (now Harare), the Department of African Administration (established in 1946) embarked upon major housing construction programmes in the 1940s and 1950s with its first schemes being 'single' men's hostels for migrant labour[311]. At that time, these were established at the city edge[312]. Prior to this, suburbanisation (or just peri-urbanisation) was synonymous with the white race as they were afforded the opportunity to have bigger plots at the city edge[313]. Suburbanisation, though happening with a small population them, was a prototype of the genesis of the impending ecological footprint and

---

income housing in Zimbabwe," *Averbury:Aldershot.(* 1991); Toriro.P, "Town Planning in Zimbabwe, History, Challenges and the Urban Renewal Operation Murambatsvina," Chapter 11, Maphosa France, Kraposy Kujinga and Sunungurai D Chingarande (eds.), (2007) "Zimbabwe"s Development Experiences since 1980: Challenges and Prospects for the Future," *OSSREA*, Addis Ababa.(2007); Musekiwa.A, "Low-income housing development in Harare: a historical perspective," Chapter 5 in ZINYAMA L, D TEVERA AND S CUMMING (eds.) 1993: *Harare: The Growth and Problems of the City*, *University of Zimbabwe,* Harare. (1993);

309 Cross in Ritchen ed, "The economics of ecosystems management," Ritchken J (ed.). The Rhodesian Science News 9(1): pp 21-22. (1975:21)

310 Patel.D, "Some Issues of Urbanisation and Development in Zimbabwe," *Journal of Social Development in Africa 3(2)* :pp17-31 (1988); ; Zinyama et al "Harare*: The Growth and Problems of the City*," *University of Zimbabwe: Harare*. (1993:85)

311 Ibid, pp8886)

312 Peck.A.J.A, *"Agora," Kingstons Limited*, Salisbury (Rhodesia). (1970)

313 Zinyama et al "Harare*: The Growth and Problems of the City*," *University of Zimbabwe: Harare*. (1993:85)

sprawling[314]. No doubt, it was concomitant with immense negative externalities - urban sprawl, pollution and congestion[315]. In Zimbabwe, generally, settlement plans tend towards sprawl given extensive parcelisation of land and general adherence to horizontal development practices[316].

The Salisbury Rural and Town Planning Authority (SRTPA), in 1956, realised the haphazard nature of non-agricultural land subdivision at the edge of the planning boundary of the urban nucleus, varying from seven to seventeen kilometres. Such urban expansion was towards Ruwa and the SRTPA decided to act strongly against this trend[317]. Guided by the philosophy of reducing the negative externalities of urban sprawl and maintaining the economic viability of the farming units in this zone, the SRTPA drafted a policy document outlining the government's wish of creating certain small areas for people wishing to "live in semi-rural surroundings"[318]. The exercise was code-named a Rural Scheme Area

---

[314] Holden.E., "Ecological footprints and sustainable urban form,".*Journal of Housing and the Built Environment 19*: pp91–109 (2004)

[315] Dixon et al. "Stewardship of the Great Lakes environment, A review of literature," *HDRU Publication No. 95-5, Dept. of Natural Resour., N.Y.S. Coll. Agric. and Life Sci.*, Cornell Univ., Ithaca, N.Y.(1995);Zorich. D.M, "Defining stewardship in the digital age, in First Monday 12(7)" <URL: http://firstmonday.org/issues/issue_7/zorich/index.html>, *Accessed on 2 August 2007.* (2007); Svendsen.E; Campbell.L, " Urban Ecological Stewardship, Understanding the Structure, Function and Network of Community-based Urban Land Management," *City and the Environment1 (1)*: pp 1-31. (2008);Powers and Peer Associates, (2009)

[316] Patel.D, "Some Issues of Urbanisation and Development in Zimbabwe," *Journal of Social Development in Africa 3(2)* :pp17-31 (1988);

[317] Ndlovu.S, "Peri-urban transformation in Zimbabwe: A review of peri-urban subdivision policy and strategy with reference to Harare, 1950-2001," *Unpublished Dissertation: Department of Rural of Urban Planning, University of Zimbabwe*, Harare.(2004)

[318] Bates 1975 cited in Ndlovu.S, "Peri-urban transformation in Zimbabwe: A review of peri-urban subdivision policy and strategy with reference to Harare, 1950-2001," *Unpublished Dissertation: Department of Rural of Urban Planning, University of Zimbabwe*, Harare.(2004) ; Satterthwaite.D;Tacoli. C, "The role of small and intermediate urban centres in regional and rural development," Paper prepared for the workshop, *Integrating Rural Development and Small Urban Centres: An Evolving Framework for Effective Regional and Local Economic Development,* March 18-19, 2003: Washington DC, World Bank/IFC Headquarters.< URL: http://www.world

(RSA). It saw the creation of seven rural small residential areas around the belt of the city (now Harare), namely Gardiner, Cromlet, Ruwa, Twentydale, Christon Bank, Merwede and Sublime. A unitary document by the Government Town Planning Department (GTPD) (now referred to as the Department of Physical Planning (DPP)) condensed these planned settlements into the "the archetypal 1957 Outline Plan. From this 1957 Outline Plan, that the contemporary Master Plans in Zimbabwe were developed"[319].

The Outline Plans informed the creation of seven Rural Scheme Areas around the peri-urban areas of Harare. The plans crafted in consultation of the Natural Resources Board (NRB) were more in favour of agriculture than urban development. Their primary objective was to secure the livelihoods of the poor white minority community group hence supplementing their urban income. They also accommodated a group of the white elite class who wanted a quiet country life, free from the hectic life of the city ('special' needs). Eventually these plans, largely, managed to arrest of urban sprawl through the creation of a "...tight girdle around the city"[320].

The RSAs demarcated the bounds and limits of the urban area. Around that same time, immigrants from Europe, particularly from England surged and increased[321]. This resulted in an increase in the price of the peri-urban land as demand subsequently increased. Some well-to-do white urbanites embarked on purchasing land for speculative purposes. Consequently, undeveloped land subdivision with the RSAs rose

---

bank.org/urban/urbanruralseminar/papers/satterthwaite-tacoli.pdf>, *Accessed on 27 June 2011.* (2003)

[319] Ndlovu.S, "Peri-urban transformation in Zimbabwe: A review of peri-urban subdivision policy and strategy with reference to Harare, 1950-2001," *Unpublished Dissertation: Department of Rural of Urban Planning, University of Zimbabwe,* Harare.(2004)pg.56 citing Mbiriri 1999

[320] Ndlovu.S, "Peri-urban transformation in Zimbabwe: A review of peri-urban subdivision policy and strategy with reference to Harare, 1950-2001," *Unpublished Dissertation: Department of Rural of Urban Planning, University of Zimbabwe,* Harare.(2004)

[321] Ndlovu.S, "Peri-urban transformation in Zimbabwe: A review of peri-urban subdivision policy and strategy with reference to Harare, 1950-2001," *Unpublished Dissertation: Department of Rural of Urban Planning, University of Zimbabwe,* Harare.(2004); Davsion, 2002)

stupendously. The Outline Plans have remained the more binding instrument than any other provisional instruments (master plans, town planning schemes, local and subject plans) for peri-urban land subdivision in the country[322].

In 1963 the Rhodesian Rural Land Board (RRLT) promulgated the economic criteria for subdividing land holdings under title. According to the criteria applicants for peri-urban land had to avail proof of capability to farm, proof of stipulated assets base, as well as, the experience of farming along with the prevailing standards then. The idea was to bottleneck the system so as to reduce tendencies of speculation. The overall effect was the screening of those who did not meet the criteria, resulting in a general oversupply of land. Utility and infrastructure provision proved very costly given the small threshold population assigned to such services[323]. Such challenges of infrastructure provision in the peri-urban areas continue to this day. They are also a cause of concern in peri-urban stewardship everywhere ([324].

At independence, in 1980, the new Zimbabwean Government repealed a number of repressive colonial legislations and policies, respectively[325]. Zimbabwe promulgated a number of development

---

322 Mbiriri, (1999)

323 Ndlovu.S, "Peri-urban transformation in Zimbabwe: A review of peri-urban subdivision policy and strategy with reference to Harare, 1950-2001," *Unpublished Dissertation: Department of Rural of Urban Planning, University of Zimbabwe*, Harare.(2004)

324 Mwesigwa.D, "Water and Sanitation in peri-urban settlements," *Paper presented at the 21st WEDC Conference with the theme:* Sustainability of Water and Sanitation Systems, held in Kampala: Uganda.(1995); Muzvidziwa. V.N, "Informal Settlement Dwellers and Environmental Problems." *UNISWA Research Journal of Agriculture, Science and Technology (Special Volume No. 1)*(2005) pp 25-37. ; Muzvidziwa.V.N; Zamberia.A.N, "Urbanisation and Development in Swaziland," *JAN Publishing Centre*, Manzini.(2006)eds. ; Tacoli. C, "Changing rural-urban interactions in sub-Saharan Africa and their impact on livelihoods," a summary, *Working Paper Series on Rural-Urban Interactions and Livelihood Strategies (Working Paper 7), International Institute for Environment and Development (IIED)*, London.(2002)

325 Jordan, "Local Government in Zimbabwe," *Mambo Press*, Gweru.(1984); TibaijukaA. K, "Report of the Fact-Finding Mission to Zimbabwe to assess the Scope and Impact of Operation Murambatsvina," *UN Habitat*, Nairobi. (2005); Chaeruka. J ; Munzwa. K, "Assessing Regulatory Framework Bottlenecks for Low-cost Housing

policies and plans like the Growth with Equity (GWE), and the Prime Minister's Directive, the Transitional Development Plans (TNDP) of 1982/3 to the First Five Year National Development Plan (FFYNDP) of 1985 to 1990. The general development policy thrust was socialist. To redress the spatial and racial disparities created by the then ousted colonial regime, the government embarked on "housing for all by 2000" campaign. It is asserted that,

> "Immediately after independence, there was a housing goal which was summed up in the slogan, 'Housing for all by the year 2000.".. Although the policy position has not always been supported by actual houses being built, there has been consistency. This is positive because it indicates ready support to housing programmes in Zimbabwe since any such development is in line with an existing desire of the government."[326]

Specifically, to redress the impacts of the colonial apartheid policy of 1890 to 1979, the new Zimbabwean government used a cocktail of instruments oscillating between technocratic-induced minimalist ideology and socialist populism. The First President of the Republic of Zimbabwe, Reverend Canaan Banana had this to say,

> "My government considers the housing of all workers as a welfare matter of paramount importance. Every worker and his family have the right to adequate accommodation. In order to achieve these objective housing programmes on both an ownership and rental basis will be worked out for those areas where this is required." [327]

At the same time, the new government was non-tolerant of squatting as a panacea to housing shortages. Canaan Banana, in his opening address to parliament in June 1983 stated that "It is the

---

in Zimbabwe, Final Draft Report," *UNHABITAT and the Government of Zimbabwe*, Harare.(2009); Davison.C, "An evaluation of existing residential layout design approaches in Zimbabwe and suggestions for alternative approaches," *Urban Forum 13(4):* pp187-204(2002)

[326] Toriro.P.," The Urban Housing Question in the Context of Operation Murambatsvina and Operation Garikai/Hlalani Kuhle," *Policy Brief prepared on behalf of the African Institute for Agrarian Studies*, Harare.(2006)

[327] GoZ, "Transitional National Development Plan 1982/83 -1984/85," *Vol 1, Government Printer*, Harare.(14 May 1980:116)

government policy to remove urban squatters and accommodate them in properly planned residential areas"[328]. This policy had earlier on been practically demonstrated when in 1980/81, the squatter settlement of approximately 30,000 people in Chirambahuyo (15 km from Harare) was bulldozed[329]. Again in 1983, an informal settlement of a further 10,000 people at Russelldene was bulldozed. Ironically, Epworth has survived this rather harsh policy for a number of decades if not more than a century now.

At independence, one must note that both local and central governments emerged as the major players in providing the public good of housing perhaps being driven by the duty to care. In no time, it emerged that the state sector had limits in such provision. Individuals began to organise themselves to house themselves. It is noted of a number of discontinuities in terms of policy pronunciation:

> "In 1980, the new policy sought to encourage home ownership... The new government changed this in order to allow blacks to become property owners in urban areas. The policy meant that housing stock under the control of both the state and councils was significantly reduced. The government also introduced a policy to control rents, thus protecting tenants from overcharging by landlords. Under this policy, rentals could only be increased within certain regulated parameters. The reaction of landlords and property developers was to shun the rental market. As a result, very few new flats were developed by the private sector during this time. The ultimate effect of that policy was to remove other players in the housing delivery system, thereby reduced housing output. In 1982, ambitious housing standards were introduced. These put the minimum stand size at 300 square metres. The impact of this policy was to make servicing expensive, thereby limiting the ability of local authorities to provide an adequate number of

---

[328] Butcher. C,)., "Urban low-income housing: a case study of the Epworth squatter settlement upgrading programme, Chapter 6 in ZINYAMA L, D TEVERA AND S CUMMING (eds.) 1993" *Harare:* "The Growth and Problems of the City," *University of Zimbabwe*: Harare. (1993))

[329] Butcher. C, "Low Income Housing in Zimbabwe," *A Case Study of the Epworth Squatter Upgrading Programme -RUP Occasional Paper No 6*, Department of Rural and Urban Planning, University of Zimbabwe: Harare.(1986); (Patel.D.H;Adams.J.T, "Chirambahuyo: A Case Study in Low Income Housing," Mambo Press: Gweru(1981),)

> stands or houses. The length of the road, water and sewer pipes to each stand was the major contributor to the expense."[330]

From the foregoing quotation is can be noted that at independence that the government came up with certain policies, which were not put to rigorous scrutiny before the change could be effective. Such decisions were more of impulsive than 'tried and tested." The result was undesired outcomes that, upon scrutiny now, one can say were unsustainable. The then Deputy Ministry of Local Government and Housing, observed the following that:

> "Despite the changes about to take place in the urban areas of both municipal and rural councils, I see a continuity need for area boards or councils. These boards or councils, operating at the neighbourhood level, are the base of urban local government structures and are important agencies of our lively environment, the maintenance of recreational and welfare facilities and self-determination of grass roots problems... The national housing shortage is one of the most pressing problems facing my ministry and I am determined that everything possible will be done to overcome the problem as rapidly as possible... My ministry is responsible for rent control for urban residential properties in the private sector, including local government areas. I am presently considering the introduction of new rent control regulations for lodgers' accommodation in the local government areas. Such controls are necessary to put a stop to the exploitation of the unhoused people by owners on tenants in those areas... All state land in the urban areas is the responsibility of my Ministry, and its disposal is undertaken in "lease with an option to purchase" basis which only entitles the lessee to take title to his land when he has completed development. This is a well-tried system, and prevents speculation in land and ensures adequate development. All disposals of land are undertaken in consultation with local authorities."[331]

---

[330] Toriro.P.," The Urban Housing Question in the Context of Operation Murambatsvina and Operation Garikai/Hlalani Kuhle," *Policy Brief prepared on behalf of the African Institute for Agrarian Studies*, Harare.pg 4(2006)

[331] Godfrey Guwa Chidyausiku, "Motion on Government Policy on Local Government and Housing, Senate Debates," *Parliament of Zimbabwe*,Salisbury. (27 August 1980 p531-532)

Chidyausiku views the grassroots organisation as a critical factor in housing production. Housing, commitment and modalities for solving it are critical in any housing policy if the delivery of this all-important good and process is to be a worthwhile reality. Though there has always been an acknowledgement of the existence of housing shortages in the country[332], the government never tolerated such *ad hoc* land invasions and improper housing developments not fitting the planning regulations and standards at hand.

Under socialism, the private sector output to housing generally decreased due to lack of incentives to do such production. The 1990s saw the liberalisation of the economy and falling of government grip in the market through the promulgation of the Economic Structural Adjustment Programme (ESAP) from 1991-1996. ESAP saw the domination of market forces and the private sector began to subdue the state's involvement in the market. The effects of the ESAP went as far as the post-1990s. The 'Housing for all' programme, thrust by the Government, in the 1980s, was to be expanded in the ESAP period. In a way, rapid expansion in the housing sector was noted especially in such places as Ruwa[333]. Yet, the same programme (ESAP) also resulted in massive retrenchments of the 'excess' labour force in many sectors of the economy whose result was the rise of the informal sector economy in many urban centres of the country. Statutory Instrument 216 of 1994 (Use Group Regulations) was created in the spirit and purpose of the liberalisation thrust. Its purpose was to try and accommodate as much as possible, non-residential functions in residential areas, for instance. This somewhat 'justified' informalisation, which was already shaping in most towns and cities in the country.

Table 8.1 is a snapshot of the major housing policy thrust by the Government of Zimbabwe for the period 1980 to 1996. There has been the shift in approaches to housing delivery based on financial and physical parameters.

---

[332] Mutanga, G., "Housing Shortages because of Legislation, Policy and Attitude," National Housing Convention Report (Public Private Partnership) Victoria Falls Nov. 1997, National Housing Convention: pp 106-108(1997)

[333] Odero.K, "Local Authorities" Response to Restructuring," *Paper presented at the 39th ISoCaRP Congress 2003*, <URL: www.isocarp.net/Data/case_studies/252.pdf>, *Accessed on 3 May 2008.*(2003)

Table 8.1: Chronology of housing policies in Zimbabwe (1980-1996)[334]

Period	Policy	Policy Effect
1980	• Homeownership • Rent restrictions	Private sector reduced investment in rental housing (This proved very difficult to monitor)
1982	• Minimum housing standards - low income plots minimum size 300m² - 4 roomed core of 50-60 m² - construction modes - self help, private, building brigades • site and services • demolition of squatter areas	Local authorities failed to provide adequate serviced plots. Due to the size of the plots, the provision of off-site infrastructure was expensive, resulting in more expensive units
1985-6	• Partnerships in housing between Government or local authorities and the private sector • Housing coops recognised	• Employers could construct houses for their employees • It still was difficult for housing coops to be registered.
1990	• Revision of housing standards - 200 m² minimum plots • Introduction of the Paid Up Permanent Shares (PUPS) to ease the problems of financing housing for low income housing	• Revision of the minimum plot size was meant to make the houses affordable to low income families • PUPS were supposed to introduce cheaper finance for low income earners because of lower interest rates
1995	• Introduction of Start-Paying-For-Your-House Scheme (better known as the Pay Scheme)	• These were supposed to be prepaid housing schemes were Government would match the money put up by the prospective home seekers. It was suitable for high and middle income earners. The policy was abused as undeserving people ended up benefiting
1996	• Direct housing construction by the government using their building units • Revision of housing standards - 150 m² as minimum plot size.	• Construction by building units was substandard. There were problems of supervision and material shortages. They could not meet their targets. IMF and World Bank asked Government not to be directly involved in housing construction • The 150 m² plots are meant to reduce costs of providing infrastructure and making housing affordable. Local authorities and politicians are opposed to the new minimum standards, as they believe that they are too low. They have not yet been implemented widely

In 2001, the Ministry of Public Works, Construction and National Housing (MPWCNH) introduced a Peri-urban Subdivision Policy (PUSP) [335]. Its objectives included what has been termed 'land democratisation and development," empowerment and redistribution primarily in favour of the urban black Zimbabweans, and maximisation of socio-political

[334] Toriro.P.," The Urban Housing Question in the Context of Operation Murambatsvina and Operation Garikai/Hlalani Kuhle," *Policy Brief prepared on behalf of the African Institute for Agrarian Studies*, Harare.pg.5(2006)

[335] Ndlovu.S, "Peri-urban transformation in Zimbabwe: A review of peri-urban subdivision policy and strategy with reference to Harare, 1950-2001," *Unpublished Dissertation: Department of Rural of Urban Planning, University of Zimbabwe*, Harare.(2004)

development and economic growth[336]. This policy did not, *per se*, determine the use of peri-urban areas as being for agricultural production. Rather, it sought to balance residential and production needs with the practice of agriculture. This has seen the introduction of mixed land-uses including commercial production, tourism and peri-urban agriculture in the clustered vicinity. The Kintyre Lake County Development (KLCD) in Harare West, for example, has been designated in light of this policy[337].

It is critical to note that the period of the introduction of the PUSP is the same time as the economic meltdown and FTLRP in the country. The economy battled due to hyperinflation and political instability. There were spontaneous land invasions by the land-hungry black population. The overall planning environment in the country during this period was messy and characterised by amplified informality including transactions in land[338]. The messy realities produced elements of 'bad stewardship' to the detriment of the sustainability cause. Overall, the post-2000 era has marked the development of a turbulent business environment in relation to the changing economic, social and political situation.

---

336 Marongwe. N, "Conflicts Over Land And Other Natural Resources In Zimbabwe," *ZERO Publications*, Harare. (2002); Mhlahlo.S.R, "The impact of housing policy on housing problems in Gweru before and after independence" *The Dyke – The Journal of Midlands State University 1(1):* 107-115.(2004)

337 Harare, "Harare Combination Master Plan: Study Report and Written Statement," *Department of Works*, Harare (1992); Ndlovu.S, "Peri-urban transformation in Zimbabwe: A review of peri-urban subdivision policy and strategy with reference to Harare, 1950-2001," *Unpublished Dissertation: Department of Rural of Urban Planning, University of Zimbabwe*, Harare.(2004)

338 Toriro.P, "Town Planning in Zimbabwe, History, Challenges and the Urban Renewal Operation Murambatsvina," Chapter 11, Maphosa France, Kraposy Kujinga and Sunungurai D Chingarande (eds.), (2007) "Zimbabwe"s Development Experiences since 1980: Challenges and Prospects for the Future," *OSSREA*, Addis Ababa.(2007) , Marongwe. N, "Conflicts Over Land And Other Natural Resources In Zimbabwe," *ZERO Publications*, Harare. (2002)Chipungu. L, "Institutional constraints to land delivery for low-income housing: a case study of Harare, Zimbabwe," in *RICS Foundation Our Common Estate Paper Series*. URL: www.rics-foundation.org, Accessed on 22 April 2008.(2005; 2011)

The year 2005 saw the mooting by the government of Operation Restore Order/Operation Murambatsvina[339]. Since 2000, the housing and land market had become highly dynamic, fluid and speculative. From late 2008 the country is slowly recovering from a period of social, political and economic crisis that has lasted from 1997-2009[340]. The Central Government diverted most of its attention to focus on stabilising the economy and striking political consensus (from 2009 to 2013). Nonetheless, housing was not prioritised. It must be underscored that the FTLRP saw a number of peri-urban housing schemes emerging in peri-urban Zimbabwe[341]. The homeless (together with the war veterans) created some housing cooperatives which they termed 'Third

---

[339] SPT, "Meltdown," "Murambatsvina one year on,"s <URL: http://www. zimbabwesituation.com/meltdown.pdf,> *Accessed on 22 July 2009.(*2006);Tibaijuka A. K, "Report of the Fact-Finding Mission to Zimbabwe to assess the Scope and Impact of Operation Murambatsvina," *UN Habitat*, Nairobi. (2005);Toriro.P, "Town Planning in Zimbabwe, History, Challenges and the Urban Renewal Operation Murambatsvina," Chapter 11, Maphosa France, Kraposy Kujinga and Sunungurai D Chingarande (eds.), (2007) "Zimbabwe"s Development Experiences since 1980: Challenges and Prospects for the Future," *OSSREA*, Addis Ababa.(2007); Potts. D, "Restoring Order"? Operation Murambatsvina and the Urban Crisis in Zimbabwe. *Journal of Southern African Studies 32 (2)* : pp 273 - 291 (2006); Chipungu. L, "Institutional constraints to land delivery for low-income housing: a case study of Harare, Zimbabwe," in *RICS Foundation Our Common Estate Paper Series*. URL: www.rics-foundation.org, Accessed on 22 April 2008.(2011)

[340] Maphosa et al. "Zimbabwe"s Development Experiences since 1980: Challenges and Prospects for the Future," OSSREA, Addis Ababa TORRES HAROLDO DA GAMA (2008)., Social and Environmental Aspects of Peri-Urban Growth in Latin American Megacities. *Paper presented at the United Nations Expert Group Meeting on Population Distribution, Urbanisation, Internal Migration and Development, Population Division, Department of Economic and Social Affairs, United Nations Secretariat*, New York, 21-23 January 2008(2007)

[341] Cousins. B, "The Zimbabwe Crisis in its Wider Context: The Politics of Land, Democracy and Development in Southern Africa," Amanda Hammar, and Brian Raftopoulos, (Eds.) *Zimbabwe"s Unfinished Business - Rethinking Land, State and Nation in the Context of Crisis, Weaver Press*, Harare (2003); Marongwe. N, "Conflicts Over Land And Other Natural Resources In Zimbabwe," *ZERO Publications*, Harare. (2002); Murowe.S; Chirisa.I, "Sally Mugabe Heights: The tale of an incidental Zimbabwean peri-urban housing scheme seeking legitimation," *Zambezia XXXIII (i/ii)*: pp71-89.(2006);Chipungu. L, "Institutional constraints to land delivery for low-income housing: a case study of Harare, Zimbabwe," in *RICS Foundation Our Common Estate Paper Series*. URL: www.rics-foundation.org, Accessed on 22 April 2008.(2011))

Chimurenga' housing cooperatives[342].However basic infrastructure for such settlements was unavailable in most cases, for instance Cowdray Park of Bulawayo[343]. To some extent, these adhered to some principles of the Grassroots Housing Model whose thrust is on incremental housing development[344].

Several housing models have been applied in Zimbabwe over the years.[345]. Their implementation has a strong bearing on the quality of peri-urban habitats given that most are produced at the city edge zone. The models include, but not limited to, Aided Self-Help Model in which local authorities provide serviced stands (with tarred roads, water and sewerage reticulation) and then individual beneficiaries construct dwellings using resources at their disposal. Low-income families have been the chief beneficiaries of this model.

- implementation of housing models also comes in as pay schemes, in which local authorities did layout plan preparation for un-serviced areas. The stands are then tendered to contractors on behalf of beneficiaries who pay up front for the necessary infrastructure. With infrastructure in place, the beneficiaries take over superstructure construction, at their own pace[346]. This is the best-suited model for middle

---

[342] Sukumar. G, "Institutional potential of housing cooperatives for low-income households: The case of India," in *Habitat International 25(2)*: pp 147-174(2001); Vakil.A.C, "Housing Co-operatives in Zimbabwe: A contribution to women"s shelter and development," *Journal of Social Development in Africa 9(1),* pp 7-17. (1994)
[343] Gumbo.T, "Eccentric housing finance sources by the urban poor in Zimbabwe: case of Cowdray Park low-income self help housing scheme in Bulawayo," *Economia. Seria Management 13(1)*: pp 89-104. (2010)
[344] Alexander. C et al. "The grass roots housing process," <URL: http://www. livingneighborhoods.org/library/grassroots.htm>, *Accessed on 22 April 2008.*(1973)
[345] Kamete.A.Y; Mubvami.T, "The contributions of cooperatives to shelter development in Zimbabwe" *UNCHS-Habitat*, Nairobi. <URL: http://www. unhabitat .org/programmes/-housingpolicy/documents/HS618.chm>, *Accessed on 21 September 2008.(*1999); ; CAGOH, "Report on a Study on the Contribution of Urban Housing to National Economic Development in Zimbabwe," *CAGOH,* Harare. (2002); Toriro.P.," The Urban Housing Question in the Context of Operation Murambatsvina and Operation Garikai/Hlalani Kuhle," *Policy Brief prepared on behalf of the African Institute for Agrarian Studies*, Harare.(2006)
[346] Alexander. C et al. "The grass roots housing process," <URL: http://www.living neighborhoods.org/library/grassroots.htm>, *Accessed on 22 April 2008.*(1973)

and high-income earners. Developers have often been cited for misappropriating the funds once it gets into their coffers.

- Employer Assisted Schemes are included as housing schemes and these involve employers getting serviced land allocated to them so that they then assist their employees in the construction of houses. In Harare, about 5 percent of the new low-income houses have been built in this manner[347]. Another criteria embarks on consortia and syndicates, and this involves groups of employers collaborating and then requesting un-serviced land from the relevant local authority. After servicing by the consortium, houses are then built for workers. The model has generally lacked in popularity in the country.
- Joint Ventures as a scheme, have occurred where local authorities have insufficient funds to service land; they provide land and invite other partners to provide other resources to service the land and construct the houses. Wet cores consist of a single room, toilet and shower on fully serviced land. The housing scheme is subject to incremental development where especially low-income families construct rooms at their own pace as funds become available.

Rental Accommodation is stipulated in policy provision by the government to constitute only 10 percent of the housing stock; the rest has to be for ownership[348]. In most low-income areas, this type of housing is in short supply. Consequently, in this scheme, households are strained to rent single rooms from landlords who stay on the same property. This is called 'lodging."

Housing Cooperatives Schemes, are increasingly becoming the main vehicle for low-income accommodation in urban areas. This approach "has become the principal hope for home seekers in the larger

---

[347] Toriro.P.," The Urban Housing Question in the Context of Operation Murambatsvina and Operation Garikai/Hlalani Kuhle," *Policy Brief prepared on behalf of the African Institute for Agrarian Studies*, Harare.(2006); Kamete.A.Y; Mubvami.T, "The contributions of cooperatives to shelter development in Zimbabwe" *UNCHS-Habitat*, Nairobi. <URL: http://www. unhabitat.org/ programmes/ housing policy/documents/HS618.chm>, *Accessed on 21 September 2008.(*1999);

[348] Mafico. C.J,C, "Urban low-income housing in Zimbabwe," *Averbury:Aldershot.(* 1991

cities"[349]. Overall, matters of housing delivery are procedurally guided by the legal framework whose essence is to ensure habitable enclaves of housing units wherever they are located.

Sustainability and appropriateness of these standards remain little understood in light of the six parameters of effective housing delivery, namely; cultural *compatibility and acceptability, social responsiveness, economic feasibility, technological suitability and feasibility, physical and biological harmony* and *temporal relevance*[350]. True stewardship in peri-urban housing should put these to the centre if sustainability is to be hailed as critical[351]. The Government, in 2003, adopted and approved a National Housing Delivery Programme (NHDP). This set out collaboration standards for local authorities, the public, housing cooperatives, professional bodies, NGOs working in housing to deliver housing to the people. Circular Number 70 of 2004 was crafted in the spirit of improving housing and encouraging densification.

The circular spells out the new standards for planning, infrastructure and house construction in all urban areas in Zimbabwe[352]. basing on the outlined standards it has been across that,

> "This [circular provisions] shall apply to new schemes, infill stands shall maintain a general character of the neighbourhood surrounding them. The maximum stand size is to encourage densification and reduce premature urban sprawl.... Peri-urban

---

[349] Toriro.P.," The Urban Housing Question in the Context of Operation Murambatsvina and Operation Garikai/Hlalani Kuhle," *Policy Brief prepared on behalf of the African Institute for Agrarian Studies*, Harare.pg 2(2006)

[350] Mafico. C.J,C, "Urban low-income housing in Zimbabwe," *Averbury:Aldershot.*(1991);Chirisa. I;Munzwa. K.M, "Collective Collateralisation, Group Democracy and the Urban Marginalised Communities in Zimbabwe," A Case of Tashinga Housing Co-operative in Harare, *Local Governance Development Journal 2(1)*: pp15.(2008)

[351] Practical Action, "Terms of Reference for Promoting Examples of Participatory Local Empowerment Urban Planning (PEOPLE-UP)," *Practical Action*, Harare.(2011); Simon.D, "Urban Environments: Issues on the Peri-Urban Fringe," *Annual Review of Environment and Resources 33*: 167-185. (2008); Toffler. A, "The Future Shock," *Pan Books Limited*, London.(1970); Young.C, "True Stewardship, Brownfields," *AG News for America*. <URL: www.brownfieldagnews.com/>, *Accessed on 4 August 2007*.(2007)

[352] Herald, "Ministry sets new standards for urban housing developments," Zimpapers, Harare. (22 February 2005)

residential plots, ranging between one and two hectares, shall ordinarily be sited outside town boundaries. They shall not form part of the urban low-density hierarchy except where they are already in existence."[353]

Specifically, the Circular makes the following stipulations:

a) The minimum stand sizes for low-cost or high-density housing range from 70 to 200 square metres. (The previous ranged from 150 to 300 square metres. Stand sizes ranging from 70 to 89 square metres apply to semi-detached and terraced housing only. For detached housing the stands sizes to range between 90 and 200 metres.
b) The minimum stands frontage for all high stands sizes is pegged at 7 metres.
c) The minimum stand sizes for middle income or medium density housing range between 300 and 500 square metres. There has been maintenance of the previously set standards.
d) Development for low-cost and middle-income housing constitutes single-family only with no outbuildings permitted on the stands.
e) All urban centres to reserve 10 percent land for medium and high-rise flats in residential areas close to the city/town centre, except where there are waivers granted by the Director of Physical Planning; 5 percent for garden and four-storey flats in other medium cost residential centres applies.
f) Stands in low-density or high cost housing range between 800 and 2000 square metres with the larger of these stands being reserved for areas with on-site sewage treatment.
g) Access roads in the high-density are to be appropriately gravelled with a cross gradient of about 5 percent. A gravel thickness of between 100 and 150 mm compared over the widths of the recommended (depending on site conditions and gravel quality). Dish drains are to be used instead of piped culverts. All the higher order roads (local and district distributors) in all areas and access roads in medium and low-density areas are to be surfaced.
h) All stands to be connected to a reticulated water supply network as a standard requirement. Communal stand pipes may be provided in semi-detached and terraced housing

[353] Herald, "Ministry sets new standards for urban housing developments," Zimpapers, Harare. (22 February 2005)

schemes as temporary measures until such a unit is independently connected subject to approval by the Department of Public Works.

i) Walls to be constructed of burnt clay brick or block, cement bricks or blocks and stabilised soil bricks or blocks. Burnt farm bricks for the construction of single storey buildings as approved by the Department of Public Works.
j) Materials for roofing to be asbestos sheet, clay tiles, zinc where available or other materials approved by Department of Public Works.

The spatial configuration of urban centres has also been changing over the years with increasing peri-urbanisation, it is emphatically stated that many households "...are moving into peri-urban areas to lessen urban living costs."[354] Enclaves of the poor outside the main city of Harare are found in Hatcliffe, Domboshawa, Epworth, Chitungwiza, and perhaps also Norton and Ruwa. In the past, the transport cost factor was not very much considered by these households[355]. It is argued that given "...low petrol prices commuting long distances to work was economically feasible even if you were poor. Thus, the spatial pattern of African outlier urban settlements remained unchallenged."[356]

The 2005 Operation Murambatsvina was a wholesale clearance campaign against illegal settlements and slums[357]. This has been described

[354] Bryceson. F. D; Mbara. T, "Petrol pumps and Economic Slump: Rural-urban linkages in Zimbabwe"s Globalisation Process, *Tijdschrift voor enonomische en sociale geographic. (Journal of Economic and Social Geography) 94(3)*: pp 335-349.(2003)

[355] Wissen-Hayek et al. "Measuring and assessing urban sprawl: What are the remaining options for future settlement development in Switzerland for 2030?" – *Applied Spatial Analysis and Policy 4(4)*(2011) pp 249-279.(2011) ; Yinger. J, "Housing and Commuting," *The Theory of Urban Residential Structure*, an e-book(2005)

[356] Bryceson. F. D; Mbara. T, "Petrol pumps and Economic Slump: Rural-urban linkages in Zimbabwe"s Globalisation Process, *Tijdschrift voor enonomische en sociale geographic. (Journal of Economic and Social Geography) 94(3)*: pp 335-349.(2003)

[357] Toriro.P, "Town Planning in Zimbabwe, History, Challenges and the Urban Renewal Operation Murambatsvina," Chapter 11, Maphosa France, Kraposy Kujinga and Sunungurai D Chingarande (eds.), (2007) "Zimbabwe"s Development

it as a "backdoor" attempt by the ZANU-PF government to carry out a "cities without slums" campaign spelt out in the Millennium Development Goals[358]. it is on record that by of 7 July 92,460 housing structures had been destroyed "... affecting 1,335,345 households at more than 52 sites; some 700,000 people in cities across the country ... lost either their homes, their source of livelihood or both with an estimated 500,000 children ... forced out of school or ... their education seriously disrupted; at least six people, including four children... dead as a result ... prolonged exposure to cold; and some 2.4 million persons -18 per cent of Zimbabwe's population have been directly or indirectly affected."[359] Thus, Operation Murambatsvina somewhat reversed the goal and path of the 2003 NHDP. Planning in Zimbabwe is a cumbersome process[360].

In light of the self-help housing before May 2005 many households, building in the peri-urban areas tried to circumvent the requirements of this process. The Operation was a government's response to try to stop peri-urban housing developments that had not followed the planning requirements. Sustainability becomes an issue of political will and support by government. If there is no political capital, efforts by grassroots are foiled. Harnessing this political capital normally requires collaborative efforts as already highlighted in this chapter. At the National Housing Convention in October 2009, all housing stakeholders came together with the idea of 'ironing out' issues in housing delivery[361].

Experiences since 1980: Challenges and Prospects for the Future," *OSSREA*, Addis Ababa.(2007); Chenga, Murambatsvina II hovers over Epworth, The Financial Gazette: URL :http: // www.financialgazette.co.zw/national-report / 3011-murambatsvina-ii-hovers-over-epworth.html, Accessed on 5 August 2010.(2010)

[358] Gumbo.T, "Eccentric housing finance sources by the urban poor in Zimbabwe: case of Cowdray Park low-income self help housing scheme in Bulawayo," *Economia. Seria Management 13(1)*: pp 89-104. (2010)

[359] ICG,"Zimbabwe"s Operation Murambatsvina, The Tipping Point?" *Crisis Group Africa Report N°97, ICG.* (2005:1)

[360] Mubvami.T ; Musandu-Nyamayaro.O, "Procedural Impediments to the Low-income Housing Land Delivery in Cities of Zimbabwe," *Department of Rural and Urban Planning. University of Zimbabwe*, Harare. (1993)

[361] GoZ/UNHABITAT, "Proceedings of the National Symposium convened by the Ministry of National Housing and Social Amenities under the theme ,"*Towards an Integrated Approach to Sustainable Housing and Social Amenities Delivery in Zimbabwe" on 28 May 2009*, Mendel Training Centre, Harare.(2009)

Following this Convention, most settlements in the peri-urban are now following the concept of incremental housing development approach. This is unlike in the 1980s when strict town planning standards of approvals first were followed.[362]

[362] Mafico. C.J,C, "Urban low-income housing in Zimbabwe," *Averbury:Aldershot.(* 1991); Toriro.P, "Town Planning in Zimbabwe, History, Challenges and the Urban Renewal Operation Murambatsvina," Chapter 11, Maphosa France, Kraposy Kujinga and Sunungurai D Chingarande (eds.), (2007) "Zimbabwe"s Development Experiences since 1980: Challenges and Prospects for the Future," *OSSREA*, Addis Ababa.(2007); Mubvami.T ; Musandu-Nyamayaro.O, "Procedural Impediments to the Low-income Housing Land Delivery in Cities of Zimbabwe," *Department of Rural and Urban Planning. University of Zimbabwe*, Harare. (1993)

CHAPTER 5
PROBLEMATISING AND CONTEXTUALISING THE STUDY

By selected cases from Mumbai, India demonstrate the possibility of moving from the culture they call "institutional pluralism" being the cooperation of the government and the civil society groups including the private sector, community and non-governmental organisations[363]. The major question is how best to achieve this institutional pluralism with a minimum number of conflicts to achieve a sustained future in housing delivery and urban development in general. The processes of urban development have largely been shaped by historical patterns of policy development and implementation. Not only local processes have mattered but also regional and global processes. Thus, while a number of continuities, discontinuities and transformations may have occurred (both in theoretical and practical terms), their relevance - in the face of new concepts, debates and policy considerations – remain little understood[364]. Among the critical and new concepts from world and allied bodies are environmental sustainability, ecological footprint and ecological debt, governance, place stewardship and housing rights. Unfortunately, like peri-urbanity, most of these terms are quite elusive and ever shifting in terms of definition and thrusts. For instance, environmental sustainability, as a concept, has been embraced with widespread euphoria and enthusiasm

---

[363] Sanyal.B;Mukhija.V.M, "Institutional Pluralism and Housing Delivery - A Case of Unforeseen Conflicts in Mumbai, India,".< URL: http://archidev.org/IMG/ pdf/ Sanyal.pdf>, *Accessed on 5 April, 2013.* (2000)

[364] Manjengwa.J, "Linking environment and development, easier said than done," learning from the Zimbabwean experience, *Development Southern Africa 24(2):* pp 225-240. (2007); Whitelaw.G., "The Role of Environmental Movement Organisations in Land-use Planning, Case Studies of the Niagara Escarpment and Oak Ridges Moraine Processes." *Unpublished PhD Thesis: Waterloo University*, Ontario.(2007)

by various actors at global, regional and local levels[365]. How it really works at more localised levels remains quite unexplored. The same predicament is true with housing, as a productive and reproductive space in urban and peri-urban areas. So, has been the emphasis on sustainable livelihoods with dwellers in a given area having to tap resources around them (natural, physical, human, and social, financial, political and spiritual) to eke an existence. In effect, housing, in terms of extractions of natural resources in the environment, is a large taker of such[366] .

One can better understand the background of this study by analysing the global, regional and local realities of peri-urban management with respect to housing and environmental developments. The city margins in Africa are difficult to manage, a development that is further compounded by the housing factor manifesting there. This echoes sentiments which state that peri-urban areas "... in most developing countries are characterised by fast population growth, a mixture of planned and un-planned settlements, inadequate service infrastructures, insecure land tenure, social tension, environmental and health problems"[367]. These create great problems for planners, service providers and social workers assigned to work in these areas[368]. In addition, these areas often fall into a responsibility gap between rural and urban authorities, leaving them in a grey zone of unclear legalities, regulations, and general lifestyles. This

---

[365] Marshall. F, "What does peri-urban sustainability mean in the context of Delhi?" <URL: http://stepscentre-thecrossing.blogspot.com/2008/12/what-does-peri-urban-sustainability.html:>, *Accessed on 2April 2009*.(4 December 2008); Manjengwa.J, "Linking environment and development, easier said than done," learning from the Zimbabwean experience, *Development Southern Africa 24(2):* pp 225-240. (2007)

[366] Pasteur. K, "Tools for Sustainable Livelihoods: Policy Analysis," *Institute of Development Studies*, Brighton(2001); Marshall. F, "What does peri-urban sustainability mean in the context of Delhi?"<URL: http://stepscentre-thecrossing.blogspot.com/2008/12/what-does-peri-urban-sustainability.html:>, *Accessed on 2April 2009*.(4 December 2008); Huby.M, "Social Policy and the Environment," *Open University Press*,Buckingham. (1998)

[367] ECOSANRES, "Adapting Planning Tools to the Peri-Urban Setting - A Combination of Existing Tools," <URL: www.ecosanres.org,> *Accessed on 2 June 2010.* (2010:1)

[368] Christie et al., *Living spaces: A vision for the future of planning*, The RSPB: Bedfordshire.(2002)

confusion leads to poor policy design and implementation, and inaccurate policy/programme evaluation.

In recent times, immense physical planning challenges associated with peri-urbanisation have been noted. The dominant physical planning challenge is urban sprawl as it brings about ecological footprint characterised by heavy losses of biodiversity and green fields and 'carbon sinks. [369] Defined loosely sprawl is, "... dispersed and inefficient urban growth"[370]. Specifically, sprawl is characterised by loss of support for public facilities and public amenities, undermining of effective maintenance of existing infrastructure and societal costs for transportation. In addition, it is marked by undesirable consumption of resources, separation of the urban poor people from jobs, imposition of a tax on time and the degradation of water and air quality. Furthermore, the permanent alteration or destruction of habitats, creation of difficulty in maintaining community, and, offering of the promise of choice while delivering more of the same distorts the natural landscape that ideally should not be displaced but integrated with urban development[371]. The ecological footprint is cause of concern everywhere[372].

In a number of countries (particularly in Asia, the Pacific and Africa) under colonialism, separate spatialised development between whites and other races, was emphasised much to the detriment of sustainability today. This left a legacy of 'divided' settlement patterns hence residents' behaviour in emergent metropolitan regions. It is prudent

---

[369] McElfish J.M, "Commentary: Ten Things Wrong with Sprawl," <URL: http://www.emagazine.com/view/?3641,> *Accessed on 22 April 2008.* (2008);

[370] Hasse.J ;Lathrop.R, "Land resource impact indicators of urban sprawl," *Applied Geography 23*: pp159–175 (2003)

[371] Cerne, (2004); Thomas. D., "Architecture and the urban environment – a vision for the new age," *Architectural Press: London* (2002)

[372] Abrams. C, "Housing in the Year 2000," Chapter 8 in Ewald William R Jr. ed. Environment and Policy: "The Next Fifty Year"s, *Indiana University Press*: Bloomington and Lo(1968);Huby.M, "Social Policy and the Environment," *Open University Press*,Buckingham. (1998);; Lenssen.N ; Roodman.M. D, "Making better buildings," Brown LR, Flavin, C, French, H, Postel, S and Starke, L, eds. State of the World 1995, Earthscan: London.(1995); Taylor.J, "Declining Life Support Systems: An NGO Response,". *WESSA, Wildlife and Environment Society of South Africa – A Celebration of 85 Years of Caring for the Earth:* pp18-20. (2011); BHP, BHP Billiton Sustainability Report.

to heed to the impacts this has had today having a strong bearing on the entailments of peri-urban stewardship. In seeking to understand peri-urban settlements in Africa, one is behoved to examine the colonial and post-colonial policy thrusts. These induced spatial and temporary change to the human settlements. Change must be understood as manifesting in three fundamental forms: transformation, continuity or discontinuity[373]. In Taylor's terms, transformation occurs when alteration involves overhaul change, for example, from one mode of production to another; continuity is change rooted in past prescriptions in which established systems remain in place and in operation longer after they were established; and discontinuity means that certain practices are immediately stopped once a new era unfolds.

Generally, and ideologically, with respect to institutions and application of standards in urban development and housing, there is a gap between the western standards sometimes labelled as colonial and 'higher up the ladder' and the needs, aspirations and capacities by low-income groups. Such a gap is more pronounced in peri-urban Africa where mosaic development than constitution informal developments are rife. The gap is now embedded in society. It has been historically defined by colonial dynamics that witnessed discontinuity when the countries attained independence and democracy in the span of years between 1957 and 1994. For example, at independence, colonial restrictions to movement of Africans to cities were removed resulting in high influx of migrants from the rural areas. This eventually saw the creation and spread of squatter and informal settlements dotted around the major city cores. Largely, the problem has been defined as a housing problem. However, the problem has disintegrated to include other challenges including those of crime, unemployment, water and sanitation, energy deficit, to name a few.

Quite a number of the low-income peri-urbanites are uncertain of their future given that their places are not adequately serviced. Many live-in fear of contracting diseases like cholera and dysentery that in certain

[373] Taylor.P.J, "Political Geography, World Economy, Nation State and Locality," *Longman*, Essex (1985)

times of the year since 2008 have been commonplace in Zimbabwe.[374] The observation is that many "... urban services (e.g. water, waste management, energy) are almost by definition dependent on a larger footprint than the city boundary. Right-fulfilling settlement services, like waste removal, often depend on the differentiated roles of a multi-agency or multi-scalar state and so a sound framework of cooperative governance is necessary if urban services are to be delivered to all."[375] This statement, in relation to the obtaining realities, reveals the great adverse effect that results from weak linkages within institutional systems that, in turn, result in poor service delivery.[376].

These multifarious problems have further produced a landscape and space architecture defined by dynamics, issues, trends and ideologies that are contradictory and elusive to deal with[377]. Unless these dynamics, issues, trends and ideologies are fully exposed, analysed and structured, formulating peri-urban housing and stewardship policies and strategies will always be a mammoth and difficult task.

Peri-urban settlements in Zimbabwe are a manifestation of the rather diametrically divergent colonial and post-colonial structural policy and ideological developments. The factors and actors that shape (and have shaped) these settlements, particularly the housing developments and management practices have not been fully analysed, conceptualised with effects and influence interrogated. In fact, traditional studies of housing in the country have focus on single actor housing processes leaving out multi-stakeholder processes in the housing delivery processes whose management and actual constructions transcend spatial, economic and

---

[374] Chenga, "Murambatsvina II hovers over Epworth," The Financial Gazette, <URL:http://www.financialgazette.co.zw/national-report/3011-murambatsvina-ii-hovers-over-epworth.html,> *Accessed on 5 August 2010*.(2010)

[375] Parnell.S Peiterse.E, The "Right to the City": Institutional Imperatives of a Developmental State," *International Journal of Urban and Regional Research 34(1)*: pp.146–62. (2010:150)

[376] Christie et al., "Living spaces: A vision for the future of planning," *The RSPB*, Bedfordshire.(2002)

[377] Rademacher. A, "When is Housing an Environmental Problem Reforming Informality in Kathmandu," *Current Anthropology 50(4)*, pp 513-533 (2009)

political boundaries. [378] The idea of a single actor in housing is supported by the assertion of the state as having had monopoly in housing delivery.[379]. In the 1970s and early 1980s, the government was the almost sole provider of housing. In the 1980s, it became necessary to open up the space for other players. It is underscored how,

> "The government's role redefined in the 1980s was to be that of "an enabler," in contrast to that of "a provider" of housing: It was to enable market agents and civil society to perform well, and encourage cooperation between private and public sectors to meet the housing needs of the urban poor. For such cooperation to flourish, the institutional monopoly of government over the lives of the urban poor had to give away to institutional pluralism, whereby multiple institutions ranging from private firms to community groups, faith-based organisations to political parties, governmental institutions to non-governmental organisations, could operate freely pursuing varying strategies to reach the urban poor. Institutional pluralism was considered a prerequisite for not merely housing provisions but to attain the broader objective of "democratization" which too had emerged as a key theme in the 1980s' development discourse."[380]

Stewardship can mean the creation of a 'common space' for operation hence the unleashing of institutional pluralism to achieve a common purpose.

---

[378] KameteA. Y,"Urban governance, poverty and urban housing," In O. Musandu-Nyamayaro and T. Mubvami, (Eds.), Urban Governance Outreach Research, pp. 13–27. *Harare: Department of Rural and Urban Planning and the Ford Foundation.*(1997), "Continuity with change: a review of Zimbabwe" public sector urban low income housing production system," in *Development Southern Africa 15(1) Autumn*: pp13-28 1998, "Government, Building Societies and Civil Society," Exploring the Interface in the Context of Urban Low-income Housing in Zimbabwe, in *African Review on Money Finance and Banking*, Felice Tambussi: Milan: pp 77-98(1999), Auret.D, "Urban Housing: A National Crisis?," *Mambo Press: Gweru.* (1995), Mafico. I, "Urban low-income housing in Zimbabwe," *Averbury:Aldershot.*(1991)

[379] Sanyal B., Mukhija.V, "Institutional Pluralism and Housing Delivery," *A Case of Unforeseen Conflicts in Mumbai,* India.< URL: http://archidev.org/IMG/pdf/ Sanyal. pdf,> *Accessed on 5 April, 2013* (2000)

[380] Sanyal B., Mukhija.V, "Institutional Pluralism and Housing Delivery," *A Case of Unforeseen Conflicts in Mumbai,* India.< URL: http://archidev.org/IMG/pdf/ Sanyal. pdf,> *Accessed on 5 April, 2013* (2000:2-3)

Examining the nature of peri-urban housing in Zimbabwe, one cannot fail to see the imprint of colonial history on urban development in the country. The country has 10 provinces two of which are Metropolitan – Harare and Bulawayo (see Figure 9.1). Urbanisation in Zimbabwe, rated at the level of 41%[381]. Peri-urbanisation in Zimbabwe, as elsewhere, has had a direct influence in the change of the spatial outlook of different areas. Specifically, it is observed that there exists "...high potential for urban development in all smaller areas [around Harare) - Mazowe, Norton, Ruwa, Arcturus and Darwendale." [382]

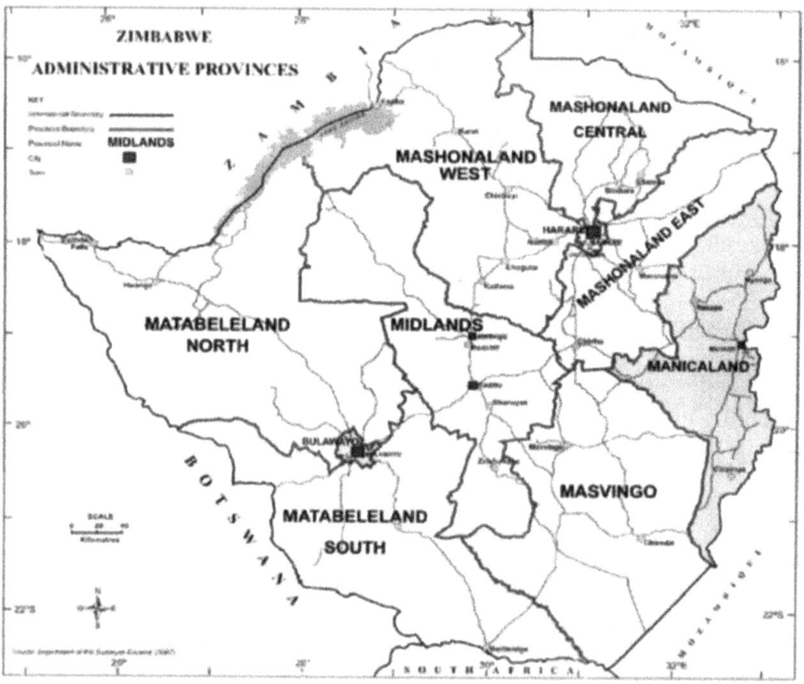

Figure 9.1: Zimbabwe's Provinces and Major Towns [383]

---

[381] GoZ/UNHABITAT, "Proceedings of the National Symposium convened by the Ministry of National Housing and Social Amenities under the theme ,"*Towards an Integrated Approach to Sustainable Housing and Social Amenities Delivery in Zimbabwe" on 28 May 2009*, Mendel Training Centre, Harare.(2009)

[382] Harare, Harare Combination Master Plan: Written Statement, Department of Works, Harare (1989:3)

[383] Department of the Surveyor-General, (2007.)

Local authorities in Zimbabwe have failed to provide basic services in waste removal especially in the decade 1997-2007 (the lost decade). Informal business operations have been marked by massive tax evasions leading to 'poverty in mutuality' (citizens and local government sharing the negative externalities of a 'broken interface'). This is largely explained by the fact that the responsible authorities have failed to engage robustness in the implementation of the plans against a background of an ailing economic performance. In addition, there have been illegal constructions in a bid to self-house households for various reasons, including capacity constraints by local authorities to provide houses and land for housing.[384]. This has resulted in the ballooning of housing backlogs. 'Land invasions' by households and various unsanctioned activities (including informal urban farming, squatter camping and marketing of wares and goods in undesignated sites) have also been a routine development. All these have destroyed the ideal stewardship of places and resources hence becoming a threat to environmental sustainability.

Matters transcending shared municipal and rural boundaries, having a 'regional dimension' in developing countries tend to receive little, if any, attention. Thus, relative to North America (the United States of America and Canada) developing countries cherish little in the notion and practice of place and regional stewardship. Scholars in North America have, in recent times, explained regional stewardship and regional collaboration stressing the centrality of such concepts in solving metropolitan problems including housing, general infrastructure provision and managing the biophysical environment.[385]. They have also stressed the

---

[384] Mapira.J, An Historical Perspective of the Problem of Housing and Some Attempted Solutions in the City of Mutare (1890-2002). *Zambezia* XXXI (i/ii), University of Zimbabwe, Harare: pp 80-103 (2004)

[385] Stoll.L, "Regional Collaboration: A framework for solving complex planning problems." *The Land Tracker 6(2):* pp 1-4. (2006)); Mckinney et al., "Working across Boundaries: A Framework for Regional Collaboration," in LeRoyer Ann ed. Land Lines 16*(3), Lincoln Institute of Land Policy,*Cambridge (USA).(2004); Zorich, "Defining stewardship in the digital age, in First Monday 12(7)."< URL: http://firstmonday.org/issues/issue_7/zorich/index.html>(2007); Wampler. B, "Participatory Budgeting in Brazil, Contestation, Cooperation and Accountability," *Pennsylvania University Press*, Pennsylvania.(2007)

need to break 'barriers and walls' erected along professional, ethnic, neighbourhood and municipal lines which tend to work against regional and area-based collaborative efforts by stakeholders. Ironically, sub-Saharan Africa countries and Zimbabwe, in particular, are riddled with challenges at transitional zones like the peri-urban. Such problems include, but not limited to tenure security among low-income groups, environmental degradation and conflicts over land, water and related natural resources. Collaborating stakeholders by way of creating forums and institutions could be useful in safeguarding the common good hence avoiding 'tragedy of the commons."[386] Both stewardship of a place and housing are in the hands of policy actors whose intentions, interests and offices often are ever changing, sometimes enhancing or cancelling past progressive efforts. Both happen in a political, social and economic environment that is sometimes volatile and less stable.

The aim of this study is to investigate peri-urban housing, in the framework of regional or place stewardship in Zimbabwe by drawing lessons from Ruwa and Epworth which are two satellites of Harare City all constituting what has been called the Ruwa-Epworth District (which is one of the seven functional districts of Harare Metropolitan Province).[387]. The study attempts to historicise processes of housing and habitat delivery highlighting transformations, continuities and discontinuities that have emerged over the years. Stewardship of housing in peri-urban settlements is a policy and practical matter which, largely, sounds ambiguous hence difficult to manage in a host of developing countries, Zimbabwe included.

The specific objectives of the study are to:

i. identify and classify stakeholders in housing delivery in the peri-urban zones with the view of explaining policy and practical bearings by each over time.
ii. explain differential processes and trends, if any, in the transformation and quality of the physical provision of shelter (stocks) in peri-urban settlements.

---

[386] Nguyen M. I,"Analyzing the encroachment process of informal settlements in the periurban of Ho Chi Minh City, Vietnam," *unpublished Master"s thesis*, Lund University: Lund(2006).

[387] Harare, "Harare Combination Master Plan: Study Report and Written Statement," *Department of Works*, Harare (1992)

iii. relate global and regional efforts in the housing and stewardship debate and practices regarding peri-urban settlements.
iv. propose practical and policy alternatives in tackling peri-urban housing and stewardship matters at different levels of analysis (local and regional).

The study seeks to answer the question: 'How is the stewardship debate shaped for the sustainable provision of shelter in peri-urban settlements?' Specifically, the sub-questions are: Who are the key actors including facilitators, sponsors and governors? Can there be deliberate stewardship in which informal and low-income peri-urban dwellers act as informed managers (stewards) whose care about their habitat reduces problems of environmental decay so that future generations will also benefit from the same habitat?

Ruwa and Epworth have some striking contrastive qualities in terms of their origins, social stratification, economic opportunities and housing and environmental management practices. The land market in Ruwa is greatly organised and formal, while that of Epworth is predominantly haphazard and informal. Though the overall focus of the study is peri-urban settlements in Zimbabwe, Ruwa and Epworth are taken as two case study areas from which the realities of housing and stewardship efforts have been drawn. The two areas are adjacent to each other and are in the same province (Harare Metropolitan Province) – Figure 9.2. Ruwa and Epworth are part of the Greater Harare Region (Figure 9.3), a region that has grown highly metropolitan in the last 50 or 60 years.

Figure 1.2: Location of Ruwa and Epworth in Harare Metropolitan Province [388]

Location factors considered in the area characterisation include distance from the city centre of Harare, the climatic, hydrologic, geologic and ecologic (floral and faunal) features of the areas. On the other hand, the historical aspects are those to do with the pre-colonial, colonial and post-colonial developments of the two areas. These contextual factors, have influenced, largely the stewardship factor around Epworth and Ruwa and they continue to have a bearing on the responses made by the settlement's dwellers on the urbanisation trends that have become part of the living arrangement. Ruwa and Epworth have evolved differently. Both Ruwa and Epworth, after independence in 1980, were run as local boards, run by government appointees called Commissioners.

[388] Adapted from the Map by the Office of the Surveyor-General (2011)

Figure 9.3: Suburbs and Peri-urban of Harare[389]

Population numbers in Epworth are debatable but for Ruwa they could be close to realistic. As of 2010, the estimated population of Ruwa was 50,000 while that of Epworth was 500,000 respectively[390]. these numbers are attributed to increasing peri-urbanisation largely explained by developments in the socio-economic fabric of the shifting economy. Specifically, it is argued that since the late 1970s Epworth has attracted a large number of poor homeless people. Numbers have grown from about 20,000 people in 1980 to 123 250 by 2002 and presently the local board has lost count, but rough estimates put the population at around 500,000[391]. However, the national population census held in 2012 puts the figures official at 161, 840 for Epworth and 56,333 for Ruwa[392]. There is thus a

---

389 Zinyama et al ,"Harare*: The Growth and Problems of the City*," *University of Zimbabwe: Harare*. (1993:85)

390 Ruwa, "Ruwa Town Council at a Glimpse as at June 2010," Ruwa. (2010); Chenga, "Murambatsvina II hovers over Epworth," The Financial Gazette, <URL: http://www.financialgazette.co.zw/national-report/3011-murambatsvina-ii-hovers-over-epworth.html,> *Accessed on 5 August 2010*.(2010)

391 Chenga, "Murambatsvina II hovers over Epworth," The Financial Gazette <URL: http : // www.financialgazette.co.zw/national-report/ 3011-murambatsvina-ii-hovers-over-epworth.html,> *Accessed on 5 August 2010*. (2010)

392 ZIMSTAT, "Census 2012 – Preliminary Report," *ZIMSTAT*, Harare. (2012)

great variance between the official statistics and statistics by journalists and independent researchers. This is an indicator of the obvious 'politics of numbers' typical of developing countries. Nevertheless, the numbers still have a bearing on the peri-urbanisation trends surrounding human settlements in this case of Ruwa and Epworth.

Epworth is located about twelve kilometres from the city centre of Harare. The settlement is easily accessible from the city centre and the eastern industrial employment nodes of Msasa and Ruwa. It lies between 1,500 and 1,600 metres in altitude. The relief consists of gently undulating ground interrupted by granite outcrops and picturesque balancing rocks that are very popular with tourists. These are some of the most beautiful balancing rocks in Zimbabwe. The former Zimbabwean bank notes had an encryption of some of these balancing rocks that are located in the Epworth local government area.

Epworth was founded in 1892. In that year, Reverend Isaac Shimmin of the Wesleyan Missions in Mashonaland was granted 1,064 hectares Epworth Farm by the British South African Company, in trust for the indigenous blacks. In 1904, the Missions purchased adjacent Glenwood Farm (981 hectares).[393] Then, in 1908, the Missions purchased two adjoining farms, one being the Adelaide Farm (1,564 hectares). These cover what is present day known as Epworth. By 1950, the settlement had about 500 families who subscribed to the Mission values and legitimately owned 4000m2 of land each allocated by the Mission for residential and cropping purposes.[394] Others also settled in, illegally, a development that was to be a cause of disagreement to the Mission business and aspirations. The growth of Epworth from 1892 and resembles 'organic' growth. The Squatter Upgrading Scheme adopted for Epworth in the early 1980s was to leave an unfinished business in this peri-urban settlement. Overall,

---

[393] Nyamvura T,Brown.A, "Epworth – an informal, unplanned and squatter settlement, Upgrading Initiatives in Epworth." Brown A and C Davidson eds. *Responsive design and plan implementation*, Department of City and Regional Planning, Cardiff University: Cardiff. (1999.)

[394] Butcher.C, "Urban low-income housing: a case study of the Epworth squatter settlement upgrading programme,"; Chapter 6 in ZINYAMA L, D TEVERA AND S CUMMING (eds.) 1993, *Harare: The Growth and Problems of the City*, University of Zimbabwe: Harare. (1983)

Epworth has populations predominantly concerned with the 'politics of the stomach." The population thus tends to forget the issues that go beyond the individual's plot or household.

Between 1970 and 1980, the population in Epworth dramatically rose to about 35,000. This coincided with the liberation war in Zimbabwe (1966-1979) which saw a huge influx of people into Epworth. The majority of the new settlers were on flight of the war that was ravaging the rural areas at the time. Epworth offered itself as an easier destination for many given that there was no direct local authority that could control movement of people and development like in other urban archetypal settlements, specifically Harare and Chitungwiza.[395] It was thus a 'natural choice' for a destination and an area for settling.

The major added advantage to this was its proximity to the capital city. This alone ascertained the settler with a strong link for those seeking for economic and social opportunities.[396] Some settlers found jobs and worked as domestic servants in the north-eastern suburbs (Hatfield, Arcadia and Waterfalls). Over the years, it has become a norm that those that fail to secure accommodation in Harare perhaps because it is too expensive for them often find their ways into Epworth. It emerged that some legal Missions tenants in Epworth rented illegally land or built shacks within their stands to rent out to desperate families. Consequently, slum conditions became a commonplace sometimes being associated with such vices as increased cases of crime, drug abuse, illegal cultivation of land and pollution. In the eyes of the Missionaries, the situation was getting out of hand. The church felt that it could not meet the demands for 'adequate housing' for the increasing numbers of peri-urban dwellers.

At the inception of the Local Board in 1986, Epworth had about 5,000 residential stands that were regularised in situ. For the residents who

---

[395] Nyamvura T, Brown.A, "Epworth – an informal, unplanned and squatter settlement, Upgrading Initiatives in Epworth." Brown A and C Davidson eds. *Responsive design and plan implementation*, Department of City and Regional Planning, Cardiff University: Cardiff. (1999.)

[396] Butcher.C, "Urban low-income housing: a case study of the Epworth squatter settlement upgrading programme,"; Chapter 6 in ZINYAMA L, D TEVERA AND S CUMMING (eds.) 1993: *Harare: The Growth and Problems of the City*, University of Zimbabwe: Harare. (1983)

had settled in areas that were deemed inhabitable, land was identified, planned and serviced and these were relocated. This exercise ended up creating about 6,000 residential stands for the whole of Epworth. But a few informal homesteads sprouted around this time. The government chipped in, demolished the illegal structures and relocated the settlers to other areas outside Epworth.[397]. Epworth covered about 3600 hectares in extent and was home to roughly 150,000 people by December 1997.

Administrative problems and lack of funds for providing infrastructure and services to the burgeoning population impelled the Mission to donate the major portion of the 3 farms of Epworth, Glenwood and Adelaide to the Government in 1983[398]. As if to confirm the Mission's justification for surrendering the farms, in 1985, a cholera outbreak occurred in the area. In 1986, the Epworth, Adelaide and Glenwood farms were gazetted as Epworth Local Government Area. The Central Government appointed the Epworth Local Board (ELB) to administer the settlement. The Zimbabwean Government that had assumed power only six years earlier welcomed the donation and directed a freeze of all non-permitted new developments. It took an aerial photograph of the whole settlement and undertook an ambitious programme to develop the area *in situ* for eventual incorporation into Harare City[399]. Even to date, the ELB runs the affairs of the settlement including all aspects of housing delivery and environmental sanitation. The Government, however, has set out two broad objectives for the Board within which most services in an urban set up are found; these were to regularise existing and future development in

---

[397] ELB, "Epworth Local Board meeting." (2002)

[398] Nyamvura T,Brown.A, "Epworth – an informal, unplanned and squatter settlement, Upgrading Initiatives in Epworth." Brown A and C Davidson eds. *Responsive design and plan implementation*, Department of City and Regional Planning, Cardiff University: Cardiff. (1999.), Epworth, Local Board Progress Report, ELB, Epworth.(1987a); "Local Board Proposed Development Report, ELB, Epworth."(1987b); Local Board Treasury Report on Debtors Databank, ELB, Epworth. (2007)

[399] Epworth, "Local Board Proposed Development Report, ELB, Epworth."(1987b); Butcher.C, "Urban low-income housing: a case study of the Epworth squatter settlement upgrading programme,"; Chapter 6 in ZINYAMA L, D TEVERA AND S CUMMING (eds.) 1993: Harare: The Growth and Problems of the City, University of Zimbabwe: Harare. (1983)

the area, and, to improve living conditions for Epworth residents[400]. Epworth 4 Area Development Committees (ADC) was elected for effective grassroots participation in the water and sanitation supply upgrading processes. The committees were each for Muguta and extension, Makomo and extension, Zinyengere and extension and Chinamano and extension. In each Area Development Committee, there were ten board members.

By 2007, Epworth had a population of around 300 000 in its seven Wards with three distinct characters of residents. Epworth is divided into 7 wards. Wards 1 and 4, that is Muguta-Makomo and Chinamano-Zinyengere areas respectively, have predominantly residents linked to the early settlers and they are colloquially referred to as 'originals. Wards 2, 3 and 5 are mainly composed of residents who moved into Epworth prior to the inception of the Local Board in 1986 but have no links with the 'originals' of the 1890s. Their areas are generally referred to as 'extensions,' for example, Muguta Extension, Makomo Extension and Chinamano Extension.

It must be underscored that when the government took over the management of Epworth in 1986, the area did not have public utilities such as water, sewer, electricity and rubbish collection.[401]. Upon taking over the management of the area, the government's Department of Physical Planning (DPP) conducted a socio-economic survey, general land-use survey. The results briefly showed that 71% of residents used unprotected wells or streams water for their domestic water consumption, 94% used pit toilets or bush for personal sanitation. The serious risk of well water being polluted by nearby pit toilets and, more particularly, by surface run-off was obvious. There were two primary schools, one ill-equipped clinic with one trained nurse, and one police post with four constables. Physically, much of the land in Epworth was unsuitable for building

---

400 Epworth," Local Board Progress Report, ELB, Epworth." (1987a)

401 Epworth, "Local Board Progress Report, ELB, Epworth." (1987a); "Local Board Proposed Development Report," *ELB*, Epworth.(1987b); "Local Board Treasury Report on Debtors Databank," *ELB*, Epworth. (2007); Butcher.C, "Urban low-income housing: a case study of the Epworth squatter settlement upgrading programme,"; Chapter 6 in ZINYAMA L, D TEVERA AND S CUMMING (eds.) 1993: Harare: The Growth and Problems of the City, University of Zimbabwe: Harare. (1983)

development. Approximately 700 existing homes were situated on such unsuitable land. Compounding the difficulties of the topography. Epworth is located on the eastern side of Harare, across the city from high-density/low income housing. As such, bulk supplies of water, electricity and sewer required to improve living conditions were not available in this side-stands were on septic tank. The median income of the residents at the time of the DPP survey was Z$90 when the elsewhere in Harare high-density, low income areas the median income was Z$194. Further, 23% of the residents were entirely economically dependent on gifts and remittances from relatives, pensions or informal sector earnings.

Overall, the Zimbabwe Government's decision not to bulldoze Epworth helped in meeting the basic shelter needs of the urban poor. Town planning layouts were done by 1987. In addition, the central government through the Ministry of Local Government Rural and Urban Development with technical and supervisory assistance from Blair Research Laboratory (BRL) (Ministry of Health) began an interim water supply and sanitation programme by drilling 290 protected tube wells and construction 1000 toilets.[402] The wells were provided at a ratio of one well to ten households and were sited in future road reserves public open spaces or next to community facilities, e.g. schools and market places and these were dug by the local people under the supervision of BRL. Wells were fitted with Blair hand pumps. These had low capital cost and low maintenance requirements and to be serviced by the locals with supervision from BRL. Blair toilets were also constructed. These were located within 8 metres of the back boundary of the stand and aligned in straight lines so that the tanker could easily drive between rows of toilets dislodging each unit as it went along the alignment of toilets also meant it would be possible in future to install sewer lines. A number of miscellaneous developments were implemented: tower lighting, tarred roads and more schools. The

[402] Nyamvura T,Brown.A, "Epworth – an informal, unplanned and squatter settlement, Upgrading Initiatives in Epworth." Brown A and C Davidson eds. *Responsive design and plan implementation*, Department of City and Regional Planning, Cardiff University: Cardiff. (1999.)

total investment for infrastructure committed by the Ministry by 1988 was Z$76 million and this converted to about £5 million[403].

Plan International was also heavily involved in construction of market stalls, sewer, electricity, water reticulation and shopping centres, tower lighting for two administrative districts, educational sponsorship for 1000 children. It also started Women's Clubs, provided book grants for two primary schools and organised management workshops for women's groups. World Vision did its work through the Epworth Local Board in training management, promotion of drama groups and coordination of churches, concentrating in Chinamano extension. The Zimbabwe Women's Bureau (ZWB) developed a women's soap making co-operative. The Red Cross and Red Crescent Society made provision of toilet kits for residents to construct their own toilets. Help-Age whose target group was those 60 years and above -provided with food grants, services, water, toilet construction and clothing.[404]

The Local Board Chairman was to be a member appointed by the Ministry. The Chairman, Vice Secretary of each Area Committee formed an Overall Development Committee, which had twelve members. Issues raised at the grassroots level were the responsibility of the ADC before they were tabled in the Board which overall comprised eight appointees who were Epworth residents and four appointees who were Government officials. To assist the board were two sub-committees namely the Lands Sub-Committee to process all applications to issue stands in Epworth (state land) for commercial, residential, agricultural and any other use; and the Finance, Works and Planning Sub-Committee to deal with the approval of building plans, development permits and layout plans. In addition, the Committee had oversight of all the work in progress including managing implementation problems faced by the contractor, new works, recommending next development stages and maintenance work.

Epworth was divided into 9 administrative areas, comprising 4 original villages, each of which has its own 'extension' in 1997. In the

---

[403] Nyamvura T,Brown.A, "Epworth – an informal, unplanned and squatter settlement, Upgrading Initiatives in Epworth." Brown A and C Davidson eds. "Responsive design and plan implementation," *Department of City and Regional Planning, Cardiff University*, Cardiff. (1999.)

[404] Ibid.

same year, Housing People of Zimbabwe (HPZ) visited a number of income projects that were being supported by the Zimbabwe Women Bureau (ZWB) since it had been working already in the area. It asked ZWB to mobilise families that were interested in a housing improvement scheme[405]. By 1999 five housing cooperatives had been established in the area including Tangenhamo which had 15 members, Kushinga, 18 members, Tichaedza, 13 members, Chiremba, 15 members and Shungu which had 16 members. All these cooperatives had to invest in the money market through the Housing Cooperative Fund managed by HPZ. By mid-1999, two cooperatives had invested Z$42,000 earning up to Z$1,300 interest per month. In a bid to build affordable houses appropriate materials like the stabilised soil blocks (SSB) were recommended and housing cooperative members were taken to an exhibition of housing in Epworth built by a local NGO, Intermediate Technology Development Group (ITDG) using SSB.[406] The cooperative members approved this technology and some of these members were trained to train others. Habitat for Humanity was providing finance for buying windows and doorframes, roofing sheets, glazing and other materials. Local builders, who had undergone training by HPZ and ITDG, did the construction.

Box 5.1: Epworth - some facts

- Located about 15km east of the capital, Harare
- Formalised into an urban residential area in 1983
- Despite paying rates to the Epworth Local Board the settlers are not recognised as being part of the residential area.
- The Methodist Church, owns the land.
- To access health and education facilities, the settlers have to pay landlords in Epworth for the use of their home addresses.

[405] Mututu.R, "The Role of Housing People in Promoting Self-Help Shelter in Epworth, Upgrading Initiatives in Epworth," Brown A and C Davidson eds. "Responsive design and plan implementation," *Department of City and Regional Planning, Cardiff University*:,Cardiff. (1999).

[406] Mututu.R, "The Role of Housing People in Promoting Self-Help Shelter in Epworth, Upgrading Initiatives in Epworth," Brown A and C Davidson eds. "Responsive design and plan implementation," *Department of City and Regional Planning, Cardiff University*:,Cardiff. (1999).

- To bury the dead, the settlers pay three-fold the normal fees charged to the other residents.
- Despite Epworth having acquired a local government board status in 1986, the settlement has hardly progressed beyond its squatter camp outlook.
- Apart from the two tarred main feeder roads much of the intricate jig-saw puzzle of hovels called Epworth are linked by makeshift nameless dust roads and paths.
- Home owners have no title deeds, electricity and access to tapped water and the spectre of displacement forever looms.
- Epworth is a complex humanitarian crisis driven by institutionalised poor governance, corruption and politics.
- Epworth was established in 1890 as a Methodist Church mission station.

Epworth, from its genesis, has continued to experience a huge influx of immigrants. The majority are of a poor background. This partly explains the growth of numerous informal dwellings in the area. Despite efforts to regularise the settlement, illegal peri-urban subdivisions persist in the area and this is to the efforts of order, harmony and amenity as put across in the planning legislation of the land, specifically the Regional, Town and Country Planning Act and allied statutes and legal instruments.[407].

Ruwa (once a growth point but acquired the status of a town in 2009), is situated 23 km east of the city of Harare along the Mutare Road. It was established as a growth point in 1986 in terms of the Income and Sales Tax Act (ISTA). Ruwa was pronounced a Local Board to manage the township was appointed by government in 1991 according to section 14 of the Urban Councils Act. Before 1991, the Goromonzi Rural District Council (GRDC) and the Urban Development Corporation (UDCORP) jointly administered Ruwa. Box 5.2 provides some facts about the establishment, growth and expansion of Ruwa. Before 1986, the town

[407] TibaijukaA. K, "Report of the Fact-Finding Mission to Zimbabwe to assess the Scope and Impact of Operation Murambatsvina," *UN Habitat: Nairobi*. (2005)

came under different rural local authorities one of them being the Goromonzi Rural District Council.

Box 5.2: Ruwa - Some Facts[408]
• Ruwa Town is located 25 kilometres from Harare. • The town falls under the Ruwa-Epworth District of the Harare Metropolitan Province. • With effect from the 3rd of January 2003, Ruwa fell under the Harare Metropolitan Province being effected through Statutory Instrument 15D and E of 2003. Before that it was under Mashonaland East Province. However, politically, Ruwa still falls under Goromonzi in Mashonaland East. • Growth Point was established in terms of the Income and Sales Tax Act in 1986. It was through Proclamation 16 of 1990 and Statutory Instrument 204 of the same year that the Ruwa Growth Point area underwent an excision from the Bromley Ruwa Rural Council and powers conferred to it as a Growth Point. • Ruwa Local Board was upgraded to a Town Council in terms of section 14(1) of the Urban Councils Act as per the letter dated 27 February 2008 from the then Ministry of Local Government, Public Works and Urban Development. This was conditional to addressing issues to do with setting a boundary of the town for the incorporation of more state land; settling the issue of the town centre on Lot A of Oaks; realigning the organogram to reflect a linear structure and with proper staff grading system; and strengthening the management system. • Administrative authority has been divided into four phases: the first being the settlement being governed under Bromley Ruwa Rural Council; the second, under the Urban Development Corporation, from 1988-1990; the third being the Ruwa Local Board, from 1990 to 2008, the last, Ruwa Town Council. • The Ruwa Local Board was established through a series of warrants which helped powers, privileges, and duties to be conferred to it. These five warrants were: Warrant

[408] RTC, "Ruwa Town Council at a Glimpse as at June 2010," Ruwa. (2010)

1 of 12 October 1990; Warrant 2 of 21 February 1992; Warrant 3 of 11 April 1997; Warrant 4 of 26 November 1997 and Warrant 5 of 17 September 1999.

- In terms of land area, Ruwa town was initial plus or minus 796.58 ha. As at June 2010, it was 3188 ha after incorporation from Goromonzi Rural District Council Area. An additional plus or minus 20,142 ha has been earmarked for incorporation.
- There are 9 wards in Ruwa.

Today, there are different residential units in Ruwa i.e. low densities e.g. Winsor and Sunway that are still under development; Damofalls that is a medium-density suburb; and, Ruwa is a High-Density suburb. The provision of infrastructure in Ruwa is mainly private sector driven. This is particularly true in one of the consortia in the town where private landowners have been seeking approval to subdivide their land. The housing backlog in the town has been growing over the year. In 2007, it had a waiting list of more than 5,000 housing applicants following the last allocation in 1995.[409]. The records of the RLB indicate that the number of serviced stands is around 10,000. Of this, only 0.5% are council-owned or on stateland. Operation Garikayi/Hlalani Kuhle scheme benefited 110 households based on the recommendations made by the local ward councillors. Thus, under OGHK, the government of Zimbabwe provided funding for the development of the superstructures but without the requisite infrastructure.[410]

Since the Ruwa Local Board faced difficulties such as the shortage of plant and equipment, financial resources and skilled workers in providing adequate infrastructure, it has established a partnership with the consortium, group of private companies for provision of the needed infrastructure. All prospective developers in Ruwa were required to contribute a development charge for the installation of off-site infrastructure such as roads, water and power. In Ruwa's up-market residential estate of ZIMRE Park, largely serviced by the Zimbabwe Reinsurance Corporation, the local board issued its developer, the

[409] RLB, "Ruwa at a Glimpse, Report prepared to support the application of Ruwa for a Town Status (Unpublished)," Ruwa (2007)
[410] Ibid. (2007)

National Real Estate, with a planning permission to develop 2,500 medium density residential stands. The developer was also obliged to provide water and upgrade the pump station. In addition, the developer paid the Board Z$19 million endowment fund.[411]

Today Ruwa has become a town whose vision is to become, "…a leading investment destination with a high-quality way of life and first choice town to live in".[412]. This vision is driven by the town's mission statement: "To administer the Town Council Area and facilitate the provision and maintenance of quality social services to residents, investors and other stakeholders." From the onset, it can be said that the settlement has strived to follow a formal tracking and in keeping with the stages of growth perhaps according to the developmentalist paradigm of modernisation. The 1990s had a strong impact on the growth given the economic reforms set by the Government. Ruwa 'gained' due to this policy of liberalisation as it managed to attract massive investments. Housing development projects like the development of ZIMRE Park emerged in this period.[413]. In succinct terms, it is observed that, between 1992 and 1999, "...the population of Ruwa grew at an average of 173 percent per year, rising from 1,447 to about 19,000."[414] This growth led to astronomical increases in demand for property development. The greatest beneficiaries of this have been private landowners who subdivided and later sold them at a profit.

While Ruwa Local Board draws levies and rates on developed properties, such developments tend to put pressure on its resources as demand for water, sewer and solid waste disposal services increases. In fact, the effect this has had on the local authority is to force it to adopt almost an all-out service-oriented strategy." It has pointed out that the centre is "…fast developing into an urban centre, housing and employing

---

[411] Odero.K. K, "Local Authorities" Response to Restructuring," *Paper presented at the 39th ISoCaRP Congress 2003* <URL: www.isocarp.net/Data/case_studies /252.pdf,> *Accessed on 3 May 2008*.(2003.)

[412] Ruwa, "Ruwa at a Glimpse, Report prepared to support the application of Ruwa for a Town Status (Unpublished)," Ruwa(2010)

[413] Odero.K. K, "Local Authorities" Response to Restructuring," *Paper presented at the 39th ISoCaRP Congress 2003* <URL: www.isocarp.net/Data/case_studies/ 252.pdf,> *Accessed on 3 May 2008*.(2003.)

[414] Ibid, pg 5

thousands of people. District industrial, commercial and residential land-uses have been developed with considerable supportive infrastructure.... The idea behind its establishment was to encourage industrial development in the area, and such industries would provide employment for disable persons mainly ex-combatants who would have received some training at the Ruwa Rehabilitation Centre (RHC).... Its proximity to Harare, which has a large consumer market and the relatively cheaper development, compared to Harare make Ruwa an attractive centre for industrial development. Furthermore, its proximity to the Harare International Airport is, indeed, an attractive feature for export- and import-related enterprises".[415] Inherent in Ruwa Town Council is the capacity to control population size, the place has little, if any, invasions on housing land.[416] Indeed, the Ruwa residents have some latent power to hold their municipal government accountable to enforce the set standards and this population control.

---

[415] Ruwa, "Ruwa Local Development – Addendum to the 1991 Study Report. Department of Physical Planning" Harare pg 2 (1997)

[416] The Times Newspaper, "Housing land runs out." <URL: www.thetimes.co.za/, Accessed on 23 July 2008.> (2008)

CHAPTER 6
THE ADMINISTRATIVE AND CULTURAL CONTEXT OF RUWA AND EPWORTH

As local boards, the Epworth and Ruwa were governed under the direct leadership of the Ministry of Local Government, Rural and Urban Development. This was before 'democratisation' in 2008. Commissioners from the ministry had oversight of local boards' business. The 2008 Harmonised Elections in which Parliamentary, Presidential and Local Government elections saw the replacement of the appointed commissioners with elected councillors in both Ruwa and Epworth. For the first time they could now have councillors instead of government-appointed commissioners. But it is important also to show that both settlements belong to the Harare Metropolitan Province though politically Ruwa is also under Mashonaland East Province (see Figure 10.1).

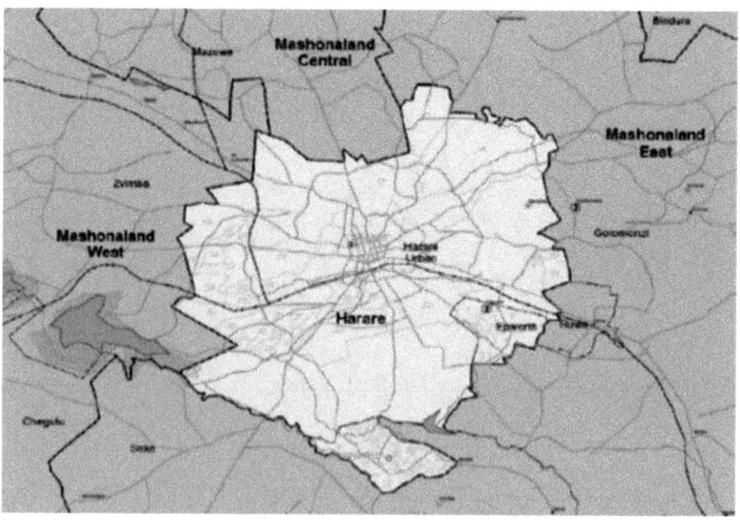

Figure 10.1: Ruwa under Mashonaland East [417]

[417] Map by the Department of the Surveyor-General (2011)

The Epworth-Ruwa District is one of the eight districts of the HMP yet Ruwa remains politically a 'constituency' of Mashonaland East Province. HMP's stewardship role is espoused in the Province's aim of the Development plan captured as the, "...improvement of urban livelihoods by providing housing and ancillary services; integrating urban agriculture in residential areas to reduce poverty; reduction of the spread of TB and HIV and other communicable diseases; improving health facilities in all the four urban areas; provision of supportive infrastructure to expand residential, commercial and industrial development; creation of job opportunities especially for school leavers and women; protection and sustainable use of natural resources; and, improving provincial resources to achieve the above."[418]

While these goals are somewhat altruistic and germane, they lack in being strategic. The Province appears to pay the role of a 'big brother' without mentioning its role in mobilising resourced to the desired end. Although the Plan does acknowledge past failures due to the ailing economy, the goals appear high sounding, perhaps only framed to appeal politically. The implication is that Ruwa and Epworth have not benefited much (in terms of housing delivery) by the existence of this structure since it was put across a few years ago. HMP is more of a political structure than a serious regional planning body that would be involved in shaping infrastructure development and attracting investment that would then see meaning housing development in the two settlements as purported in its development plan.

Evidence shows that residents in Ruwa have been more active in their affairs than those of Epworth[419]. This is, in terms of visioning[420] ,

---

[418] HMP, "Harare Metropolitan Provincial Development Plan 2011," *Government of Zimbabwe*, Harare (2011:4)

[419] RLB, "Ruwa at a Glimpse, Report prepared to support the application of Ruwa for a Town Status (Unpublished)," Ruwa (2007) ; "Ruwa Town Council at a Glimpse as at June 2010," *Ruwa.* (2010); Chenga, "Murambatsvina II hovers over Epworth," The Financial Gazette<URL:http://www.financialgazette.co.zw/national-report/3011-murambatsvina-ii-hovers-over-epworth.html>, *Accessed on 5 August 2010.*(2010)

[420] MIT, "Just Jerusalem Competition, Jerusalem 2050," *Cambridge*,(2007) <http://web.mit.edu.justjerusalem/> *Accessed on 23 August 2007.*(2007)

budget formulation and implementation[421]. These are critical determinants in housing delivery and management as well as habitat maintenance. Yet, before independence in 1980, both settlements were in the hands of different administrative arrangements: Ruwa was a rural centre governed by a rural local authority while Epworth was a squatter settlement in the hands of a church organisation. It is most likely that as a 'refugee camp' of some type, Epworth was managed with a lot of leniency and permissiveness by the church acting as a philanthropic organisation, tolerant on building and settling patterns by the incoming residents. In this aspect, it can be said that the settlement developed on a 'soft ground' in which planning standards were seen as 'another yoke' on the shoulders of the residents which in the view of the church was perhaps unethical and intolerable. Ruwa has managed to maintain the peri-urban dwelling housing conditions for the residents relatively high and in consistent with the urban planning and housing standards stipulated in government statutes and policy documents.

There is also bounteous evidence showing that Harare Metropolitan Province is experiencing high rates of urbanisation-cum-peri-urbanisation (Box 6.1 and 6.2). These processes are central in urban governance where the government should treat citizens as equal partners in matters of development to achieve sustainability. In Box 6.1, the growth of the metropolitan region is satirised. This is the story that explains the immense growth of Epworth[422]. The growth puts pressure on the administrative capacities of the settlements to ensure that service delivery is addressed as a pressing need.

---

[421] Chirisa. I, "Population Growth and Rapid Urbanisation in Africa: Implications for Sustainability." *Journal of Sustainable Development in Africa 10(2),(*2008*)* pg.364-391 ; Munzwa et al. "Participatory Budgeting and Participatory Planning," Defining the theoretical and practical emphases in the two approaches, in *Local Governance Development Journal 1(2)*: pp 45-72.(2007)

[422] Chenga, "Murambatsvina II hovers over Epworth," The Financial Gazette, <URL:http://www.financialgazette.co.zw/national-report/3011-murambatsvina-ii-hovers-over-epworth.html,> *Accessed on 5 August 2010.*(2010)

Box 6.1: Harare: A Growing Metropolitan Area - Emerging Issues and Implications[423]

"Unless the Government and city council introduce apartheid-style pass laws, and simultaneously removes the constitutional guarantees of freedom of movement, both the city and its metropolitan area are going to continue growing faster than the population as a whole and urbanisation continues relentlessly. More land will go under brick and concrete, since all these extra people will need somewhere to live. The rich and many in the middle-income group will probably be catered for by private developers, some the owners of empty land already within the city. But most of those who need land to build homes will have to rely on the city council, and not just the lower paid. With land reform almost all the rural land around Harare is State land, leased to farmers. Developers of new suburbs for the better off will probably have to go into partnership with the city council, perhaps by putting in services for a council estate in return for being granted land to develop for more upmarket housing. Harare and its satellite towns need land to expand."

"The Government has now designated certain farms to the northwest and northeast of the city for future urban expansion. Some of the satellite towns such as Chitungwiza have already had adjacent rural land designated for urban development. Farmers are upset; much of the land is highly fertile and productive. The city expands into someone else's backyard. But almost all land around Harare is productive and fertile. That is why the city was established where it was. No one in his right mind selects a desert for a future capital if there is something a lot better. There did not appear to be much choice, should Harare be expanding than the farms designated. The Chitungwiza corridor to the south of the city is not suitable. The airport is there and while industrial development can be allowed, living under a flight path can be hell. In any case there is need for a "green belt" to separate Zimbabwe's first and third largest urban centres, otherwise life could be intolerable for those too far from the urban edge. In any case, urban land is always more valuable than rural land. Obviously, bulldozers are not going to move onto these newly designated farms tomorrow. "

423 The Herald, "Harare"s Expansion Inevitable" <URL: http://allafrica.com/stories/201007280723.html>, *Accessed on 2 April 2012.(*28 July 2010)

> "But the holders of that land have been warned that one day they will come. They have some time to sort themselves out and apply for new farms elsewhere. This is what has always happened. The owners of the land that most of the western and south-western suburbs are built on lost their land to the city council. Some went gracefully, accepting compensation. Some had to be forced to go, which is why Budiriro was built so late. The only serious question over the Government move to designate these farms is whether Harare City should continue to grow, or whether growth should be pushed into a ring of satellite towns, such as Norton, Mazowe, Beatrice and the eastern edge of Ruwa. All these centres are on the line of rail, so it would seem logical to have them taking up the growth of the metropolitan area. But huge investments in commuter rail transport are needed before such centres can become small cities, and there is no sign that this is going to happen overnight. Allowing Harare to expand a bit more is therefore the only practical option, and the designated farming land is the only practical choice for such expansion. Almost all of Harare, bar the central business district and the Avenues, is built on a couple of dozen farms that surrounded the original town. About half those farms had to be acquired by the State. So, what is happening now is not new."

Box 3.2 speaks of the urban expansion reality in terms of incorporation of farmland into urban land which, describing the situation in peri-urban areas of Botswana outlined as 'eating farmland, growing houses'[424]. This is so because the major reason for the farms' acquisition has been that the 28 farms, with close to 21,000 hectares of land, will be developed mainly for residential purposes[425]. The incorporation means that all developments on the farms are now subject to approval by Harare City Council." Both Epworth and Ruwa as my study area, as local government areas, have been administered by respective Local Boards (LB) as proclaimed by Statutory Instrument 75/1986[426]. Nevertheless, Ruwa attained its town status in 2009.

---

[424] Home.R, "Eating farmland, growing houses": *Peri-urban settlements and customary land tenure in Botswana, Southern Africa,* <URL: http://www.n-aerus.net/web/sat/workshops/2001/papers/home.pdf>(2001);
[425] Chideme (13 July 2010)
[426] (Chakwizira, 2001)

Box 6.2: "City of Harare Boundaries Extended"[427]

"The City of Harare's boundaries have been extended following the incorporation of 28 farms previously under Mazowe and Goromonzi rural district councils. The 28 farms, with close to 21 000 hectares of land, will be developed mainly for residential purposes. The incorporation means that all developments on the farms are now subject to approval by Harare City Council. The additional farms will result in additional wards and possibly more parliamentary constituencies under Greater Harare. Housing construction is ongoing at some of the farms such as Rumani Estates (Charlotte Brooke) and Acorn. More farms will be acquired to meet the rising demand for housing and industrial growth. The council committee on environment management met on July 2 to deliberate on Government's offer and agreed to accept 27 farms from Mazowe RDC and another from Goromonzi. "The Greater Harare municipal boundaries be altered by incorporation of the tracts of land listed in the table below," read part of the committee meeting resolutions."

"A full council meeting scheduled for the end of July is expected to officially adopt the resolution and make it binding. The lands are Mgutu, Ingleborough, Esk Bank, Calgary, Lot 1A Thorn Park, Lot 1 Thorn Park Estate, Teviotdale A, Teviotdale1A, Teviotdale 2 and 3 and Teviotdale. Others are Buckland Estate, Welston Township, Riet Poort Georgie, Sunray, Killarney, Rumani, Nijo, Charika Extension of Borrowdale, Happy Valley Estate, Lot J of Borrowdale, Acorn, Echo Farm, Lot1A Chakoma, Chakoma Estate B, The Springs and Stuhm. All these farms were under Mazowe Rural District Council with the exception of Caledonia Farm, which fell under Goromonzi. The committee recommended that council advise the Local Government, Rural and Urban Development Ministry of its acceptance of the farms and request expedition of the statutory requirements. At its full council meeting in April this year, the council resolved to approach Government to acquire peri-urban land for residential purposes. Town clerk Dr Tendai Mahachi wrote to the Government requesting incorporation of 72 properties, mainly farms, around Harare. The national housing backlog stands at over one million family units against an urban population estimated to be

---

[427] Source: Chideme Michael"City of Harare Boundaries Extended," The Herald, *Zimpapers*, Harare (also found <http://zimbabwefood.blogspot.com/2010/07/city-of-harares-boundaries-have-been.html; http://www.zimbabwesituation.org/?p=15736> (13 July 2010).,).,

> increasing at a rate of between 6 and 7 percent annually. The huge backlog is a result of increased rural-urban migration, the high cost of building materials, shortage of housing finance, unaffordable mortgages and lack of capacity by many councils to deliver accommodation."

Operations of the two are guided chiefly by the Urban Councils Act (Chapter 29: 15). Like any other typology of local authority in Zimbabwe, the core duties of LBs include delivery of services to their inhabitants. At the helm of the LBs are the persons of the Secretary in keeping with section 132 (3) of the Urban Councils Act stipulating that "...a town council shall appoint a person approved by the Local Government Board to be the Secretary of the Council". The Secretary is there to steer development by ensuring the proper administration of the council and managing the operations and property of the council as well as supervising and controlling the activities of the employees of the council in the course of their employment. In this case, the Secretary is a liaison officer hence the 'chief steward' with powers to implement organisational policies, advise the board on all issues as well as direct all functions of the body and ensure staff supervision like a town clerk would do in major cities and towns of the country.

Local boards have administrative departments responsible for keeping local board standing committee registers, security of the local board areas and all clerical duties (e.g. typing and reception services). According to section 212 of the Urban Councils Act, local boards are mandated with responsibilities including street addressing (numbering of stands and naming of roads). This can be done, by notice, in writing to the owner or occupier of a house or any building, direct the owner or occupier at his or her own expense to mark at the main entrance or in some other conspicuous position on such land the number specified in that notice. All will be done in keeping with any by-laws or renew any housing number in line with any by law. Another key responsibility they have is of conflict resolution. This is stipulated in section 282 of t the Urban Councils Act. Cases and queries dealt with may cover issues to do with the allocation and management of residential, commercial and industrial stands. Other matters include encroachments and boundary disputes.

Day-to-day operations with respect to housing by the boards cover water meter readings, distribution of statements of water rates and charges (in keeping with the Urban Councils Act Section 183 and 184; the Water Act, Chapter 20:22). Furthermore, the administrative departments must 'monitor' stand developments as well as manage council land (land subdivision and consolidations). This is as guided by the RTCP Act (Chapter 29:12) and the Urban Councils Act. To develop land in the area under the board's jurisdictional power, one has to apply for a planning permission in line with section 26 of the RTCP Act and sections 39 and 40 of the Urban Councils Act. Moreover, the administrative departments of local boards must arrange of committee meetings, the writing of minutes and preparation of meeting agenda as well as preparation of staff salaries and handling of all personnel issues such as recruitment, selection and managing the collective bargaining processes. The departments are also mandated with the management of transportation within the local board area.

Like all other local authorities, local boards have security services according to section 142 of the Urban Council's Act. They must also manage transportation services. In addition, local boards have finance and accounts departments responsible for budget preparation, financial management, revenue collection, licenses, stores control as well as monthly statements preparation and issuing such as water, stands in keeping with sections 285, 286, 287 and 289 of the Urban Councils Act. According to section 287, councils can borrow money from government or private sectors and in such circumstances the books of accounts and the records would be the prima facie evidence of the credit worthiness of the council. When one examines the foregoing functions, one wonders why discrepancies in development progress between Ruwa and Epworth yet they are both guided by the same instruments of power and legitimacy. This wonderment can only be explained by embedded socio-economic and political factors. Epworth has developed organically hence weak institutionalism while Ruwa has been a diametric opposite in which institutionalism is strong and the bulk of development progression is pre-determined and ordered.

In basic terms, the council accounts department maintains the finance of the local authority and thus where subdivision fees, rents and rates, development application fees, are deposited. In essence, the accounts department is the service department for all developmental activities. The other important department in local boards is the Engineering Department broadly mandated with the management and maintenance of the council area infrastructure at its hard-core level. The Engineering Department is also responsible for water supply and sanitation as well as plumbing and drainage activities for the council area (Urban Councils Act parts 12 and part 13). Local boards also have Health Departments whose principal task is defined as the provision of health facilities and services to the local board area.

Cultural factors are important in understanding housing and related developments. As argued humans "...make frames that delimit what they perceive, and those frames determine what is important, irrelevant, good, bad, and so on, about those perceptions - that is, some things are ruled in, and others are thrown out."[428] Although prefers to call the frameworks worldviews, we can call this culture. People tend to behave or embrace, resist, reject or accept change because they hold a certain view, which, then becomes institutionalised to constitute a form of culture. This culture also changes through time tending towards equilibrating the behaviour of the whole gamut of community that observe it. The desire to have one's own home or house has roots in tradition and culture. Whether people stay in or move away from a place, they normally try to maintain how they behave in their culture sometimes for identity sake[429]. In Zimbabwe, the urban farming that we see in open spaces around cities can be taken for a culture transfer from rural areas to urban area[430].

---

[428] Goldberg, How Our Worldviews Shape Our Practice, ." Conflict Resolution Quarterly26 (4): pp. 405-431. (2009:408).

[429] Gienow-Hecht, Cultural Transfer. Chapter 16 in Hogan Michael and Thomas G Paterson (eds.)," Explaining the History of American Foreign Relations (Second edition), *Cambridge University Press*, Cambridge, pp. 257-278(2004).

[430] du Toit.F., "Musha: The Shona Concept of Home: Aspects of Zimbabwe Architecture Monograph 1," *Zimbabwe Publishing House*, Harare. (1981); ; Mbiba.B, "Urban Agriculture in Zimbabwe," *Avebury*, Aldershot.(1995); Mougeot, 2000, Tawodzera et al. 2012)

Traditionally, in the culture of the Shona (the dominant ethnic group in Zimbabwe), the concept of *musha* (home) is at the centre of the *unhu/ubuntu* wisdom[431]. Without a home, the community wonders what kind of a person one is, in terms of character and wisdom. Thus, in the traditional Shona wisdom, having a *musha* is a sign of maturity. As such, this has a bearing on one's status within a community. Having a home adds to one's dignity. In the past, having a homestead with a built house in a rural home was a very critical virtue for many[432]. However, with increasing urbanisation, this 'myth' is slowly waning off. But that someone must have a house, a built structure of his/her own somewhere remains a critical aspect in the life of a 'right thinking' Zimbabwean108. This partly explains the construct of the housing need in today's urban centres in the country. It is argued that, in urban Zimbabwe "access to land is mainly by purchase, though some people inherit from family or relatives. This [...] is not necessarily true for Epworth as there are different forms of land acquisition and tenure systems."[433].

Regarding indoor housing space arrangements, the issue of the nature of the social relationships in the home is very critical[434]. It provides a pointer to issues of cultural underpinnings underlying the use of indoor

---

[431] Dube.C, "Housing coops frustrated over land," *Zimbabwe Independent*. <URL: http://www.thezimbabweindependent.com/business/14311.html>, *Accessed on 22 April 2008.*(2004)

[432] Potts.D, "Viewpoint: What do we know about urbanization in sub-Saharan Africa and does it matter?" *International Development Planning Review, 34 (1):* pp. v-xxi.(2012); "Making a Livelihood in (and Beyond) the African City: The Experience of Zimbabwe" *Africa: The Journal of the International African Institute, 81 (4)*: pp. 588-605(2011) Making a Livelihood in (and Beyond) the African City: The Experience of Zimbabwe" *Africa: The Journal of the International African Institute, 81 (4)*: pp. 588-605(2011); Viewpoint: What do we know about urbanization in sub-Saharan Africa and does it matter?" *International Development Planning Review, 34 (1):* pp. v-xxi.(2012)

[433] Sigauke.N, "Improving Urban Livelihoods: Epworth Sustainable Livelihoods Benchmark Study,"< URL: http://practicalaction.org/docs/region_southern_africa/ Epworth_Benchmark_Study.pdf>, *Accessed on 27 June 2011.(2002:20)*

[434] Grant.M. R, "Rental Shelter as a Coping Mechanism in Gweru, Zimbabwe," *PHD Thesis, Queen"s University*, Ontario, Canada.(1991)

housing space[435]. In most African contexts, the extended type of relationship is quite typical. This extended family structure usually attaches importance to kinship[436]. With respect to urban and peri-urban areas where the economy is usually inclined towards the cash economy, peri-urban dwellers also entertain relatives from the rural areas coming to seek opportunities in towns[437]. Sometimes they also have to help them attend to certain critical matters on their behalf while they are away. In the general context of Zimbabwe in the past five years or so where outmigration was greatly phenomenal, this may come in the form of a relation being asked to take care of the property while the owner was away in the Diaspora[438]. Social relationships may point to how housing stock passes through hands from generation to generation. Parents who leave for the rural homes after retirement often choose to leave their properties in the hands of trusted relatives or children. Such a pattern, as already stated is of importance with regard to basic things: indoor space use, caring for members of the extended family, and, rural-urban linkages (local-Diaspora relations) as homeowners who are retirees or pensioners may have to live their properties with trusted relatives and friends, and whether households hire servants or not.

Peri-urban dwellers in both Ruwa and Epworth maximise on the existing open spaces around them, including the wetlands for peri-urban farming and even for worship as illustrated in Chapter 4 and 5, respectively. The chief reason for urban farming by household is to boost

---

[435] Gwagwa, "Women as "home-makers and men as "heads" of households: Who is responsible for housing improvements," Chapter 4 in Sithole-Fundire S.A. Zhou, A. Larsson & A. Schlyter, 1995: Gender Research on Urbanisation, Planning and Everyday Life, *Zimbabwe Women"s Resource Centre Network*, Harare.(1995)

[436] Dube.C, "Housing coops frustrated over land," *Zimbabwe Independent*. <URL: http://www.thezimbabweindependent.com/business/14311.html>, *Accessed on 22 April 2008.*(2004)

[437] Potts.D,, "Viewpoint: What do we know about urbanization in sub-Saharan Africa and does it matter?" *International Development Planning Review, 34 (1):* pp. v-xxi.(2012)

[438] Potts.D, "Viewpoint: What do we know about urbanization in sub-Saharan Africa and does it matter?" *International Development Planning Review, 34 (1):* pp. v-xxi.(2012); Irurah.D, "Urbanisation and Housing Challenges: Cities in Africa Conference." *Parallel sessions on urban land management – Rapporteur"s Report;* December 8, 2003. (2003))

the livelihoods and supplement of food supply away from the conventional markets. This has been studied previously of which this study confirms it[439]. The open spaces can be on-plot and off-plot space. Most of these activities emerged and got boosted during the post-ESAP era, especially from 1997 when the economy of Zimbabwe plunged and many people were retrenched from formal employment[440]. Newer activities include, for example the provision of private lessons by private tutors in the homes, and especially after the public-school system suffered staffing setbacks, a situation which became worst in the period 2007/2008. Some homes have taken over the role of schools though space requirements for other activities synonymous with schooling cannot be accommodated (like sport fields). Overall, most, if not all, of the activities observed and being done by the residents, fall in the informal sector category[441].

A critical dimension to the living conditions of peri-urban dwellers is to do with their relationship with the environment. Today's peri-urban challenges ought to view stewardship in the framework of collaborating of actors[442]. Peri-urban areas are 'contested zones' and they are riddled by a number of conflicts. Conflict management helps build trust among especially the peri-urban dwellers themselves. The prime land

---

[439] Mushamba et al. "Urban and Peri-Urban Agriculture: Prospects for Food Security and Growth in Eastern and Southern Africa," Report prepared for the Ministers" Conference on August 28-29, 2003, Sheraton Hotel – Harare - Zimbabwe. <URL: http://www.ruaf.org/files/ministers_conference.pdf>, *Accessed on 2 April 2007. (2003)*

[440] Branom-Zwick, "Food vs. Shelter: The Planning Debate," *Sightline Daily*. <URL: http://daily.sightline.org/daily_score/archive/2006/01/30/food_vs_shelter,> *Accessed on 22 April 2008.* (30 January 2006)); Brook. R.M;Dávila. J.D eds., "The peri-urban interface: a tale of two cities, School of Agricultural and Forest Sciences," *University of Wales and Development Planning Unit, University College,* London. (2000);Houston.F, "Housing America State by State: How Governors Are Leading the Way," in *Housing Facts and Findings 7(1)*: p1.< URL: www.fanniemaefoundation. org/programs/hff.html>(2005); Mushamba et al. "Urban and Peri-Urban Agriculture: Prospects for Food Security and Growth in Eastern and Southern Africa," Report prepared for the Ministers" Conference on August 28-29, 2003, Sheraton Hotel – Harare - Zimbabwe. <URL: http://www.ruaf. org/ files/ ministers_conference.pdf>, *Accessed on 2 April 2007. (2003*

[441] Williams; Round, "Re-theorising the Nature of Informal Employment: Some Lessons from Ukraine," in *International Sociology 23(3):* pp367-388 (2008).

[442] Stoll.L, Regional Collaboration: A framework for solving complex planning problems. *The Land Tracker 6(2):* pp 1-4. (2006))

contestation process is fight between farming and urban development land ([443]. Actors also work with their numerous stakeholders. One major social challenge is managing migration to the area itself. Whereas colonial policies aimed as completely halting mass movement to urban centres, post-colonial policies have gone contrary hence the spill over effect into the peri-urban zone. It is therefore not clear as to what instruments are social in the management of peri-urbanisation[444].

Ideally, policies help shape the practice by the stewards of peri-urban human settlement development[445]. Indeed peri-urban governance is enshrined in the legislative and institutional framework of Zimbabwe yet it remains less explicit[446]. Stewardship in peri-urban settlements is a function of the knowledge, attitudes, perceptions and practices by the different actors in the environmental policy and spatial management framework. Over the past years, the government of Zimbabwe has tried to 'bend' regulations to accommodate the low-income population. But the extent to which these programmes have benefited the group remains debatable. The blame has often been laid on the standards that subscribe to western and colonial values[447]. Housing policy and amendments thereto, in Zimbabwe, have tended to be regarded highly as technical, emphasising on standards and related material.

Culture is tied to technological progress and institutional development. In technological terms, it can be noted that infrastructure is

---

[443] Toriro.P, "Town Planning in Zimbabwe, History, Challenges and the Urban Renewal Operation Murambatsvina," Chapter 11, Maphosa France, Kraposy Kujinga and Sunungurai D Chingarande (eds.), (2007) "Zimbabwe"s Development Experiences since 1980: Challenges and Prospects for the Future," *OSSREA*, Addis Ababa.(2007)

[444] UNFPA, "State of World Population 2007."*Unleashing the Potential of Urban Growth.* UNFPA: New York. (2007) ;Tibaijuka A.K, "Building Prosperity – Housing and Economic Development Earthscan" London. (2009); Chipungu. L, "Institutional constraints to land delivery for low-income housing: a case study of Harare, Zimbabwe," in *RICS Foundation Our Common Estate Paper Series*. URL: www.rics-foundation.org, Accessed on 22 April 2008.(2011)

[445] de Valk. P, "An Analysis of Planning Policy in Zimbabwe (Unpublished Paper)," *Department of Rural and Urban Planning, University of Zimbabwe*, Harare. (1986:5-6)

[446] TibaijukaA. K, "Report of the Fact-Finding Mission to Zimbabwe to assess the Scope and Impact of Operation Murambatsvina," *UN Habitat*, Nairobi. (2005)

[447] Tipple, (2004)

a major handicap in peri-urban areas[448]. Sustainable peri-urban development informed by the appropriate technology criteria, rooted in the grassroots-housing model, is one, which puts the environment, social group (including children) and local availability of raw materials into picture. In most of these settlements, materials like used plastics, cardboard boxes and wood are used extensively for housing. They are 'cheap' to get but difficult to maintain. Sophisticated technologies including the applications of remote sensing or aerial photographs and techniques in geographic information systems (GIS) are critical in peri-urban stewardship[449].

Overall, and currently, most settlements in the peri-urban surroundings are following the incremental housing development approach. This is unlike in the 1980s when strict town planning standards of approvals first were followed. The peri-urban development, taking place today in the country regarding shelter development, indeed, follows the Alexanderian (1973) Grassroots Housing Model. Thus, Zimbabwe in the last 12 years has witnessed immense developments in its city-edges. The contribution of cooperatives in peri-urban housing is most noted. It has been noted that most of these housing schemes are named after liberation war heroes to 'legitimise' their existence. This is in direct response that most of these settlements were formed during the Fast Track Land Reform period, specifically around 2000[450]. A combination of forces

---

448 Mafico. I, "Urban low-income housing in Zimbabwe," *Averbury:Aldershot.(* 1991)

449 Ward.P. M; Peters.P. A, "Self-help housing and informal homesteading in peri-urban America: Settlement identification using digital imagery and GIS,." *Habitat International 31(2)*, pp205-218 (2007:16) ; Wilmersdorf.E, "Spatio-Temporal GIS-Design For Real-Time Processes," *Geographia Technica, 2,(2010)*

450 Marongwe. N, "Conflicts Over Land And Other Natural Resources In Zimbabwe," *ZERO Publications*, Harare. (2002) ; Marongwe.N, "The Fast Track Resettlement and Urban Development Nexus: the case for Harare," Paper Presented at the Symposium on Delivering Land and securing Rural Livelihoods: Post Independence Land Reform and Resettlement in Zimbabwe, Mont Clair, Nyanga, 26-28 March 2003. <URL: http://www.sarpn.org.za/documents/d0000617/P624-nelson.pdf>, *Accessed on 22 April 2008*.(2003);Chipungu. L, "Institutional constraints to land delivery for low-income housing: a case study of Harare, Zimbabwe," in *RICS Foundation Our Common Estate Paper Series*. URL: www.rics-foundation.org, Accessed on 22 April 2008.(2011); Murowe.S; Chirisa.I, "Sally Mugabe Heights: The tale of an incidental

from the urban homeless, the rural landless and other desperate groups have worked together to claim land in the peri-urban for housing. In addition, the formal land market has failed to be robust to accommodate these desperate groups of people. The FTLRP has seen a number of farms being grabbed by 'land invaders." The Deputy Director[451] of the Department of Physical Planning (DPP) observes:

> "When we look at how land was acquired in the peri-urban before Operation Murambatsvina, we see the land occupiers getting into some conflict. They were divided among themselves; some wanted the land for farming and others for housing. This is history repeating itself. Exactly this was the situation with Churu Farm. I think you know the story. [The politician] Ndabaningi Sithole allowed people to build houses [informal] on his farm. We see this type of housing - the informal type - that which comes through mass action, through farm occupations. Thus, before Murambatsvina we see people coming together. We see them forming some cooperatives. We also see cooperatives becoming a requirement by the local authorities themselves to allow people to acquire land to build. Thus, if home-seekers needed local authority attention they had to organise themselves into cooperatives. Indeed, these cooperatives had to undergo some registration. This was to guarantee them recognition by the local authorities. When Operation Murambatsvina came in 2005, it was a sweeping wind. Even our minister [the Minister of Local Government] could not stop it. It was an operation. ... Peri-urban areas were the worst affected. Though within town there were stands on which were some outbuildings, the main target was the peri-urban. I should say that Murambatsvina was a peri-urban story. What was happening there [in terms of land acquisition and informal building] was unsustainable.... After Murambatsvina we again see again the peri-urban land occupiers re-organising. They had no option but to get organised. This time there were now many checkpoints: You could have a well-built building structure but if it stood on an unapproved stand it could be destroyed. Perhaps your stand plan was approved but the way it had been approved did not meet the required standards. I can liken the whole process to a police roadblock. When you get there, he may ask for a driver's licence…then the vehicle

---

Zimbabwean peri-urban housing scheme seeking legitimation," *Zambezia XXXIII (i/ii)*: pp71-89.(2006)

451 Interview 11 March 2011

> licence…then check on the bearings [here normally they are not always fit]. You see…There will always be the next step."

Evident in this text by the Deputy Director are four things that can be noted. First, planning in Zimbabwe is a cumbersome process and there have always been cases where individuals have sought to circumvent the process[452]. The case of Ndabaningi Sithole cited by the Director echoes the Epworth story in this study. It is a settlement that began on philanthropic grounds, a church offering space for 'refugees' and the homeless[453]. Secondly, self-help housing became commonplace before May 2005 could not meet most of the requirements of this planning process. This was a development building from the process of the agrarian 'revolution." It involved violent land grabbing from the whites. As something that began impromptu, there was little if any planning involved hence haphazardly, defying basic tenets of sustainable development. Such was to stumble with the coming of the Operation Murambatsvina in 2005.

The Deputy Director argues that the Operation was chiefly engineered to stop peri-urban housing developments that had not followed the planning requirements. This may be true to a great extent. Thirdly, there is a general belief that if planning standards are followed, then sustainability will automatically follow. Yet, a number of factors must be taken aboard. Such factors include adopting appropriate technology and collaboration by partners in financing different activities in housing. Fourthly, the role of political capital must not be underestimated.

---

[452] Mubvami.T ; Musandu-Nyamayaro.O, "Procedural Impediments to the Low-income Housing Land Delivery in Cities of Zimbabwe," *Department of Rural and Urban Planning. University of Zimbabwe*, Harare. (1993);Toriro.P.," The Urban Housing Question in the Context of Operation Murambatsvina and Operation Garikai/Hlalani Kuhle," *Policy Brief prepared on behalf of the African Institute for Agrarian Studies*, Harare.(2006)\; Toriro.P, "Town Planning in Zimbabwe, History, Challenges and the Urban Renewal Operation Murambatsvina," Chapter 11, Maphosa France, Kraposy Kujinga and Sunungurai D Chingarande (eds.), (2007) "Zimbabwe"s Development Experiences since 1980: Challenges and Prospects for the Future," *OSSREA*, Addis Ababa.(2007)

[453] Butcher. C,)., "Urban low-income housing: a case study of the Epworth squatter settlement upgrading programme, Chapter 6 in ZINYAMA L, D TEVERA AND S CUMMING (eds.) 1993" *Harare:* "The Growth and Problems of the City," *University of Zimbabwe*: Harare. (1993)

CHAPTER 7
LEGAL AND POLITICAL PARAMETERS DEFINING DEVELOPMENTAL PROCESSES IN ZIMBABWE

In terms of legislation, Zimbabwe has a number of laws, which provide for managing urban and regional space. These include primarily the Regional, Town and Country Planning Act (29:12), Urban Councils Act (29:15), Provincial Councils and Administration Act, Housing Standards Control Act (Chapter 29:08), Land Acquisition Act (20:10), Mines and Minerals Act (21:05), Environmental Management Act (EMA) (20:12), to name but a few. Overall, these instruments (the legislations) are applied wholesale hence, in most cases, are not be specific to peri-urban areas only. I present a snapshot on the provisions of some critical legislation in Zimbabwe.

The Regional, Town and Country Planning Act (RTCPA) (29:12) provides guidelines to planning in Zimbabwe[454]. It facilitates housing and environmental stewardship initiatives as it defines and lays out procedure for regional planning, master planning, and local development planning (GoZ/UNHABITAT, 2009). It also directs how development control must be carried out; provides for subdivisions and consolidations (which are critical for defining space provision for including for housing and related services)[455]. However, the statute has been lambasted as being rigid and

---

[454] GoZ, "Development and Building Control – Control, Applications, Permits, And Enforcement: Building Plan Appraisal and Regulations." *Government Printers*, Harare.(1990);TibaijukaA. K, "Report of the Fact-Finding Mission to Zimbabwe to assess the Scope and Impact of Operation Murambatsvina," *UN Habitat*, Nairobi. (2005); GoZ, "Study and Review of the Current Minimum High-density Housing Standards," *Government Printers*, Harare.(2001)

[455] O"Donnell.P.M, "Preservation of the Spirit of Place" <URL: http:// www. international.icomos.org/quebec2008/cd/toindex/77_pdf/77-hFCw-13.pdf>, *Accessed on 27 June 2011.pg8.* (2008)8

flexible for 'accommodative' development[456]. In recent years, Statutory Instrument 216 of 1994 (Use Group Regulations) has been mooted as an instrument under the RTCPA permitting formerly unpermitted commercial and industrial activities within residential areas[457]. This instrument partly explains why vending and informal manufacturing in urban and peri-urban neighbourhoods have been tolerated for livelihoods support of households in the recent years[458].

The Urban Councils Act (UCA) (29:15) which is administered by the Ministry of Local Government, Rural and Urban Development, provides urban local authorities with a wide range of powers and responsibilities for the provision of services and functions including water supply[459], health (both personal and environmental health including sanitation and refuse removal), public lighting, creation and maintenance of recreational parks, and housing for citizens[460]. Another kind of bye-laws in the ambit of the UCA is the Model Building Bye-laws of 1977. The byelaws also fit in the Rural Councils Act. They cover issues on structural design and control, foundations, masonry and walling, miscellaneous materials constructions, water supply, lighting, drainage and sewerage, ventilation, fire protection and public safety[461]. The

---

[456] TibaijukaA. K, "Report of the Fact-Finding Mission to Zimbabwe to assess the Scope and Impact of Operation Murambatsvina," *UN Habitat*, Nairobi. (2005)

[457] Kamete.A.Y, "Restrictive control of urban high-density housing in Zimbabwe, deregulation and challenges for urban design," *Housing, Theory and Society,* 16(3): 136–151. (1999c); Chaeruka. J ; Munzwa. K, "Assessing Regulatory Framework Bottlenecks for Low-cost Housing in Zimbabwe, Final Draft Report," *UNHABITAT and the Government of Zimbabwe*, Harare.(2009)

[458] UNCHS, "Proceedings of the International Conference on Urban Poverty, 9 – 13 November 1997," *Florence, Italy. UNCHS*, Nairobi. (1998);World Bank, "Voices of the Poor: Can anyone hear us?" *Oxford University Press:* New York.(2000);; Merrill, (2007)

[459] Mara ; Alabaster, (2008)

[460] Mhlahlo.S.R, "The impact of housing policy on housing problems in Gweru before and after independence" *The Dyke – The Journal of Midlands State University 1(1):* 107-115.(2004); Tevera et al 2002; Mapira.J, An Historical Perspective of the Problem of Housing and Some Attempted Solutions in the City of Mutare (1890-2002). *Zambezia* XXXI (i/ii), University of Zimbabwe, Harare: pp 80-103 (2004)

[461] Musandu-Nyamayaro.O," Housing Design Standards for Urban Low-income People," *Third World Review 15(4),* Liverpool University Press (1993)

existing Model Building By-Laws have been considered very rigid, outdated and inhibitive to the smooth implementation of infrastructure development works in local authority areas. The same byelaws are cited as being contradictory to some sections of the existing housing policy.[462]

The Provincial Councils and Administration (PCA) Act defines a region as a spatial entity marked out according to administrative purposes at a provincial level following the levels of planning (national, provincial, district and ward). It shows a hierarchy in terms of functionality, responsibility, powers or appointments and in terms of roles. In terms of membership the PCA Act section 14 part (a) and (b) highlights the members in hierarchical order that is Governor, councillor, chiefs, etc. It is important to note that both Epworth and Ruwa are now part of the Harare Metropolitan Province, established in 2004[463]. The person of the Governor and Resident Minister is a political appointee of the President.

The Housing Standards Control Act (HSCA) (Chapter 29:08) of 1974 outlines the minimum standards which provide for repair, demolition or closure of buildings of an unsatisfactory standard and abatement of overcrowding of dwellings[464]. Overall, this legislation endeavours to bring sanity to the housing sector by regulating the number of people who can live in a certain dwelling by specifying the minimum number, some kind of determining the 'carrying capacity' of buildings so as to ensure that overcrowding and unhygienic conditions which define squalor are avoided. Contemporary urban planning discourse aims at facilitation of

---

[462] Walt. G, "Health Policy – an introduction to process and power," *Zed Books. London.*(1994); Marshall. F, "What does peri-urban sustainability mean in the context of Delhi?" <URL: http://stepscentre-thecrossing.blogspot.com/2008/12/ what-does-peri-urban-sustainability.html:>, *Accessed on 2April 2009.*(4 December 2008); Siyeni.Y.M, "Expanding Water Service Delivery through Partnership between Water Utility and Small Scale Water Providers in Lusaka, Zambia" *A Case of Lusaka"s Peri-Urban Areas.* University essay from Linköpings universitet/Tema vatten i natur och samhälle<. URL: http://www.essays.se/essay/4d116540c8/,> *Accessed on 14 August 2010.* (2008)

[463] HMP, "Harare Metropolitan Provincial Development Plan 2011," *Government of Zimbabwe*, Harare (2011:4).

[464] Mhlahlo.S.R, "The impact of housing policy on housing problems in Gweru before and after independence" *The Dyke – The Journal of Midlands State University 1(1):* 107-115.(2004)

urban development and housing provision, for example as stipulated in the Millennium Development Goals[465].

The Public Health Act (PHA) (Chapter 15:09), administered by the Ministry of Health and Child Welfare (MOHCW), provides local authorities with the power to take all lawful or necessary precautions for the prevention of the occurrence of any potential outbreaks of any infections or communicable and contagious diseases[466]. In Epworth, the squatter upgrading programme which was introduced for the settlement in the 1980s was an attempt to bring sanity to urban development in the area as well as to provide 'adequate housing' to the inhabitants. However, due to financial and related challenges, the programme has not gone much further than the expectations of the actors then[467]. High influx of squatters and land invaders makes it difficult to monitor and manage health concerns[468]. In general terms, peri-urban settlements may be very difficult

---

465 Tibaijuka A.K, "Building Prosperity – Housing and Economic Development Earthscan" London. (2009)[465] Payne.G, Majale. M, "The Urban Housing Manual: Making Regulatory Framework Work for the Poor," Earthscan, London. (2004)

466 Walt. G, "Health Policy – an introduction to process and power," *Zed Books. London.*(1994) ; Hood, 2005;Marshall. F, "What does peri-urban sustainability mean in the context of Delhi?" <URL: http://stepscentre-thecrossing.blogspot.com/ 2008/ 12/what-does-peri-urban-sustainability.html:>, *Accessed on 2April 2009.*(4 December 2008); ;Siyeni.Y.M, "Expanding Water Service Delivery through Partnership between Water Utility and Small Scale Water Providers in Lusaka, Zambia" *A Case of Lusaka"s Peri-Urban Areas.* University essay from Linköpings universitet/Tema vatten i natur och samhälle<. URL: http://www.essays.se/essay/ 4d116540c8/,> *Accessed on 14 August 2010.* (2008))

467 Chenga, Murambatsvina II hovers over Epworth, The Financial Gazette: URL:http://www.financialgazette.co.zw/national-report/3011-murambatsvina-ii-hovers-over-epworth.html, Accessed on 5 August 2010.(2010) ;Matovu.G, "Upgrading Urban Low-Income Settlements in Africa," *Constraints, Potentials and Policy Options. Paper presented at the Regional Roundtable on Upgrading Low-Income Settlements, Johannesburg, South Africa: October 3-5 2000.*< URL: http://www.worldbank.org/ urban/upgrading/afrnd/docs/mdp_low_income_upgrading_paper_2000_final_doc.pdf, >*Accessed on 22 April 2008.(* 2000);Butcher. C,)., "Urban low-income housing: a case study of the Epworth squatter settlement upgrading programme, Chapter 6 in ZINYAMA L, D TEVERA AND S CUMMING (eds.) 1993" *Harare:* "The Growth and Problems of the City," *University of Zimbabwe*: Harare. (1993); (1986)

468 Marshall. F, "What does peri-urban sustainability mean in the context of Delhi?" <URL: http://stepscentre-thecrossing.blogspot.com/2008/12/what-does-peri-urban-

to ensuring that public health is hailed to high standards given the differing status of the inhabitants.

The Zimbabwe National Water (ZINWA) Act (Chapter 20:25 of 1998) has the core purpose of harmonisation, water development and management. In particular, Section 5 of the Act compels the authority to advise the Minister to formulate national policies and standards on water pricing, planning, management and development as well as water quality, pollution control and environmental protection[469]. This Act gives ZINWA the right to exploit, conserve and manage the water resources of Zimbabwe so as to ensure equitable accessibility and efficient allocation, distribution, use and development of water resources[470].

The Land Acquisition Act (20:10) provides for the acquisition of land in the country. It has been noted that the procedures for land acquisition were cumbersome, lengthy and fraught with many legal technicalities before Constitutional Amendment Number 17 of 2005, which came into force on the 14th September 2005[471]. About the acquisition of land for urban expansion, the very same process used initially to acquire rural agricultural land before the Constitutional

---

sustainability.html:>, *Accessed on 2April 2009.*(4 December 2008); \;Siyeni.Y.M, “Expanding Water Service Delivery through Partnership between Water Utility and Small Scale Water Providers in Lusaka, Zambia” *A Case of Lusaka”s Peri-Urban Areas.* University essay from Linköpings universitet/Tema vatten i natur och samhälle<. URL: http://www.essays.se/essay/4d116540c8/,> *Accessed on 14 August 2010.* (2008); Chirisa. I, “Prospects for the asset-based community development approach in Epworth and Ruwa, Zimbabwe,” A housing and environmental perspective. *African Journal of History and Culture 1(2):* pp028-035. (2009:30)

469 Zingoni et al., “Effects of a semi-formal urban settlement on groundwater quality: Epworth (Zimbabwe),” Case study and groundwater quality zoning. *Physics and Chemistry of the Earth, Parts A/B/C 30 (11-16),* pp 680-688 (2005);

470 O”Donnell.P.M, “Preservation of the Spirit of Place” <URL: http://www.international.icomos.org/quebec2008/cd/toindex/77_pdf/77-hFCw-13.pdf>, *Accessed on 27 June 2011.pg8.* (2008) Mwesigwa.D, “Water and Sanitation in peri-urban settlements,” *Paper presented at the 21st WEDC Conference with the theme:* Sustainability of Water and Sanitation Systems, held in Kampala: Uganda.(1995); Mara ; Alabaster (2008)

471 Marongwe. N, “Conflicts Over Land And Other Natural Resources In Zimbabwe,” *ZERO Publications*, Harare. (2002) , Chipungu. L, “Institutional constraints to land delivery for low-income housing: a case study of Harare, Zimbabwe,” in *RICS Foundation Our Common Estate Paper Series.* URL: www.rics-foundation.org, Accessed on 22 April 2008.(2011)

Amendment Number 17, applies. The relationship between Ministry of Lands and the Ministry of Local Government, Rural and Urban Development in this process; the Ministry of Lands gazettes farms for urban expansion only on the basis of written requests from the Ministry of Local Government Rural and Urban Development. Statutory Instrument on Farm sizes Number 288 of 2000 works hand-in-glove with the Land Acquisition Act[472]. Access to land is critical for housing development[473].

The Mines and Minerals Act (21:05) vests power in, and gives official rights of the approved prospectors to extract minerals[474]. The Act consolidates and amends the law relating to mines and minerals. Section 240 of the Mines and Minerals Act abrogates the construction or erection of any works on the registered mining location in contravention of the conditions attached to the approval of plans. The mining commissioner is provided with powers to order the miner of such mining location, to remove such works or to discontinue their use. Sand extraction is categorised as a mining activity[475]. However, in Epworth, illegal sand and quarry dealers tend to mine these important resources for supply to

---

472 Murerwa. H, "Speech by The Minister of Lands and Rural Resettlement, Hon. H. M. Murerwa (MP) On Land Delivery For Housing," *Housing Convention Victoria Falls 26 – 30 October 2009* (2009)

473 Kawonga.A. J.C, "Access to land for low-income housing in Malawi: The case of Zomba Municipality, in Municipal Development Program – MDP, undated," *Addressing poverty in the context of decentralisation in Eastern and Southern Africa – Case studies in Malawi, Uganda, Zambia and Zimbabwe: MDP Working Paper 3,* Municipal Development Programme for Sub-Saharan Africa: Harare, pp 65-81.(1996); Kombe.W.J,)., "Land-use dynamics in peri-urban areas and their implications on the urban growth and form: the case of Dar es Salaam, Tanzania,". *Habitat International 29(1)*: pp 113-135 (2005); Chipungu. L, "Institutional constraints to land delivery for low-income housing: a case study of Harare, Zimbabwe," in *RICS Foundation Our Common Estate Paper Series*. URL: www.rics-foundation.org, Accessed on 22 April 2008.(2005); Lupala. A, "The peri-urban poor as land development managers, in *id21": Insights 41*.(2005)

474 GoZ, "Zimbabwe Millennium Development Goals," *2004 Progress Report, UNDP*, Harare.(2004)

475 Huby.M, "Social Policy and the Environment," *Open University Press*, Buckingham. (1998); ; Houston.F, "Housing America State by State: How Governors Are Leading the Way," in *Housing Facts and Findings 7(1)*: p1.< URL: www.fanniemaefoundation.org/programs/hff.html>(2005)

builders, sometimes at odd hours including the night. The result is massive land degradation in various spots of the peri-urban vicinities.

The Environmental Management Act (EMAact) (20:12) provides for the protection of the environment, conservation, preservation of natural resources (land, air, water, flora and fauna) and control of development in a given area (urban and rural). Section 97 states that the carrying out of development of projects requires the carrying out of an Environmental Impact Assessment (EIA). The legislation also makes provision for the protection of wetlands. The Minister of Environment is mandated to prepare Master plans which are partly for the purpose of promoting facilitating and coordinating of strategies, and planning activities relating to the environment and ensuring the protection and sustainable management of Zimbabwe's environment[476]. It should be stressed that the Environmental Management Act is the watchdog, an instrument used to achieve the objectives of planning as far as environmental planning is concerned encompassing issues such as sustainability and preservation. The environment is the major determinant of sustainable housing development[477]. It also determines the livelihoods activities that can be supported in it[478].

---

476 Harare, "Harare Combination Master Plan: Study Report and Written Statement," *Department of Works,* Harare (1992)

477 Huby.M, "Social Policy and the Environment," *Open University Press*, Buckingham. (1998); Lopez.T; Nugent. P,;"African Cities. Competing Claims on Urban Spaces," Brill: Leiden. (2009);Lawrence. R. J, "Housing and health: Beyond Disciplinary Confinement," *Journal of Urban Health 83(3):* pp540-549(2006); Magigi. W; Majani.B.B.K, "Housing themselves in Informal Settlements: A Challenge to Community Growth Processes, Land Vulnerability and Poverty Reduction in Tanzania," *Paper presented at the 5th FIG Regional Conference, Accra, Ghana*, March 8-11, 2006 (2006);Muzvidziwa. V.N, "Informal Settlement Dwellers and Environmental Problems." *UNISWA Research Journal of Agriculture, Science and Technology (Special Volume No. 1)* (2005) pp 25-37. ; Mbiba. B, "Contentious development: peri-urban studies in sub-Saharan Africa," in *Progress in Development Studies 2(2),* pp113-131 (2002); "Zimbabwe"s Global Citizens in "Harare North": Some preliminary observations," Palmberg Mai and Ranka Primorac eds., *Skinning The Skunk – Facing Zimbabwean Futures, Discussion Paper 30, Nordiska Afrikainstitutet*: pp 26-38.(2005)

478 Mbiba.B, "Urban Agriculture in Zimbabwe," *Avebury*, Aldershot.(1995) ; Kretzmann. J.P, "Building Communities from the Inside Out.". <URL: http:// www.

The Land Survey Act (Chapter 20:12) was promulgated in May 1933 and revised in 1996, its two main purposes are to effect the registration of any land as provided for in the Deeds Registry and to predetermine the position of a curvilinear boundary, or of any beacon defining the terminal of any boundary of piece of land registered in the Deeds Registry as outlined in section 3 of the Act. According to section 25 of the Act, any land is to be subdivided to effect separate registration of one or more portions of that land in the Deeds Registry. The Land Survey Act is critical for land-use planning through enabling the effective registration of land thereby establishing rights over the land such as ownership and servitude rights. But critics have noted the rigidity and inflexibility of the statute especially in the face of emerging informal settlements especially in the peri-urban areas[479]. Epworth, though partially upgraded to date, the bulk of land occupiers on the entire settlement remain without title[480]. Ironically, much of the land is vested informally in private individuals and institutions. Land is indeed a 'thorny issue' in Zimbabwe[481].

The foregoing instruments, among others, are useful for orderly development, promotion of health and amenity in human habitats including those located in the peri-urban. Land taxation is a critical

---

thecommunityconnection.org/CC_aboutpubs/14_Bldg_Comms_InsideOut.doc>, *Accessed on 22 April 2008,* (1995)

[479] Mlalazi. A, "Residential Development: Public and Private Sector Involvement: Some Preliminary Thoughts," *Paper presented at the ZIRUP Annual School*, Harare. (1990); Musandu-Nyamayaro. O, "Legal Audit, Key Finding and Recommendations, Appendix5, HPZ (HOUSING PEOPLE OF ZIMBABWE) (2001).," *Report on the National Stakeholder Validation Workshop held on 24-25 November 2001 at the Management Training Bureau*, Harare. (2001); TibaijukaA. K, "Report of the Fact-Finding Mission to Zimbabwe to assess the Scope and Impact of Operation Murambatsvina," *UN Habitat*, Nairobi. (2005)

[480] Chenga, Murambatsvina II hovers over Epworth, The Financial Gazette: URL:http://www.financialgazette.co.zw/national-report/3011-murambatsvina-ii-hovers-over-epworth.html, Accessed on 5 August 2010.(2010)

[481] Dube.C, "Housing coops frustrated over land," *Zimbabwe Independent*. <URL: http://www.thezimbabweindependent.com/business/14311.html>, *Accessed on 22 April 2008.*(2004)

instrument in land stewardship[482]. However, the issue remains little understood and studied in Zimbabwe and Africa in general. In most cases, it is not the provisions of the instruments that matter but lack of enforcement. The 'environmental issue' has been topical. Evidence for this is the coverage of such news daily in the media[483]. The Environmental Management Agency (EMA) is the principal determinant of steering environmental initiatives in the country. The continuum of action ranges between regulation or control and facilitation or promotion[484]. There may also be traces of inaction and ambivalence. It is important to take note of some of these instruments in a bid to find out the role of the public institutions in fostering and enhancing environmental stewardship in the public affairs of the nation. Instruments used by EMA include the National Environmental Policies and Strategies (NEPS), National Environmental Plan (NEP), the Local Environmental Action Plans (LEAP), some statutory instruments and the Environmental Impact Assessment (EIA).

---

[482] Aristizabal. N; Gomez.A.O, "Chapter 6: Are services more important than titles in Bogotá?" In PAYNE GEOFFREY (ed.) (2002)., *Land, Rights and Innovation – Improving tenure security for the urban poor*, ITDG Publishing: London. (2002); Armitage.L, "Customary Land Tenure in Papua New Guinea," *Status and Prospects*. <URL:http://dlc.dlib.indiana.edu/archive/00001043/00/armitage.pdf,> *Accessed on 22 April 2008.*(2000)

[483] Examples include, the Herald, "Gvt gets tough on veld fires," The Herald, Zimpapers, Harare(16 August 2010a); "Projects benefit over 280 villagers," The Herald, Zimpapers, Harare,(16 August 2010b); The Herald, "Use Powers to save Environment, Chiefs Urged,"The Herald, Zimpapers, Harare.(17 2010); The Herald, "Sewage catastrophe looms, EMA," The Herald, Zimpapers, Harare(18 August 2010); The Herald, "Shurugwi Town Council owed US$120 000," The Herald, Zimpapers, Harare.(19 August 2010a); "Wood poaching rife in Hwange West," The Herald, Zimpapers,Harare.(19 August 2010b); Herald, "Veld fires destroy National Parks estates: Chadenga," The Herald, Zimpapers, Harare.(20 September 2010); Herald, "EMA drags city council to court," The Herald, Zimpapers, Harare. (24 August 2010); The Herald, "Tobacco Firms Urged to Plant Trees," The Herald, Zimpapers, Harare. (8 February 2010); The Herald, "200 000ha destroyed by veld fires — EMA," The Herald, Zimpapers, Harare.(8 September 2010); Kadzere. M, "Woodlots - Alternative Source of Curing Tobacco," The Herald, Zimpapers, Harare. (1 April 2010); Kashawo.L, "Let"s save our environment from veld fire," The Sunday Mail, Zimpapers,Harare. (22 August 2010.)

[484] Mapedza.E, "Forestry policy in colonial and postcolonial Zimbabwe: continuity and change," *Journal of Historical Geography 33(4)*:pp 833-851 (2007)

There are 60 guiding principles spelt out in the country's National Environmental Policy and Strategies (NEPS) document. The NEPS is a framework that Zimbabwe has adopted in keeping with "its commitments made under Rio Convention on Environment and Development (Agenda 21)"[485]. According to the NEPs document, the purpose of NEP is to "... promote and facilitate the consolidation and coordination of strategies, plans and activities developed at different levels (provincial, district and community) and in different sectors across the country." The sectors include mining, agriculture, real estate development including housing estates, to name but a few. Once adopted, the NEP binds everyone including the state. In essence, the NEP, as any other plan is an ongoing process, time-bound and subject to the stages of planning life cycle[486] . In discussing environmental stewardship and sustainability, these instruments are integral to peri-urban development.

Indeed, Zimbabwe faces a number of interlinked environmental challenges, which local communities must tackle. In peri-urban areas, specific challenges include increased deforestation, increased sewerage disposal and river systems, solid waste management challenges, the climate change issue, subsequent personal and environmental health challenges and unbridled tendencies in town expansion explaining the problems associated with the ecological footprint. The Ministry of Environment and Natural Resources Management (MENRM) is the primary arm of government fighting against environmental maladies in the Zimbabwe. Yet, actions and policies crafted in the name of environmental resources protection are meaningless and fruitless unless certain attitudes and knowledge gaps in the stakeholders, particularly communities are addressed[487]. The Environmental Management Act speaks Environmental Management Plans (EMPs), Local Environmental Action Plans (LEAP) and Environmental Impact Assessment (EIA). In the forthcoming

---

[485] GoZ, "National Environmental Policy and Strategies," *Ministry of Environment and Natural Resources Management*, Harare.pg. 26(2005), Nhema. F, "Foreword. GoZ, National Environmental Policy and Strategies," *Ministry of Environment and Natural Resources Management*: Harare. (2005)

[486] EMA Act, "Local Environmental Action Planning Manual,"*Environmental Management Agency/UNDP*, Harare,(2007).

[487] Savory.A, "Holistic Resource Management," *Gilmour Publishing*. Harare, (1988)

paragraphs I make a quick analysis and synthesis as to how these instruments have been useful in shaping places to achieve sustainability.

According to the EMA Act, section 96, every specified authority "shall an environmental management plan within such a period as the ministry may specify." An Environmental Management Plan (EMP) contains a description of the functions exercised by the specified authority in respect of the environment, a description of the environmental standards set or applied, a description of the policies, plans and programmes that are designed to the plan. In addition, it must state the degree of compliance required of other persons. Moreover, are arrangements for cooperation with other persons or environment management and a description of the manner in which the specified authority. Such ensures that its functions are exercised in a way that ensures compliance with the statute, other relevant enactments and environmental standards somas to achieve environmental management and protection. The preparation of EMPs is to conform to set prescriptions. These guidelines are very specific to the requirements, yet, doing these on the ground may not be as easy as the paper says it. The major setback with EMPs is that they are time-bound. Thus, they can expire. They also get abandoned. With sustainability, the long-range picture matters more than the snapshot picture of human reality.

Local Environmental Action Plan (LEAP) is defined as "...a process which addresses an area's environmental threats or problems [involving] the local community coming together, identifying their problems and concerns, and working together to solve them"[488]. It is thus a collaborative process involving community visioning most likely informed by an analysis of the place and the community's strengths, weaknesses, opportunities and threats. In itself, a LEAP fosters and enhances community resilience to possible disasters and risks. LEAP in Zimbabwe is linked to the country's National Conservation Strategy (NCS) which was launched in 1987 by the then Prime Minister, Robert

[488] EMA, "Local Environmental Action Planning Manual," *Environmental Management Agency/UNDP*, Harare.(2007:1)

Gabriel Mugabe[489]. It is acknowledged that LEAP responds to the tenets and requisites of Agenda 21[490]. The idea of LEAP was first introduced in the rural areas under the District Environmental Action Plans (DEAP) process. The belief then was that environmental problems were in synonym with rural areas. However, upon realising the challenges urban areas also face, the idea was taken urban[491].

To date, the idea of LEAP has been enshrined in the Environmental Management Act (CAP, 20:27). the challenges associated with the LEAP process have been identified. These include the fact that: the process is time consuming, costly and raises high hopes among members of the community, which however may not be corresponding with the resources available to execute the expected[492]. However, there is a justification as to why local authorities should develop LEAPs, particularly that they form a baseline and serve as blueprints upon which future investments in the place are to be based. Secondly, it's 'people-centricism," in terms of the participants involved in producing the plan, providing the local people and key stakeholders an urge and sense of ownership, perhaps, not only of the plan document, but also of the place and its investments[493]. it is spelt out the importance of LEAPS as: a forum for bringing diverse groups and individuals, and individuals with different interests, values and prospective together for a shared vision and a tool for sustainable development[494]. All these resonate the essence of sustainable practices hence inculcation of stewardship among members of a community. In the peri-urban settlements of Zimbabwe, these tenets are

---

489 EMA, "Local Environmental Action Planning Manual," *Environmental Management Agency/UNDP*, Harare.(2007:1) ; Nhema. F, "Foreword. GoZ, National Environmental Policy and Strategies," *Ministry of Environment and Natural Resources Management*: Harare. (2005)

490 EMA, "Local Environmental Action Planning Manual," *Environmental Management Agency/UNDP*, Harare.(2007)

491 Ibid.

492 Section 95 of the Environmental Management Act; EMA, "Local Environmental Action Planning Manual," *Environmental Management Agency/UNDP*, Harare.(2007)

493 Cunningham.G; Mathie. A, "Asset-Based Community Development-An Overview Coady International Institute." <URL: http://www.synergos.org,> *Accessed on 22 April 2008*. (2002)

494 EMA, "Local Environmental Action Planning Manual," *Environmental Management Agency/UNDP*, Harare.(2007:1)

yet to realise as operational guidelines for these are not yet fully developed.

Pollution, in its various forms of water, noise, land and air, is a serious matter of concern. Use of artificial fertilisers often leads to high levels of eutrophication in rivers and brooks[495]. This has often been associated with environmental health challenges. In addition to extractions of stones and sand for construction from rivers and wildernesses, households also dump wastes in the environment. Sections 97 to 108 of the Environmental Management Act provide for EIA. In the National Environmental Policy and Strategies document, EIA is defined as,

> "...both a process and a tool for Project Planning and decision making... (Whose) ... purpose is to ensure that during development planning, possible impacts on biophysical, economic and social cultural elements of the environment are taken into account [with the] aim to identify, likely impacts, estimate their security, indicate which impacts may be significant and what opportunities there might be to avoid or minimise negative impacts and enhance potential benefits."[496]

EIA is a prerequisite for development projects of a given scale hence it is central to housing development projects. Part 3 of Statutory Instrument 7 of 2007 on Environmental Management Regulations spells out how EIAs must be conducted. Everywhere EIAs are carried out, the idea is to promote environmental sustainability by providing a 'platform' over which harmful developments can be avoided in the environment. It is unfortunate that, because of the political situation surrounding especially the FLRP-induced housing in the peri-urban not many EIAs have been done. Some of the settlements, no doubt, are sitting on environmentally sensitive areas, while others have already begun to induce high levels of erosion into river bodies. All such are indicators of 'bad stewardship' hence a threat to the cause of sustainability and sustainable development of human settlements. Indeed, when decisions are made without careful thought (emotionally and being politically motivated), they tend to work

---

[495] Zingoni et al., "Effects of a semi-formal urban settlement on groundwater quality: Epworth (Zimbabwe)," Case study and groundwater quality zoning. *Physics and Chemistry of the Earth, Parts A/B/C 30 (11-16),* pp 680-688 (2005);

[496] GoZ, "National Environmental Policy and Strategies," *Ministry of Environment and Natural Resources Management*, Harare.pg 27(2005)

strong against issues of building 'lasting solutions," which, in essence, is about sustainable development.

In contemporary Zimbabwe, the overall concern among estate developers and home-seekers has been that the laws governing housing and its delivery are archaic hence inelastic to accommodate the new demand for shelter as well as accommodating new technologies that may be required to ease the pressure[497]. With this concern in view, the National Housing Convention in October 2009, saw housing stakeholders advocating for change in the regulatory framework governing housing, specifically low-cost shelter delivery. To reduce inefficiency and there was a resolution to: "...amend the RTCP [Regional, Town and Country Planning] Act and Model Building Bye-laws to allow for alternative building technologies and material; [to] operationalise pro-poor frameworks in terms of service delivery procedures and arrangements; [and to] formulate relevant pieces of legislation to recognise and effectively regulate private land developers and the planning profession"[498].

Housing has been described as a 'political hot potato'[499]. A few housing projects (Epworth included) which have survived destruction in Zimbabwe yet the majority have been demolished[500]. We must also acknowledge that from 1980 to 1999, the Zimbabwe Africa National

---

497 TibaijukaA. K, "Report of the Fact-Finding Mission to Zimbabwe to assess the Scope and Impact of Operation Murambatsvina," *UN Habitat*, Nairobi. (2005)

498 GoZ/UNHABITAT, "Proceedings of the National Symposium convened by the Ministry of National Housing and Social Amenities under the theme ,"*Towards an Integrated Approach to Sustainable Housing and Social Amenities Delivery in Zimbabwe" on 28 May 2009*, Mendel Training Centre, Harare.pg.5(2009)

499 Bourne.L. S,, "The Geography of Housing," *V H Winston and Sons Ltd*, London. (1981)

500 (Patel.D.H;Adams.J.T, "Chirambahuyo: A Case Study in Low Income Housing," Mambo Press: Gweru(1981),Butcher. C, "Urban low-income housing: a case study of the Epworth squatter settlement upgrading programme, Chapter 6 in ZINYAMA L, D TEVERA AND S CUMMING (eds.) 1993" *Harare:* "The Growth and Problems of the City," *University of Zimbabwe*: Harare. (1993); Toriro.P, "Town Planning in Zimbabwe, History, Challenges and the Urban Renewal Operation Murambatsvina," Chapter 11, Maphosa France, Kraposy Kujinga and Sunungurai D Chingarande (eds.), (2007) "Zimbabwe"s Development Experiences since 1980: Challenges and Prospects for the Future," *OSSREA*, Addis Ababa.(2007)

Union (Patriotic Front) – ZANU-PF – rule almost single-handedly the country. 1999 saw the formation and rise of the Movement for Democratic Change as a resilient opposition party.

By 2008, MDC had taken over all the urban local authorities in local government elections. Loyalty to ZANU-PF continued albeit precariously in the rural areas. in the post-2008 harmonised elections the country plunged into serious post-election violence and polarisation was very rife. On 15 September 2008, after more than six months of great impasse between the two camps (ZANU-PF and MDC), a Global Political Agreement (GPA) was signed with the former South Africa President Thabo Mbeki being the guarantor and facilitator. The GPA birthed the Government of National Unity (GNU in 2009 which saw the stabilisation of the economy that had deteriorated in a span of a decade (c. 1998-2008). The manner in which the GNU has operated to date (2013) has been on characterised by bickering, animosity and distrust. Despite this unsteady relationship of the parties, scholars would argue for contestation that works towards creation of development dividends than that of co-optation[501]. A rapid evaluation of the GPA in Zimbabwe (2008-2013) would indicate that the agreement helped in saving the economically 'sinking titanic," Zimbabwe. It also quenched the political skirmishes that we tending towards a civil war-like situation. However, in terms of improving urban and peri-urban environments, it is maintained that there has been increasing squalor and the development of slum like conditions[502].

In an interview with the DPP Deputy Director, the role of political will is noted in sustaining settlements. The Deputy Director argues,

> "A cooperative called Nehanda [in Dzivaresekwa] was quite advanced when Operation Murambatsvina came. At least they had some draft layout plans. They had built their houses according to standards.... I should say *housing is shelter meeting a certain standard.* Nehanda as a cooperative, on government land, the approval was easy. *Sezvaunoziva nyoka*

---

[501] Wampler .B, "Participatory Budgeting in Brazil: Contestation, Cooperation and Accountability," *Pennsylvania University Press*,Pennsylvania.(2007)

[502] Chirisa. I, "Epworth in Zimbabwe; Inclusivity, Housing and the Stewardship Concept." *The Built & Human Environment Review 6*: pp 18-29. (2013)

> *huru haingaizvirumi.* (As you may know, the Government as a Big Snake could not bite itself). That is how Nehanda survived the Operation. Dzivaresekwa and Hatcliffe are on government land, that is, stateland. You must however bear it in mind that it's only after everything has been planned and allocation of stands has been done that stateland then becomes private land. As we speak Dzivaresekwa and Hatcliffe stand beneficiaries are still making payments [for the land] to government. Their plans have to be approved at two stations. First, it is us (the DPP) which approves the layout plans and then the engineering department of the local authority approves the building and civic design plans (for roads and storm water designs). Thus, there is approval of designs and civic works"[503].

The text indicates the significance of government approval of people settling in a defined area. Payment cements the stay. Conversions of stateland to private land are achieved on a rent-to-buy basis. The cases of Nehanda and Hatcliffe, largely, demonstrate how the political factor has been the basis for which some peri-urbanites have justified their stay in the areas they occupy. Most of these dwellers are there 'on a ZANU-PF ticket' as it has emerged. Reference to the term 'Government' is rather misleading as it should be 'party." The question is: Is place sustainability achieved through allocations made by political parties or it is the survival of some political parties that hinges on parcelling out land to the homeless, hopeless and landless? Peri-urban dynamics in most African states are politically driven. Politics can be involving traditional leaders as in the Ghanaian and Botswana cases or it may involve modern institutions like political parties as in this case[504]. When these institutions are at loggerheads, an unsustainable picture of development is built. Politicians in most cases avoid following planning standards just before elections. They may follow them latter after the election or even use them as a punitive tool against those who may not have voted them. Such is a 'shaky'

---

[503] Interview of the Deputy Director on 11 March 2011

[504] Akroffi.E.O., "Urbanisation and the Urban Poor in Africa,". *Paper presented at the Promoting Land Administration and Good Governance, 5th FIG Regional Conference, Accra, Ghana, March 8-11, 2006*
(2006)Home.R, "Eating farmland, growing houses": *Peri-urban settlements and customary land tenure in Botswana, Southern Africa,* <URL: http://www.n-aerus.net/web/sat/workshops/2001/papers/home.pdf>(2001); ; (2002)

terrain for individuals and households to make sustainable developments at the micro-scale.

Sustainability, in the built environment, indeed, has to focus on issues of building technologies and materials. However, current observations from most peri-urban settlements around Harare indicate that the incremental approach to housing development has in effect ushered in a wave of building of temporary structures and in most cases without adequate infrastructure in the form of roads, water and sanitation and power utilities. This contradicts the Grassroots Housing Model which sees 'sustainability' as a product of a close working partnership between a housing cooperative and its 'consortium' of qualified civil engineers, planners, architects and financiers[505]. However, in the Zimbabwean case, it has been observed that:

> "At the moment, the housing demand in the country is increasing. There is a shortage of housing and people are talking of the option of having *parallel development*. Others want to call it *phased development* and others *incremental development*. I must say there is no written policy about this. Nevertheless, because of the increased demand home-seekers are saying we can bypass the standards and have infrastructure later. It is in this debate where there is increasing peri-urban housing. Yet, I don't want to call it peri-urban housing. Let's call it urban expansion. I still remember when Glen View was being built. We never called it peri-urban. Everything was done instantly: infrastructure was provided and houses were immediately built. The term peri-urban was not used. It was just a new scheme. Sometimes the term is used with reference to how a new area is opened up for new development. With reference to the areas occupied by the housing cooperatives, there is no readiness for servicing"[506].

The Deputy Director is lamenting on the inaptitude associated with peri-urban shelter in Zimbabwe. He argues that there is no written policy on its adoption. Without a written code, it becomes difficult for one to draw informed analyses and discourses. Even when stakeholders speak of revision of existing codes, the issue of peri-urban sustainability is more

---

505 Alexander. C et al. "The grass roots housing process," <URL: http://www.living neighborhoods.org/library/grassroots.htm>, *Accessed on 22 April 2008.*(1973)

506 Interview 11 March 2011

implied than explicit. Focusing on the instruments may not be issue but the actors. Stewardship as a policy and technical dimension to sustainability would require that there are strong policies, legislative instruments and law enforcement for meaningful peri-urban development[507].

Sustainability is achieved by collaborative action. Compliance to set standards is important. True stewardship would expect that players operate willingly and in compliance of the set standards. Nevertheless, Zimbabwe has had the problem of squatting for a long time. Squatters normally defy principles of good stewardship as is prescribed in literature. This is because, the way squatters normally degrade the environment by their practices including dumping of solid waste in areas they deem as underutilised. Stewardship is having a sense of responsibility, in this context of human habitats, about caring for the environment. Critical in all the peri-urban developments that have happened in Zimbabwe, as elsewhere, is the centrality of the question of sustainability. This concept is highly enmeshed in the stewardship paradigm and practice as it seeks to strike a balance between people's development needs in the framework of ecological and social parameters. However, context matters. Context, as discussed in this chapter entails historical, geographical and psycho-social factors working in combination to produce certain fundamental outcomes. In this case, I poise sustainability is a matter of many factors, not only the three well documented (market, people and the environment) but also institutional, policy and the strength of instruments designed to enhance it. Appropriate technology and respect for cultural tendencies are also very critical. Although there are basically three income groups worth considering in seeking understanding of human settlements, the low-income groups always stand out as normally lacking in terms of decent jobs, houses, health, to name but these three.

---

[507] Gough.K; Yankson, "Land Markets in African Cities, The Case of Peri-urban Accra, Ghana," *Urban Studies* 37(13): 2485 – 2500 (2000);Kombe.W.J, "Land-use dynamics in peri-urban areas and their implications on the urban growth and form: the case of Dar es Salaam, Tanzania,". *Habitat International 29(1)*: pp 113-135 (2005); ; Howlett. M;Ramesh.R, "Studying Public Policy: Policy Cycles and Policy Subsystems and Political Organisations," *Princeton University Press*, Princeton. (1995)

Overall, the foregoing discussion of parameters shows the context of peri-urban housing and stewardship in Zimbabwe. It must be underscored as a historical fact that Zimbabwe as a country has borrowed heavily from its former colonial master especially with respect to administrative and legal structures. These structures have remained unchanged such that they no longer respond to the needs of the current populations who are surviving in the context of increasing poverty and pressing economic challenges. Taken as a whole, the existence of instruments, policies, legislation and institutions is not a guarantee that sustainability is going to be easily attained. Rather, it takes finances, collaboration of effort, political will and enforcement that is not arbitrary to achieve it. In addition, the political environment generally shows the extent to which progressive development can be noted on the ground. The more than ten years of economic and political stability in Zimbabwe has derailed a lot of urban and progress that one could expect [508]. Poverty and squalor define the context of peri-urban spaces at the moment. In the next chapter, focus will be put on one case study area, Ruwa after which the next other chapter will focus on housing and stewardship in Epworth.

---

[508] Chirisa. I, "Epworth in Zimbabwe; Inclusivity, Housing and the Stewardship Concept." *The Built & Human Environment Review 6*: pp 18-29. (2013), b, "Politics in Environmental Stewardship in Zimbabwe," Reflections on Ruwa and Epworth. *African Journal of History and Culture* 5(1): pp13 – 26, DOI: 10.5897/AJHC11.026 , c,"Increased Squalor in Urban and Peri-urban Zimbabwe since 2009" Assessing the Rhetoric, Practices and Contradictions of the Government of National Unity, *Southern Peace Review Journal* 2(1): pp118-135

CHAPTER 8
HOUSING AND STEWARDSHIP IN RUWA

It is suggested that the private sector "should have access to land for housing development for the public in general and own employees in particular on a cost recovery basis without causing premature expenditure of public funds." [509] The purpose of this chapter is to describe and explain the realities in Ruwa with respect to stewardship and housing. There are debates whether we should regard Ruwa as a peri-urban or simply as a town hence defined settlement. While this debate cannot be overlooked, at least, as one examines how the town is trying to get more land for urban expansion, it becomes quite imperative that the peri-urban of the town itself is part of the process of transformation and change in both temporal and spatial terms. The first part of the chapter tries to capture the administrative and management strides by the town. The second part deals with the experiences and perceptions of the Ruwa residents in their habitats.

Ruwa was until the 1980s preserved as a rural landscape. It was then declared a growth point pointing to urbanisation of this centre. Ruwa has transitioned from being a growth point into becoming a town. Such development implies an increase in the number of human-built structures hence also more concrete and tarmac structures. Evidence on the ground indicates that this expansion in the built environment has had an effect on the ecology of the environment as evidenced by the population increase with massive forests' destruction to pave way for development. Due to the dominance of private sector investment, the place has grown in the span of about thirty years to become not only an investment centre but also a home for mainly the middle-income groups. Although critics have pointed

---

[509] Policy Number 12 in Harare (1989) Harare, "Harare Combination Master Plan: Written Statement," *Department of Works*, Harare(1989)

out that the town does not deserve a town status according to the provisions of the Urban Councils Act, for example in that it does not yet have a defined central business district (CBD), the town in terms of its population, estimated to be plus or minus 50,000. In the very recent years Ruwa has been growing chiefly in terms of the development of high-class housing estates (for example, in suburbs like Zimre Park and Windsor Park).

The administration and management of Ruwa are at crossroads. Politically, the town is under Mashonaland East Province where is has always belonged. Administratively it is under Harare Metropolitan Province. This problem poses a number of stewardship challenges as clearly outlined by the town planner in the following excerpt:

> "We are in a dilemma. This is because we are defined differently depending on whether it's politics or administration. We see our town needing more land to accommodate new urban development and housing needs. For your own information, we applied for some farms for these purposes [urban development and housing]. Mashonaland East said that it could not attend to such application. It said its [the province] thrust on Ruwa is rural. In this regard, the province said it is prepared to allocate farms that we applied for, to farming. This it did to gain political mileage. As you may know, Ruwa is under an MDC council. ZANU-PF has therefore been fighting hard to make sure that we do not then get immersed in the affairs of Harare though administratively we are under Harare Metropolitan Province. The argument by ZANU-PF is: Why boost a council which belongs to a party [MDC] that opposes it. This struggle has created challenges for us already – we cannot acquire land for housing. Our cemetery is located right in the rural land. We brought in the Minister (Comrade Chombo) to assist and ease our dilemma. He seems to side with Mashonaland East given that he is also from ZANU-PF. It seems we are fighting a losing battle. When two elephants fight, it is the grass that suffers."[510]

From the foregoing description by the town planner of Ruwa, there has been stalled development for Ruwa as it ought to have developed or acquired land for urban development. This is the politics in housing development that is explained by political jitteriness and agitation which are defined at two levels. The first is to do with two provinces or regions

---

510 Interview on 03 March 2013.

failing to collaborate and resolve common issues or at least find a common ground to have resolve the pressing challenge. The second is to with the political hidden agendas in which the MDC and ZANU-PF have taken the town for a battleground on which they express their feuds and jealousies over each other. While collaboration and stewardship theorists argue for creating a level play ground in which differences – political, professional, creed, etc – have to be set assist to build a common good, actors on the ground, particularly politicians see room for political mileage if they do not come close to each other[511]. In the map (Figure 4:1), Ruwa applied to expand the town to almost double its size. It received no positive response regarding this proposal.

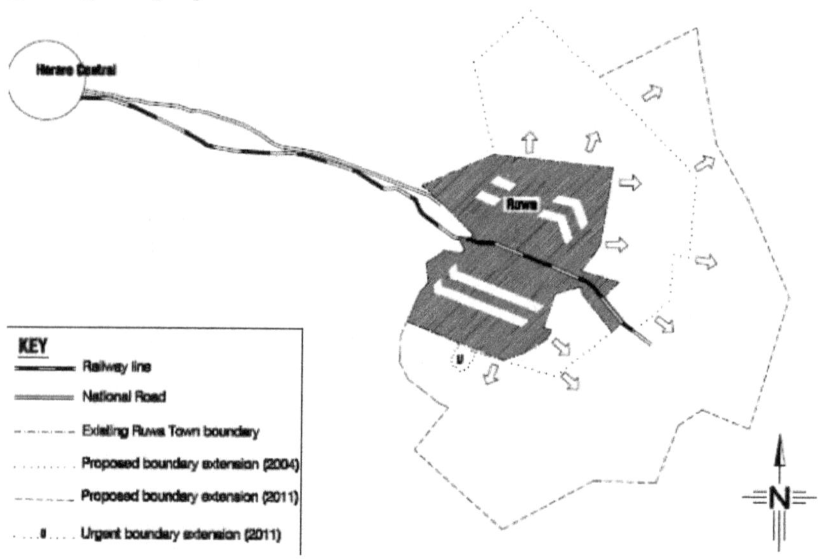

Figure 8.1: Ruwa's Existing and Proposed Land for Urban Development and Housing [512]

In 2011 the town applied for more land in keeping with its prospects for growth. Still the application remains pending as the politics previously mentioned brew to the disappointment of the town planners and council administration. While the halt may be taken as purely

[511] Mckinney et al. Working across Boundaries: A Framework for Regional Collaboration, in LeRoyer Ann ed. *Land Lines 16(3),* Lincoln Institute of Land Policy: Cambridge (USA).(2004)

[512] Adapted from Map of Ruwa, 2012

retrogressive, from an ecological planner's viewpoint, it is important for the halt in keeping with the philosophy of 'putting the brakes to sprawl'[513]. Despite the struggles to negotiate to have land for housing and urban development, Ruwa has over the years worked diligently to collaborate with other private sector players. Through the private public partnership arrangement, the town has, of late, managed to exploit water resources of the dam in its immediate vicinity through augmenting water supplies to that by the City of Harare. The ability to attract a PPP arrangement in the settlement is largely a function of the income status of the inhabitants of the place. Thus, the town being predominantly middle-to-high income classes (unlike Epworth predominantly low-income) gives it privy towards partnering for sustainable solutions to their place. Private companies being profit-driven tend to shun working with the poor unless, their operations are heavily subsidised and incentivised.

Ruwa Town has brought about significant development through the Public Private Partnership (PPP) showing how concerted effort of different institutions can shape developmental aspirations. To a great extent, housing provision in Ruwa is both a responsibility of largely the private sector. Although Wards 1, 2 and 3 are public sector housing schemes, Wards 5, 6, 7, 8 and 9 are private sector initiatives. The total existing stands add up to 12,000, while stands with houses under construction are 5,500. Only 7,862 of the stands have development permits. The current stock of stands being serviced by the private add to 4,929, most of which are partially serviced. Stands whose development is at a standstill are 1,076. The council-built houses amount to 46 in the entire town[514]. The challenges in Ruwa habitat and housing delivery include the fact that the waiting list servicing has been very slow since 1995. The town has no formal dump site for waste disposal. The one in use is neither properly planned nor formally acquired. In addition, the privately-owned land is a case of speculation, thus resulting in large tracts of undeveloped stands. Such undeveloped plots pose problems to the urban fabric of the town including illegal dumping on them; the menace of uncut grass

---

[513] McElfish J.M, "Commentary: Ten Things Wrong with Sprawl," <URL: http:// www.emagazine.com/view/?3641,> *Accessed on 22 April 2008.* (2008);

[514] Ruwa, "Ruwa Town Council at a Glimpse as at June 2010," Ruwa (2010)

especially during the rainy season a problem which creates havens for thieves, and is also a breeding ground for mosquitoes. These environmental challenges militate against the aesthetic values of the town[515]. Some plot occupiers in Ruwa are trying as much as possible, to preserve the indigenous trees (*musasa, mutondo, muzeze*) as noted by the shrubbery within and outside their plots.

Remarks by the principal officials in the town management (stewards) are critical to indicate the extent to which the PPP arrangement has worked as a magic bullet to development. The Secretary and Chief Executive Officer (CEO) observed that the "...town encourages both regional and local investors to bring their proposals as this will help us in the enhancement of the town…. We have as special working relationship with our investors as we have agreed on the Build, Operate and Transfer (BOT) model as opposed to the Build, Own, Operate and Transfer (BOOT)."[516] In the same sources, the Town Engineer argues: "We can safely say that Ruwa is one of the few towns in Zimbabwe which has an effective refuse collection system and the town authorities are concerned about the health of the residents." Again, in the same, the Town Chairman raises the concern that "…many people mistake Ruwa to be part of Harare; this is an unfortunate misnomer as we are a standalone town…. Ruwa needs its own charity funds and calls for all well-wishers to come forward their gifts during the festive season."[517]

The town holds some critical events in its calendar and has a number of projects in its steering. For example, during its annual Ruwa Agricultural Show (RAS) held in September, farmers in the vicinity of the town and industrialists are given an opportunity to showcase their products. Besides, the town has reserved a "large chunk of land" for the development of a new industrial park whose focus is geared to the transformation of Ruwa into "a prominent manufacturing powerhouse in the country". Put in place has been a sound water management system and is an ongoing project. The town's water supply is sourced from 30 cubic metres per day "enough to supply Ruwa Town without any problem".

---

[515] ibid, (2010)
[516] The Business Diary, "PPP key to development of Ruwa," p42. (December 2010)
[517] Ibid,(December 2010)

Phase 1 of the project, which includes 11.5-kilometre pipeline from Norah Dam to Green Sykes holding dam, 10 megalitre Reservoir and a 2 by 5 megalitre reactor (treatment plant), requires a huge capital injection amounting to US$4 million. Moreover, the Town is building a local primary school, a "unique scenario in Zimbabwe as most town authorities are struggling to cope with the hardships of the economic recession and in most cases assisted by carrying out such products"[518].

Ruwa has some unique features which have worked as success factors to its growth and management. It is argued that the town offers "excellent services to its residents despite being owed over US$3,8 million by the rate payers. It addresses residents on pressing issues[519]. This is in keeping with the philosophy of Policy Number 12 which stipulates that, "The private sector should have access to land for housing development for the public in general and own employees in particular on a cost recovery basis without causing premature expenditure of public funds."[520] Generally, there is positive partnership interplay between Ruwa and her inhabitants. This collaboration between the governors and the governed brings an element of trust hence internal cohesions that works as a factor for strong cohesion and dictates a trajectory of certainty. For this reason, it is argued that the town continues to be "the trump card of economic development in Zimbabwe" signalling its significance as an industrial town "for export promotion and economic growth" for the country[521].

Having shown the external, administrative and political dynamic shaping Ruwa besides the town's abilities to organise internal players with whom it works with in an atmosphere of trust and solidarity, I dig further into the internal dynamics regarding how the Ruwa community is structured and relates to housing and stewardship matters. According to the household survey (see Table 8.1), most of the respondents indicate that they bought stands or houses (37%). Six percent (6%) and 25% state that they are tenants and lodgers, respectively. Others state that they were

518 The Business Diary, "PPP key to development of Ruwa," p42. (December 2010)
519 ibid, (December 2010:42)
520 Harare, "Harare Combination Master Plan: Written Statement," *Department of Works*, Harare(1989)
521 The Business Diary, "PPP key to development of Ruwa," p42. (December 2010)

'hired' out as caretakers of the stands where they resided (being the 12% that say property they are residing on belongs to a friend and the 5% that indicate other arrangements).

Table 8.1: Household Tenure Status of Respondents in Ruwa [522]

Status in Accommodation	Frequency	Percentage (%)
Owner/Purchaser	57	37
Tenant	9	6
Lodger	38	25
Tied Accommodation	9	6
Property belongs to friend	18	12
Property belongs to parents	13	8
Other	10	5
Total	154	100

The caretakers indicate that they are responsible for monitoring the construction of the houses some of which are visibly still work-in-progress at the time of the survey. In the case of absence from a property, property owners hire lodgers, tenants or caretakers whose role becomes of stewardship, taking care of all matters of the health of the property including settling rates and bills, cutting grass and having oversight of the construction processes in the case where construction is in progress. Sometimes commitment to contributing to the welfare and development of a place depends on the manner in which people are having no divided attention especially between rural and urban. I sought to check on the frequency of the people going to rural homes (Table 8.2). More than 60% of the inhabitants only visit once a year or never go either because they have completely abandoned the idea or they are foreigners who do not even have a rural home.

Table 8.2: Frequency of going to the rural home (%) [523]

Aspect	Percentage (%)
Once a week	26.0
Once a month	9.1
Once a year	14.2
Once in two years	13.0

522 Field Survey (2010)

523 Field Survey (2010)

Aspect *(contd…)*	**Percentage (%) *(contd…)***
Never	14.29
N/A	16.88
Total	100

N=154

Tagara, a homeowner staying in Damofalls observes that, "Going rural these days depends on many factors. As a country, we have since undergone a serious economic crisis. Who, in this environment will afford keeping two homes – the rural one and the urban one? Just see what I am trying to achieve here – to finish this house and also to send my children to school. We only go to the 'villages' when we hear there has been a funeral." From Tagara's words, which are also echoed by Emily in Ruwa Township and Zuze in ZIMRE Park, double-rootedness in the rural and the urban appears to be dismantling. However, there is Lucia who works in a hair salon in Harare, lodging in Chipukutu who says, "Business is low these days. Competition is stiff. When you calculate the amount you spend on rent, food, school fees and transport, you think twice about continuing in this place. My father who owns a farm in Banket was saying it is more profitable to come and do tobacco farming. I am considering taking this opportunity seriously." This testimony by Lucia implies that we cannot rule out completely the fact that faced with hardships; some households will consider relocating to the rural areas. In Zimbabwe because of the fast-track land reform programme embarked upon by government in 2000, the rural area provides a window of opportunity to those willing to practice small-scale agriculture. Charles says, "But have you been to the reserves of late? The squeezing that used to be the norm has just disappeared. A number of fields formerly owned by the people that left for A1 and A2 farms are just lying idle. I am thinking of going back to Wedza and practice farming on such pieces of land that my uncles and brother left there." Potts (2006) has raised some of the issues and concerns indicated here by the respondents regarding patterns of circular migration in Zimbabwe. Despite hardships with respect to urban life as mentioned by a number of respondents, a good number of the respondents in Ruwa maintain that they were attracted to the town by the affordability of the shelter there (28.6%, peacefulness of the town (30.52), closeness to Harare (10.39%), closeness to their jobs (9.1%) and a combination of these factors (14.29%). Table 8.3 is a summary of these aspects.

Table 8.3: Percentage Rating of Pull factors to Town (%)

Aspect	Percentage (%)
Affordable shelter	28.6
Peacefulness	30.52
Closeness to Harare	10.39
Closeness to job	9.1
Affordable life	6.5
Semi-rurality	0.65
Opportunities	0.0
Most of the above	14.29
Total	100

N=154

Most people moving into Ruwa as home owners state that they are attracted by expansive residential space mainly for the medium to high income classes. In Ruwa the issue of rental escalations (22.73%) is noted as the prime determinant for intra-urban migration. Table 8.4 provides a snapshot of the causal factors of why the respondents left where they used to stay. The largest number (22.73%) mention rising rentals in Harare as the main push factor.

Table 8.4: Push and pull factors (%) (Survey, 2010)

Aspect	Percentage (%)
Poor sanitation	0.00
Poor water availability	1.95
Rising rentals	22.73
Strictness of property owner	10.39
Search for own property	1.18
Eviction/Murambatsvina	7.14
Marriage	1.95
Employment opportunities	7.14
Most of the above	3.9
N/A	41.0
Total	100

N=154

The table shows the extent to which peri-urbanisation is explained by the cost of living in whose ambit is unaffordable rentals. On trying to understand whether the inhabitants have moved from one place and the other since coming to Ruwa 59.85% of the respondents indicate that they have done so, some several times (Figure 8.2). This is mainly in the cohort of lodgers, tenants and caretakers. There are also lodgers and tenants who have 'graduated' from tenancy and lodging to become plot owners. Kasikai testifies,

> "When I came here in 1998, and I was lodging, I never thought I would own this beautiful house in ZIMRE Park. I was getting tired of shifting from one place to the other in this neighbourhood until Gede offered me to buy his stand. He moved to Borrowdale Brookes from here. Because of the erratic water supplies here, he said he could not keep this stand. Gede gave me an opportunity to by the stand on basis of instalments. The instalments were indeed favourable and with my salary I managed to clear the payment. I bought the stand at the equivalence of US$2000. Today, a similar stand (500m^2) you get it at not less than US$10,000. After 2009, I managed to acquire three more stands here in Ruwa. I am smiling is there prices are rising each day. The cost of these stands has trebled in less than five years. What a fortune!"

Kasikai's experience is also shared by Nyemudzai, Clemence and Taguta. They used to be 'wanderers' in Ruwa but they had a sudden experience of becoming plot owners. They became builders and developers and by a serial of experience, they have seen the possibilities of building fortunes through by serviced stands and selling when they feel it is worthy doing so.

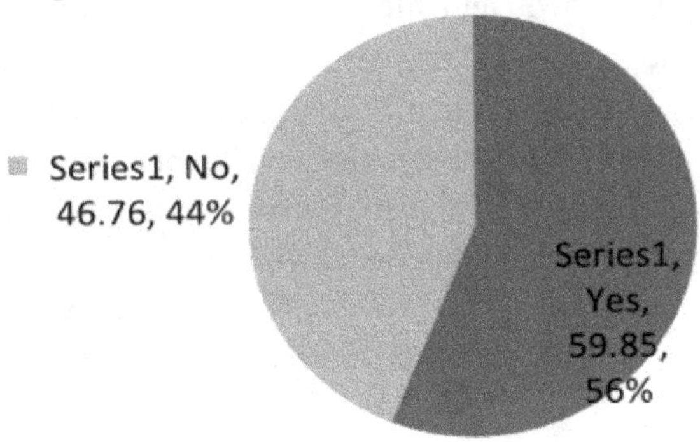

N=154

Figure 8.2: Intra-settlement migration in Ruwa (%) (Survey, 2010)

Nevertheless, this explains speculative behaviour in which idle land will fetch high prices with little having been invested in them.

Speculation is a bad practice of space stewardship and this brings about strong sentiments against it especially from the angle of Marxist theorists who regard it as exploitative and anarchists who take property as theft[524].

In the forthcoming section I provide the experiences of the Ruwa peri-urban dwellers and this is important to understand how, in keeping with the Housing Adjustment Theory, the inhabitants have 'adapted' themselves or their shelters in the peri-urban settlement. Place stewardship has strong elements of adaptation and making oneself comfortable even sometimes in hardships hence resilience based on capacity (Shinn, 1999).

In Ruwa, particularly Zimre Park, Damofalls and Chipukutu, there are constant sounds of dynamite rock blasting which one can easily mistake for borehole drilling. The explanation by Chakari, one of the respondents, is that this occurs on stands with rocky surfaces to allow for construction. Consultations with the neighbours in this development are not done as it is taken for a norm in the area. In keeping with the provisions of the town and environmental planning legislations, when such 'developments' happen, neighbours must be consulted first[525]. Ruwa Industrial Area, which is next to Maha Shopping Centre, accommodates a number of industries. This industrial area is one of the major sources of effluent that is treated at a local sewer plant in Sunway City.

The impact of the effluent to the ecological environment is that living organisms such as fish, found in Ruwa River, are affected by the foreign elements thrown into the water. The question "when does a steward become a nanny?"[526] resurfaces. It seems the responsible authorities are not doing enough. Although they are backed by a host of laws and institutions, enforcement and development control are not being effected. In some instances, the local communities have taken steps to protect and manage their immediate environments. In Zimre Park, some plot occupiers have always made attempts to cut grass in a way to reduce obscurity with access roads, hence increase visibility for drivers and also

---

[524] Hodkinson.P. H, "The return of the housing question" *Ephemera - Theory & Politics in Organization, 12(4)*: pp. 427 (2012)

[525] (Section 22 of the Regional, Town and Country Planning Act)

[526] Saltman ; Ferroussier-Davis, "The concept of stewardship in health policy," *Bulletin of the World Health Organisation, 2000*, 78 (6): pp 732-739. (2000),

'scare away' mischievous elements in the form of thieves and muggers. The cut grass is then used for thatching.

Chamunorwa stays in Damofalls, Ruwa. His rural home is Gokwe-Sanyati. Chamunorwa says. Before he started 'breaking stones' to make quarry, he was working with a certain bricklayer by the name of Nhongwa; he was an assistant to this Nhongwa. Chamunorwa complains the Nhongwa was not paying him commensurately. At that time, he stayed in Mabvuku and they were building a house from Moyo in Ruwa. Chamunorwa informed Moyo of his plight and begged him to accommodate on his plot standing they were building. He asserts that, "I told him that my stay on his premise would help that his materials for construction would not be stolen. He agreed. I parted ways with Nhongwa, the oppressing bricklayer. Now I stay with my whole family and this is my new workplace. You know how I pay my rentals? Just keeping this place is the rental. Things are now better for me. Now I can afford a decent livelihood together with my family."

Chamunorwa is quarrying on somebody's stand next to Moyo's plot. He says the owner of this plot comes time and again and has allowed him to go ahead with digging, heating and breaking the boulders on-plot. He says that this is a way to clear up the land before the actual construction begins. Chamunorwa remarks, "He has just asked me not to disturb his peg. The advantage with this stand is that the owner won't spend much on the foundation as others. The rock here is already a good foundation." Prices for the quarry stones in Damofalls are eighty dollars per five cubic. Chamunorwa argues that "I don't enjoy monopoly in this business. This is what all bricklayers here do when their construction business is on the low. We are more than one hundred in this business, just in this area. You see!" This story is also a matter of social capital building. There are a number of caretakers on Ruwa and Epworth plots who are mere keepers in return for accommodation. In some cases, the plot owners live in Harare, in more decent accommodation and they refer to these peri-urban plots as the bush *(kusango)*.

Fanuwero, an old man in his late sixties, lives in Ruwa Township. On his plot is a barber shop. Fanuwero claims that he is a member of the Jehovah's Witnesses' sect. Like Aphiri, his origins are Malawi. Before retirement, he was working for some private company in Ardbenie, Waterfalls in Harare. In his working days he had rented accommodation in the same area as his workplace. Some years down his labour service, the company gave him a loan to build a house after he got a stand in Ruwa. The house is not yet 'finished' in the sense of painting and cladding. But Fanuwero managed to get to this present stage of completion as he was still employed. Now that he is retired, he has not been in a position to finish as he had planned. He no longer hopes that he will ever get money to get this work done.

In a bid to address 'bread and butter' issues Fanuwero is renting out the barbershop. On the plot, Fanuwero has planted some fruit trees. He has two lodgers in the house. The proceeds are inadequate in terms of meeting family daily needs. Ruwa Township, at the time of the study, is experiencing frequent power-cuts. Fanuwero's household sometimes uses firewood as an alternative energy source. But Mbuya Mubatsiri from the neighbouring farm often sends Melody, her servant with the wood to Fanuwero's place. This arrangement is explained by the friendship between Mbuya Mubatsiri and Fanuwero's wife. Though Fanuwero is not part of that friendship deal, he and the whole household are enjoying the fruit of the friendship.

Fanuwero's story shows how social capital is embedded in the housing and habitat provision. In addition, it shows the importance of financial capital in the development of shelter in peri-urban settlements. Employer-assisted housing is an important dimension to housing and as such overlooking its role may be detrimental in addressing the housing needs of the poor. A roof over a poor man's head makes a very big difference to that person and entire household. As well, there are financial flows that accrue to households which have space to let. Partly this is sanctioned through the provisions of Statutory Instrument 216 of 1994 (Use Group Regulations)[527].

---

[527] Chaeruka. J ; Munzwa. K, "Assessing Regulatory Framework Bottlenecks for Low-cost Housing in Zimbabwe, Final Draft Report," *UNHABITAT and the Government of Zimbabwe*, Harare.(2009); Kamete.A. Y, "Restrictive control of urban high-density housing in Zimbabwe, deregulation and challenges for urban design," *Housing, Theory and Society,* 16(3): 136–151. (1999c)

In Plate 4.1, Ray, one of my research assistants is captured assisting Charity and Rumbidzai, to shell their maize by the roadside during the survey. The two women sell vegetables and fruits by the road junction just close to Old Windsor Primary School. Charity and Rumbidzai explain the reasons for placing their market by the junction. The reasons are two-fold: firstly, to capitalize on it as a meeting point of people from all directions, secondly, its proximity to their homes (just less than two hundred metres away). Charity and Rumbidzai elucidate that:

> "Takadzidziswa kuchechi kwedu kuti tishandise maoko edu. Takatoonawo kuti zvinotibatsira kuti tisasweronyeya vanhu nemakuhwa. Munoziva kuswera pamba usina chaunoita zvinokutuma kuita makuhwa." [We have been taught in our church to work with our hands. But we have also realised that this saves us from backbiting and gossiping. Just being at home and doing nothing is the reason why people end up gossiping.]

Plate 4.1: 'Capturing' customers by a road junction in Old Windsor Park. Charity and Rumbidzai explain why they have chosen the site in which they sell their goods (mainly vegetables). It is strategic and allows them to attend to customers while doing part of their household chores. In this photograph, they are shelling maize as they wait for customers. Their homes are just some 50 metres away from their working site. While their husbands are at their formal

jobs, these women do street trading partly to supplement household income and partly to occupy themselves. This is part of the story in gender relations in housing where men are said to 'build houses' and women 'make homes." The junction on which Charity and Rumbidzai have chosen could be a critical point for the supply of customers from all direction of the roads but road junctions should generally be free from obstructions especially to motorists. Good stewardship implies taking on board the concerns of the other users of the road or space and preventing accidents and environmental risks especially in neighbourhoods. (Survey, 2010)

These women have linked up their activities to what women are commonly known for – gossip. But they have learnt that spending much time at home can be gainfully converted into bringing extra money into the household by selling some goods to the neighbourhood. Also, in the era when formal jobs are scarce, young men have also learnt to enterprise. John and Michael are in their mid-twenties. They live in Zimre Park, Ruwa. We meet them pushing a wheel barrow full of firewood. It is an order by someone in Zimre Park. Michael explains how they operate and says, "This wheelbarrow, when full, costs only five dollars. Just tell us where you stay and we deliver them at your doorstep. We do all our work in preparing this firewood just across the road, in Sunway City. We can reduce the price for you." Gauging the size of the bundle of firewood with bundles in Epworth, going for about a dollar, this is five times more expensive than in Harare. The income-base of the clientele applies.

Unlike John and Michael who are mobile suppliers, other young men like Gamuchirai are 'hooked to the place' of operation. Gamuchirai lives in Ruwa Township. He is a young man in his late twenties who is working as craftsman as well as the marketer of a number of crafts that he makes. Plate 4.2 shows some birds on display for marketing. Gamuchirai is lodging on this plot where he produces and markets his birds and other crafts. Lodging means the landlord also stays on-plot. Chawada, the landlord is a man of understanding. He gave space to Gamuchirai for him to work and to market his products. However, the contract states that Gamuchirai must pay a fee for this space. Practically, it means Gamuchirai is paying rent for accommodation and for the space that he uses for market displays and production. Gamuchirai has accepted the offer and he is doing his operations on-plot. However, there are a few challenges he faces regarding marketing his products. He says that in the neighbourhood the prices are rather suppressed relative to selling in established and designated market places for crafts (for example at Avondale and Newlands shopping centres in Harare).

In recent times, Gamuchirai has observed that the landlord is arbitrarily hiking rentals as and when he feels that must happen. He thinks that Chawada's believes he is making super-profits yet his returns are just below expectations. In effect, the business is actually troubled in many ways. There are many other poor entrepreneurs working on-plot and have similar challenges as those of Gamuchirai. Like Gamuchirai, most of these are entrapped in the places they reside and operate at the moment. They fear to move because the chances are high that they might not find an accommodative place. Gamuchirai believes staying at Chawada's place is the solution. He says, "Better the devil that you know than the angel that you don't know." Indeed, local embeddedness does not only apply to big firms but also to household entrepreneurs. People are rational and will always calculate the benefits or lack of benefits associated with moving or staying in a place.

Plate 4.2: Residential areas as space for manufacturing and marketing crafts, Ruwa Township. In this photograph, Ray, my research assistant holds a piece of 'bird' craft made and being marketed by Gamuchirai. The stand belongs to

Chawada. Stand owners as stewards of places decide activities that they can allow on their stands or plots and those they do not. Overall, this is in keeping with Statutory Instrument 216 of 1994 (Use Groups) which allows certain uses to be done with the residential areas. We can trace a hierarchy of stewardship in which the central government has allowed local authorities to allow residents to use residential space partly for residential and partly for industrial (especially light manufacturing as services) purposes. This 'right' has been extended to 'landlords' who then allow their tenants and lodgers to enjoy the rights but at a fee. Sometimes this manufacturing brings with it certain nuisances particularly noise as welding, in this case, is synonymous with neighbourhood noise. To allow for such noise in a neighbourhood requires great solidarity and tolerance. Stewardship becomes a neighbourhood concern which must be communicated and shared among the neighbours. Without such communication, it becomes a matter of the prisoner's dilemma in which households think rationally and try to find out what they may lose by not doing what the rest are doing. (Survey, 2010)

Marjorie is a housewife who stays in Zimre Park. She now displays her fruits and vegetables in her veranda (see Plate 4.3). The reason for using the veranda is that it ensures that the vegetables do not wilt in the heat of the sun. It also allows her to do other duties in the home (like cleaning the rooms and utensils and cooking) without having much to bother as customers come to buy from her place. This is a distance-reduction measure. Marjorie says, "Customers just knock at the door and I can hear that loudly and clearly. Thus, I attend to them instantly." In Ruwa, peri-urban dwellers make maximum use of the space in and around their plots. This has an important bearing on their livelihoods as well as the general quality of the habitat[528]. In a habitat, on important factor is the quality of houses themselves.

---

[528] Neefjes, "Environments and Livelihoods for Sustainability," *OXFAM GB*, London.(2000);); Nhema. F, "Speech By The Minister Of Environment And Natural Resources Management Hon. Francis Nhema (MP) At The National Housing Convention at Victoria Falls, 28 October 2009." (2009);

Plate 4.3: Vegetable on sale in a veranda, ZIMRE Park. In a neighbourhood, households will identify items that are missing and enterprise in such. The house becomes not only a place for sleeping, cooking and resting but also a place on which commercial enterprise is conducted. Issues of public health can be overlooked by those enterprising. In this picture, the veranda in which the vegetables on sale are displayed has, in its immediate vicinity, a structure which serves as toilet in times when running water is not available. This is dangerous especially after cases of diarrhoea, cholera, typhoid and dysentery are common in the peri-urban settlements. (Survey, 2010)

It is important to look at quality from the angle of house or plot use conversions. Residential conversions are a common feature in Ruwa. In Ruwa, there are a number of cases where residential plots have been converted to 'commercial' or 'institutional' space usage. The usual expectation is that such conversions are peculiar to inner-cities where space has become too limited for new expansion[529].

---

[529] Geraedts;Van der Voordt, (2007);Gappert,"The future of urban environments: implications for the business community," *Business Horizons*. Available:< http://findarticles.com> (1993); Fry, (2004);Garau et al. "A Home in the City: Urban Millennium Project Report on Improving the Lives of Slum Dwellers,". *Global Urban Development Magazine 2(1)*, Global Urban Development (GUD): London. URL: http://www.globalurban.org, Accessed on 22 April 2008.(2006); Grant. J, "Encouraging mixed use in practice. Paper prepared for, International Planning Symposium on *Incentives, Regulations, and Plans –The Role of States and Nation-*

Near Old Windsor Primary School, there is a seemingly very big house (Plate 4.4). It is Westview Primary School whose operations began in January 2010.

Plate 4.4: House-turned-school in Old Windsor Park. Converting houses for other purposes is common but especially in city centres as location plays an important role in price (rental) determination. Nevertheless, conversions are also part of the peri-urban story. Where multiple home-owners, despite the existence of a policy that one who owns a residential property in Harare cannot own other properties within Greater Harare, it is still possible through having a political muscle to own many houses. Politicians tend to short-change voters as they put policies which they (the politicians) violate. This is bad stewardship. While the superstructure here is bigger enough for the requirements of a small family, it is smaller for a school which requires more space to accommodate uses including for sport and recreation. The question remains if proper town planning procedures have been followed in the acquisition of the space outside the building to accommodate the ground for sports and recreation. Corruption paints a bad picture to good stewardship endeavours. (Survey, 2010)

The new school has Grades 1 to 6 classes and one of the teachers explains: "A new school does not start with Grade 7..." For a town planner, a number of questions can be raised regarding use of the facilities, conversion procedures followed, numbers of pupils hence demand,

---

States in Smart Growth Planning," National Centre for Smart Growth Research and Education, University of Maryland, Habiforum Foundation, The Netherlands, Maryland Department of Planning, September 30 – October 1, 2004: Available:< http://www.smartgrowth.umd.edu>(2004)

provision of attendant and supporting facilities (including adequacy of playgrounds for extracurricular activities). All these factors arise given the smallness of the stand in which the school stands. The "whole process of conversion" is purported to have gone through the town planning procedures and "no objections have been made about the school by the community"[530]. Inside the building, the kitchen has been converted to a computer laboratory. This laboratory is furnished with all sorts of flat screen computers and walls are inscribed with some messages about the Yahoo search engine.

This 'converted big house' (Westview Primary School premise) belongs to one of the late Zimbabwean ambassadors. It was on one of ambassador mission trips to Zambia that he saw the guest house that his fellow Zambian ambassador had built. He was so impressed that he decided to have a similar design. He imported and implemented it on one of his stands in Ruwa. The guest house is designed like a hotel. As he was almost completing this grand project, the ambassador unfortunately died. The widow to the late ambassador, found the 'house' too big for family use. As such, she decided to lease it out for other purposes. A certain Mr. Nyama has taken over the premise which he now runs a private school, Westview Primary School.

Mr. Marata purports that the local board (now Ruwa Town Council) has been in full support of the developments taking place at the new school. As a goodwill gesture to the school project, the council made a donation of a piece of land (more than 2000 square metres outside the premise for the development of school grounds). No doubt this is a case of converting a passive open space to an active open space. Apparent, in this virgin land is its placement within the radius and catchment of a wetland. Obviously, the wetland has been lost paving way to a human-induced development and this, in a way, is a vote towards ecological harm as opposed to protection[531] .

---

[530] Interview, Mr. Marata, 18 March 2010

[531] de Sherbinin. A;Martine.G,"Urban Population Development and Environment Dynamics," *Committee for International Cooperation in National Research in Demography*, Paris.<URL:http://www.cicred.org/Eng/Publications/pdf/Policy papers /PP3.pdf>, *Accessed on 22 April 2008*.(2007)

Again, in Zimre Park, Ruwa, there is also private secondary school called Rose of Sharon. It is owned and run by a local organisation which is registered as a Trust. Fees are pegged at two hundred dollars (US$200) per term. The premise is residential hence has limited space for support of lessons in the extramural bracket. School children attending Rose of Sharon indicate that they carry out sporting practice at local primary school grounds. This is similar to the situation of the Westview Primary School where extra-curricular activities are sacrificed because the space for such is not available.

In Ruwa, near the Town Council offices, just about hundred metres to the north, along Chiremba Road, the Guru family converted their residence into vehicle servicing centre (a garage). A host of cars 'litter' the yard. The family now occupies the cottage. The main house has been compartmentalised to house the office and the storehouse. In no uncertain terms, this is a case of business and materials (spares) displacing the dwellers. Muchengeti, the garage manager indicates that it is more rewarding having the house as a garage than renting it out to people. In other words, the house is more useful in enhancing the income requirements of his household than using it for residence only. Families can sacrifice their comfort for money.

Paintings and decorations are part of investment made in human habitats. Yet not all cases are matters of housing conversion In Zimre Park, for example, there is a church building like structure which has an inscription JESUS IS LORD on it. Much of the structure is glassy in outlook. Being in juxtaposition with the Seventh Day Church premise, indeed one is made to think this area is a church site harbouring so many church buildings. But the beautiful house is owned by a Nigerian businessman, Ochukwu whose shops are found in the CBD of Harare. Unlike Epworth, Ruwa has managed to attract many foreigners who can be labelled as 'the haves," that is, people of the elite class. When such classes are in a place, they are less constrained in terms of speaking their voices up and demanding accountability on the property tax which they contribute. Yet, Ruwa has remained for years without adequate water supplies. Instead there have been individual efforts on plots by households providing water. It is only now that the Town Council is seriously considering piped water connections[532]. Ruwa, on the other hand, is different; the settlements are greatly planned though some maintenance challenges have emerged in the past ten years or so. As Plate 4.5 shows some of the services like telegraph wires are in a forlorn state of repair. With the economic doldrums that Zimbabwe as a country has experienced in the past fifteen years or so, the place has also had a lot of developmental setbacks.

Plate 4.5: Part of Old Windsor Park. Peri-urban farming is now a common feature. Houses are normally situated in the obscurity of plants growing, in this case maize. The roads are filled with potholes. Electricity pylons are not well attended to. These are all the responsibilities of the local authority which must enforce measures to ensure that environmental quality is achieved including street lighting, clean environments. From the year 2000 to 2013, local authorities are working with limited budgets leading to their incapacity to provide basic services to residents who are the tax payers. Strategies including participatory budgeting and good governance could assist but they work best if the macro-economic environment is conducive to allow for progressive development. People embark on informal urban and peri-urban farming to cushion themselves against the vagaries of macro-economic instability such as typified Zimbabwe, between 2006 and 2008. (Survey, 2010)

---

[532] (Ruwa, 2010)

Humankind always interferes with nature for critical developmental needs. One relevant case in point is the blasting of rock outcrops in Sunway City, Ruwa to pave way for housing development (Plate 4.6). For low-income housing development, while blasting is affordable and to allow for the laying of pipes (water and sewer) by public utility providers, it is not 'cheap' for individual poor households, particularly illegal land occupiers in this case in Epworth[533]. Sunway City, at the time of the fieldwork, has been proposed for housing development.

Plate 4.6: Blasting the Rocks: Paving way for residential development in Sunway City. Housing construction results in the destruction of the natural physical environment. Source: Field Survey (2010)

Rock blasting to pave way for housing development is a function of income and individual discretion. For some relatively wealthy households in Ruwa, a notable sense of preservation of the natural environmental features like rock outcrops is noted in areas such as Winsor Park and Fairview. Inhabitants of such areas aim at preserving the already

---

533 Mapira.J, An Historical Perspective of the Problem of Housing and Some Attempted Solutions in the City of Mutare (1890-2002). *Zambezia* XXXI (i/ii), University of Zimbabwe, Harare: pp 80-103 (2004); UNCHS, "An Urbanising World: Global Report on Human Settlements," *Oxford University Press*, United Kingdom, (1996); UNCHS, "Proceedings of the International Conference on Urban Poverty, 9 – 13 November 1997," *Florence, Italy. UNCHS*, Nairobi. (1998)

present plant species with little, if any harm to the natural environment. As such, they act as 'good stewards' of the environment. Predominantly the houses in Ruwa (59.1%) are brick and mortar under tiles followed by those of brick and mortar under asbestos (Table 8.5) on the next page.

Table 8.5: Materials used on Main Dwelling on Plot (%) (Survey, 2010)

Aspect	Percentage (%)
brick and mortar under tiles	59.1
brick and mortar under asbestos	32.47
brick and mortar under corrugated iron sheets	5.84
pole and dagga under thatch	0
pole and dagga under asbestos	0.65
pole and dagga under corrugated iron sheets	0
wood under thatch	0
wood under asbestos	1.95
wood under plastic	0
Other	0
Total	100

N=154

Inhabitants of Ruwa used the plots for various purposes but the main activity (74.5%) is gardening (see Table 8.6).

Table 8.6: On-plot activities by Ruwa peri-urban dwellers (Survey, 2010)

Activity	Frequency	Percentage (%)
Gardening	114	74.03
Welding	4	2.6
Poultry	1	0.65
Church	0	0
Extra lessons	0	0
Other	6	3.9
N/A	29	18.83
Total	154	100

N=154

This is probably explained by the fact that the area is historically known for peri-urban farming most which was done for market gardening.

However, the plots have significantly been reduced in the town so that the gardening that takes place there is more for subsistence than commercial basis. Converting land for urban development 'shrinks' space that initially afforded activities for farming to take place. A Munwahuku Stream passes between Damofalls and ZIMRE Park in Ruwa and Mabvuku (Harare). This tributary stream is in a horrible state in terms of degradation. Most times, the water looks dirty. Lorries negotiate the way on the swampy terrain to ferry sand from the Munwahuku's banks and bed. The miners say river sand is more expensive than pit sand. In Ruwa, river sand is pegged at sixty dollars per five-cubic while pit sand goes for fifty. Firimoni, the sand marketer says, "Our clients come here to buy. We have heaps and heaps of sand down there. Once we get a buyer, we load the truck for delivery. We have to be strategic and organised otherwise we scare our customer."

As the employment issue is of critical concern in Ruwa the majority of the peri-urban dwellers have embarked on informal means for survival. The need for livelihood enhancement has led them to seek 'maximum' utilisation of space around[534]. Among the peri-urban dwellers there are others who believe that seeking formal employment is still a viable option. A case in point, are the hordes of employment seekers sitting outside industrial premises in Ruwa (Ruwa Industrial Area). At one premise a group approaches us with questions indicative of the desperation they have for jobs and one man in the group asks, "What business can we give you today? Don't you want to hire us for help?"

In the industrial areas, people wait eagerly for opportunities to occur. Yet not everyone who sits by the gate is a (formal or even informal) jobseeker. For instance, a certain group of women who belong to white garment church (*mapositori*) are sometimes seen sitting by some gates. I ask them what they intend to do. They indicate to me that the premise whose gate they sit by is a furniture manufacturing company. They point out that they are from Epworth and are queuing to buy saw-dust - a waste

[534] Rubin. M, "Inner-city redevelopment programmes and its impact on housing and evictions. Presentation made at Refresher Course on Urbanising Africa," *the city centre revisited at Witwatersrand University, Johannesburg: 16-27 August 2010* (2010:1)

product from the timber processing. One of them says that, "In Epworth, where we stay, we don't have electricity. We buy the saw-dust and we use in place of electricity. It is our source of energy. This sack, I am holding, is filled at a cost of a dollar. Firewood is expensive; the same with paraffin. It's a story of survival hence we look for what is cheap for us."[535] To confirm the woman's words, Tariro, one woman in Solani some three days later, demonstrates how they use a heating devise in which they pour saw dust. I have also discovered that the selling of saw-dust is a common feature in Epworth. They buy a little firewood and put it together with the sawdust. To them, this is a cost-saving measure as this lessens the cost of energy for consumption by their households.

Although, it is a constitutional right to enjoy resources endowed in a habitat, the place is under grave environmental assault. River and pit sand extraction is the order of the day. White garment churches are also everywhere in the area. The vleis are heavily cultivated and a host of dumps have been created on the ground. They get filled with water, especially during the wet season. Heavy goods trucks used in the transportation of building materials disturb vegetation and soils. This triggers massive soil erosion which in turn results in enormous siltation of the rivers and streams in the area. This concurs with one study in peri-urban Maseru in Lesotho which associates urban development with the negative externalities of massive soil erosion[536]. Nevertheless, the same sands deposited in the rivers is mined and transported away from the rivers to plots. The miners are not really mindful of the degradation processes but are mainly after making money. Firimoni says these dumps are a residue of actions by brick moulders. Along the tarmac, on the edge of ZIMRE Park are some dumped ramshackle and out of use cars and piles of bricks.

The foregoing paragraphs have shown indicated that while Ruwa cannot be purely taken as peri-urban because of its built-up qualities (having been established more as a defined 'urban' development in recent years), it is a settlement that rapidly turned urban. To explain its growth, the role of the private sector in the development of the town is the major

535 Interview 12 February, 2011

536 Rownstree et al (1991)

driver in spatial development. Moreover, the area is in administration and political ambivalence threatening housing endeavours as it belongs to two provinces simultaneously. Such an ambiguity has also meant that the provision of housing attendant services (cemeteries, for example) is also under threat given the existence of indistinctness in authorities. Politically such a move is done by political parties to ensure that development is patterned by the wishes of such parties rather than the peri-urban dwellers themselves. Nonetheless, in Ruwa, the town management strongly believes in partnerships with its stakeholders. In this regard, one can categorically pinpoint that the town, from its genesis in the late 1980s to date, has been run largely as corporatist basis where business contracts including memoranda of understanding define the scope and purse of development.

Besides, in Ruwa, the internal process in community dynamics are major explanation as to why Ruwa has grown well (relative to Epworth), for example the majority of community member (37%) are owners of the existing housing stock as depicted in this study. Relative to Epworth, the other study area, Ruwa has higher quality housing the reason being the dominance of the middle-income classes in the areas. The Ruwa community base implies strong ownership of the development processes taking place in the area. Indeed, the spearheading of the processes by community leaders including ward councillors cannot be underestimated. The chapter has also shown that, like any other place in Zimbabwe, a good number of residents in Ruwa embark on a number of livelihood activities some of which show good stewardship of place (for example paintings and decorations of houses and grass cutting) while other practices (like streambank cultivation and dumping of waste on undesignated sites) are symptomatic of bad stewardship.

Housing conversions to accommodate non-residential uses are rampant in Ruwa. This is further compounded by the fact of the existence of a gap between in land uses. For instance, there are fewer schools in Ruwa which may explain the rampancy of conversions as business-minded people take advantage of such. In a way, this may be a pointer to the fact that they acknowledge that their 'eyes are open' to see gaps needing attention within their communities. Wherever houses develop, it follows as night follows day that, attendant services must also be provided. That conversions take place and the local authority seems to sanction or give a blind eye to 'unwanted' developments that produce eye sores and also do not need to sound environmental practices that is a sign of bad stewardship. However, there are limits to which the local authority can determine behaviour of community member especially in the context of high levels of poverty, politically-driven misdemeanours, corruption.

Finally, the chapter has also revealed that the fact that households buy by-products like saw dust for use in their homes for energy, show good products stewardship meaning that even waste can still be utilised for in other everyday processes of life. With respect to waste management, this follows the principles of the 3 Rs – Reduce, Reuse and Recycle. However, the same materials used can be a cause of concern with respect to human health as the result in increased carbon footprint in the environment. Overall, the study has revealed a number of defined aspects in peri-urban stewardship of Ruwa. Some dimensions have to do with physical processes, others with the political and administrative processes while others are based on contractual hence legal parameters. It is very clear that historical and contemporary dynamics help to define the processes and institutional responses that define place stewardship. The next chapter will focus on the realities and experiences in Epworth.

CHAPTER 9
HOUSING AND STEWARDSHIP IN EPWORTH

It is observed that physical space is "… social, cultural and political space: a space that offers, enables, triggers, invites, prescribes, proscribes, polices or enforces certain patterns of social behaviour; a space that is never no man's land but always somebody's space; a historical space, therefore, full of codes, expectations, norms and traditions; and a space of power controlled by as well as controlling people. We know all of that. Yet, it is not enough to merely exclaim this; it needs to be demonstrated and therefore requires careful and meticulous moves."[537] The chapter demonstrates housing and stewardship in Epworth showing the different processes in housing and place stewardship in the peri-urban settlement. In keeping with the assertion, the "social, cultural and political space" of Epworth has largely, contrary to beliefs by both some locals and outsiders, as "...never no man's land but always somebody's space..."[538] Over the years there have been efforts to regularise the settlement so that it may be fully incorporated as part of Harare City. Despite efforts to regularise the settlement, challenges of new settlers coming into Epworth continued. The settlement's seven wards (see Figure 9.1) are marked by a mosaic of house structures that detail is as more slum than anything. The largest group of the newcomers are harboured in Ward 7 of the settlement others have settled in portions of the other Wards. Ward 7 and these other areas are informally referred to as 'Gada,' loosely translating to *'free riders.'* It must be stressed that this 'new breed' of settlers are illegal and informal.

---

[537] Blommaert. J, "Chronicles of complexity - Ethnography, superdiversity, and linguistic landscapes," *Tilburg Papers in Culture Studies, Paper 29*, Tilburg University and Ghent University.(2012:7)

[538] Ibid, pp7)

By 2007, it is reported, that the Local Board was finding it difficult to carry out planned developmental projects, the informal settlers sat on most of the sites earmarked for development projects (school sites, hospital sites, electricity substations and other areas)[539]. It is also estimated that in 2008, Epworth had over 18,000 informal or illegal settlers. Interestingly the officially approved residential stands have not increased significantly from the originally regularised 6000 stands[540]. In this vein, the matter of concern is that illegal and informal settlements have continued to flourish despite the establishment of the Epworth Local Board whose very purpose of establishment was to ensure that no future non-permitted development would take place in the area with in mind the long-term objective of incorporating a regularised Epworth town into City of Harare. Presently, close to 70% of the Epworth residents largely live in overcrowded non-permitted, unplanned and un-serviced areas. The squatter settlements continue to have very high levels of challenges related to health, poverty and crime.

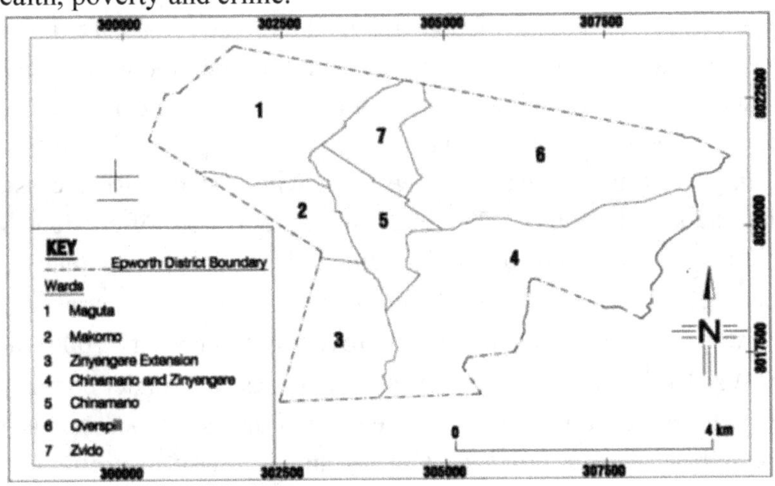

Figure 9.1: Wards in Epworth[541]

[539] Epworth, "Local Board Treasury Report on Debtors Databank," *ELB*, Epworth.(2007)
[540] Ibid, 2007
[541] Chanza ; Chirisa. I,, "How Will Climate Change Transform African Local Governance?"Assessing the Role of Civic Engagement. *Journal of Public Administration and Policy Research* 1(2): pp 035-046.(2011)

In post-2000 Epworth, a number of housing and environmental issues have been discussed in a number of meetings of the area. The following paragraphs are devoted to the unravelling of some of these issues. But it must be noted that when the Government mooted Operation Murambatsvina in 2005, Epworth was to be treated as something sacrosanct hence remained untouched. This is despite the poor housing structures that Epworth has relative to other settlements in the country. Several times 'clean up' campaigns missed it: first in the 1980s, then in 2005 and then after 2009. This is partly explained by the investment made to upgrade the settlement with the Government working in partnership with various players in the upgrading projects of the 1980s.

Little progress is reported having been made in housing development apart from the opening of roads and beacons for 420 stands in the first sub-phase being spearheaded by Shelter Zimbabwe at the Mabvazuva Housing Development[542]. In this respect only two residential building plans and one commercial plan were approved by the Local Board, during the month of September 2004. Yet, it is stated that ten residential building plans were approved during the month of June 2005. It is shown that the Building Inspectorate Division had notified on an increase in the submission of building plans for approval due to the then on-going clean-up campaign. Eleven residential stands were cessioned during the month of June. The increase in the number of cessions being recorded was attributed to the clean-up campaign. This saw many stand holders regularising their illegal subdivisions[543]. Ten residential building plans were reported to have been approved as of February 2006, mostly from Ward 4[544]. In the same feedback, 14 houses were under construction during the period under review; twenty-two and sixteen cessions were processed during the month of January and February respectively. This decline noted was attributable to the number of owner-initiated cessions during the same period. Initiatives to spearhead the electrification of

---

[542] Epworth, "Minutes of the Land and Environmental Management Committee," Meeting Number 103 (3 November 2004)

[543] Epworth, "Minutes of the Land and Environmental Management Committee," Meeting Number 107(13 July 2005)

[544] Epworth, "Minutes of the Land and Environmental Management Committee," Meeting Number 125(25 July 2007)

Epworth were suggested to match the realignment of the servitude at the proposed power station. It is further pointed out that beneficiaries of Operation Garikayi were listed by this period based on conformation. A claim for stand 1786 by a certain man (resident) was dismissed[545].

Twelve building plans, seven cottages and two main houses were approved during the month of June 2007 with fourteen cessions for residential stands being processed during the same period[546]. Meanwhile, 100 houses under the first phase of Operation Garikai were handed over to beneficiaries. The minutes point out to one application for claim of stand. It was alleged that stand 2434 (with a possible subdivision) allocated to Mr Gwande (not real name) and Mr Gomo (not real name) under Operation Garikayi was allocated to him by the headman in 1982. However, the claim was dismissed citing that the stand was vacant the time it was allocated to the beneficiaries of Operation Garikayi. Eleven residential building plans, eight of them in Glenwood were approved during the month of October 2008. It was reports that most construction activities were confined to Rockview Park with very little activity in other areas. Thirteen cessions for residential stands were processed during the month of October. The building inspectorate reports that three beneficiaries of the Glenwood housing project had started constructing approved structures while 905 beneficiaries were shown their stands. Five residential and two garage building plans were approved during the month of October 2009. Seven cessions of residential stands were processed during the same month. The need to issue title deeds to all areas with approved plans was discussed and consolidations were to explore the possibility of doing that. Twenty-five residential building plans were approved during the month of June 2010. Five cessions of residential stands were processed during the same month. It was reports that housing and engineering sections had started bookings for physical handover of stands to beneficiaries of the Glenwood Housing Project. Contractor for roads was on site for the Rockview Park Housing project

545 Ibid.

546 Epworth, "Minutes of the Land and Environmental Management Committee," Meeting Number 2(13 November 2008)

Idle sewer ponds in Chinamano are sited in the middle of the residential area, making them a health hazard if used[547]. In addition, informal settlers have built dwelling structures on the edge of ponds. In addition, deep gullies left by illegal extraction of sand recognised in Glenwood housing project. Sand extraction by illegal or sand poachers has been observed along Jacha River[548]. One application for renewal of sand extraction permit from Shamwari Cooperative was received and subsequently turned down. A Chinese construction company also applied for a permit to extract 500 cubic metres of pit sand from Epworth. This was turned down as well. Epworth could not afford to provide such huge quantities. The board notes with concern that sand extraction was likely to add to the environmental challenges caused by lack of capacity to reclaim areas damaged by illegal sand extraction. The Building Inspectorate Department encouraged residents in Solani to build ecological sanitation (shortened as *ecosan*) toilets[549]. These, as argued, do not pollute the ground water sources.

Open spaces are very useful in residential development for providing the urban space with 'breathers' and recreation by the residents. However, sometimes such open spaces are 'invaded' by other uses like peri-urban farming, open air worshippers' services and dumping of waste (Plate 9.1) on the next page.

---

[547] (Epworth,) "Minutes of the Land and Environmental Management Committee," Meeting Number 111,9 March 2006)

[548] Epworth, "*Minutes of the Land and Environmental Management Committee," Meeting Number 12,(4* November 2009)

[549] Epworth, "*Minutes of the Land and Environmental Management Committee," Meeting Number 19,(10 July 2010)*

Plate 9.1: Worship time in Cell 7. A white garment church is in a time of worship in a vlei area in Cell 7. This is a common feature with these churches which identify certain sites in open spaces. Such spaces are treated as 'holy grounds' by the churches and do not allow other members of the community to use the places. This development brings about the notion of 'privatisation' of public space. Good place stewardship is shown by the groups protecting the spaces and blocking others and putting 'holy tags' to the space. That such places are usually without supportive infrastructure like toilets and water supply systems and that they are encroachments in wild spaces and wetlands, may be taken for bad place stewardship. (Survey, 2010)

One important observation as well is the use of open spaces. Religious groups, especially the white garment apostolic sects *(mapositori)* mostly have 'sacred shrines' in the vleis and small hills which they refer to as kuMasowe (the wilderness). Once the *mapositori* identify a shrine, some mark their worshipping place by graffiti. The public open space becomes privatised hence exclusion of any other person who may want to come and worship on such 'holy grounds' or use it for a different purpose. The disquieting observation is that of the absence of toilets and ablution on these off-plot sites of religious importance. This poses health and environmental challenges hence the fear for such water-borne diseases like cholera, diarrhoea, typhoid and dysentery. Other groups like the Jehovah's Witnesses use streets and crossroads to preach and sell books and pamphlets. Domboramwari in Epworth is a colony for church activities with a host of church buildings under construction. All these have a bearing on the living environment in the peri-urban just like anywhere else. On the other hand, the major part of Epworth is not serviced by proper roads, except the upgraded area and the new section being developed by Shelter-Zimbabwe. Overall, in both settlements, the display of goods for sale by roadsides is a common feature. Roads in urban development are part of modest planning considerations. In the development of a neighbourhood unit, of which housing is the dominant constituent, roads service the neighbourhood. But over the years, informal traders have 'invaded' the roadside for marketing their different wares and commodities (see Plate 9.2).

Plate 9.2: Street trading in Overspill. Households have turned public spaces like roadsides as spaces in which they display their wares and goods for sale. Under normal circumstances, such spaces should be reserved for vehicular traffic only and that physical markets are provided for by local authorities. Street traders take advantage of the people using the road to be buyers of their goods. Ideally, the locally authority should have control of areas like roads and open spaces so that they are not abused by the public. Nevertheless, high unemployment rates in the country put local authorities in a fix and dilemma since windows like employment creation by luring foreign investment is a taxing challenge including to the central government. (Survey, 2010)

In Epworth, there is an array of the types of housing tenure arrangements. The dominant tenure arrangement is the owner/purchaser type - 37% - (though for Epworth this is not in the strictest sense of freehold titling). This is followed by the lodging arrangement (27%). Lodging and tenants are taken as separate tenure arrangement in this study where the former refers to the housing arrangement in which the owner uses part of the stand or house and then sublets the other rooms. Tenancy is taken to mean that the owner is completely absent on-plot. Normally, he or she only visits (from where he/she resides) to collect rentals. It emerged in both towns that some houses belong to friends or parents, 7% and 9% percent, respectively. These two (houses belonging to friends or parents) are perhaps extensions of the owner/purchaser category. It is argued that the land tenure system in Epworth has been "... abuse with a number of illegal land disposal involving self-appointed headmen, con-artists and the occupants changing hands without following the requisite procedures. This has resulted in a number of untraceable absent registered occupiers who have either sold stateland or unpaid huge debts for rates and services."[550]

The immediate occupants hold properties in trust as the real owners are away. In a number of cases the owners are found to be residing in other parts of the town, in the rural area or having gone abroad. Table 9.1 summarises the housing tenure arrangements in Epworth. As already indicated in the owners/purchaser is the lead category (37%) followed by lodger type (30%), followed by tenancy (15%) and held in trust by a friend (2%).

Table 9.1: Household Tenure Status of Respondents in Epworth (Survey, 2010)

Status in Accommodation	Frequency	Percentage (%)
Owner/Purchaser	50	37
Tenant	20	15
Lodger	41	30
Tied Accommodation	4	3
Property belongs to friend	3	2
Property belongs to parents	13	10
Other	6	4
Total	137	100

N = 137

[550] Epworth, "Epworth Local Board Development Proposals," ELB, Epworth ,(2002:8)

The survey has sought to understand how peri-urbanisation manifests itself through migration patterns. It has revealed that Zimbabwe, like most developing countries, is undergoing a process of rapid urbanisation[551]. The frequency of visiting rural homes is noted in the study as a key indicator in describing urbanisation. Very few (2.75%) from both Ruwa and Epworth indicate that they visit their rural homes once week (Table 9.2). Quite a significant number of the respondents (37.11%) show that they visit once in a year. Twenty-point two seven percent (20.27%) are unclear in their responses. The general trend and pattern are that rural ties with the majority of the peri-urbanites are dying out. This concurs with the researches that people are increasingly becoming *homo urbanus*, i.e. tending towards living in urban areas. It is in this process, that the shelter question and its provision become an issue[552].

Table 9.2: Frequency of going to the rural home by Epworth respondents (%) (Survey, 2010)

Aspect	Percentage (%)
Once a week	2.92
Once a month	8.03
Once a year	29.2
Once in two years	6.57
Never	29.2
Not Clear	24.1
Total	100

N=137

Overall, the migration pattern emerging from the study is: rural-urban, then urban (core city) to peri-urban. People are pushed or pulled to certain places for various reasons. Asked where they stayed before coming

[551] UNHABITAT, "*The state of African cities 2008: A framework for addressing urban challenges in Africa,*" UNHABITAT: Nairobi.(2008); UNHABITAT," Global report on human settlements 2009," *Planning sustainable cities*: UNHABITAT, Earthscan (2009);Tibaijuka A.K, "Building Prosperity – Housing and Economic Development Earthscan" London. (2009); Shildo.G, "Housing Policy in Developing Countries," *Routledge*, London. (1990)

[552] UNHABITAT, "*The state of African cities 2008: A framework for addressing urban challenges in Africa,*" UNHABITAT: Nairobi.(2008); UNHABITAT,"Global report on human settlements 2009," *Planning sustainable cities*: UNHABITAT, Earthscan (2009),

to Epworth, the majority (48%) state that they came from the capital city, Harare (Figure 9.2).

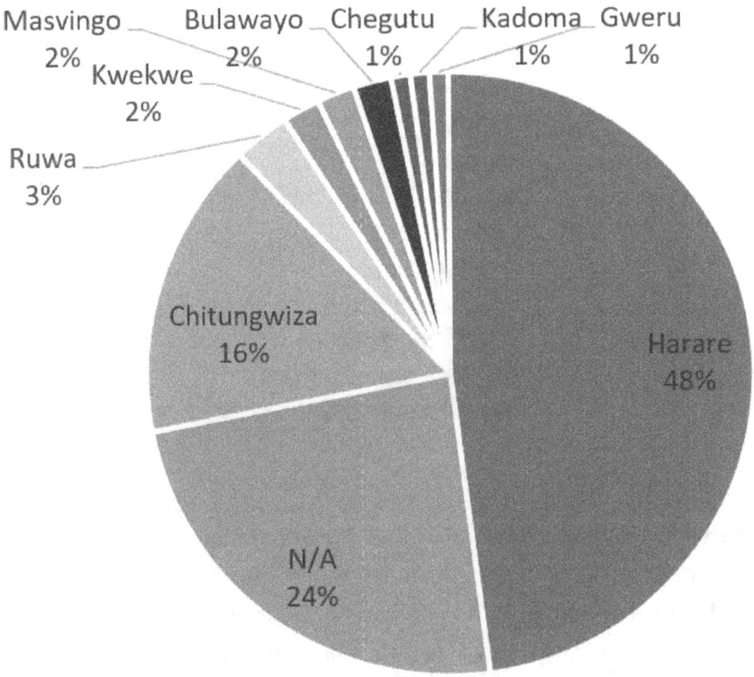

N=137

Figure 9.2: Place of Stay before coming to Epworth (%). (Survey, 2010)

The majority for Epworth, most respondents state that they came because they were looking for cheaper accommodation or freer conditions of dwelling. A significant percentage of the respondents (16%) came from Chitungwiza. Chitungwiza is Harare dormitory town that was established in the colonial days. The other respondents (24%) indicated that they were born and bred in Epworth. As such, they have not moved in from anywhere. Rather they are products of the natural increase. A very insignificant number (9%, in total) indicates that it stayed in towns and cities like Kwekwe, Chegutu, Masvingo, and Bulawayo before coming to Epworth. Further on, the survey sought to establish the places where the respondents were born. Figure 5:3 shows the distribution pattern of respondents in Epworth regarding their places of birth.

Figure 9.3: Place of birth

N=137

Figure 9.3: Percentage Rating of Pull factors to Town (%) (Survey, 2010)

For Epworth, the majority of the residents were born in Harare (21%). This is followed by those born in the three Mashonaland Provinces (East, 14%; West, 10% and Central, 9%) totalling 33%. Sixteen percent (16%) were born in Manicaland and 8% from Masvingo. Only 2% were born in other countries, like Malawi and Zambia. Most of the respondents who migrated into the two peri-urban settlements indicate that Harare was their first destination before they relocated to the two towns (54%). For the recent migrants, the pull factors by Epworth are shown in Table 9.3.

Table 9.3: Pull factors by Epworth respondents (Survey, 2010)

Aspect	Percentage (%)
Affordable shelter	24.82
Peacefulness	7.3
Closeness to Harare	8.03
Closeness to job	8.03
Affordable life	27.7
Semi-rurality	2.9
Opportunities	4.4
Most of the above	18.25
Total	100

N=137

In summary, the main reasons cited are: affordability of shelter in the town (26.8%), general peacefulness of the area (19.59%) and closeness to Harare the capital city (17.5%). A sub-group of ancillary factors include: proximity to the place of employment (8.59%), general affordability of living in the peri-urban zone (16.49%), the semi-rural state of the settlement (1.72%), and availability of other opportunities, particularly self-employment and trade (2.06%). Some of the respondents (7.22%) indicate that they were attracted by a combination of these factors herein highlighted. Because they perceive that life in the peri-urban is 'reasonably' affordable, they offer better space for living than the city centres[553]. The reasons for moving away from the town of initial settlements are rated as in Table 9.4 and include: poor sanitation (1.95%), poor water availability (1.75%), rising rentals (14.78%), strictness of property owner (7.9%), search for own property (11%), eviction/*Murambatsvina* (7.22%); marriage (2.1%), employment opportunities (19.93%) and a combination of these other factors (2.41%).

Table 9.4: Push factors (%) (Survey, 2010)

Aspect	Percentage (%)
Poor sanitation	2.19
Poor water availability	1.46
Rising rentals	5.84
Strictness of property owner	5.11
Search for own property	2.92
Eviction/Murambatsvina	7.3
Marriage	2.19
Employment opportunities	34.31
Most of the above	0.73
N/A	37.96
Total	100

N=137

These factors are important matters to consider whenever the planning of settlements is to be achieved with some considerable strides of sustainability. This means ignoring such social factors will be prove heinous over time. Although, as noted in Chapter 4, most people moving

[553] Nabutola.W, "Affordable Housing – Some Experiences from Kenya," *Paper presented at the FIG Working Week 2004, Athens, Greece*, May 22-27, 2004 (2004)

into Ruwa state that they are attracted by expansive residential space mainly for the medium to high income classes, for Epworth, it is due to cheaper rentals for the low-income earners. The study has revealed that the poor are usually more footloose than well-to-do classes. This is evidenced by the fact that even upon arrival into Epworth, they still move from one plot to another (Figure 9.4). Such behaviour brings in a new pattern of intra-(peri-)urban migration. Reasons for the intra-urban movements include issues of sanitation, search for even lower rentals or marriage. In Epworth study respondents mention employment opportunities. Some respondents still cite eviction in the form of Operation Murambatsvina, which took place in[554].

Figure 9.4: Intra-settlement migration in Epworth (%) (Survey, 2010)

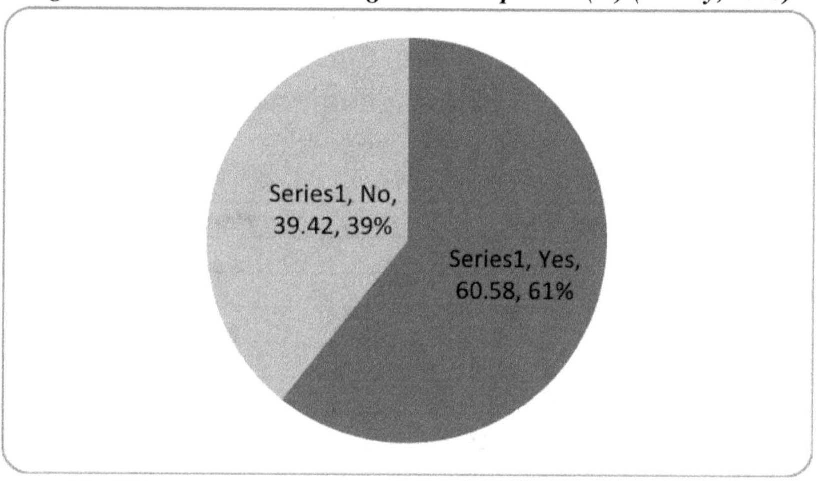

N=137

Overall, as people are becoming more permanent urban dwellers, it is important that the issue of 'adequate housing' be carefully examined[555]. To further describe the situation of housing in the two

---

[554] TibaijukaA. K, "Report of the Fact-Finding Mission to Zimbabwe to assess the Scope and Impact of Operation Murambatsvina," *UN Habitat*, Nairobi. (2005); Murowe.S; Chirisa.I, "Sally Mugabe Heights: The tale of an incidental Zimbabwean peri-urban housing scheme seeking legitimation," *Zambezia XXXIII (i/ii)*: pp71-89.(2006)

[555] Chirisa. I, "Population Growth and Rapid Urbanisation in Africa: Implications for Sustainability." *Journal of Sustainable Development in Africa 10(2),(2008)* pg.364-

settlements, it is important to examine the experiences and perceptions of the peri-urban dwellers, through life stories that some of them told in the course of the study.

Immediate west of Domboramwari is a place called kwaMadhonoro (Plate 9.3). Further west, a silhouette of the Harare International Airport can be seen. This name (kwaMadhonoro) is a corrupted version of MacDonald. Jambo (a respondent) says MacDonald was a farm owner on whose farm this Madhonoro settlement has sprouted.

Plate 9.3: A bird's eye view of the Magada of Madhonoro Area. Structures built follow a haphazard plan which defies a low-income residential layout plan that would emerge if existing town planning standards were applied – be it those stipulated by Circular No. 70 of 2004 or otherwise. Roofs are made of various materials – some corrugated iron sheets, others asbestos yet others grass. Plots are a mosaic of various shapes and sizes. Plot possessors use their space for various purposes the dominant one being peri-urban farming. In line with greening of peri-urban spaces, the plants grown play a pivotal role of being carbon sinks albeit being done unconsciously. This should be encouraged given that is part and parcel of good environmental stewardship. However, the fact

---

391 ; Jenkins. P,"African Cities: Competing claims on urban land," *News for the Nordic Africa Institute no. 3*: Nordic Africa Institute: Uppsala.(2006) ;Mbiba, "Contentious development: peri-urban studies in sub-Saharan Africa," in *Progress in Development Studies 2(2),* pp113-131 (2002);)

that some houses are located in wetlands and wildernesses, they tend to disrupt the ecological balance leading to biodiversity loss. (Survey, 2010)

Madhonoro is one of the settlements that are referred to as MaGada. Jambo explains his understanding of the word 'gada." To him it is derived from a Shona idiophonic construction meaning "purposeless sitting". Exactly this describes the way people just settled in the areas as in other areas in Epworth, the settlement which was informal and arbitrary. They settled wherever they wished, without seeking the permission of the authorities. This is a common development especially in Latin America with the Brazilian or Argentinean *favelas*, being the close parallel to the 'gada' style in Epworth.

In Chinamano area, in Epworth, Practical Action, a developmental oriented non-governmental organisation working in the area developed a 'demonstration house with an outside toilet' (Plate 9.4).

Plate 9.4: NGO 'demonstration house with an outside toilet' in Chinamano. The demonstration house appears to have been constructed using materials which most of the residents in Epworth cannot afford. Sustainable construction that takes on board good stewardship should be that which uses low-cost materials which last long. Without decent incomes, it is somewhat difficult to enforces the Grassroots Housing Process as explained by Alexander et al (1973), the one in which households have to build over time as and when they get resources to build. This demonstration house ought to have accommodated the concept of 'appropriate technology." Without the appropriateness of technology hence adhering to the concept of Payne and Majale's (2004)

'lowering the ladder," it remains a 'pie in the air," unreachable to man. Good stewardship is one in which responsible institutions are sensitive to the needs and requirements of the groups and communities whose cause they champion, advocate and lobby for. (Survey, 2010)

While the demonstration by Practical Action is very good looking and strong, in terms of both the strength and type of materials used, it remains very 'unreachable' for the generality of the people in Epworth whose household incomes, according to the survey, are predominantly around $74 (US dollars) per month[556]. If the NGO could source funds to try and provide for everyone, its targets are the 'poorest," there are other issues difficult to grapple with, for instance, the management and maintenance of the housing structures themselves. The question of scale for provision remains central. Perhaps that explains why the demonstration house has remained for quite some time without many replicas emerging in the settlement. There are limits to what NGOs can do. It is critical to look at the general living conditions of the peri-urban dwellers. However, it must be noted that in peri-urban and urban development, it is not only the local authority that is the determinant of what type of houses or materials can be used on them[557]. Non-governmental organisations can also be instrumental in determining materials that can be used, especially targeting the low-income earners.

Aphiri, of Malawian origin, lives in Magada, Epworth. He tells his story in which, among other things, migration, landlord-tenant relationships, use of rooms and outdoor space are highlighted. When his father came to Zimbabwe in the 1940s, he joined the labour force in the country as a farm worker. Aphiri thus grew up on a farm just outside

---

[556] Payne.G, "Urban Land Policy Options: Titles or Rights?" *Paper presented at the World Bank Urban Forum Westfields Marriott, Virginia, USA: 03-05 April, 2000.* (2000) <URL:http://www.worldbank.org/html/fpd/urban/forum2000/papers/ realestate.pdf> *Accessed on 27 June 2011*; Payne G. (ed.): "Land, Rights and Innovation – Improving tenure security for the urban poor," *ITDG Publishing*, London.(2002); [556] Payne.G, Majale. M, "The Urban Housing Manual: Making Regulatory Framework Work for the Poor," Earthscan, London. (2004); Kundu. A., "Chapter 8: Tenure security, housing investment and environmental improvement: the cases of Delhi and Ahmedabad, India. Payne Geoffrey (ed.), 2002: "Land, Rights and Innovation – Improving tenure security for the urban poor," *ITDG Publishing*, London.(2002)

[557] Stoll.L, "Regional Collaboration: A framework for solving complex planning problems." *The Land Tracker 6(2):* pp 1-4. (2006)

Salisbury (now Harare). As time went by and Aphiri also sought to find own employment, he got into the city, stayed in Dzivaresekwa HDRA for quite some time and then got married from which marriage he fathered five daughters. Since he was dependent on casual jobs as and when he got them, the inconsistent hikes in rental forced Aphiri to look for alternative accommodation elsewhere. Someone told him that in Epworth life could become bearable for him. In 2006, Aphiri moved to Epworth. Compared to Dzivaresekwa, the rentals are 'ridiculously low' (three times lower, per room). (see Plate 9.5 shows the 'house' that Aphiri is renting in Epworth.

Though all his daughters are married now, Aphiri regrets why he suffered in the hands of merciless landlords for years in order to meet the huge rental obligations against a small income he earned then. Aphiri stresses that "...the landlord was...hiking rents every month. My income was so low. Surprisingly, now I find this place free and guess what? For these two rooms I pay only fifteen dollars for rent." To him Epworth is more affordable in rentals. The house is a three-roomed structure but of the rooms, his family is using two. The other room, Aphiri says is occupied by another family.

Plate 9.5: On-plot Stewardship. In this photograph, the researcher poses with Aphiri under an avocado tree which is part of the features at the homestead on which Aphiri is renting. Planting trees in the age of the encouragement of

greening the environment and the creation of carbon sinks is a sign of good stewardship. However, this has been done unconsciously by the plot owner who was doing it to have fruits rather than for greening. The walls of the housing structure in which Aphiri stays are peeling off and the owners seems less concerned about maintaining it. The ventilation and provision of windows are poor. These aspects point to bad stewardship on the part of the owners of informal housing structures. They are merely concerned with reaping off benefits from tenants in the form of 'rentals' than with 'investing' in the aesthetics and habitability of the structures. (Survey, 2010)

When Aphiri says that the place is 'free," he means that they are not subject to close monitoring as households by the landlord. He says that the plot owner (Esther) is supposed to be staying on her brother's plot which is just some five hundred metres away. Yet, at the beginning of the year something terrible happened; Esther's shelter succumbed to the incessant rains. This forced her to seek temporary residence with a friend just in the same area. New construction is underway on Esther's brother's plot. Esther has no intention to come and stay on her premise because she is getting rentals ($45) from the three rooms she is letting to Aphiri and his co-tenant, Jerry. She has calculated the importance of this monthly income and seen that it can cushion her for subsistence needs of a month.

On the premise where Aphiri and Jerry are staying, there are some mango and avocado trees. Also, there are some mealies growing on-plot. Aphiri says all belong to Esther and she is very strict on regarding the products from trees and the mealies alike. No-one is allowed to harvest the fruits without her consent. However, she allows her tenants to fetch water for household use from her brother's plot. This, Aphiri says is an honourable gesture from Esther. Sometimes Aphiri and Jerry's families fetch water from some of their neighbours, just in the immediate vicinity to their homes.

Islam is Aphiri's religion. He and his family get to the mosque some five kilometres away on foot for worship. Regarding the possibility of some special needs in his housing and habitat, Aphiri indicates the home and its grounds are sufficient for everything needed for their worship and prayer. Aphiri is a smoker and he justifies this by saying that men are allowed to smoke in "... our religion only if they heed that the smoking poses no harm to women and children [through passive smoking]. As such, it must not be done in an enclosed place. Actually, it [smoking] is good. It shows that someone is at peace or in deep meditation."

Aphiri is employed as a security guard in Highlands (Harare). He cycles to work (bicycle). It takes him an average of an hour to get to the workplace. The story of Aphiri indicates a number of advantages at his disposal after he came to Epworth. An outsider would worry about the small size of the house he occupies, but to him, though not adequate, is better than 'lodging' where the landlord is around to monitor every activity that he has to do. He is satisfied with the rentals he now pays. But the story also shows how kinship ties can be of significance in the acquisition of plots. Normally such plots are found located close to each other. Sometimes this creates multi-plot ownership of which this is common in this part of Epworth. In real terms, this has created a new class of people, the slumlords. They speculate and get land where they put 'tenants' who pay them rentals monthly. Since there are always desperate home-seekers especially from Harare, these slumlords are assured of rent every month. They have a grip on this land. Some slumlords get this land on ZANU-PF ticket. Once they obtain land, they create no-go areas for example '*Kumawovheti*' (a place of the war veterans) which is a difficult area for outsiders (for example, researchers) to get to.

Another story in the same place of Magada is that of Mbuya Todii. She lives with her grandchildren. Mbuya Todii is in her seventies. She does not own many assets. But she owns a field across the river and some hoes to till it. Before coming to Epworth Mbuya Todii lived in Seke Unit D, in Chitungwiza. Her Catholic Church diocese, under the tutelage and direction of the late Archbishop Patrick Chakaipa, bought her a stand in Epworth. This was done on humanitarian and compassionate grounds. The church fully paid for stand; she purports. To date, not much had been done to build a more permanent structure (a house). Mbuya Todii laments that this lack of development is attributed to the fact that her children (who could have assisted her in improving the property) have, one by one died. Almost in tears, she moans:

> "*Vana vangu vapera. Mumwe akashaya, mumwe akashaya, mumwe akashaya, mumwe akashaya, mumwe takamurasa mwedzi wapera uyu, mumwe akanoudza vasekuru vake nezveuyu akashaya mwedzi wapera. Nanhasi haasati adzoka.*

> *Ava vaunoona vazukuru.* [My children are finished up, now. One died, then another, and the other and the other. Just last month we buried the other. The only remaining of my sons went to tell his uncle of the death of his brother who passed on last month but hasn't come back. These, you see, are my grandchildren.]"

None of the grandchildren is going to school. Mbuya Todii expresses the desire that the grandchildren must be in school but the money for that is just not there: *"Mari yacho ingawanikwepi, mwanangu?"* ("Where can I get the money?"). The old woman and her family thrive on peri-urban agriculture[558]. The grandchildren help her with cultivation and harvesting. The structure belonging to this poor family comprises two rooms. One of the rooms is used as a granary, for keeping the harvested crops. The other is used as a kitchen, dining room and bedroom and grandmother says, "*Tinonongorindirana tokwana nezvinhu zvedu. Mbeu dzedu tinotochengetera mumba imomo*. (We have no option but to squash ourselves in this one room. Otherwise, where else can be put our belongings? We must keep our harvested crops indoors)."

Mbuya Todii's story indicates the degree of the housing challenges among the poor. They live miserable lives and tend to lack in hope for the next day. Livelihood coping strategies (like in this case, peri-urban farming), create other problems and constraints like storage space for the harvests. They have no option but to manoeuvre in the little space available. In addition, to find the old age in the peri-urban settlements is often associated with them having the battle to raise 'trailers' of grandchildren as an effect of the HIV and AIDS scourge. The cohort (of the old age) has no option but to be creative in order to address the three basic needs of food, shelter and clothing. In addressing the food aspect come the small fields and plots for farming as indicated in this case of Mbuya Todii.

Zoro is middle-aged man in his late thirties. He stays in Overspill and often visits the Quarry Dam which some sections of the community also refer to as the 'pool of death." As he refreshes himself on the banks

---

[558] Mbiba.B, "Urban Agriculture in Zimbabwe," *Avebury*, Aldershot.(1995)

of the dam, he enjoys sight-seeing including of men and boys fishing or bathing. He enjoys catching a siesta by the dam-side (see Plate 9.6).

Plate 9.6: Recreation on the banks of a dangerous 'lake." Zoro, a resident of Epworth finds time to rest by the lakeside. As the researcher speaks to him, the realities of landscapes that result after extraction of raw materials to build (quarrying) are revealed. Quarry miners target peri-urban areas as sources of the raw materials for housing and related infrastructure. This form quarry resembles an oxymoronic development which, on the one side has recently been converted by residents into a place where they derive certain benefits including a bath place and recreation. On the other hand, it is a 'pool of death' where a number of corpses, at least according to reports from the residents of Epworth have been found. The place was a permanent eyesore in space. Measures to try and bar people from getting near it have proved futile as the fence around have been stolen. Vandalism is a sign of bad stewardship of common assets. This concept points to the challenges of the Prisoners' Dilemma and the Tragedy of Commons. (Survey, 2010)

Behind his usual place of 'resting' is a pole which he says once supported a fence. It has, however, since 'disappeared." Zoro explains that the purpose of the fence was to prevent people from getting into the pool and then remarks, "But you just know what people are like. They stole it for own domestic use."

The explanation by Zoro indicates that, in peri-urban areas just like other places in the inner core of the cities, are problems of vandalism and lack of care for public property. Whereas this fence was put to protect them against a dangerous 'dam," the vandalisers never even considered the safety of children and other members of the community. Indeed, they went ahead to use the fence for selfish reason. At community level, it means stewardship of place is endangered by selfish perceived gains of existing common pool resources. This confirms observations in peri-urban Zambia that ignorance and lack of civic awareness is the major explanation for vandalism of common assets in peri-urban areas[559]. Such is a direct attack against Follet's 'model of unified pluralism." Such brings into picture the dangers of tragedy of the commons and the prisoner's dilemma as put across in literature. But still behind the Dam is a story which Zoro enjoys sharing with people who do not know it.

Zoro says that, long ago in the colonial days, a certain quarry mining company owned a granite mining claim here. Its heavy machinery, one day 'accidentally' hit the underlying rock. This triggered water to gush out. The company brought equipment to try and drain out the water. This was to no avail hence an unstoppable spring and pool was born. It is unfortunate that as this happened the firm disbanded its operations. Zoro is of the opinion that it is the quarry stones from this site that were used for "the construction of Salisbury". There is a general belief by the local people that the dam has mermaids. A number of people have drowned and this is common problem with this pool. Zoro rebuffs this idea. He acquiesces that indeed many people have died. But Zoro explanation is somewhat contrary to the common myth and he argues, "You should know this, that: some of those people are stressed up with life. Such are the ones who come and commit suicide here. They drown themselves. As well, robbers and thieves know about this dam. After they have killed someone (and to destroy the evidence for murder), they come and throw corpses into the dam.... The depth of this dam is known by the aquatic police team. People who swim in the dam usually do not go very deep. It is said that deep down the waters is the quarry machinery left behind by the miners."

The Quarry Dam, just like one in Odar Farm in Harare South and with the same name, is associated with a number of tragic incidences.

---

[559] Mwanamakondo.B.Y, "The state of resettlement areas in Zambia," *A paper presented at the Swedish Cooperative Centre (SCC) at the Chrismar Hotel, 27-28 February 2007*, Lusaka.pg3. (2007)

Around the pool are all sorts of different other kinds of activities happening: the selling quarry stands, pit sand and bricks, fishing and leisure making. The story by Zoro is insightful of the myths and realities surrounding the dam. Zoro sees vandalism and 'sabotage' as key challenges in the area. For example, this issue of the stolen fence he explains. This is important when examining the realities surrounding common pool resources. Sometimes people have learnt to live with 'danger' in their environments. This is a sign of 'adaptation." The dam has now become a dangerous spot yet men and boys in the area use it as a recreational facility. In addition, the dam is a scar left by processes of ecological footprint of colonial city construction. This is the evidence of the dependence that big cities have on their immediate peri-urban areas on 'cheap' building materials and other resources.

Mai Chimuti stays in kwaSolani. She has a maize field across the river that borders Epworth and Ruwa. I meet her on her way in MaGada (Overspill). Today she is carrying on her head a bundle of fresh sticks. She has just cut them near her field. In her bundle, I notice that some of the fresh sticks are not for firewood as they do not burn well. She explains that, "I come from Manicaland. What you have just noted is a tree we use for herbs. Its name is *mupomboshori*. It has medicinal value particularly for pregnant women. Remember that every herb that God created is of good use for people. It is only improper to use herbs to kill. When you kill, heaven will severely punish you." This statement by Mai Chimuti is revealing of the different reasons different people give when they use resources around them. They attach certain values to their actions and all is done in the name of utility. Yet, in the process, forest destructions are also incurred. As acknowledged, the settlement "... has serious environmental problems among them land degradation, siltation and gullies."[560] It is somewhat amazing though that there is some residual dense forest of the indigenous *musasa* trees located North West of the Domboramwari rock outcrop. It embroils the Police Station and the Local Board offices. Its resilience to the indiscriminate practice of cutting down of indigenous species by the peri-urban dwellers is probably due to fear of

---

[560] Epworth (2002:8)

prosecution. Mai Chimuti's story is revealing to the religious and environmental dimensions of stewardship. In legal and constitutional terms, local people are entitled to the resource endowments in their area of dwelling. Yet the definition of a local person is marred with its own challenges given that most of them are immigrants. On the other hand, their 'right to the city' must also be respected and is the dimension that gives them an urge of dependence on their immediate environment.

In the vleis near Stopover (kuCell 7) are two young men in their mid-thirties. They 'hammer' granite rocks to produce quarry stones (Plate 9.7). One is Phinias and the other James. They say that they 'own' the site jointly.

Plate 9.7: 'Grinding' the rocks for quarry in Cell 7. The researcher listens to Phinias as he explains how he operates on the ground where he grinds rocks for quarry stones. This ground is now a private space of a kind. There is exclusion of other players interested in dealing with quarry stones. The operations are run as a micro-enterprise. The major market of the stones is the 'export market' of housing developments in the big city, Harare. Peri-urban areas have strong links with core cities as they supply raw materials required in construction. Bad stewardship is expressed in the form through which tyres and rubber are burnt to allow for the 'softening' of hard rocks. Micro-entrepreneurs in building supplies drawn from the natural environment, like Phinias are mainly worried about ekeing a living from the diligence they express rather than the cleanliness of the air in the atmosphere. Such knowledge could only be brought to them by way of stewardship education. Nevertheless, the fact they use materials like used tyres could be a sign of 'good stewardship' given that

they resort to recycling which is one of the ways of sustainable waste management practices. (Survey, 2010)

Anyone who wishes joining them would be subject to the conditions that they put across to him or her. Their job requires a lot of physical strength for one to qualify as opposed to academic or professional credentials. Phinias explains that, "Once you get hold of a site like this one then no one can now easily join. Someone can only join if he is prepared to work with or for us. Our job does not need you to be educationally qualified, only your stamina and power... I stay just across that stream. I am renting on someone else's property. My rural home is Honde Valley (Manicaland).... I was born in 1975 and I am married. I have just one kid. Here in Epworth, I stay with my whole [nuclear] family." He goes on to say that he once worked for a fertilizer company in Harare, as a truck loader. When the business in the company dropped, the company could no longer afford having a huge workforce, Phinias decided to move to Epworth. When he came here, he began on this job he is doing right now. This is the occupation that has made his family have 'bread and butter' since 2004. Phinias tells how he identified this particular site for work. He, then, tells the processes involved in producing the much-needed quarry stones for building construction. Also, he reveals the quantum of the stones and the price and supply mechanisms associated with the production.

> "In this place were dumped rocks from Dombo [These could have been dumped by quarry suppliers]. We saw an opportunity in the rocks as we discovered that quarry stones are on high demand in and around Epworth. Now, for goodness' sake we have made use of what was useless to the [formal] quarry producers. This is what we do with the boulders: We first heat up the rock to excessive heat. This softens it. In the process, we use tyres for this heating. Per month, we can produce as much quarry stones as five cubic metres. Each cubic costs ninety dollars. Our competitor big companies sell the same amount of quarry stones at one-hundred twenty dollars."

Phinias is of the opinion that it is more profitable to sell the stones by gauging the loads in wheelbarrows than anything. He says they 'judge' their customers before the sale. This is all about price discrimination. Phinias says that those "...who are well-to-do [the rich], we charge five dollars a wheel barrow, those without [the have-nots], we charge three dollars." For Phinias and James (and others in the industry) quarry stone production and distribution is a highly involving task. Phinias and James believe it is their all-important source of livelihood; they have no option but to work hard for them to survive. Their sphere of influence stretches as far as Snake Park [a high-density suburb west of Harare, about 30 kilometres from Harare City Centre where new housing constructions are also in progress]. They have a fairly stable customer base. James stresses that those "... who once bought from us always come back and also refer others to us."

Phinias and James' story shows important aspects related to housing and stewardship in peri-urban settlements. First, there is a lot of exportation of peri-urban resources to the big cities for the sake of their residential and other purposes of expansion. Second, the heating of tyres is a process that is a concern of air pollution in the area and the surrounding vicinities. However, the concentration and focus are not on negative externalities from this production but on the 'politics of the stomach." Third, those involved in the production and marketing of peri-urban products like quarry stones, have also learnt to devise ways to merchandise their products. Similar to this story by Phinias and James in Epworth is a story by Chamunorwa in Ruwa. In Epworth, Stopover, there is a similar example of a privately-owned crèche (Plate 9.8).

Plate 9.8: Creche in Stopover. The possessor of this space has put effort in 'beautifying' this place to make it attractive to those people intending to bring

their children for early childhood education through the crèche. This betterment of a place is an indicator of good stewardship. However, the major reason is for profit. The functional and space requirements for a crèche, unlike for a school, can be accommodate on a relatively small plot. Parents in the neighbourhood will welcome the development of crèches within their vicinities given the need for having cost-cutting measures especially in sending their children to crèches by bus or car. (Survey, 2010)

Kuda, a secondary school boy (about 15 years of age) remarks, "This crèche appears to be new because of the well-decorated and new durawall they put but it is very old in the neighbourhood. I also went to the same crèche years ago." This statement shows that maintenance is part of place stewardship. A well-maintained place will last its purpose and serve a wider a community.

Although a number of structures in Epworth can fall under the category of brick and mortar under asbestos, most of them are by no means reaching to the standards as stipulated in the Model Building Bye-laws which require materials to be tested and approved by the local authority. The materials used on structures have a bearing then on the general nature of the housing stock in thethe area (see Table 9.5). Housing structures (the main structures on stands) in Epworth fall in the following classifications:

i. brick and mortar under tiles only 6.57% of the surveyed lot of stands,
ii. brick and mortar under asbestos (44.33%), the majority being in Epworth, especially the upgraded sites,
iii. brick and mortar under corrugated iron sheets (11.34%) being 17.52% of Epworth's surveyed stock, ivandiv). pole and dagga under thatch, 0.69%.

Table 9.5: Materials used on Main Dwelling on Plot (%) (Survey, 2010)

Aspect	Percentage (%)
brick and mortar under tiles	6.7
brick and mortar under asbestos	56.66
brick and mortar under corrugated iron sheets	17.52
pole and dagga under thatch	1.46
pole and dagga under asbestos	5.11
pole and dagga under corrugated iron sheets	2.19
wood under thatch	0.73

Aspect (*contd…*)	**Percentage (%) (*contd…*)**
wood under asbestos	1.46
wood under plastic	0.73
Other	6.57
Total	100

N=137

The remainder of structures are: pole and dagga under asbestos, pole and dagga under corrugated iron sheets, wood under thatch, wood under asbestos and wood under plastic being synonymous with Epworth. Evident in this classification, is that the type of materials chosen by the peri-urban builders are dependent on the income level of the household. But other factors include whether or not such a structure is considered permanent or temporary or the purpose to which the structure is being put to use. Families and households normally begin with temporary structures before embarking on putting up a more permanent structure. Generally, houses in Epworth (especially in the part with new informal settlers) are characterised by irregular stands, in terms of shapes and sizes, coupled by poor construction materials (grass, plastics, poles and dagga) having been used. Table 9.6 shows that the dominant activity by households is gardening (54%) followed by poultry (6.57%).

Table 9.6: On-plot activities by peri-urban dwellers (Survey, 2010)

Activity	**Frequency**	**Percentage (%)**
Gardening	74	54.01
Welding	1	0.73
Poultry	9	6.57
Church	2	1.46
Extra lessons	1	0.73
Other	16	11.68
N/A	34	24.82
Total	137	100

N=137

Like in Ruwa, peri-urban farming in Epworth is dominated by these activities which require relatively large plots for them to take off. In Stopover, Epworth, Munyukwi, who teaches agriculture at a local school, is engaged in serious on-plot farming. He nurses seedlings and grows vegetables. Margaret, the wife is full time on the garden while he spends most of his time in the classroom. Yet the wife gives all credit to the husband. Margaret says: "*Baba* is a trained teacher for Agriculture. Instead of just teaching in the classroom he decided to benefit us as a family and this is getting to even the wider community. Who does not know us here, as suppliers of seedlings and vegetables? *Baba* is always ready to advice those who want to go and do it on their own." Munyukwi has invested at the on-plot a deep well for watering the garden as well as for water for domestic use. Margaret says that the local market for seedlings is not that vibrant. Consequently, she has agreed with her husband to transplant mature seedling into an off-plot garden some three hundred metres away from their house. Exotic trees are still in their infancy of growth showing the little time most of them had in the settlement. Even, in Overspill Magada, some people have planted some orchards (see Plate 9.9).

Plate 9.9: Orchard development in Overspill Magada. Orchards serve two basic functions – providing families and households with food and extra-income in the event of them yielding the expected fruits and greening the environment hence acting as carbon sinks. Greening in the age of increased carbon footprint is a good stewardship of the natural environments or emerging 'artificial ecosystems' with increased urbanisation and urban expansion. (Survey, 2010)

The overall picture of Epworth is that of an eyesore. Plate 9.10 on the next page shows the researcher standing with Chamu and Sam in Stopover, Epworth. The two are putting up a structure that is to be used as a tuckshop on their plot. They are not following an architectural plan but building 'from the head." In light of this, it is noted that the poor tend to build just to satisfy the immediate needs they apprehend. This explains why a place like Epworth would be considered quite 'vernacular' in terms of architectural designs and general settlement pattern as has put across[561]. Linked to stewardship, such an unfolding picture provides a framework for defining parameters through which settlements are designed by the poor whose use value of the space outstrips exchange value that the well-to-do often emphasise.

Plate 9.10: Tuckshop under construction on a residential stand in Stopover. The researcher is being told that what he is seeing under construction is

---

[561] Highlands. D., "What"s Indigenous? An Essay on Building" in Turan, M. (ed.) "Vernacular Architecture: Paradigms of Environmental Response," *Aldershot, Avebury*, 31-62.
(1990) , Gough.K, "From Bamboo to Bricks: Self-Help Housing and the Building Materials Industry in Urban Colombia," PhD thesis, University College London. (1992), Kellett "Constructing Home: Production and Consumption of Popular Housing in Northern Colombia," PhD thesis, University of Newcastle upon Tyne. (1995), "The Construction of Home in the Informal City," in F. Hernández, M. Millington, and I. Borden (eds.), Transculturation: Cities, Space and Architecture in Latin America. *Amsterdam and New York*, Rodopi, pp 22-42(2005), "Contemporary Vernaculars: Informal housing processes and vernacular theory," *Journal of the International Society for the Study of Vernacular Settlements - ISVS e-journal 2(1)*: pp 1-12. 2001),Kellet ; Nappier "Squatter Architecture: a Critical Examination of Vernacular Theory and Spontaneous Settlement with Reference to South America and South Africa," *Traditional Dwellings and Settlements Review 6(2) May 1995*: pp 7-24. (1995)

tuckshop. In the discussion it emerges that the two bricklayers are not qualified but just know how to improvise on structures. This is typical of vernacular architecture. The two do not even have a drawn plan but they have what they need 'in the head." Levelling has not been properly done and the upcoming structure will, no doubt, be bending. They are also 'economising' on the cementing in the mortar that they are using reducing the structure to a mere temporary structure. Temporary structures according to the provisions of the Regional, Town and Country Planning Act (1976, revised 1996) should last only for six months. But Chamu and Sam insist that they are building for 'permanence." (Survey, 2010)

Regarding the state of layout mapping in Epworth, the lamentation has been that, "... a number of the proposed land-use proposals have been affected by the squatters. Though the Board had, prior to the invasions, requested the Department of Physical Planning to make layout maps for Adelaide Farm, unfortunately the area has been settlement and it would mean planning with and around these settlers. This makes it difficult for Epworth to benefit from the sale of undeveloped land"[562]. It becomes counterproductive to continue planning and illegal settlers continue to violate the proposed plans. Such violation is driven by largely two factors – political and housing poverty. Politically, settlers are normally 'permitted' to do as they ought, given that politicians will be 'hiding' for votes hence tend to tolerate the nuisances posed by squatters. Moreover, without options for housing, people are forced by circumstances beyond their control encapsulated in the notion of 'urban penalty' to get to peri-urban settlements like Epworth where they can seek land to build or alternative rental housing from the slumlords.

In Overspill, Epworth the survey reveals heaps of logs being cut into fuel wood (Plate 9.11) on the next page.

---

[562] Epworth, "Epworth Local Board Development Proposals," ELB, Epworth, (2002: 6)

Plate 9.11: A Wood Market in Magada. The 'energy crisis' is part and parcel of the peri-urban story. Wood has become scarce in most peri-urban settlements and firewood vendors 'import' wood from places as far as Marondera, Beatrice and Mvuma which they then sell to residents. The wood is cut to pieces that are sold to households. In this picture, some men are cutting wood to small pieces to be sold in a 'retail market' of firewood. The physical market is a home which belongs to a certain Mr. Mudiwa. (Survey, 2010)

The woodcutters indicate that they bring the wood from the surrounding farms. This shows the symbiotic relations between the Ruwa, Epworth and the surrounding farms. The farms are close to Epworth and this echoes the narrative by Fanuwero. Energy, water and sanitation are critical concerns among peri-urban dwellers.

Off-plot activities are manifold. Streams and rivers are used variously for swimming by children, car washing and river-sand extractions, among others. Sand mining in both Ruwa and Epworth is a 'cash cow' for a number of peri-urban dwellers. A common sight in river banks is of heavy goods trucks parked for buyers to hire or loaded to various destinations. Buyers are asked what they prefer for the day. One 26-year-old Jackson says to me, "What is it that you need today? River sand or pit sand? These trucks are for its transportation to wherever you want it taken." This aggressive style of marketing is a common characteristic of informal sector operators. It is common sight to see some young man hawking for brick customers. But the bricks are stockpiled somewhere; here is just pointer of the real stocks away (Plate 9.12).

Plate 9.12: Rain-damaged brick kiln in Stopover. This implies loss because the brick moulders used their physical energy and then energy to light up the brick kiln but the products have not received much care as they should leading to their damage and ultimate disuse. In the same place where the kiln stands, is a sunflower field. This development points to contestation of space where different uses compete for the same space. Conflicts are the primary cause of bad stewardship which explains ills like vandalism, neglect and tragedy of the commons. (Survey, 2010)

Nevertheless, brick moulding has seriously scarred the peri-urban landscape. Moulding bricks and leaving them to 'disintegrate' unused is itself is a sign of bad place stewardship and also a cause of health concern. When residents take open spaces as no-one's space of responsibility, it becomes a serious cause of concern. In Epworth, the chief cause of environmental degradation is the quest to have building materials. As already noted, portions of land within or immediately away from the built area are in serious disfigurement. In Epworth such places like the Quarry Dam and south of Stopover are badly marred due to sand extractions. The peri-urban dwellers feel that the Quarry Dam area has contributed immensely to the establishment of the city of Harare given the vast quantum of the quarry that was used in the building constructions of the city. Today, though at much lower scale, some informal operators have resuscitated the quarry extraction industry. Children tend to like swimming and playing is these waters just as the Quarry Dam in Epworth had been turned by some residents to be a fishing, scenic viewing, swimming and bathing pool.

Overall, humankind always has a utilitarian perspective over the resources in its vicinity. But the same pool was a serious threat to life and health of the residents[563]. Chief among these wastes are non-biodegradable materials which include plastic and tin cans (Plate 9.13).

Plate 9.13: Informal dumpsite in Cell 7. With local authorities failing to deliver services as stipulated in the Urban Councils Act (Chapter 29:15), households

[563] Walt. G, "Health Policy – an introduction to process and power," *Zed Books. London*.(1994);Marshall. F, "What does peri-urban sustainability mean in the context of Delhi?" <URL: http://stepscentre-thecrossing.blogspot.com/2008/12/ what-does-peri-urban-sustainability.html:>, *Accessed on 2April 2009*.(4 December 2008); ; Siyeni.Y.M, "Expanding Water Service Delivery through Partnership between Water Utility and Small Scale Water Providers in Lusaka, Zambia" *A Case of Lusaka"s Peri-Urban Areas.* University essay from Linköpings universitet/Tema vatten i natur och samhälle<. URL: http://www.essays.se/essay/4d116540c8/,> *Accessed on 14 August 2010*. (2008)

resort to informal dumping in those open spaces which they deem can accommodate their waste. Household waste is a major cause of concern as consumerism increases. Improper waste disposal is an indicator of bad environmental stewardship. Where proper dumping was done, the same land can then be reclaimed for other uses in future. In the stewardship debate, waste management is a critical factor for consideration. (Survey, 2010)

This picture coincides with the sentiments raised which argue that "...uncollected waste attracting disease vectors and high occupancy rates, which increase the risk of communicable diseases makes Epworth Local Government Area a time bomb to its environs and being extremely a low-income suburb, it is the most poverty-stricken area."[564] Some of the wastes including plastics, tins and cans are dumped in pits left after sand extractions or farm brick moulding. The same provide breeding ground for mosquitoes which are vectors for malaria. Mosquitoes are known for breeding in stagnant waters. Although, the study has not sought to find out the incidences of water-related diseases, bilharzias included, the same dangerous pools of stagnant water (Plate 9.14 and 9.15) can be the ground upon which such diseases are brewed.

Plate 9.14: 'Measuring' up the depth of a pit from which river sand has been extracted, Cell 7. Informal extractions of building materials including pit sand

[564] Epworth (2002:1)

and quarry are usually not accompany with corresponding reclamation measures. Environmental degradation is symptomatic of bad environmental stewardship. Housing construction that is sustainable is that which takes on board measures to provide an aesthetically pleasing environment. Bad stewardship on the environment, as explained, by the Environmental Management Agency (EMA) happens because responsibilities are not clearly defined and there are departmentalised approaches to managing common problems. Sand mining and quarrying are identified as the responsibility of the Ministry of Mines. The question is whether such a ministry has any concern of environmental management. (Survey, 2010)

As river-bank grasses grow thicker and thicker, that creates dangerous spots for human safety in the environment as people are raped or mugged in these grasses or tall growing crops like maize. There is one thing that remains unresolved in Epworth. Stands are being pegged. Officers from the office of the surveyor-general are busy on the ground, to pave way for proper town planning. This implies loss of some of these orchards. Literature shows that slum upgrading will result in displacement of the slum dwellers together with some of their 'investments'[565] .

Plate 9.15: Pits as water collectors during the rainy season. After extractions of quarry and sand are done on the land, this leaves out huge 'scars' on the land

[565] Tibaijuka A.K, "Building Prosperity – Housing and Economic Development Earthscan" London. (2009) ; UNHABITAT,"Global report on human settlements 2009, " *Planning sustainable cities*: UNHABITAT, Earthscan (2009)

surfaces which then accumulate water. The water when stagnant is a serious health concern as it may harbour bilharzias and can be a breeding ground for mosquitoes that cause malaria. Such diseases are costly to households as infected members seek treatment. Good stewardship which seeks to prevent such dangerous disease-brewing places is a requirement not only in peri-urban settlements but everywhere where communities are in habitat. (Survey, 2010)

This chapter has demonstrated how Epworth typifies a place that has organically developed. Epworth has had a treatment of the place as 'no man's land' yet in reality there are so many individuals who want to treat it as 'private' property. Those who hold cards from the local authority call themselves 'landlords' though they are not so in the strictest of the sense since they do not hold title to the land. Landlordism in Epworth is partly a result of the behaviour of politicians who use land as a political tool to woo votes for themselves and partly a historical fact in which those who call themselves 'originals' have had claims to land informally leading to the emergence of 'slumlords' in the areas.

By and large, Epworth, as a settlement presents itself as a 'soft spot' upon which anyone who is fleeing the high rentals in Harare, thinks of getting information. Its high receptivity of refugees has seen it grow in leaps and bounds over the more than 110 years of its existence. Evidence from the minutes analysed in this chapter, having been a record from various local board meetings, indicate that housing, environmental pollution and degradation are major areas of concern in place stewardship of Epworth. Religious groups like *vapositori* tend to use open spaces which map resemble a move towards the protection of wildernesses. However, the factor that these areas are not serviced with the toilets and water facilities reduce them to places of potential environmental hazards.

Furthermore, street vendors in Epworth, by their using of road space to display their goods and wares for sale pose traffic dangers and this—of public space by private individuals. Such informal trading by the road sides is a sign of bad stewardship of the public space. This is further compounded by the local authority is also failing to control such behaviour. It has also been revealed that most of the housing stock in Epworth is of substandard quality despite efforts in the mid-1980s to upgrade the settlement. As new settlers' stream in, the problem continues unabated the problem remains cancerous and spreading. Around 48% of

Epworth dwellers propose to have come through Harare. They claim they have been attracted by affordable housing and affordable life in the settlement. As noted from literature, haphazard settlement in Epworth resembles informal housing in Latin America and East and West Africa. Efforts by some NGOs to provide in housing in Epworth are in direct contradiction with the concept of 'lowering the ladder'[566]. Generally, and like in Ruwa, the livelihood activities in Epworth point to both good and bad stewardship practices. The next two chapters are devoted to state, corporate and civil society partnerships as they play a role in shaping peri-urban settlements in Zimbabwe.

[566] Payne Geoffrey (ed.), 2002: "Land, Rights and Innovation – Improving tenure security for the urban poor," *ITDG Publishing*, London.(2002)

CHAPTER 10
DEPARTMENTALISM AND THE BUSINESS OF STATE INSTITUTIONS

It is being suggested that planners "… need to work in new ways. They must get out of their 'departmental boxes' and forge or join multi-disciplinary teams. We need to develop an agreed common purpose amongst planners, architects, engineers, developers and politicians, and within communities, that will help to revitalise urban and rural places. The development process and its effects are extremely complex; development professionals, including planners, must cast off their specific focus and lose their 'silo mentality.'" [567] Peri-urban housing development and maintenance require a pluralistic and collaborative approach[568]. Normally, as peri-urban households build, rent and live the consumptions of the peri-urban space and its resources are part of the issues of sustainable development that are not explicitly put into consideration. These households have different experiences and realities as micro-space stewards. But the story by households is incomplete if 'gatekeepers' involvement is not put into perspective. As mentioned in Chapter 3 on the administrative context of the study, local Authorities, in this case Ruwa Town Council and Epworth Local Board are local government structures which spearhead local service delivery (water, roads, health facilities, etc). They are empowered to do so by the Urban Councils Act.

The participation of the state is not per se defined as restricted to this geographical space. Rather, the processes so happen as they apply everywhere. General indications from the study indicate that these departments though aiming to achieve the primal state goal of public

---

[567] Christie et al.)., *Living spaces: A vision for the future of planning*, The RSPB: Bedfordshire.pg 47(2002))

[568] Lawrence. R. J, "Housing and health: Beyond Disciplinary Confinement," *Journal of Urban Health 83(3):* pp540-549(2006)

interest, the efforts are usually so compartmentalised that conflicts and ambiguities in purpose often arise. This makes the planning of peri-urban areas even more cumbersome and hectic than is just put across in literature. Planning plays a coordinative role to spatial orderliness. This chapter is shaped is specifically influenced by stewardship that shifts development operating partners from their "'departmental boxes'[to] cast off their specific focus and lose their 'silo mentality'"[569]. Specifically, the chapter examines the contribution of the following state departments and agencies in peri-urban housing: Environmental Management Agency (EMA), Ministry of Local Government, Rural and Urban Development (MLGRUD), Harare Metropolitan Province (HMP), Department of Physical Planning (DPP), Urban Development Corporation (UDCORP), Ministry of Lands and Rural Settlements (MLRR), and the Ministry National Housing and Social Amenities (MNHSA. At the end of the chapter, an attempt is made to show the inter-linkages between these existing state departments.

From this study, it has emerged that "EMA's entry point is Section 97 of the Environmental Management Act"[570] regarding housing development. This Section 97 of the legislation spells out that housing is typical of one development project which requires an environmental impact assessment (EIA) before it is initiated. The Act is generic in its approach. Nevertheless, there are a number of environmental statutory instruments specifying the details of how to do the assessments. According to one senior EMA officer the EMA's role is to safeguard and promote environmental sustainability and one method of doing this is the encouragement of green building. The senior officer notes that green building is today encouraged the world over; the idea is to mitigate the negative impacts of air pollution.

However, in Zimbabwe, green building is little recognised and, in light of this, the senior officer with EMA notes with concern that:

> "Instead of our people planting hedges around their houses, they are in fact removing the hedges and replacing them with

---

[569] Christie et al.)., *Living spaces: A vision for the future of planning*, The RSPB: Bedfordshire.pg47(2002)

570 Interview with Senior Environmental Officer, 24 March 2011

> walls – durawalls. This is addition of concrete to the already existing concrete jungle. We are removing the green! The result is that the excessive carbon gases emitted have no place for absorption. The whole debate is part of the climate change and the aspect of the ecological footprint debate. That some settlements are located further away from places of jobs or other social and economic activities means people have to travel using either buses or cars. There is pollution emission posed cars and buses. It infuses carbon in the environment. .... Our Climate Change Office [located within our parent ministry], I am sure, has a way to make calculations of carbon content in the atmosphere. This explains why motorists have to pay carbon tax. All this is part of the ecological footprint and how we link it to settlement development, like those which are outside the main city"[571].

Clear from this statement is that housing development is located within a broader sphere of environmental planning and stewardship. Besides, environmental sustainability is a broad subject that involves managing atmospheric processes. It is unfortunate that we are living in a 'consumer society' in which the waste management problem associated with settlements is an issue of serious concern. Peri-urban settlements become 'dumping' grounds for various kinds of waste. The Senior Officer at EMA says that the term 'peri-urban' is not important as they take a uniformised approach in managing places, unless they have to strictly classify their actions as rural or urban. As such the senior officer opines:

> "As you may have read, the ecological footprint is that impact associated with increased human action in space.... Imagine the waste that is generated after goods have been bought for household consumption. The peri-urban areas have generally been the chief place where such waste is dumped. We use a blanket approach to our environmental management endeavours. Thus, we don't specifically look at peri-urban areas as a separate space. Some of our policies, however, are specific to rural areas and other urban"[572].

The sentiments raised by the senior EMA office about the definition and specification of policy to peri-urban reveal the reality of how planning for the peri-urban normally escapes the minds of various

---

571 Interview with Senior Environmental Officer, 24 2011

572 Interview with Senior Environmental Officer, 24 2011

agencies. Such escapism may also explain why most of these areas are neglected by sometimes only to receive attention when things really get out of hand for example the Presidential Commission of Inquiry in Botswana (Home, 2001). Revealed as by the study is that EIAs are differently applied to peri-urban settlements like Epworth and Ruwa as explained by their different origins and shapes. Another Senior Officer (female) notes that: "A settlement like Epworth has been in existence for quite a long time. If you look at the EIA initiative, it is quite recent in the country. For such a settlement, which developed informal, and as a rural set up, we cannot enforce the law in retrospect. But new projects are subject to the law so, a place, like Ruwa, one can safely say, most of the projects have gone through EIA. In older settlements we encourage the local authorities to work with CBOs so that they identify the community challenges and strive to act together towards redressing the challenges"[573].

From this snippet, it is clear that EMA does not work alone in addressing environmental issues. A number of ministries, agencies, departments and local authorities are part of ensuring that environmental sustainability is achieved. EMA says it has trained local authorities to engage CBOs within their areas of jurisdiction. Thus, CBOs are critical in identifying problems and identifying the solutions and implementing those solutions. One way is development Local Environmental Action Plans (LEAP) in which locals and their stakeholders are the agents for improvement and change. In this case, EMA's role is to facilitate the process by providing guidance. Local people implement the plans. Thus, LEAP is not solely about the environment but includes local communities identifying challenges (including socio-economic) affecting them. Explicitly, the Senior Officer stresses that the challenges "... may be poverty and the locals have to seek to find means to address this poverty in their community. In environmental terms, it may be about managing waste. "[574].

These days use of GIS to address environmental impacts affecting communities (for example, flooding, deforestation, climate change) is seriously considered. But the EMA Senior Officer asserts that: "... our

573 Interview on 28 July, 2011

574 Interview with Senior Environmental Officer, 24 2011

Environmental Planning and Monitoring section does GIS applications. We are at a stage of installing a laboratory to allow such operations. As for the climate change concern, we have a department of Climate Department which is in the Ministry." [575] While stewardship aims to break walls of professionalised services and delivery, the mention of sister agencies in one ministry that focus on different things may be a source of 'gray areas' that are left unattended. The senior officer asserts that, "As EMA we are mainly concerned with the implementation part. Our aim as EMA is of reducing or mitigating negative impacts to the environment, if not moderating them. Deforestation is a concern of our sister agency, the Forestry Commission. As you may know we are three agencies under the Ministry of Environment and Natural Resources Management. There is EMA, to manage the environment as it were; Forestry Commission to encourage planting of trees and guarding against deforestation, and the Department of National Parks and Wildlife mainly to manage the fauna"[576]. This is departmentalism at its worst and would require serious coordination of conduct and practice if conflicts and neglect of critical aspects of environmental stewardship are to be avoided.

In its duties, EMA is guided by a number of statutory instruments including the following:

I. Statutory Instrument 7 of 2007 which is a general guide to environmental management looking specifically on issues like the setting of fireguards, doing EIA, sand abstraction, and waste management,
II. Statutory Instrument 6 of 2007 dealing with water and effluent, solid waste and industrial and mining waste,
III. Statutory Instrument 10 of 2007 sets standards for Hazardous Substances,
IV. Statutory Instrument 12 of 2007 is about Hazardous Substances like fuels and chemicals,
V. Statutory Instrument 72 of 2009 on Air Pollution, and,
VI. Statutory Instrument 3 or 5 of 2011 (not totally new, but just adding value to Statutory Instrument 7).

575 Interview with Senior Environmental Officer, 24 2011
576 Interview with Senior Environmental Officer, 24 2011

The instruments are critical for EMA operations and industries must comply with the benchmarks stated in these. The Ministry of Health assists EMA a great deal in the implementation, monitoring and evaluations linked with the enforcement of these instruments. That EMA acknowledges the role of the Ministry of Health is in itself a worth practice. There is mention of private industries of which the issue of ISO Certification is explored. The Senior Officer explains that, "ISO Certification is voluntary. That one is the baby of SAZ [Standards Association of Zimbabwe]. It is about global compliance standards for industries... We are a public institution. We enforce public laws!" [577]

Some private corporations sometimes dump their liquid and solid waste in water bodies. The EMA Senior Officer contends that, "this issue is not about companies dumping their waste. It is about dumping that waste without a license. Before dumping they must be licensed to do so. They must have their waste tested in a laboratory so as to determine which band the waste belongs to. We have several bands for example the Blue Band, Green Band, Yellow Band and the Red Band. Each band stipulates the type of licence required in terms of how much the polluter must pay. I encourage you to grab those statutory instruments that I mentioned to you from Government Printers....I don't remember what is now called. Oh ...it's PrintFlow! All the specifications are in those statutory instruments"[578].

Observations around the City of Harare and its peri-urban (Ruwa and Epworth included) indicate extensive housing constructions. Two issues are connected to this: quarrying by households for concrete requirements; and, deforestation due to perhaps increased power cuts and also perhaps most of the upcoming settlements do not have access to electricity yet. The EMA Senior Officer admits that indeed such developments are happening yet makes the following reservations:

> "Indeed, these are interesting observations but I have this to say to you: First, about quarrying, that is not administered by us but the Ministry of Mines. So, I don't have much to comment there. Second, regarding deforestation, again, that is the issue for the Forestry Commission. But I should point to you, overall, what

577 Interview with Senior Environmental Officer, 24 2011

578 Interview with Senior Environmental Officer, 24 2011

> the Communal Forest Resources Act says. It states that communities have a right to the resources that are available in their areas. So, communities can exploit these resources, for example woodfuel. In fact, this is also a provision in our [National] Constitution. Perhaps the question is the rate of exploitation which is problem to really tackle. That is where the question of sustainability comes in. They [communities] must use these resources within their areas of living. They are not allowed to transport these to other places without a licence. It becomes a big challenge when resources are commercialised"[579].

These issues raised by the key informant here point to the complexity associated with agencies in the environmental business that of striking a balance between the three needs in the environmental sustainability equation: people, prosperity and planet. Indeed, housing development has a marked ecological impact[580]. The impact is noted even after the houses have been constructed as households seek to manage waste produced in the houses or when they seek to find firewood in those cases when electricity has not yet been connected to the houses. The work to combat these challenges is somewhat also too compartmentalised among the 'environmental subsidiaries' making it difficult to achieve a coordinated sustainable management practice. Having discussed the role of EMA, I examine that of the MLGRUD.

The promotion of local governance, provision of coordinated and orderly spatial development; provision of professional and technical construction and maintenance services in property development, facilitation of the provision of affordable and functional residential accommodation, the promotion of mitigation and preparedness planning for emergencies and disasters, and, the coordination of central and local government programmes and development initiatives are tasks at the core of the Ministry of Local Government, Rural and Urban Development (MLGRUD). it is observed that provision of off-site infrastructure (roads,

---

579 Interview on 28 July, 2011

580 Huby.M, "Social Policy and the Environment," *Open University Press*, Buckingham. (1998); ;Lenssen.N ; Roodman.M. D, Making better buildings. Brown LR, Flavin, C, French, H, Postel, S and Starke, L, eds. *State of the World 1995.* Earthscan: London.(1995);)

sewer and water) are entailed as part of the greater housing mandate, taking cognisant of the fact that in terms of "Maslow's hierarchy of needs thesis," housing is indeed a basic need[581]. The MLGRUD administers, among other regulations, the Regional Town and Country Act, the Urban Councils Act and Rural District Councils Act whose thrust is the production of functional spaces with the necessary infrastructure and services. The Minister acknowledges that:

> "The successful execution of the National Housing Programme has a very delicate relationship with the provision of affordable offsite infrastructure of an approved standard. Thus ... we must collectively strive to provide consistent with the noble tenets enshrined in the habitat agenda.... In terms of the Regional Town and Country Act, the Urban Councils Act and Rural District Councils Act, local Authorities are mandated to proffer off-site infrastructure. The installation of on-site services is ordinarily the responsibility of the developers. Where the private developers put in place such infrastructure, the same is handed over to local authorities for maintenance upon certification that the workmanship meets the approved standards of the local planning authority. The need to off-site infrastructure provision ought to be construed within the context of spatial planning, premised on the professional commitment to develop integrated land-uses. Infrastructure is an integral part of the land-use configuration as informed by operative master and local plans. And project specific design details. Among other considerations the planning process must of necessity respond to matters of cost, transport segregation, densification and demand thresholds to strengthen the functionality of the planning area whose major land-use could be housing"[582].

Peri-urban housing has suffered over the years in phase of macro-economic instability in the country (1997 to 2009). The period was a trying time not only for the local government ministry but every department and sector. However, in the same period, two metropolitan provinces (Harare

[581] Chombo. I, "Presentation on the Challenges Pertinent to the Provision of Off-Site Infrastructure by Local Authorities," Honourable Minister of Local Government, *Rural And Urban Development on 28 October 2009.*(2009)

582 Extract from Speech at the National Housing Convention, October, 2009.

and Bulawayo), run within the MLGRUD, emerged. The metropolitan provinces are part of the MLGRUD.

The Urban Development Corporation (UDCORP)was established in 1986 through an Act of Parliament (The Urban Development Corporation Act, No 14) to assist local authorities throughout Zimbabwe with a variety of specialised services in land and property development. It was the First Five Year National Development Plan (FFYNDP) covering the period 1986-1990 that put forward as a first priority the establishment of UDCORP. This was in keeping with a recommendation made in 1981 by the United Nations Commission for Human Settlements (UNCHS) which commissioned a feasibility study on the spatial planning for Zimbabwe. This was soon after the country's independence from British rule in 1980583. The idea for setting up this institution was meant to encourage the setting up of growth points, employment generation, provision of housing and social services, creation of supporting environment for development, financial and technical assistance to local authorities and cooperative, commercial, industrial and other enterprises584.

UDCORP is a government state-owned enterprise under the ambit of the MLGRUD. UDCORP, like most other government departments is headed by a Director who is appointed by the Minister of Local Government Rural and Urban Development. Under the Director is the Deputy Director who assists the Director in running the corporation and under the deputy-director are other officers and technicians in defined areas of speciality. Technicians (engineering, electrical and surveying) are at the lower ramp of the organisational ladder. UDCORP has several departments or sections including Human Resources, responsible for recruiting and training new staff development programs and the Properties and Technical Services Division which has three sections namely; Physical Planning, Project Planning and Management and Property Development Consultancy. The Properties and Technical Services

[583] Wekwete.K.H, "The case for an Urban Development Corporation in Zimbabwe – a preliminary assessment,," *Department of Rural and Urban Planning, University of Zimbabwe*, Harare. (1987)
[584] ibid, (1987)

Division is the development arm of the corporation. It offers services in Urban and Regional Planning, Real Estate Development from the inception of development projects (that is, identification of land for development) right up to the provision of infrastructural services and the subsequent transfer of stands to beneficiaries. The Division also offers services in Project Planning and Development Consultancy. The study has revealed that UDCORP has involved a number of actors (international, national and local) over the years. An Officer interviewed asserts:

> "As a parastatal of the Ministry of Local Government, our budgets are approved by the ministry. We used to get part of our funding from some international NGOs like DANIDA, one Belgian NGO and SIDA. The last time we worked with these NGOs was in 1995. Our relationship with SIDA just died a natural death. We worked with this other Italian NGO (Molisv) in one project in Manicaland. That project was based on the Central Place Theory. It was organised just like flea markets. The markets were on a rotational basis and beneficiaries were drawn from people of the surrounding local authorities. We called a periodic market. There were sellers of different products including agricultural products. It was a very noble idea. It brought activity to the rural areas (*waitoonawo kuti kumaruzevha kwatove ne*activity). However, the project just died as well. I think local businessmen were the greatest threat to this noble project. This is because the market was drawing away a lot of their customers. I am not saying that it was so. It's just my opinion. .... We survive from projects which are locally funded."[585]

Evident in this report is that Zimbabwe has lost international initiatives over the years. By inference, UDCORP is an urban planning agency responsible for undertaking preparation of master, local and subject plans. Master plan preparation is provided for in the Regional Town and Country Planning Act Section 13. Whereas the DPP is concerned about offering planning service to local authorities, it has little to offer in terms of highly technical services such as engineering and survey services, UDCORP offers them. In the following shred of paragraph, the UDCORP Officer provides an overview of the work of UDCORP since its inception in 1986:

---

585 Interview 24 March 2011

> "Since inception we have assisted local authorities with preparation of plans including master and layout plans. Specifically, Bindura Municipality, Kadoma and Chinhoyi have benefited from us in this regard. We have also been involved in what were called 'development areas," particularly their identification. For instance, in Gokwe and Gutu we built workshops for rental purposes.... We did feasibility studies for small income generating projects throughout the country. These included supermarkets, horticulture, and cattle projects. We were heavily involved at growth points e.g. Gwanda. Our mandate was to go into what were called development areas so that they grow: from district service centres, to growth points, to towns. I still remember I joined UDCORP as an intern. At Ruwa, for example, UDCORP used to provide advisory services including day-to-day planning issues, construction of houses, particularly inspection. There were [UDCORP] engineers who were stationed in Ruwa, even Murewa and Kotwa. We had secondments to local authorities everywhere. Some ended being permanently employed there"[586].

From this brief, it can be noted that UDCORP has really been on the ground to spearhead spatial processes in physical development of local government areas. In terms of residential development, it was involved in the construction of garden flats in Bindura, Marondera and Harare. In land development, in Harare it has had projects in Borrowdale involving various pieces of land. It participated in a 200 stands joint venture project with Chitungwiza Municipality. In its consultancy endeavours UDCORP was heavily involved with assisting various local authorities preparing their layout plans. This includes preparation of layouts for regularisation, for example in Epworth. Another example is the Kadoma Nissan Housing Project (for the Nissan Company), where the workers were on land that had no title, its involvement was to facilitate settlement upgrading. In the same town, in 1992, UDCORP prepared layouts for industrial development.

The officer provides a view about UDCORP's involvement in Epworth:

> "In Epworth we have been doing a lot of work and I can say it is ongoing work. At the moment we are working there on an advisory basis. *Takamboenda nevekuBotswana vakati* why do

586 Interview 23 June, 2011

> you call this a squatter settlement? In Kenya they call such a settlement an informal settlement. In Epworth, in preparation for the physical upgrading, we first had a socio-economic study to form the basis of the upgrading. *Panguva yatakaita izvi, kwaitove nemombe, vanhu vachigara kumamisha.* We had to generate from the people ideas, to prepare them into getting into an urban setting. This was around 1989. Preparations for layouts began in 1989 through to 1995. As of the implementation, it is ongoing. There were 8 settlements that emerged. Maguta, the original, had bigger stands and we proposed stand owners to subdivide them. The new areas, we called extensions. I must say that the shapes in the original settlements were irregular and unique. We had to formalise the [stand] boundaries for us to come up with a more workable plan. Currently we are assisting the local board with its planning issues, for example, the operative plan proposal formulation given that the current local plan is now outdated"[587].

In more recent times one peri-urban housing development of a consultancy type in which UDCORP has contributed to is the Odar Housing Development Consortium. The settlement is called Southlea Park, located on Odar Farm and comprising about 7,000 stands. The Odar Housing Development Consortium is made up of 54 companies. Land was allocated to it by the Ministry of Local Government, Rural and Urban Development (MILGRUD) as an employer-assisted programme. The project comprises low, medium and high-density housing including ancillary services. The project started in 2006. Layout plan preparation was done in 2006. In 2007, the plans were approved including civil engineering designs. A survey was also carried out in the same year. UDCORP as the project planners and managers has shaped the vision on an advisory basis. The consortium formed some committees including the Project Committee to deal with the development issues hence UDCORP is not project managers on a full-time basis. It prepared a project plan which it reviews on a regular basis to see the extent it is being followed. Servicing of the stands is done in-house as members contribute monthly subscriptions (US$15 high-density and US$20 medium and low density) and the officer explains:

587 Interview 23 June, 2012

> "Engaging a contractor on a full-time basis was found to be too costly. The consortium engaged a site agent to monitor developments on the ground. We supervise on a regular basis, Monitoring and Evaluation. The project is being implemented in phases, beginning with those ideas [we deem] easier to handle, for example, water and sewer reticulation. We started with major roads, the 15 and 20 metre roads.... They applied for a Parallel Development Permit. The City of Harare gave some conditions about water and accessibility. Only paid-up beneficiaries are already on site. They have built temporary structures and put up structures. They have also established a primary and a secondary school. The secondary is now operational up to Form 4 or Form 2." [588]

UDCORP was also involved in the layout preparation of ZIMRE Park. It planned for 3,000 stands and the officer explains:

> *"Isu takaita* planning, *ivo vakaita zvimwe voga.* We did the planning of National Real Estate (ZIMRE) but in consultation with Ruwa Local Board and DPP. We had to incorporate considerations by the Ruwa Local Board. They were just minor considerations.... for example, that we should include stands for flats and industrial development. They also told us to reserve land, adequate land for commercial stands, which would enable the development of modern shopping malls. They said we should not demarcate individual [commercial] stands but just to live the land open. Theirs was a radical and modern approach *yema*shopping malls so we left vast land for shopping centres, leaving room for expansion. We were trying to avoid problems of space such as what you see at Arundel and Groombridge. These shopping centres are too crammed and when you consider expanding then you have to demolish some of the structures. "[589]

> "UDCORP has provided diversified services to different projects and settlements. The corporation has gone a full cycle. In the 1980s, its mandate was more of consultancy than anything. In the late 1990s to early 2000, it had to diversify into land and property development as consultancy work was hard to come by due to a shrinking economy. It decided to get into actual development such that from 2000 to 2006 it was heavily involved into this (actual development). In 2007, at the peak of economic meltdown, UDCORP put some of its projects on

588 Interview 23 June, 2012
589 Interview 23 June, 2012

hold. It only resumed work after the dollarisation (in 2009). The officer says, "we provide auditing services to local authorities. This is so that the local authorities have their accounts in order, to allow them to borrow. We have been auditing since inception, though others have since hired their own auditors. We used to have offices in almost all towns but now we have two UDCORP offices: one here in Harare and the other in Gweru. Gweru services the southern region and Harare *kuno*. Ruwa, Epworth, Bindura, Mutare, Harare....still depend on us"[590].

It can be noted that the corporation was established with a broad agenda of creating functional urban spaces in the country, those where real development and growth were taking shape[591]. Unfortunately, the problem of under-capitalisation has continued with UDCORP from its inception to date. This was further exacerbated by the country's economic crisis which last for more than a decade. Yet, its contribution in peri-urban development remains quite visible. In both Ruwa and Epworth, UDCORP has contributed much. It continues to do so in a number of upcoming settlements at the city-edge.

Harare Metropolitan Province (HMP) was established in 2007, it covers eight districts and of these, seven are functional.[592] These are; Harare Central, Harare South, Harare North, Mabvuku-Tafara or Harare east, Highfield, Chitungwiza and Ruwa- Epworth. There are four local authorities within the metropolitan province, Harare, Chitungwiza, Ruwa Town Council and Epworth Local Board. The metropolitan government has a charter,[593].which is itsitsvehicle to the operation of the system. The charter proposes to:

I. create a new legislative board and determine its powers and organisational and operational procedures, establish

590 Interview 23 June, 2012

[591] Kessides.C, *The Urban Transition in Sub-Saharan Africa: Implications for Economic Growth and Poverty Reduction*, The Cities Alliance: Washington D. C. (2006); Habitat Platform, "Treasures in your neighbourhood: International exchange at neighbourhood level." *VNG Uitgeverij: The Hague.*(2002)

[592] HMP, "Harare Metropolitan Provincial Development Plan 2011," *Government of Zimbabwe*, Harare (2011:4)

[593] Ibid, (2011)

legislative districts determine and set the qualification of its members.

II. establish the position of top executive or administration officers set requirements of the position, determine how the people will be selected and establish the position powers.

III. outline the fiscal, budgetary and financial administration procedures.

IV. determine the public work responsibilities to be assumed and their operations and as well as to establish an education system and how it will be governed and staffed.

V. outline the new government's judicial system and its staffing and determines the scale of other governmental concerns, such as utilities, file protection, public and safety planning

The administration of the Ruwa-Epworth District as part of the metropolitan province raises pertinent issues worth of analysis in the housing, stewardship and peri-urbanisation discourse. The Provincial Administrator (PA) coordinates the operations of the province with the district administrators (DA) having oversight of the districts. The coordination also includes all government activities that emanate or are channelled through the different line ministries. At the time of the research the topical issue was a tree planting programme. The flow of resources for development follows the decentralised path so that budgets and policy issues translate to development on the ground. One Local Government Officer had this to say:

> "Harare Metropolitan Province is headed by a PA. But he cannot be everywhere at the same time hence the principle of decentralisation has informed what happens and how information flows in the system. Under the PA are seven district administrators- DAs. These DAs report to the PA and that is how he gets informed of what is happening on the ground. The PA reports to the Permanent Secretary of the Ministry of Local Government which Permanent Secretary then reports to the Minister.... When it comes to how the province is funded, I must say that we make our requests through our parent ministry, the Ministry of Local Government which puts the request to the Ministry of Finance. When financial resources are allocated, we get these via the same channel"[594].

594 Interview on 9 March 2011

At the time of the study (March 2011), Harare Metropolitan Province did not have a vision statement of its own but was just using one from the MLGRUD. Even the mission statement was one of the ministry, namely: "...to promote local governance, to provide coordinated and orderly spatial development, to provide professional and technical construction and maintenance services in property development, to facilitate the provision of affordable and functional residential accommodation, to promote mitigation and preparedness planning for emergencies and disasters, and to coordinate central and local government programmes and development initiatives." This is just an expression of the province as an operational arm of the MLGRUD. The Local Government Officer shows the relationship of the province and Harare City Council and its sister local authorities (peri-urban satellites) and reiterates:

> "Like I indicated earlier on, the province coordinates all the activities done in Harare. This includes budgeting. In the councils' budgeting committees, the DA is the vice chairperson. He or she has a special role in those council committees and meetings, namely to control deliberations and to safeguard the interests of the public. As you might know, sometimes these local authorities try to advance their own selfish interests ahead of those of the citizens and the public. The DA is just the person to ensure that residents are not suffocated by bills which may be pushed to them. The DA also oversees expenditure by the local authorities; he also guards against instances of corruption. We go to council full board meetings. The DA has the final say.... In fact, he can rescind certain resolutions if they are harmful to the public."

To a great extent, the presence of the DA in council meetings reflects a voice of dissent and agitation to the independent function of local authorities. What is referred to as public interest could perhaps rather be called political interest rather than public interest at least from the expression of most local authority councillors in urban local authorities who are from the MDC and not ZANU-PF. Apart from the coordination function, the province administers all stateland. The Local Government Officer argues that:

> "I am sure that you are aware that there is private as well as stateland; we administer the stateland! Harare City Council or Ruwa Town Council cannot sell to whomever, stateland. The

> Province can allocate that to housing cooperatives; it can also allocate the same to peri-urban farmers but on a temporary basis. For the farmers the allocation is temporary because the farms acquired are for urban expansion. I must say to you that we also work closely with EMA. We tell the farmers that if they cut trees indiscriminately or burn vegetation, they will face the full wrath of the law. We may also force them to leave the land we will have given them."

The temporary use of land designated for urban planning by the peri-urban farmers is a critical peri-urban development aspect in Harare Metropole. Sometimes farmers have grouped to form cooperatives. The key informant could not however disclose the number of cooperatives that had benefited from the Province as that was deemed confidential information. The officer could only say that in her Ruwa-Epworth District there was only one such cooperative. In the district, there were huge numbers of peri-urban farmers pressing demands on the existing available land as exposed by the following statement that:

> "As for peri-urban farmers, we have more than 4000. On average each farmer should have 2 hectares each. However, a much broader definition of the beneficiaries includes even those who have pieces of land as small as this room. Given a big number of people that come to us for land, we have also embarked on borrowing land from other [adjacent] provinces.... There are instances where Mashonaland East Province has said you can make use of vacant land located in such and such an area because we are not yet using it but is adjacent to you [Harare Metropolitan Province]. The farmers are not allowed to build. They cannot build because they are told that their presence there is temporary. Overall, not all the districts have access to farms or have farms. For example, Harare Central; much of its space is already built up. But my district is privileged in this respect."

Although Ruwa and Epworth are in one district (Ruwa-Epworth District), the officer of the Harare Metropolitan Province admits that they do not treat the two settlements as equal. To the province, Epworth is more defined as a rural setting while Ruwa is more developed upcoming modern settlement[595]. The variation in the level of infrastructure development is the major indicator to explain this. The officer has this to add that, "Recently we were having some budgeting consultations. We had to consider these differences. How, for example can you treat a place where there are no roads, where there is no water, no street lighting…no tower lights, where there is no solid waste collection as that which has? Even when we get money through the PSIP, we just have to apply the principle of equity... give more to those without. Epworth lacks in a number of basic elements of infrastructure. The people are poor…"

From the foregoing quotation, it can be noted how the issue of participatory budgeting has not brought results on the ground as has been the case of Brazil where local inhabitants of a place have a voice in shaping their places[596]. Stewardship that shapes the sustainable development of human settlements is one which is inclusive and integrating different components of human, financial and physical resources. Although Harare Metropolitan Province works with a number of actors, the key informant is not keen to comment on Operation Garikayi and Operation Maguta and says, "I cannot answer on the issues of Operation Garikayi, or even Operation Maguta. Though, I know that they somehow report to the province on what they do, I am not in a position to answer on their behalf. Offices have been created to deal with Operation Garikayi and Operation Maguta. You can approach them and ask them on what you are asking"[597].

Again, under the MLGRUD is the Department of Physical Planning which is an arm of government responsible for managing the spatial planning system of the country as well as giving technical advice for the implementation of the development planning system in the country. The Department manages the spatial planning system by making sure that

---

595 Kellett. P,, "Contemporary Vernaculars: Informal housing processes and vernacular theory." *Journal of the International Society for the Study of Vernacular Settlements - ISVS e-journal 2(1)*: pp 1-12.,(2011); Murowe.S; Chirisa.I, "Sally Mugabe Heights: The tale of an incidental Zimbabwean peri-urban housing scheme seeking legitimation," *Zambezia XXXIII (i/ii)*: pp71-89.(2006)

596 Wampler. B, "Participatory Budgeting in Brazil: Contestation, Cooperation and Accountability," *Pennsylvania University Press*,Pennsylvania.(2007) ; World Bank , Brazil: "Toward a More Inclusive and Participatory Budget in Porto Allegre Volume 1: Main Report," *World Bank*, Washington DC., (2008)

597 Interview on 9 March 2011

local authorities are executing their spatial planning functions as prescribed by the Regional, Town and Country Planning Act (Chapter.29:12) and related Regulations. It is also responsible for guiding the Minister to interpret planning provisions and to execute planning functions under the Minister's reserved powers of the said planning legislation[598]. Though there was much involvement in the early years of independence in Epworth, over the years its role has somewhat diminished. For Ruwa, much of the planning is done through private consultancy. Overall, DPP's role in Ruwa and Epworth has been more indirect than direct.

The DPP is the primary steward for planning. The Department's work is defined according to the following specific parameters:

I. Formulation and review of Spatial Planning Policy and supportive legislation that promotes on-going socio-economic and other Government programmes,
II. Setting of Standards that are universally applied by all local planning authorities across the country,
III. Being a watchdog hence monitoring local planning authority compliance with provisions of the Act, set Standards and procedures,iv). Supervising spatial planning activities of local planning authorities,
IV. Executing planning functions under the reversed Powers of the Minister in the RTCP Act (section 29,40,43 and 49),
V. Facilitating sites for the development of government, state enterprises and parastatals;
VI. Detailing planning of housing estates on state land,
VII. Technical evaluation of plans (master plans, local plans and layout plans) originating from local planning authorities for the Minister's decision;
VIII. Mediation role on stakeholder conflicts arising from spatial planning decisions of local planning authorities that interfere with other people's land rights, and

---

598 Mlalazi.E, "Employment of Planning Graduate and Gaps:7-8 October 2010, Harare: Perspectives from the Department Of Physical Planning," *Paper presented an the Workshop On Strengthening Planning Education In Zimbabwe,* 5th October 2010 (Ref: B/2/3)9(2010)

IX. Providing technical assistance to plan preparation structures for the development planning system which is prescribed by the Provincial Councils and Administration Act of 1984.

In practice, though, the department finds itself assuming the role of the local planning authority, undertaking direct planning functions on behalf of those local planning authorities who lack professional capacity to carry out that function in their own areas of jurisdiction (Mlalazi, 2010). This predicament is likely to remain unchanged until that time when small towns and RDCs are financially sound to recruit own professional staff and have planning departments in their structures. Service delivery takes place at different levels, being: head office, and 10 provincial stations. The head office staff is drawn from experienced staff from Provincial Stations while for the provincial Offices is recruited from the job market. As at October 2010, the department had a structure for 172 posts covering professional and technical staff constituting: 3 managerial posts (Director and deputies), 14 lower management (Chief Planning Officer/Chief Technician) and 155 support staff (Town Planning Officers/Town Planning Technicians). It is unfortunate that the department has over the years been experiencing high staff turnover hence has been a "training ground for some other institutions" – public and private, alike. Such a turnover compromises quality of delivery as the inexperienced take the reins of planning.

The director and deputy director express bitterness towards this development of high staff turnover, and also even blame the curriculum at the University of Zimbabwe, Department of Rural and Urban Planning which allows planners to be generalists hence venture into other sectors including the real estate, construction, transport, planning advocacy and information and communications (Mlalazi, 2010). I must declare that much of the discourse and text in writing this chapter has been obtained from the Deputy Director of the DPP and as well derived from the paper by the Director of Physical Planning. Perhaps, we should also see how the macro-economic environment contributes to the sustainability of institutions. For Zimbabwe, the years from 1997 to date have been years of economic destabilisation which explains, partly, why there are so many Zimbabweans, abroad (Maphosa, Kujinga and Chingarande, 2007).

There are a number of ways to define peri-urban. The Deputy Director, DPP has mentioned that:

> "Basically, there are three ways in which we can define the term peri-urban, first as *a zone of transition* between the rural and urban areas; second as *a zone that cannot do without the city* (this can be in terms of dependency on education facilities or jobs offered in the city); lastly as hinging on the rural as a resource, primarily looking at land as a resource and not defined in terms of urban stands. Overall, the term implies interdependence of the rural and urban areas, looking at the immediate influence which these have one on another. Criteria for determination must be looked at from the angle of distance and impact. I am sure you have heard of Von Thunen. When you look his model, even though he didn't mention the term peri-urban, his model vividly implied it. This is in terms of the sphere of influence and impact criterion"[599].

It is implied in this text that the peri-urban zone is a place of spatial interdependence. Lifestyles of individuals and households are part and parcel of this interdependence. Recent developments in peri-urbanisation in Zimbabwe have been characterised by changing lifestyles especially of the black Africans in Zimbabwe. Again, as illustrated by the words of the Deputy Director, DPP, the issue of 'upward mobility' of citizens (shifting from a lower class to the one above) has a bearing on how one relates to peri-urbanity. The Deputy Director opines that:

> "In the colonial days, peri-urban Ruwa was considered as a place for poor whites. These were given an opportunity to leave here because they could not afford going for holiday or weekend retreats as rich whites. Today peri-urban plots are not for the poor. They are for the rich people; *munhu mutema akapfuma anoti anoda* plot. Blacks are not keen on retreats or holiday homes. *Vanoda pavanoti ndepangu apa. Ndinoita zvandinoda kuita pasina anondikanganisa.* So, some people have been coming to us requesting for plots. But we have had to be very tactful.... [As a department], we are now discouraging building that is of a compound style. We do not want too many buildings. We want order near the town. We are discouraging kraals [*kuti munhu anoti anoda kuchengeta mombe* though *Hapana mutemo unoramba mombe*]. Imagine Tynwald. If it is a new proposal!

599 Interview, 11 March 2011

> We are saying that low-density housing should not be more than 2000 square metres unless it is a departure, say because of the terrain. On the plot we are encouraging the construction of only one building perhaps plus a servant quarter. *Komboni ndiyo yatiri kuramba.* It has to go. Plots are also generally discouraged on private land [earmarked] for urban expansion. When it comes to allowing processes for urban expansion, a farm is faster to deal with than plots. It's faster in the sense that, suppose there are fifty (50) mansions having been built with servants' quarters as well... Think of the boreholes. We can have a borehole in the midst of a road; tanks of fuel; windmills...there are so many infrastructural contents to deal with. If the number of plots increases that causes urban sprawling. Towns should thrive on cost-effectiveness. You are not cost-effective if you run a road only to serve five families"[600].

These sentiments by the deputy director are also important in highlighting the role of DPP as a key agency in spatial management of human settlements in the country. That preferences and tastes of space demanders have changed according to changing times (colonial to independence) is a critical pointer for policy and practice in peri-urban housing. DPP is against haphazard compound-like housing construction on plots. Stewardship is a management factor. On stewardship, the deputy director, DPP stresses that, "You call it stewardship; I call it management. For instance, there are people who say planning does not involve management. I personally disagree with that. Management is inseparable from planning. We oversee spatial matters.... Check with the preamble [of the Regional, Town and Country Planning Act, Chapter 29:12]. There is a talk about health, amenity and safety. We have to ensure that in our design standards such are safeguarded. Our designs should ensure that there is delivery of health, amenity and safety. We also demand the carrying out of Environmental Impact Assessments (EIA). All this is part of management, the management of space"[601].

Overall, planning as an instrument of human settlement policy in Zimbabwe has been blamed for stifling housing delivery in the country. These have been termed "planning failures" (Toriro, 2007). This may be

600 Interview 11 March 2011
601 Interview 11 March 2011

the principal reason of the poor's exclusion from housing delivery systems (Chaeruka and Munzwa, 2009). Specifically, the factors that explain poor delivery of urban housing are: the cumbersomeness of the process due to constraints in the poor managing to meet the high standards, separation of land-uses causing inefficiency in the general urban system, urban sprawling effects, insensitivity to low-income groups including planning regulations excluding the informal sector in the urban centres and the mismatch between what the poor can afford in terms of resource mobilisation and what the regulations prescribe. Planning, in the context of increasing urban and peri-urban poverty, has tended to pose challenges to the enhancement of stewardship of place.

The definition of peri-urban in Zimbabwe has shifted. Today there is a growing demand for shelter. The Deputy Director of DPP argues that,

> "... to define peri-urban [as a planning department], we have standards that define the area. A plot has to be 1-2 hectares in size. Sometimes these standards have been compromised. But when we look at places like Christon Bank and Ruwa, one average they are of size 1.6 hectares. The standards stipulate that they have to be of a uniform character.... In Ruwa, these plots were defined on the basis of being viable agricultural units and sometimes these came in different sizes. The farming viability was to be defined by AGRITEX on the basis of land capability and infrastructure requirements. The plot thus had to be of a considerable small size. But that does not disqualify certain farms, which may not have been 'chopped' to get to small-sized units. Even when not subdivided they are still peri-urban farm by virtue of their location.... Let's put in view the new context in which peri-urban has applied in Zimbabwe. Farms acquired recently have been used for housing. This bring about what I call the home-seekers' definition of peri-urban. I am talking of the housing cooperatives and occupiers which took over farms like Whitecliffe, Caledonia, and Odar-Stoneridge...We now have 'peri-urban layouts' because of these. This is a *de facto* definition. There are two types of land falling in the zone we are calling peri-urban that you have to understand about: stateland, like Hatcliffe which has come about by some lank banking; and, land that has been designated

by Master plans (sometimes this type has not yet been acquired)"[602].

That DPP technically defines peri-urban is critical for this study. However, the definition is elitist hence ignores that current developments whose characterisation as informal is undisputed. The Deputy Director speaks of the 'home-seekers' definition of peri-urban housing as well as 'peri-urban layouts." Behind this nomenclature are the forces of the fast-track land reform programme in the country which availed land for the poor to start building and investing housing in the peri-urban areas. To some extent this explains the failure of the urban master planning procedures in creating space for housing of the poor classes in society. This echoes the observation by the Abrams (1964) that the poor are less concerned about what they build but where they build. This is an issue in housing land delivery.

The Urban Development Corporation (UDCORP) was established in 1986 through an Act of Parliament (The Urban Development Corporation Act, N° 14) to assist local authorities throughout Zimbabwe with a variety of specialised services in land and property development. It was the First Five Year National Development Plan (FFYNDP) covering the period 1986-1990 that put forward as a first priority the establishment of UDCORP. This was in keeping with a recommendation made in 1981 by the United Nations Commission for Human Settlements (UNCHS) which commissioned a feasibility study on the spatial planning for Zimbabwe. This was soon after the country's independence from British rule in 1980[603]. The idea for setting up this institution was meant to encourage the setting up of growth points, employment generation, provision of housing and social services, creation of supporting environment for development, financial and technical assistance to local authorities and cooperative, commercial, industrial and other enterprises[604].

602 Interview on 11 March 2011

[603] Wekwete.K.H, "The case for an Urban Development Corporation in Zimbabwe – a preliminary assessment," *Department of Rural and Urban Planning, University of Zimbabwe*, Harare. (1987)

[604] ibid, (1987)

UDCORP is a government state-owned enterprise under the ambit of the MLGRUD. UDCORP, like most other government departments is headed by a Director who is appointed by the Minister of Local Government Rural and Urban Development. Under the Director is the Deputy Director who assists the Director in running the corporation and under the deputy-director are other officers and technicians in defined areas of speciality. Technicians (engineering, electrical and surveying) are at the lower ramp of the organisational ladder. UDCORP has several departments or sections including Human Resources, responsible for recruiting and training new staff development programs and the Properties and Technical Services Division which has three sections namely; Physical Planning, Project Planning and Management and Property Development Consultancy. The Properties and Technical Services Division is the development arm of the corporation. It offers services in Urban and Regional Planning, Real Estate Development from the inception of development projects (that is, identification of land for development) right up to the provision of infrastructural services and the subsequent transfer of stands to beneficiaries. The Division also offers services in Project Planning and Development Consultancy. The study has revealed that UDCORP has involved a number of actors (international, national and local) over the years. An Officer interviewed asserts:

> "As a parastatal of the Ministry of Local Government, our budgets are approved by the ministry. We used to get part of our funding from some international NGOs like DANIDA, one Belgian NGO and SIDA. The last time we worked with these NGOs was in 1995. Our relationship with SIDA just died a natural death. We worked with this other Italian NGO (Molisv) in one project in Manicaland. That project was based on the Central Place Theory. It was organised just like flea markets. The markets were on a rotational basis and beneficiaries were drawn from people of the surrounding local authorities. We called a periodic market. There were sellers of different products including agricultural products. It was a very noble idea. It brought activity to the rural areas (*waitoonawo kuti kumaruzevha kwatove ne*activity). However, the project just died as well. I think local businessmen were the greatest threat to this noble project. This is because the market was drawing away a lot of their customers. I am not saying that it was so. It's

> just my opinion. .... We survive from projects which are locally funded."[605]

Evident in this report is that Zimbabwe has lost international initiatives over the years. By inference, UDCORP is an urban planning agency responsible for undertaking preparation of master, local and subject plans. Master plan preparation is provided for in the Regional Town and Country Planning Act Section 13. Whereas the DPP is concerned about offering planning service to local authorities, it has little to offer in terms of highly technical services such as engineering and survey services, UDCORP offers them. In the following shred of paragraph, the UDCORP Officer provides an overview of the work of UDCORP since its inception in 1986:

> "Since inception we have assisted local authorities with preparation of plans including master and layout plans. Specifically, Bindura Municipality, Kadoma and Chinhoyi have benefited from us in this regard. We have also been involved in what were called 'development areas," particularly their identification. For instance, in Gokwe and Gutu we built workshops for rental purposes.... We did feasibility studies for small income generating projects throughout the country. These included supermarkets, horticulture, and cattle projects. We were heavily involved at growth points e.g. Gwanda. Our mandate was to go into what were called development areas so that they grow: from district service centres, to growth points, to towns. I still remember I joined UDCORP as an intern. At Ruwa, for example, UDCORP used to provide advisory services including day-to-day planning issues, construction of houses, particularly inspection. There were [UDCORP] engineers who were stationed in Ruwa, even Murewa and Kotwa. We had secondments to local authorities everywhere. Some ended being permanently employed there"[606].

From this brief, it can be noted that UDCORP has really been on the ground to spearhead spatial processes in physical development of local government areas. In terms of residential development, it was involved in the construction of garden flats in Bindura, Marondera and Harare. In land development, in Harare it has had projects in Borrowdale involving

605 Interview 24 March 2011
606 Interview 23 June, 2011

various pieces of land. It participated in a 200 stands joint venture project with Chitungwiza Municipality. In its consultancy endeavours UDCORP was heavily involved with assisting various local authorities preparing their layout plans. This includes preparation of layouts for regularisation, for example in Epworth. Another example is the Kadoma Nissan Housing Project (for the Nissan Company), where the workers were on land that had no title, its involvement was to facilitate settlement upgrading. In the same town, in 1992, UDCORP prepared layouts for industrial development.

The officer provides a view about UDCORP's involvement in Epworth:

> "In Epworth we have been doing a lot of work and I can say it is ongoing work. At the moment we are working there on an advisory basis. *Takamboenda nevekuBotswana vakati* why do you call this a squatter settlement? In Kenya they call such a settlement an informal settlement. In Epworth, in preparation for the physical upgrading, we first had a socio-economic study to form the basis of the upgrading. *Panguva yatakaita izvi, kwaitove nemombe, vanhu vachigara kumamisha.* We had to generate from the people ideas, to prepare them into getting into an urban setting. This was around 1989. Preparations for layouts began in 1989 through to 1995. As of the implementation, it is ongoing. There were 8 settlements that emerged. Maguta, the original, had bigger stands and we proposed stand owners to subdivide them. The new areas, we called extensions. I must say that the shapes in the original settlements were irregular and unique. We had to formalise the [stand] boundaries for us to come up with a more workable plan. Currently we are assisting the local board with its planning issues, for example, the operative plan proposal formulation given that the current local plan is now outdated"[607].

In more recent times one peri-urban housing development of a consultancy type in which UDCORP has contributed to is the Odar Housing Development Consortium. The settlement is called Southlea Park, located on Odar Farm and comprising about 7,000 stands. The Odar Housing Development Consortium is made up of 54 companies. Land was allocated to it by the Ministry of Local Government, Rural and Urban

607 Interview 23 June, 2012

Development (MILGRUD) as an employer-assisted programme. The project comprises low, medium and high-density housing including ancillary services. The project started in 2006. Layout plan preparation was done in 2006. In 2007, the plans were approved including civil engineering designs. A survey was also carried out in the same year. UDCORP as the project planners and managers has shaped the vision on an advisory basis. The consortium formed some committees including the Project Committee to deal with the development issues hence UDCORP is not project managers on a full-time basis. It prepared a project plan which it reviews on a regular basis to see the extent it is being followed. Servicing of the stands is done in-house as members contribute monthly subscriptions (US$15 high-density and US$20 medium and low density) and the officer explains:

> "Engaging a contractor on a full-time basis was found to be too costly. The consortium engaged a site agent to monitor developments on the ground. We supervise on a regular basis, Monitoring and Evaluation. The project is being implemented in phases, beginning with those ideas [we deem] easier to handle, for example, water and sewer reticulation. We started with major roads, the 15 and 20 metre roads.... They applied for a Parallel Development Permit. The City of Harare gave some conditions about water and accessibility. Only paid-up beneficiaries are already on site. They have built temporary structures and put up structures. They have also established a primary and a secondary school. The secondary is now operational up to Form 4 or Form 2." [608]

UDCORP was also involved in the layout preparation of ZIMRE Park. It planned for 3,000 stands and the officer explains:

> *"Isu takaita* planning, *ivo vakaita zvimwe voga.* We did the planning of National Real Estate (ZIMRE) but in consultation with Ruwa Local Board and DPP. We had to incorporate considerations by the Ruwa Local Board. They were just minor considerations.... for example, that we should include stands for flats and industrial development. They also told us to reserve land, adequate land for commercial stands, which would enable the development of modern shopping malls. They said we should not demarcate individual [commercial] stands but just to live the land open. Theirs was a radical and modern approach

608 Interview 23 June, 2012

> *yema*shopping malls so we left vast land for shopping centres, leaving room for expansion. We were trying to avoid problems of space such as what you see at Arundel and Groombridge. These shopping centres are too crammed and when you consider expanding then you have to demolish some of the structures… UDCORP has provided diversified services to different projects and settlements. The corporation has gone a full cycle. In the 1980s, its mandate was more of consultancy than anything. In the late 1990s to early 2000, it had to diversify into land and property development as consultancy work was hard to come by due to a shrinking economy. It decided to get into actual development such that from 2000 to 2006 it was heavily involved into this (actual development). In 2007, at the peak of economic meltdown, UDCORP put some of its projects on hold. It only resumed work after the dollarisation (in 2009). The officer says, "we provide auditing services to local authorities. This is so that the local authorities have their accounts in order, to allow them to borrow. We have been auditing since inception, though others have since hired their own auditors. We used to have offices in almost all towns but now we have two UDCORP offices: one here in Harare and the other in Gweru. Gweru services the southern region and Harare *kuno*. Ruwa, Epworth, Bindura, Mutare, Harare....still depend on us"[609].

It can be noted that the corporation was established with a broad agenda of creating functional urban spaces in the country, those where real development and growth were taking shape[610]. Unfortunately, the problem of under-capitalisation has continued with UDCORP from its inception to date. This was further exacerbated by the country's economic crisis which last for more than a decade. Yet, its contribution in peri-urban development remains quite visible. In both Ruwa and Epworth, UDCORP has contributed much. It continues to do so in a number of upcoming settlements at the city-edge.

Ministry of Lands and Rural Resettlements (MLRR) is primarily in the rural areas, when it comes to rural land conversion, it is this ministry

---

609 Interview 23 June, 2012

[610] Kessides.C, *The Urban Transition in Sub-Saharan Africa: Implications for Economic Growth and Poverty Reduction*, The Cities Alliance: Washington D. C. (2006); Habitat Platform, "Treasures in your neighbourhood: International exchange at neighbourhood level." *VNG Uitgeverij: The Hague.*(2002)

which has a great stake for reference. The role of the Ministry of Land and Rural Resettlement in the transfer and governance of land is very critical as a peri-urbanisation move and process. Minister Hebert Murerwa at the National Housing Convention in 2009 presented on the topic: 'Land delivery for urban expansion.' The Minister highlights that the Ministry of Lands and Rural Resettlement (MLRR) has focussed more on the land reform programme whose thrust has been the provision of land for rural resettlement and agricultural production. The minister stresses that, "Indeed the bulk of the land acquired by Government has gone towards rural resettlement. However, the land acquisition process has made available some land for urban expansion. As you may be aware.... Government took a deliberate decision to also acquire land for urban expansion as part of the land reform programme after realising that this was a way of availing land of the size required for urban expansion at reasonable cost"[611].

The MLRR, in its mandate, works in close contact with the MLGRUD. This has been followed throughout, in the implementation of the land reform programme. The procedure is that the MLGRUD represents urban and local authorities which, when land is provided, proceed to re-plan for housing development. The MLRR receives regularly submission of lists of farms that the MLGRUD and its local authorities require for urban expansion. The MLRR administers several pieces of legislation enabling the process of land acquisition of which the principal one is the Land Acquisition Act (Chapter 20:10). It is asserted that this Act, in section 3, empowers the President or any Minister duly authorised by the President for that purpose, to compulsorily acquire:

a) "Any land, where the acquisition is reasonably necessary in the interests of defence, public safety, public order, public morality, public health, town and country planning or the utilisation of that or any other property for a purpose beneficial to the public generally or to any section of the public."
b) "Any rural land, where the acquisition is reasonably necessary for the utilisation of that or any other land (i) for resettlement for agricultural or other purpose, or (ii) for the purposes of

611 Extract from Speech at the National Housing Convention, October, 2009.

land reorganisation, forestry, environmental conservation or the utilisation of wild life or other natural resources or (iii) for the relocation of persons dispossessed in consequence of the utilisation of land for a right to that land. This was followed by an acquisition order or section 8 notice"[612].

In certain instances, where the land owner objects to the acquisition and indicates this in writing within a period of 30 days after the preliminary notice, the Acquiring Authority applies to the Administrative Court for confirmation of the acquisition order. The challenges associated with the procedures are that they are cumbersome, lengthy and were fraught with many legal technicalities. Constitutional Amendment Number 17 of 2005, which came into force on the 14th September 2005, changed the legal procedures in respect of the compulsory acquisition of agricultural land for resettlement purposes, and the Section 16 B of the Constitution has barred any legal challenges in respect of agricultural land compulsorily acquired for resettlement purposes[613]. Acquisition of land for urban expansion is characterised by the very same process used initially to acquire rural agricultural land[614]. Murerwa underscores that before the Constitutional Amendment Number 17, a notice was served on the owner and the latter objected, the Acquiring Authority had to apply to the Administrative Court for an order to confirm the acquisition in terms of Section 7 to the Land Acquisition Act. This process, in the terms of Murerwa, has unfortunately turned to be cumbersome also requiring the Minister of Lands and Rural Settlement (as Acquiring Authority) to fully justify the need for acquiring the land for

---

612 Murerwa. H, "Speech by The Minister of Lands and Rural Resettlement, Hon. H. M. Murerwa (MP) On Land Delivery For Housing," *Housing Convention Victoria Falls 26 – 30 October 2009* (2009)Extract from Speech at the National Housing Convention, October, 2009.

613 Murerwa. H, "Speech by The Minister of Lands and Rural Resettlement, Hon. H. M. Murerwa (MP) On Land Delivery For Housing," *Housing Convention Victoria Falls 26 – 30 October 2009* (2009)

614 Chipungu. L, "Institutional constraints to land delivery for low-income housing: a case study of Harare, Zimbabwe," in *RICS Foundation Our Common Estate Paper Series*. URL: www.rics-foundation.org, Accessed on 22 April 2008.(2005); Mubvami.T ; Musandu-Nyamayaro.O, "Procedural Impediments to the Low-income Housing Land Delivery in Cities of Zimbabwe," *Department of Rural and Urban Planning. University of Zimbabwe*, Harare. (1993)

urban expansion or housing to counter objections lodged by former owners. The result has been that the process of acquiring land for urban expansion has been rather slow. In light of this Murerwa affirms that:

> "I need to highlight the relationship between my Ministry and the Ministry of Local Government, Rural and Urban Development in this process. My Ministry gazettes farms for urban expansion only on the basis of written requests from the Ministry of Local Government Rural and Urban Development....We have on record a list of peri-urban properties identified by the same Ministry and it was on the basis of this that previous gazetting was carried out. I am reliably informed that a majority of the farms involved were subsequently allocated to housing cooperatives for development.... The Ministry of Local Government Rural and Urban Development would also valuate the farms acquired and be expected to pay full compensation for both land and improvements at the current market rate.... With the recent restructuring of Ministries under the inclusive Government it becomes necessary to clarify the roles of the Ministry of Local Government Rural and Urban Development and that of National Housing and Social Amenities in this whole process"[615].

As at 2009, the MLRR had gazetted 68 farms of which forty-four (44) are in Harare, one (1) in Ruwa, one (1) in Chinhoyi and the balance is in the Bulawayo Metropolitan Province. Yet, the challenges the Administrative Court still had to hear cases and confirm the acquisition. For this reason, only 4 farms in Harare Metropolitan Province had, by then, been confirmed in the Administrative Court (Murerwa, 2009). The Minister asserts, thus,

> "The question that needs to be asked is what the position of all other farms whose acquisition has not been confirmed is? The legal position however is that for all the farms whose owners were served with preliminary notices (section 5 notices) the process of acquisition is still live as such notice expire after 10 years from the date of first publication. What is required is the re-service of acquisition orders (section 8 orders) for those farms following which applications are made to the Administrative Court for confirmation." For my Ministry to proceed with this process we need the responsible Ministry to

615 Extract from Speech at the National Housing Convention, October, 2009.

> indicate whether the farms initially identified are still required for purposes of urban expansion and national housing. Supporting affidavits to support identification of these farms for urban expansion will also be required from the responsible Ministry to substantiate and support the need to acquisition. In submitting this detail, the responsible Ministry will need to work closely with urban local authorities who have to take particular note of the location of the farm's vis-a-vis their prescribed and gazetted urban boundaries.... "There have been numerous other challenges encountered of late in the process of availing land for housing developments and urban expansion. One of these challenges is the purported changes in ownership or attempts to change ownership of some of the farms identified for housing and urban expansion. On realising that their properties have been gazetted, some owners have made frantic efforts to "sell" the farms and apply to the Registrar of Deeds for change of ownership with intentions, we believe, to scuttle the acquisition process. The Ministry's position is that once the acquisition process has begun transfer of title should not and cannot be allowed to proceed"[616].

The submission[617] has been resonated in the explanation of the prevalence of housing poverty in Southern Africa which observes that:

> "For Harare, the procedures and processes of converting peri-urban land to urban uses are highly technical and painstakingly administered involving land feasibility studies, purchase, land transfer, land-use planning, cadastral surveying, land servicing and allocation to developers. However, processes are extremely slow due to institutional weakness, including the fact that residential layout plans cannot be prepared while land is still in private ownership. Time spans of four or more years between land identification and commencement of construction are the norm in the context where squatting is not tolerated. This inevitably has led to very high land prices, speculation, 'downward raiding' (gentrification and high-income groups occupying housing land intended for lower income groups), and overcrowding of the housing stock"[618].

---

616 Extract from Speech at the National Housing Convention, October, 2009.
617 Murerwa. H, "Speech by The Minister of Lands and Rural Resettlement, Hon. H. M. Murerwa (MP) On Land Delivery For Housing," *Housing Convention Victoria Falls 26 – 30 October 2009* (2009)
618 UNHABITAT, "*The state of African cities 2008: A framework for addressing urban challenges in Africa,*" UNHABITAT: Nairobi.(2008)

Some peri-urban farms including Breamar, Dunotar, Longlands and Edinburgh were initially set aside for the expansion of Chitungwiza. As a stopgap measure the MLRR had to take a decision to re-plan these farms converting them into A2 model farms. The MLRR has also encountered challenges on peri-urban farms identified and reserved for future expansion but allocated to urban beneficiaries specifically for peri-urban agriculture. Under this arrangement one-hectare plots are demarcated and allocated for urban agriculture. Beneficiaries are allowed to utilise their plots but are not allowed to construct permanent dwellings thereon. They are expected to relinquish use of the plots when the farms are required for housing development. It is argued that, though this arrangement is plausible, it is faltered as the beneficiaries want only to destroy the vegetation on these farms leading to serious deforestation[619].

Ministry National Housing and Social Amenities (MNHSA) as it stands today (from 2009) is the outcome of merging the Ministry of Rural Housing and Social Amenities (MRHSA) established in 2005 and the Department of Urban Housing Development (DUHD) which was in the Ministry of Local Government, Public Works and Urban Development (MLGPWUD). It became as stand-alone ministry combining the functions of the former MRHSA and DUHD functions (MNHSA, 2009a; Mhashu, 2009; Munyoro, 2009). Before 2005, the housing agenda was mainly urban-orientated such that anything to do with rural housing and social amenities was "...assigned to agencies tasked with lands, rural settlement, community and general rural development functions" (MNHSA, 2009:5). The role of the MNHSA to coordinate the task is heavily involving, tapping from a variety of stakeholders as much as possible. A stewardship and partnership model is the anchor to such an endeavour.

The MNHSA's vision is: "A nation with sustainable human settlements". Like most vision statements, this sounds utopian and romanticised, should one look into the challenges that the country has gone through let alone the fuzziness associated with the term "sustainability"

---

619 Mwanamakondo.B.Y, "The state of resettlement areas in Zambia," *A paper presented at the Swedish Cooperative Centre (SCC) at the Chrismar Hotel, 27-28 February 2007*, Lusaka.pg3. (2007)

whose usage has become stretched and ever-shifting[620]. This vision is tied to the mission statement of the ministry which reads that the ministry "...facilitates, promotes and provides affordable and accessible housing and social amenities in Zimbabwe." Again, these statements are packed. They give a critic the impression that the ministry is burdening itself with responsibilities, especially of providing when perhaps it should just be concentrating on facilitating and promoting the development and management of human settlements in the country.

Facilitation and promotion are in keeping with the Habitat Agenda, a policy adopted by 171 governments at the United Nations Conference on Human Settlements, Istanbul in June 1996 whose objectives were outlined as ensuring adequate shelter for all and sustainable development of the world's urban areas and achieving these objectives through enablement and participation, gender equality, financing shelter and human settlements, international cooperation and the assessment of progress (Payne and Majale, 2004). State provision takes us back to the 1960s and 1970s where shortcomings in this approach were to be noted in the years that followed. Yet, it remains true that the MNHSA provides houses given that it enjoys a huge stock of rented shelter developed in the past years which are now in its custody.

Specifically, the MNHSA has the following mandate to formulate and implement housing and social amenities policies at household, business centre and growth point level, to mobilise resources for implementation of housing and social amenities, to administer housing estates, to administer the National Housing Fund, Housing and Guarantee Fund, Rural Housing Fund and Social Amenities Development Fund, to develop and implement strategies that ensure community mobilisation and participation for purposes of providing and maintaining social amenities infrastructure, and to acquire land for urban housing development[621]. a

---

[620] Mitlin. D,, "Sustaining markets or poverty reduction?," *Environment and Urbanisation 14(1):* pp 173-177.(2002)

[621] GoZ/UNDP/UNHABITAT, "Proceedings of the National Symposium convened by the Ministry of National Housing and Social Amenities under the theme ,"*Towards an Integrated Approach to Sustainable Housing and Social Amenities Delivery in Zimbabwe" on 28 May 2009*, Mendel Training Centre, Harare. (2009)

longer list of the functions of the ministry which are spelt out as its terms of reference are provided as follows:

i. formulating and implementing relevant policies,
ii. developing and implementing strategies in consultation with other ministries and stakeholders,
iii. providing housing and social amenities infrastructure,
iv. coordinating and mobilising communities for the provision and maintenance of infrastructure,
v. mobilising resources for the implementation of programmes,
vi. coordinating implementation of the Rural Housing Delivery Programme (RHDP)
vii. administering government housing estates, managing and accounting for relevant housing funds,
viii. administering rent control regulations for residential accommodation,
ix. developing and monitoring housing allocation criteria for all local authorities, and,
x. facilitating the purchase of land for urban housing development[622].

These terms of reference are drawn mainly from the Housing and Building Act (Chapter 22:07), the Housing and Building Amendment Act of 1994 (Sales in Execution), the Immovable Property (Prevention of Discrimination Act, Chapter 10:12) and the Housing Standards Control Act (Chapter 29:08). These are important in the drawing of the key result areas of the ministry[623]. The Housing and Building Act empowers the MNHSA to construct buildings and infrastructure in support of real estate development by other actors while the Housing Standards Control Act gives it regulatory powers, that is, to "monitor and maintain housing standards nationally"[624]. In a quest to ensure fairness and equity in the

---

622 MNHSA, "2010 to 2014 Strategic Plan," *Government of Zimbabwe*, Harare. (2009a:8)

623 MNHSA, "The Ministry"s MNHSA (Ministry of National Housing and Social Amenities) (2010),Integrated Performance Agreement for the Year 2010," *Government of Zimbabwe* Harare.(2010a)

624 MNHSA, "2010 to 2014 Strategic Plan," *Government of Zimbabwe*, Harare. (2009a:8)

letting of residential property, Statutory Instrument (SI) 32 of 2007 (Rent Regulations) empowers Rent Boards, to arbitrate in cases of rent disputes, evictions and the consideration of applications for rent reviews or variations.

Though administered by other arms of the government, the other critical laws and policies guiding the work of the MNHSA include that National Constitution, local governments statutes (the Urban Councils Act, Chapter 29:15; the Rural District Act, Chapter 29:13; the Traditional Leaders' Act); land and related legislation (the Land Acquisition Act, the Land Survey Act and the Deeds Registration Act); the Environmental Management Act; the Regional, Town and Country Planning Act; Model Building Bye-Laws of 1977; the Building Societies Act (Chapter 24:02); and statutes governing the conduct of professionals in t professional he built environment sector (the Architects Act, Chapter 27:01; Engineering Councils Act, Chapter 27:22, and the Quantity Surveyors Act, Chapter 27:13)[625]. Having a clear understanding of the provisions of the legislations and statutory instruments helps the ministry towards a smooth running of its operations.

However, the increased number of players with different possible conflicting points of entry makes the whole business of the ministry a bit cryptic and obscure. Some of the areas for emphasis, as provided say by the National Constitution are more socially and ethically rooted than anything. Others are technical in economic, legal and engineering terms. For instance, when the ministry came into office in 2009, the treasury "...instructed that ministries implementing capital projects should merely concentrate on securing quick wins and move away altogether from embarking on new ones"[626]. This was to cater for the non-performance in such projects as explained by the more than decade of economic meltdown and stagflation in the country. Such is a tight rope for walking. Yet there is also considerable strength in working with partners of diverse

---

[625] MNHSA, , "2010 to 2014 Strategic Plan," *Government of Zimbabwe*, Harare. (2009a:8) ; ; MNHSA, "The Ministry"s MNHSA (Ministry of National Housing and Social Amenities) (2010),Integrated Performance Agreement for the Year 2010," *Government of Zimbabwe* Harare.(2010a),

[626] MNHSA, "The Ministry of National Housing and Social Amenities Annual Report for 2009," *Government of Zimbabwe*, Harare.(2009h:2)

backgrounds and interests provided there is more of consensus-seeking in business as enabled by adopting partnership linkages. In effect, a healthier situation is when all the actors frankly contribute and sometimes argue towards informed consensus. Some scholars have written on the role of contentious politics rather than falling into the trap of co-optation[627]. This is possible where cooperation and accountability are treated as mutual elements leading to transparency in business. This perhaps is further elaborated through the organisational structures that the ministry has at head office, provincial and district levels.

The ten departments in the MNHSA are: Finance and Administration, Human Resources, Housing, Social Amenities, Construction and Operations, Estates Management, Research and Planning, Audit and Legal Services. Delivery is pursued through a decentralised system with the Head Office in Harare spearheading the coordination of policy formulation and evaluation as well as "...technically backstopping field offices; and the sub-national level involved in hands on business – programme and projects implementation[628]. It is stressed that the ministry applies the systems approach in its operations, being buttressed by participatory methodologies. It also believes in a flexible approach of continuous improvements in its internal capacity. It can be noted that this is influenced by its firm belief in the application of the analysis of Strengths, Weaknesses, Opportunities and Threats (SWOT). In this respect, it acknowledges the critical role and contribution made by the strategic links with both local and international partners. Figure 10.1 shows the organisational structure that the ministry has at head office and is quite vertical signifying the hierarchy in the chain of command within the ministry. Another structure is also there and it applies at the provincial and district levels. This is horizontal coordination at localised project levels[629].

---

627 Wampler. B, "Participatory Budgeting in Brazil: Contestation, Cooperation and Accountability," *Pennsylvania University Press*,Pennsylvania.(2007)

628 MNHSA, "2010 to 2014 Strategic Plan," *Government of Zimbabwe*, Harare. (2009a:10)

629 MNHSA, "2010 to 2014 Strategic Plan," *Government of Zimbabwe*, Harare. (2009a:8); MNHSA, "The Ministry"s Organisational Structure - Head Office,"

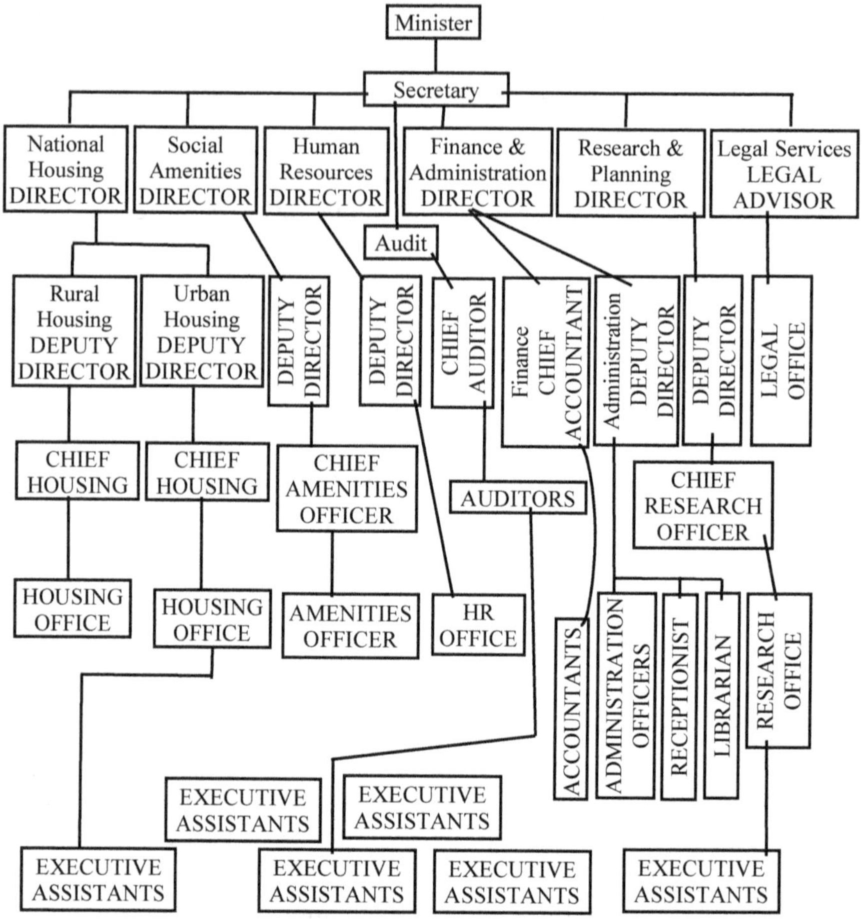

Figure 10.1: MNHSA Organisational Structure – Head Office – Source: adapted from Several MNHSA documents

The organisational structure of the MNHSA provides critical offices for factoring in the different actors it has to involve in housing and amenities delivery. Government, under the Inclusive Government agenda, is divided into five clusters - Economic Development, Infrastructure, Social Services and Reconstruction, Human Rights and Governance. The Infrastructure Cluster, in which the housing ministry is, has ministries interdependent on each other. It has 8 sector ministries in it, namely, public

---

Government of Zimbabwe, Harare.(2009e); MNHSA, "The Ministry"s Organisational Structure - Provinces and Districts," *Government of Zimbabwe*, Harare.(2009f)

works, energy, water, transport, information and communication technologies, housing, public works, science and technology and public services. Infrastructure is the "key enabler and driver" for growth and expansion in any economy[630]. No doubt that the different departments in the MNHSA have a critical role in 'unlocking value' from both the sister ministries in the Infrastructure Sector and those outside this sector.

The MNHSA is at the centre-stage in facilitating the construction of houses by both the state and non-state actors in the country. It strives to bring to realisation to its dream of having a nation with sustainable human settlements, albeit among many challenges. It is noted that only 11,000 units were built between 1999 and 2009 in the country against an effective demand for structures as evidenced by the highly urbanising population (pegged at 7% urban population growth per annum)[631]. It goes further to outline, how, under the 100-day programme under STERP, the ministry defined three issues for operations namely: the review existing policies, assessment of the housing delivery programme, and the management of the Operation Garikayi /Hlalani Kuhle (OG/HK) housing units.

As the primary actor in housing and habitat delivery, in a space of about ten months, the ministry embarked on intensive and widespread engagement of stakeholders which saw the holding of a housing symposium in May and the National Housing Convention in October 2009[632]. Yet the engagement with stakeholders is not an end itself. The idea was for the process to feed into future plans and programmes for the sector. At the National Housing Convention in 2009, the stakeholders formulated a set of recommendations to tackle aspects raised under the five thematic areas of the conventions, namely: policy and legislative

---

[630] GoZ/World Bank, Proceedings Report of the Workshop held under the theme, "Infrastructure Recovery and Development in Zimbabwe: Current Needs, Medium Term Solutions and Long-Term Vision," on Wednesday 25th November 2009, Wild Geese lodge.(2009)

[631] GoZ/World Bank, Proceedings Report of the Workshop held under the theme, "Infrastructure Recovery and Development in Zimbabwe: Current Needs, Medium Term Solutions and Long-Term Vision," on Wednesday 25th November 2009, Wild Geese lodge.(2009)

[632] Ibid.(2009)

framework, land for housing, housing finance, superstructure, infrastructure and technology, and the role of community-based organisations.

Indeed, there is a lot of rhyme in these thematic areas to the objectives of the MNHSA. Each of these puts actors to the housing and habitat sector in the limelight. These, in the assignment of responsibilities to the action areas cited by the convening actors, show a wide range of who should be involved in the quest for answers as indicated by the labyrinth of shelter provision expectation. A quick rundown of some of these actors include:

i. the MNHSA, the port of call for all housing matters
ii. Local government associations, in this case the Zimbabwe Local Government Association (ZILGA) and the Urban Councils Association of Zimbabwe (UCAZ).
iii. Non-governmental organisations (NGOs) chiefly geared in housing provision, technical advice, and infrastructure development, particularly water and sanitation.
iv. Community based organisations (CBOs) including housing cooperatives, microfinance institutions and sometimes burial societies that may have an interest in housing development.
v. The Ministry of Justice, Legal and Parliamentary Affairs (MJLPA) whose role in legislative reform is central.
vi. The Zimbabwe Republic Police (ZRP) whose involvement in eviction of squatters and land invaders was noted to be done in a humane manner, in keeping with the internationally set standards of evictions.
vii. The Ministry of Local Government, Rural and Urban Development (MLGRUD) which spearheads local governance in urban, peri-urban and local government areas, and also supervises local authorities.
viii. Local authorities, which, in keeping with the principle of subsidiarity, are close to citizens and manage their affairs including housing as a basic right.
ix. The Ministry of Finance (MoF) which regulates national finance systems and transacts with regional and international finance institutions including those which may want to invest in housing or infrastructure development.

x. The Corporate world which includes all private sector institutions including banks, insurance companies, building societies which, in housing and social amenities may provide a window to housing finance including mortgage arrangements or contribute to housing development by way of social corporate responsibility (SCR) or engagement in public-private partnership (PPP) arrangements. In some countries, the corporate world is a critical provider for social and rental housing programmes.

xi. Multinational corporations (MNCs) and investors that are usually key players in foreign direct investment (FDI) and which should have a leading role in housing their own employees or extend the same to local communities.

xii. Tertiary education institutions whose role is to train labour and manpower critical to the housing sector. These include planners, housing project management officers, architects, land surveyors, quantity surveyors and civil engineers – those of the technical fields of the built environment. The role of the University of Zimbabwe (UZ), the National University of Science and Technology (NUST) and Polytechnic colleges was stressed in terms of labour training and research.

xiii. Interest and pressure groups which do advocacy work in terms of advancing concerns of human rights including the right to adequate shelter.

xiv. Parastatals whose major contribution is seen in infrastructure provision and management including the Zimbabwe Electricity Supply Authority (ZESA) for electricity supply, TelOne for communication lines, the Zimbabwe National Water Authority (ZINWA) for regulating water resources, the Urban Development Corporation (UDCORP) for advancing the work of the MLGRUD in projects specific thematic and spatial areas.

xv. The Ministry of Land and Rural Resettlement (MLRR) being the chief steward of land and from which land for urban development and housing must be acquired in keeping with the provisions of the Land Acquisition Act. However, evidence on the ground shows that there are a number of bureaucratic impediments to lead to expedited land delivery for housing.[633]

xvi. The Ministry of Public Works (MPW) being the primary state functionary in infrastructure development.

xvii. The Infrastructure Development Bank of Zimbabwe (IDBZ) for financing especially offsite infrastructure.

xviii. The African Development Bank (ADB) being a regional body sometimes responsible for advancing loans to national financial institutions including those to do with housing and mortgage financing.

xix. Insurance and Pension companies, whose contribution to the housing sector had traditionally been greatly significant as a source of 'locked up' funds critical for shelter development.

xx. The Scientific Institute for Research and Development Corporation (SIRDC) whose role in researching own aspects like affordable and durable building technologies are very critical to the housing sector.

xxi. The Attorney General's office being the facilitator for law development of which housing and planning laws have been pointed out as needing speedy change to afford the generality of the population improved and sanitary housing conditions.

xxii. The Department of Physical Planning (DPP), housed under the MLGRUD, being responsible for the spatial development of areas in terms of offering planning services to ensure sustainable settlements in the country.

---

[633] (GoZ/UNDP/UNHABITAT, "Proceedings of the National Symposium convened by the Ministry of National Housing and Social Amenities under the theme ,"*Towards an Integrated Approach to Sustainable Housing and Social Amenities Delivery in Zimbabwe" on 28 May 2009*, Mendel Training Centre, Harare. (2009) ; GoZ/UNHABITAT, "Proceedings of the National Symposium convened by the Ministry of National Housing and Social Amenities under the theme ,"*Towards an Integrated Approach to Sustainable Housing and Social Amenities Delivery in Zimbabwe" on 28 May 2009*, Mendel Training Centre, Harare.(2009); MNHSA, "An Abridged Version of the Second National Housing Convention Held from 26 to 30 October 2009," *Government of Zimbabwe*, Harare.(2009c); Mubvami.T ; Musandu-Nyamayaro.O, "Procedural Impediments to the Low-income Housing Land Delivery in Cities of Zimbabwe," *Department of Rural and Urban Planning. University of Zimbabwe*, Harare. (1993)

xxiii. The Surveyor- General's office being responsible for land surveying services.

xxiv. The Zimbabwe Institute for Regional and Urban Planners (ZIRUP) being a professional body for planners, advancing professional practices in keeping with ethical norms for the profession and safeguarding the clients, in this case communities to be accommodated in set settlements.

Table 10.1 on the next page spells out the role (as number 1) MNHSA has in housing delivery, however in keeping with other players. Issues and actions that appear in this Table are directly emanating from the 2009 Victoria Falls National Housing Convention deliberations – what stakeholders recommended as policy and action points of intervention to ensure sound housing delivery in the post-crisis era (1997- early 2009 economic meltdown). Thus, Table 10.1 maps the recommendations to who can act in a given housing specific problem. What can be noted from this list is the multi-faceted nature of issues and contributions which the MNHSA has to grapple with in its efforts to ensuring the development of sustainable settlements in the country. A challenging task is that more of a stewardship or partnership model applies than working as a single actor (monopoly). This implies the need for coordinative capacities on the part of the ministry to avoid unnecessary duplications, conflicts and wastage of resources. As the spearheading agent for housing and habitat sector, MNHSA is in all expectations supposed to make the first moves in terms of initiating and championing its mandate as the principal actor having to account for performance and overall delivery (of the processes and outputs) in the sector.

		STANDARDS		FINANCE			
		Revision of Housing Standards **1,7,8, 20, 22, 24**	Incremental development of infrastructure and housing	Affordable low-cost housing finance **1, 3.4. 8, 9, 11, 10, 17, 13, 19**	Social and rental housing options **1, 2, 7, 8, 9, 10, 11, 13, 14,**		
LABOUR	Capacitating planning departments **1, 2, 8, 10, 12, 24**	Standards differentiation without compromising health **1,7,8, 20, 22, 24**		Housing micro-finance schemes **1, 3.4. 8, 9, 11, 10, 17, 13, 19**		Adherence to international standards in conducting evictions **1, 2, 3, 4, 6,13**	
	Registering planning practitioners along statutory lines **7, 22, 24**	Councillors involvement in the revised standards: policy from below **1, 2, 4, 7, 8, 22**		Contribution of remittances to housing **1, 3.4. 8, 9, 11, 10, 17, 13, 19, 12**		Modelling by-laws with climate, health and alternative technologies in mind	**TECHNOLOGY**
MANAGING BOTTLENECKS	Establishing a one-stop shop for plan preparations and approval **7, 22, 1**	Constitutionalisation of housing as a basic right and local government as the implementer of housing policies **1, 2, 3, 4, 5, 7, 8, 13, 21, 24**	Capacitating land surveying institutions **12, 10, 12**	Revitalizing the National Housing Fund (NHF) **1, 7, 8**		Expedition of dissemination of information to key stakeholders **1, 2, 7, 8, 12**	**RESEARCH**
		Appropriation of compensation for peri-urban land **1, 7**	Land acquisition for land expansion **1, 7, 8, 15, 22, 23**	Research on appropriate design and technological parameters **1, 2, 3, 4, 7, 8, 12,**	Research on demographic and socio-economic variables **1, 2, 8, 12, 24**		
		URBAN AND HOUSING LAND		**RESEARCH**			

Key

1.MNHSA	2.ZILGA, UCAZ	3.NGOs	4.CBOs	5.MJLPA	6.ZRP
7.MLGRUD	8. Local authorities	9. MoF	10. Corporate world	11. MNCs and investors	12.Tertiary education institutions (UZ, NUST, Polytechnics)

13.Interest and pressure groups	14.Parastatals (ZESA, TelOne, ZINWA, UDCORP)	15.MLR	16. MPW	17. IDBZ	18. ADB
19.Insurance and Pension companies	20.SIRDC	21.Attorney General's office	22. DPP	23. Surveyor-General's office	24. ZIRUP

Table 10.1: Actors and their Contribution to/ in the Housing and Habitat Sector in Zimbabwe[634]

Local authorities as well as the households interact with other players including NGOs like Practical Action Southern Africa in Epworth; (Practical Action, 2011), private housing developers, in the case of Ruwa, and government ministries and departments (refer to Figure 10.2).

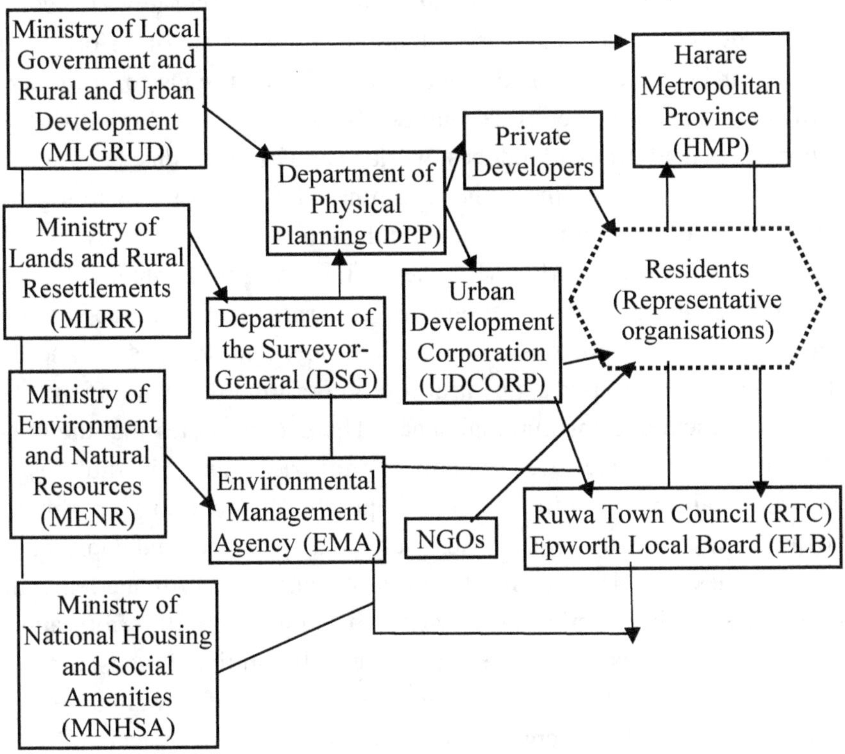

Figure 10.2: Stakeholders in Peri-Urban Zimbabwe: An Interactive Model (Fieldwork, 2012)

634 MNHSA,"Integrated Performance Agreement for the Year 2010," *Government of Zimbabwe*, Harare (2010).

Each actor is guided by a certain own philosophy. For instance, the Environmental Management Agency (EMA) is concerned with the sustainable upkeep of the natural and physical environment, endeavouring to reduce the negative effects caused by the ecological footprint. Next, the Urban Development Corporation (UDCORP), as a state-owned enterprise responsible for overseeing urban development, has often provided technical services with this regard. The Department of Physical Planning (DPP) is responsible for ensuring order, amenity and safety in the development of human settlements. The Ministry of National Housing and Social Amenities (MNHSA) has the overall task of housing delivery. Overall, the MLGRUD has oversight on issues of local governance and service delivery. In most cases, there is duplication of effort in the endeavour by the actors to do their duties and this tends to bring about confusion and wastage of resources. It is clear that capitalising on synergies is healthful and reduces overlaps and duplications.

In this chapter, the author examined the role of the state together with the factors inhibiting and enhancing housing delivery and stewardship in the peri-urban settlements. It is noted that state involvement is achieved through the institutions of government, that is, departments and agencies and ministries. The notion of public interest, as advanced in statist development, plays a central role in defining the work of the state in geographical and institutional space. The chapter notes that the major problem with state departments, ministries and institutions is departmentalism as the framework of operation is done in 'departmental boxes." These 'departmental boxes' defy principles of sound coordination hence issues are dealt within a disparate and uncoordinated manner, sometimes falling victim to vagaries of duplication of effort and in efficiency with respect to resource use. Institutional gaps are thus inevitable during planning and implementation of programmes and projects. Besides, there remains in Zimbabwe, a 'technological lag' in the manner in which space governance should be used, specifically the use of GIS, remote sensing and other earth observations tools.

Some institutions, like the Harare Metropolitan Province serve more of 'political interest' than anything such that there is poor stewardship hence detriment of peri-urban management. This has been amply demonstrated by the manner in which peri-urban space, specifically stateland, has been 'dished' out to ZANU-PF party loyalist at the expense of other people needing it. There is rampant violation of sustainable land use practice in certain instances. The chapter notes specifically that the Harare Metropolitan Province accommodates 4,000 farmers (as urban and peri-urban farmers). The allocation of such land (though temporary) is based on political affiliation (in this case to ZANU- PF rather than on competency of farming as would be expected. Moreover, in the chapter, it is clearly noted that issues of capacity to handle peri-urban housing and environmental hinge on the macro-economic performance of the country as well as political will to do so. In this respect, some departments, agencies and ministries are failing to fulfil the mandates as they are not supported by the requisite tools and human resources. For example, the DPP, instead of playing a watchdog role and overall coordination of planning, continue to do plans for small towns and rural district councils. This translates to a steward becoming a nanny. In its own right, such a development adds to inefficient in planning practices.

Furthermore, the chapter has shown how the definition of peri-urban in Zimbabwe, according to the DPP, has shifted due to political, economic and institutional dynamic of change. There is thus, a *de facto* and *de jure* definition of peri-urban. Such a gap shows that there are ambiguities that result to the detriment of easy policy articulation and ultimate implementation of set plans and goals. Above all, the chapter stresses how, when confronted with economic upheavals, institutions and organisations tend to 'metamorphose' or set to become resilient so as to remain relevant. Exclusively, the case of UDCORP shows this development. Nevertheless, the danger is when an organisation's role deviates from the expected and exact reason for its existence. More so, despite, the fast-track land reform in Zimbabwe, the delivery of land for urban development and housing remains cumbersome to the detriment of the cause of the right to housing especially to low-income group. Emphasis in this study has been placed on the MNHSA to show its linkages with stakeholders. This ministry in 2009 and in 1997, held National Housing Conventions with the idea to bring together its partners in development. These forums have provided an opportunity to dialogue in keeping with the notion of breaking walls' hence removing 'departmental boxes." However, what follows after discussions and dialogue ought to correspond and with practice on the ground. Nevertheless, just the idea of bring together stakeholders is important and one would wish every ministry would endeavour to do the same. The next chapter will be devoted on housing and peri-urban stakeholders outside the framework of the state. It serves to show housing contractual, negotiated and concessionary windows may assist and have assisted in the development of areas in Zimbabwe with special reference to the peri-urban.

CHAPTER 11
CAN THE CONCESSIONARY MODEL REALLY WORK?

The involvement of the private sector and civic organisations in human settlements planning and peri-urban development has contributed more towards infrastructural development especially roads, water and sewer reticulation in various settings. Civic organisations pay particular focus on social improvement of communities for example water and sanitation provision as well as provision of 'aid' and donations to disadvantaged groups. On the other hand, private corporations often contribute to urban development as part of their corporate social responsibility. In this chapter, the author describes and explains the work of the private sector like Shelter Zimbabwe and a number of building societies and banks. After, this I examine the role of voluntary organisations like Practical Action Southern Africa (PASA). The contents of the chapter are premised on the argument for concessionary urban development[635].

From this argument, it is clear how local authorities as apparatuses of the state, play a role to host interested played who want to bring housing and other development in their areas of jurisdiction. Some of the players are from within the country while others are international and transnational. Some are multi-lateral while other bilateral. Such engagements are made possible through negotiated agreements. State apparatus in the form of local authorities remain in situ long after the other players have long gone. The central government often allows local government units to enter into concessions with players through various

[635] Gijzen (2009) in Heurkens. E, "Changing Public and Private Roles in Urban Area Development in The Netherlands,". *Paper prepared for the 4th International Conference of the International Forum on Urbanism (IFoU) , 2009, Amsterdam/Delft under the theme "The New Urban Question – Urbanism beyond Neo-Liberalism": pp 1263 – 1272.* (2009: 1268)

avenues including decentralised cooperation or twinning arrangements, emergency cases like the 2008/9 Cholera case in which for example, some local authorities signed contracts to receive supplies of chemicals to curb the spread of the epidemic, or statutorily via the section on borrowing powers as prescribed in the Urban Councils Act (Chapter 29:15).

Historically, local authorities in Zimbabwe, with the funding support from central government and co-operating partners such as the World Bank and UNDP, have provided off-site infrastructure especially in the sphere of roads, water and sewer. For example, under the Urban I and Urban II Programmes, such projects were done in Harare, Mutare, Bulawayo, Gutu-Mupandawana and Marondera. From the late 1990s, a negative phenomenon set in with the ability of "...the local authorities to cope with the exigent dictates of provision and maintenance of truck infrastructural services in the face of ballooning urban populating trends"[636]. The besetting macro-economic challenges of the 2000s progressively diminished the capacity of Government to anchor local authorities through the Public Sector Investment Programme (PSIP) window. It is further asserted that:

> "Support to councils via the borrowing powers was drastically reduced in nominal and real terms, a situation exacerbated by the fizzling out of multilateral input. The economic challenges rendered it difficult for councils to mobilise financial, material and technical resources, as would enable councils to provide infrastructural services. Consequently, the country experienced a marked deterioration in the state of local authority roads, sewer and water facilities, while efforts to implement new projects were significantly stunted. This scenario impacted adversely on the realisation of the housing delivery programme. The current dispensation calls for a paradigm shift in the design and operationalisation of strategies for infrastructure provision, and the ensuing discourse shall deliberate on possible options that may be considered"[637].

---

636 Chombo. I, "Presentation on the Challenges Pertinent to the Provision of Off-Site Infrastructure by Local Authorities," Honourable Minister of Local Government, *Rural And Urban Development on 28 October 2009.*(2009)

637 Chombo. I, "Presentation on the Challenges Pertinent to the Provision of Off-Site Infrastructure by Local Authorities," Honourable Minister of Local Government,

On the contribution of the United States Agency for International Development (USAID) to human settlements in Ruwa, the Ruwa Town Planner remarks that,

> "The involvement of USAID in Ruwa brought 600 low-cost housing units in Ward 1 [Ruwa]. It has also assisted the town by donating money to improve the water situation in Ruwa and other residential areas including Chitungwiza and Norton. In 2003, a sum of US$200 000 was donated to purchase water treatment chemicals. This donation was divided equally between the town of Ruwa, Chitungwiza and Norton. The assistance from USAID greatly improved the water situation then and averted the risk of disease outbreak."[638]

International aid for housing and habitat has been affected by the controversial policies by the Zimbabwean Government between 1997 and 2009. This may explain the poor delivery of housing and urban deterioration in this period. The National Housing Convention in 2009 tried to bring together the different players in housing. Very few international players attended. The major observation was that inclusion of international players was critical to spurring meaningful housing development.

For Ruwa, since its establishment, as already highlighted, major developments have taken place, and those underway have not been the sole responsibility of Ruwa Local Board (and now town council) alone. This work is attributed to strong partnerships with, especially, the private sector including building societies, real estate firms, and private land developers. Non-governmental organisations have also played their part. Notable private organisations include ZIMRE Properties, Damafalls Investments, ZB Building Society (in conjunction with Intermarket and Wentspring Investments) Chipukutu Properties, Mashonaland Holdings, National Housing Trust, and USAID only to name but a few.

Intermarket Building Society is reported to be developing a shopping complex in Ruwa. In terms of design, the shopping complex is said "... to allow residents of the town access to different services under

---

Rural And Urban Development on 28 October 2009.(2009) Extract from Speech at the National Housing Convention, October, 2009.

[638] Telephone Interview on 01 May 2013

one roof." To build this complex, Intermarket Building Society is reported working in partnership with other three stakeholders namely StarAfrica corporation, ZB Bank and PG Industries. In the same paper, Ruwa is acknowledged as "a fast-growing suburb"[639]. Consequently, the town has gained tremendous physical growth. Indeed, questions have been raised as to the environmental sustainability of the town and the role being played by the private organisations and developers in maintaining and upgrading the quality and aesthetic value of the town. The hard work and commitment placed in the growth of Ruwa is of immeasurable quality hence the need to place great care in proper development. The Ruwa Town Planner in acknowledging the contribution of the private sector in Ruwa explains that:

> "In recent times, as before, the private sector has not only assisted in developing and servicing stands but also road maintenance, which has seen potholes being filled up and having a better road network within the town. However, the town still faces some challenges that are affecting the day-to-day lives of the people and the businesses. Although Ruwa took over the in 2010 operations of water supplies from the Zimbabwe National Water Supply Authority (Zinwa) and from the Harare City Council, the town is still faced with inadequate water supply, as their plant is limited. The water plant is only providing two mega litres per day when the town needs at least seven mega litres. Residents and industry are seriously affected by inadequate water supply. Now rationing is the measure that the town is currently undertaking. The water problem has made them to critical think of how to resolve their common problems by way of creating partnerships."[640]

In July 1966, the Mashonaland & Provincial Trust Company (Pvt) Ltd and Mashonaland Real Estate (Pvt) Ltd merged and incorporated into Mashonaland Holdings. This company has the record of having been the first property company to be listed on the Rhodesia Stock Exchange (now Zimbabwe Stock Exchange) in 1969[641]. In terms of its contribution to property development, it is noted with succinctness that, "In 1987

---

[639] In the Herald of 11 August 2008, "Shopping Complex for Ruwa," Zimpapers, Harare.(2008)

640 Telephone Interview on 01 May 2013

[641] Interview with Project Manager, 14 May 2013

Mashonaland Holdings acquired land at Ruwa which it transformed into the Ruwa Growth Point. The brainchild of the then Chairman, Mr T C Hardy, a satellite town east of Harare was established, incorporating industrial and commercial stands, as well as large residential areas for low, medium and high-density housing. The entire infrastructure and many of the factories and houses were built by Mashonaland Holdings." On being asked of its role now, in Ruwa, the property manager of Mashonaland Holdings argues, "The holding has pulled out now. Its role was that of a developer. Since all the properties are now sold out, it no longer has a role to play."[642] This development is noteworthy in that private players' role in a defined area are usually on concessionary grounds after which the task is done, they have to pull out. Nevertheless, the local government structure will now have the role to manage and provide demands and expectations of the residents and users of the space that defines it jurisdiction. In this regard, the role of the private or civil sector is that of a 'nanny' while that of the local government structure (or local authority) is that of a steward, having to oversee the smooth operations of the area and its people with the overall goal of sustainability. The respondent argues,

> "Mashonaland Holdings driven by its quest for development acquired Ruwa in 1987 and transformed it into the Growth point. By then it incorporated industrial and commercial stands as well as large residential stands for low, medium and high-density housing. The entire infrastructure and many old houses were built by Mashonaland Holdings. To date, Mashonaland Holdings has taken the lead in availing all stands found in Ward 1 to 7 which is almost 50% of the total population of Ruwa. It is currently the private sector with the largest share in terms of land acquired for residential development. The firm assists in servicing of residential as prescribed in the development permit. Despite, availing more stands than other private organisations, the firm has little to show in terms of promoting the environmental sustain inability of the area as there is nothing more to talk about despite servicing of the stands."[643]

The partnership between Ruwa Local Board and ZB Building society started as early as year 2000[644]. The partnership resulted in ZB

---

642 Interview with Property Manager, 13 May 2013.
643 Interview with Project Manager, 14 May 2013
644 Interview with the Projects Manager, 5 June 2013.

bank acquiring the entire residential area of Springvale. The development of Springvale was done in two phases, that is, phase 1 and 2. Phase 1 has 425 residential whilst phase 2 has up to date 395 stands. Upon acquiring land for the development, the bank serviced the land following the requirement of the development permit they were granted. The permit states satisfactory servicing of the area with both water and sewer reticulation system and storm water drains. More so, the roads had to be well tarred and in some extreme cases with culverts, rails/barricades by the roadside.

Moreover, to reduce the shortage of water because of erratic water supply from the City of Harare, ZB Bank sank two boreholes in Springvale. This was also meant to reduce the insurgence of unprotected wells, which were being sunk by the residents. Routine test on borehole water to check its safety is done after every six months. More so, in creating environmental safety to the residents of Springvale, the Bank claims that they do routine grass cutting soon after the rainy season. This is also done to reduce the rate of crime rate and to improve the aesthetic value of the area. To date, the ZB Bank has employed security to guard the area from to reduce extraction of sand for building purposes, which has left dangerous pits, and gorges that are harmful to the residents themselves. In addition, the Bank claims that it has, at one point in time, donated money to Ruwa specifically for refuse collection and plans are still there to spearhead clean up campaigns once development is complete. Against this background, the longevity of ZB Bank operation in Ruwa is determined by the satisfaction of the terms and conditions of the development permit[645].

Previously known as ZIMRE Holding Limited (ZHL) Group, ZIMRE Properties was incorporated on 27 January 2003 following the successful disposal of National Real Estate (Pvt) Limited[646]. ZIMRE Properties is driven by the vision of becoming the first-choice provider of real estate solutions in Zimbabwe and in the region. The firm has developed more than 2000 residential stands in Ruwa both medium and

[645] Interview with the Projects Manager, 5 June 2013.

[646] Interview with the Projects Manager (Property Development and Project Management), 27 May 2013

low density. It acquired undeveloped land and improved in onsite and offsite infrastructure. This has further provided the base for future developments of built structures on serviced land, which is subdivided and then sold piecemeal, to other developers or individuals. Real estate development by ZIMRE Properties is currently happening in Ruwa. In recent times, ZIMRE Properties has spearheaded the servicing of land in Ruwa and assisted the town with money to improve refuse collection. Zimre Properties also claims to have assisted in borehole drilling to improve the water situation in the Town[647].

The Contribution of Damafalls Investments and Chipukutu Properties

Damafalls Investments has currently involved in the growth of Ruwa Town by developing the Damafalls community. To date it has serviced 1000 occupied stands so that they are reticulated with water and sewer[648]. Roads have also been well developed; major distributors are tarred. Unfortunately, at the time of research, this community had not electricity. This unavailability of electricity partly explains the increasing deforestation in the area. The area has experiences massive sand extraction by poachers in the recent past and this problem continues almost unabated. Despite these challenges, security has been set up by Damafalls investments in order to reduce this negative trend. Heavy fines are set to anyone found extracting sand for construction especially near the watercourse in the area with the money channelled to the Damafalls development fund. Chipukutu Properties is also involved in the development of Ruwa. To date, it has developed up to 600 residential stands with reticulated water and sewer pipes[649].

Shelter Zimbabwe was established in 1988 with the mandate to provide housing in the country. The housing company had delivered a number of residential stands between 1988 and December 2008. It has a new housing development project in Epworth named Rockview Park

---

[647] Interview with the Projects Manager (Property Development and Project Management), 27 May 2013.

648 Interview with Property Manager, 23 May 2013.

[649] Interview with Property Manager, 21 May 2013.

Phase 1 was launched in October 2005. The anticipation is that at the end of the project, 5,000 medium density residential stands would have been serviced. Table 11.1 is a matrix showing the achievements by Shelter Zimbabwe, in areas where residential suburbs have taken shape and the projects have been completed and duly awarded certificates of compliance by City of Harare as well as some which are 'work in progress." The Assistant Operations Manager points out that,

> "Our thrust is to develop virgin land into a fully serviced land, in partnership with local authorities and we call such joint ventures (JVs). In this arrangement, local authorities provide land and Shelter Zimbabwe provides infrastructure. Our final product is a fully serviced land, a titled stand (I mean a stand with title deeds). We also have what we call Land Maximisation. In this approach, the idea is of increasing the housing stock in Harare without extending the frontiers. We negotiate with landowners [stand owners] who have big stands say 4.000m^2 to subdivide them to produce two or three other stands out of it." [650]

Table 11.1: Achievements by Shelter Zimbabwe 1988- 2011[651].

Period	Number of Stands Serviced	Location (Residential Area)	Socio Economic Status	Project Status
1988-1993	586	Glen View 2 & 3	High-density	Completed
1993-1995	362	Glen View 2 & 3 Infill	High-density	Completed
1996-1997	325	Glen View 101 & 224	High-density	Completed
1998-1999	837	Glen View 7 Extension	High-density	Completed
2000-2002	14	Hatfield	Medium density	Completed
2000-2002	20	Prospect	Medium Density	Completed
2000-2002	328	Railway reserve Phase 1	High-density	Completed
2004-2005	371	Railway Reserve Phase 2	High-density	Completed

650 Interview with the Assistant Operations Manager on 18 March 2011
[651] Shelter Zimbabwe records (2011)

Period	Number of Stands Serviced	Location (Residential Area)	Socio Economic Status	Project Status
2004-2005	222	Hopley	High-density	Completed
2007-2009	238	Section 1A of Rockview Park Phase 1	Medium Density	Completed
2009-2011	257	Section 1B of Rockview Park Phase 1	Medium Density	Nearing Completion
Current	720	Rockview Phase 1C	Medium density	Work in progress
Upcoming	3 700	Rockview Phase 2	High-density	
Current	500	Mvurwi	High-density	Work in Progress
Up Coming	10 000	Chizhanje Harare	High-density	
Up Coming	1 000	Marondera	High-density	
Land-use maximisation	64	Harare	Subdivisions	Completed units

Shelter Zimbabwe has done Land Maximisation projects in Harare, in places including Prospect, Malbereign, Bluff Hill and Borrowdale. Such subdivisions are not possible in high-density areas. The Assistant Operations Manager explains the rationale of 'cutting' the big stand: "Our argument is the stands of size 4.000m^2 were ideal then [in the colonial times] but not now, when there has been [great] population increase in the urban centres. Nevertheless, the success of Land Maximisation hinges on the goodwill of the landowner. Once the landowner agrees we know already that the Local Authority is going to approve. Local authorities [we deal with] are well approved of the approach."[652]

The disposal of the serviced stands is normally specified by the partners of the housing company, particularly the local authorities. The purchases must service the housing waiting list of the local authority. Thus, high and medium density stands are disposed through the open market system. With respect to the Land Maximisation Approach, the

652 Interview with the Assistant Operations Manager on 18 March 2011

manner in which the open market works is somewhat different. The seller normally finds own buyers or sell through an estate agent. Apart from the Joint Venture arrangement, which is by a memorandum of understanding (MoU), Shelter Zimbabwe also has what it calls a Special Purpose Vehicle (SPV). It is explained as follows:

> "This is about the local authority, Shelter Zimbabwe plus other professional partners. These come together and form a company to deliver the special project at hand only for the company to dissolve after delivery. Roles and functions of each partner, as well as the profit-sharing arrangement is agreed upon. We have partners that we call permanent partners and these are: PlanAfric, for planning, Brian Colquhoun and Company, for civil engineering, Genesis Bank, for banking and project financing, and Kashangura and Associates, for land surveying. Our temporary partners are contractors we hire. They normally depend on their performance in the assigned tasks. They may include estate agents for selling stands. Contractors are normally excluded from special purpose vehicle arrangements."[653]

The advantage with SPV is that it is a way of financing the company's housing projects; partners are assured of their rewards to be at the end of the project. This aids financing y et, the banker needs some certification of agreed milestones for them to release funding. The surveying partner can be called upon any time to provide their service. For instance, if pegs are removed, the surveyor comes to replace them. The justification, as noted by the Assistant Operations Manager is that "… because [he] is still a partner until the project ends."

Since Shelter Zimbabwe does not put up superstructures, the services of architects are *ultra vires*. The Assistant Operations Manager points out that: delays in project implementation are inevitable. The main reason is bureaucracy, though there are mechanisms to try and manage the setbacks. He points out: "Local authorities, through their structures have to follow laid down procedures. Nevertheless, as you know, their structures are a mixed bag of people. They work through committees and committee meetings happen at spaced times. This is a cause of concern and delay to expected progress. But once we engage a local authority as a

653 Interview with the Assistant Operations Manager on 18 March 2011

partner, it is also a way of managing the bureaucracy. For example, when we have site meetings, the local authority must send its representative and usually that is an engineer. *Kana project ikafoira navowo vafoira.* Proof of presence at site meetings aids approvals... They have a duty to deliver." [654] Besides setbacks posed by bureaucratic tendencies, which are somewhat, exogenous to the project, there are also those poised almost within the project set up. These tend to escalate projects costs. The Assistant Operations Manager argues that, "In Epworth, the rate of vandalism and theft has been very high. *Vonogona kuchera nokudzura ma*pipe *achererwa pasi.* This means that we then have to invest more in security and that in turn means more costs to the project". [655]

In Epworth, Shelter Zimbabwe has a project called the Rockville Park Housing Project. Its prospective outcome is a medium to low-density residential area. The project site is located adjacent to Mutare Road, that is immediately south of the road. It is the land between Mutare Road and Epworth. The area is adjacent to Sunway City and the Shelter Zimbabwe Assistant Operations Manager opines that Sunway City is in Harare. The land where Rockview Park is was once stateland and was granted to Epworth Local Board, which then decided to collaborate with Shelter Zimbabwe in order to deliver houses. Phase A of Rockville is complete now and we are in Phase B. Stands cost \$12 per m^2. The serviced stands are then sold on terms, that is, instalments for 36 months. Can it be that Rockville is the first low-medium density in Epworth? The Assistant Operations Manager argues that, "I should believe so. In fact, we are giving Epworth a new look. In addition, it is from this side from Mutare Road. [Towards] as we get to the existing Epworth, we intend to service high-density stands. It is our hope that the local authority will resettle people living in areas without the facilities to [our high-density serviced stands in that time in the future]. But that depends on the local authority."[656]

One of the challenges in Epworth has been noted as the disbandment of the Zimbabwe National Water Authority (ZINWA). This

---

654 Interview with the Assistant Operations Manager on 18 March 2011
655 Interview with the Assistant Operations Manager on 18 March 2011
656 Interview with the Assistant Operations Manager on 18 March 2011

body was operating with a cross-jurisdictional approach; it took no notice of municipal boundaries. It had a regional approach[657]. But the return of ZINWA to its core functions, as a water management body, has been a blow to the management of peri-urban towns and in particular, Epworth.

> "ZINWA was not administering water looking at [local authority] boundaries. We now have three [independent administratively] authorities. Supplying water to the three authorities [Harare, Ruwa and Epworth] has not been without challenges.... Now we have to negotiate with Harare for water rights. We have to negotiate with the three local authorities because some of the pipes belong to Ruwa. Shall I say that the relationship between the three local authorities is not one of the best? Regarding the water situation, I must say that then [when ZINWA was managing], we had an overall authority over water. Things were moving. But now without that water supply, there is a big challenge in the area. "[658]

The other challenge for housing developers like Shelter Zimbabwe is political partyism, which tends to bring unnecessary tension between principal housing delivery players. The Assistant Operations Manager says, "We also have to look at the history of the two settlements. For example, Ruwa was for white farmers. With the prevailing political tension in the country most of the things with some sympathy with the whites is taken to be from MDC and that sparks tension." [659] Shelter Zimbabwe has other projects in Marondera and in Mvurwi. The complete list of the areas therefore includes Harare, Epworth, Marondera and Mvurwi (Table 11.1). Although the company has tried in other towns, a

---

[657] Horenz.J.W.G, "An approach to regional planning,". *Zimbabwe Science News 13(11):* pp261-264. (1976), ; Catanese ; Synder eds.,"Urban Planning (Second Edition)," *McGraw-Hill Inc,* New York (1988); Forster, (2001); Malizia.E.E, "City and Regional Planning: A Primer for Public Health Officials," *The Art of Health Promotion,* May/June 2005: pp 1-12.(2005); Seemann. K;Marinova. D, "Understanding Connectivity of Settlements: Implications of the Power Curve," *Paper presented at the 18th World IMACS / MODSIM Congress, Cairns*, Australia 13-17 July 2009. <URL: http://mssanz.org.au/modsim09, 27 June 2011>. (2009); Simon. D, "Urban Environments: Issues on the Peri-Urban Fringe," *Annual Review of Environment and Resources 33*: 167-185. (2008); ; Chapman. I, "Closing thoughts, *The Art of Health Promotion, May/June 2005*," pp 13-14(2005)

658 Interview with the Assistant Operations Manager on 18 March 2011

659 Interview with the Assistant Operations Manager on 18 March 2011

number of constraints have been noted. The constraints have to do with the composition of the councils that has a bearing on the reaching of critical decisions, the capital position of Shelter Zimbabwe, and the past performance of the economy. To counter some of the challenges to do with mistrust by clients, Shelter Zimbabwe speaks of 'phasing development." The Assistant Operations Manager narrates:

> "We have also had an attempt of Kadoma City but it proved difficult to convince them. It is not easy to establish relations with local authorities like we have done with Harare and Epworth. Some are very sceptical about our approach. Also, there is the committee system which I once talked about. We have had cases where there was some agreement and then we find after a while some letters being written back to us to reverse the agreements. Debates in committees end up not being rational but something else. I think most of our local authorities are very rigid. They are not ready to try new approaches. When we approach them, we don't tell them we have money. Well tell them we have a formula. Some then demand bank statements. However, we say we have a financier. They want to see the cash flow statement.., which we do not have. *Mari yavanotarisira kuona apa kana mari yakadaro munyika hamhuna*... We once tried *ma*pay schemes. However, those do not work. They have their own challenges. Pay schemes! You get land. You look out for clients. The clients begin to contribute [money]. Moreover, they have their stands serviced. Nevertheless, they were heavily discredited *panguva yeZimdollar* due to the hyperinflation. *Mari ine value nhasi mangwana haina, haichatengi chinhu asi client ari kutarisira chinhu nokuti akachibhadharira*. To start this approach now [in the dollarisation period], *vanhu vanokuti muri matsotsi*. Pay schemes were associated with what we called escalation costs. Such escalation would be passed to the stand beneficiaries who would then resist paying.... Due to those shortcomings, we now talk of phasing development so that we manage with resources we have at hand. With development phasing, we will service stands and sell them at, say 50% to completion, where we can recover our costs as clients begin to pay instalments." [660]

Shelter Zimbabwe says it has no projects in Ruwa except one Etosha Project, which is still on the cards: "I should say we have no

---

660 Interview with the Assistant Operations Manager on 18 March 2011

projects there. We had one on the cards [Etosha Project]. Nevertheless, its feasibility failed due to water challenges. Underground water supplies were insufficient and water could only be brought there at a very high cost. Though we are still working around what can be done, we have no project on the ground [in Ruwa] yet." [661] Despite challenges and setbacks, Shelter Zimbabwe's vision is to expand into all towns and cities in the country and eventually Southern Africa. Nevertheless, the story of Shelter Zimbabwe is a tale of seeking innovative practices in housing delivery in the country amid socio-economic and political challenges. In this real, aspects of trust, mistrust, confidence and suspicion, to say the least, are the real shapers of stewardship. Shelter Zimbabwe remains convinced that with transjuridictional approaches to a problem, change for the better is possible. In its own right, such an approach and initiative, is in line with the thinking of pundits of the stewardship model. How to raise finances and how to gain political will remain central to the whole idea. Indeed, addressing these challenges, no doubt, answers the sustainability question of the projects, programmes and outcomes[662].

I also take the case of Practical Action Southern Africa (PASA) as the epitome of such efforts.

In 2009, PASA mooted a Promoting Examples of Participatory Local Empowerment in Urban Planning (PEOPLE-UP) which is a four-year project[663]. The project is funded by the European Commission through Practical Action Southern Africa. The goal of the project is that of improving the living conditions of the poor and marginalised people living in urban and peri-urban areas by way of ensuring their access to basic municipal infrastructure. PASA's demonstrations are being implemented with Epworth and Mutare. To realise its goal, PASA has a

661 Interview with the Assistant Operations Manager on 18 March 2011

662 Mitlin. D,, "Sustaining markets or poverty reduction?," *Environment and Urbanisation 14(1):* pp 173-177.(2002), Brookings Institution, "The Housing Crisis and Lessons for Monetary Policy," *The Brookings Institution,* Washington, D.C. (2008), Gappert,"The future of urban environments: implications for the business community," *Business Horizons*. Available:< http://findarticles.com> (1993)

663 Practical Action, "Terms of Reference for Promoting Examples of Participatory Local Empowerment Urban Planning (PEOPLE-UP)," *Practical Action*, Harare. (2011)

firm belief anchored in the tenet that the fostering of relevant institutional structures at both municipal and community level will help in capturing the needs, views and priorities for infrastructure will enhance service delivery. The existing and new residents' associations, cooperatives and small-scale businesses are envisaged to be the delivery vehicles of the PEOPLE-UP mission whose thrust is the planning and delivery of basic infrastructure levels at ward level. The idea is to "...strengthen community voices and promote more participation by residents through their representative structures and enhance their input in selecting technological and delivery options in service delivery"[664]. The primary object is to put the 'targeted' people on the driving seat of the processes so that the initiative automatically gets owned up by them.

The target groups and beneficiaries are 62,000 of the 302,000 residents in Sakubva Mutare and 240,000 in Epworth. The majority of the beneficiaries in Mutare are the elderly, orphans, and vulnerable children. In Epworth, the beneficiaries are segmented between the originals and the new migrants due to failure to secure accommodation in Harare, the capital city. It is envisaged that 12 local authorities will have benefited from the PEOPLE-UP project initiative in the long run. The overall results are strengthened local authorities with established structures and processes to consult and fully integrate infrastructure service delivery needs and priorities of poor urban and peri-urban residents, enhanced capacity and voices of local community and their leaders to understand and demand improved service delivery[665]. Moreover, the partnerships formed increase income and employment opportunities for urban poor from service delivery, and inclusive approaches in service delivery for the poor and marginalised documented and disseminated to influence policies and practices of other 10 local authorities in Zimbabwe

In an endeavour to achieve this, Practical Action has involved Civic Forum on Housing (CFH) and Mutare Housing Cooperatives District Union (MHCDU) as the main project partners with strong grassroots links. From PASA's objectives, one can see exactly the 'spirit'

---

[664] Ibid, pg 22
[665] Ibid, (2011))

of stewardship as put across by stewardship pundits[666]. However, on the ground there seems to be more hurdles and constraints than those expected. This is explained by the little scope covered in terms of actuating these goals. Largely, one can attribute the little progress to the political ‘bickering’ happening on the ground as evidenced by the polarity at national level. It is unfortunate that in a politically volatile milieu it is the poor who suffer most, worst in violation of the development agenda that different agencies purport to hold[667].

Dialogue on Shelter for the Homeless in Zimbabwe Trust is shortened Dialogue. It was formed in 1997 and registered in 1998. The Project Coordinator for Land and Housing explains that, “It was an initiation by Beth Chitekwe-Biti and others who, having made contacts with the South Africa Homeless People’s Federation got to understand that, indeed, the marginalised groups fail to find space in urban areas. With this insight, Dialogue was formed to trumpet the voice of the poor so that they can negotiate for access to land. Since the organisation was organised as a private voluntary organisation [PVO], Dialogue had no direct interface with the communities. That gaps have since been filled in by the Zimbabwe Homeless People`s Federation who now work us our face.”668 The mission of Dialogue is thus of ensuring that urban poor communities work, through their initiatives and self-determination, to create own habitats. In terms of partnerships, Dialogue works with community organisations that constitute an autonomous network –called the Zimbabwe Homeless People`s Federation. The network does community mobilisation such that, to date, it “... is working in 74 areas,

---

[666] Parr, J et al. “The practice of stewardship,” *Developing leadership for regional action. Denver,* CO: Alliance for Regional Stewardship: March. (2002) ;Stoll.L, “Regional Collaboration: A framework for solving complex planning problems.*” The Land Tracker 6(2):* pp 1-4. (2006);Mckinney et al. Working across Boundaries: A Framework for Regional Collaboration, in LeRoyer Ann ed. *Land Lines 16(3),* Lincoln Institute of Land Policy: Cambridge (USA).(2004)

[667] Potts.D, , “Restoring Order”? Operation Murambatsvina and the Urban Crisis in Zimbabwe. *Journal of Southern African Studies 32 (2)* : pp 273 - 291 (2006); Sigauke.N, “Improving Urban Livelihoods: Epworth Sustainable Livelihoods Benchmark Study,”< URL: http://practicalaction.org/docs/region_southern_africa/ Epworth_Benchmark_Study.pdf>, *Accessed on 27 June 2011.(*2002:20)

668 Interview on 23 May 2013.

has an active membership of 52,000 families who are grouped in 582 saving schemes across the country." 669 In terms of its modus operandi, Dialogue works as a development facilitator. It engages in negotiations with an identified local authority on behalf of the urban poor. The Project Coordinator elucidates that:

> "In our engagements with local authorities, we remind them [local authorities] that the urban poor exist. We speak on behalf of the poor. *Tisu tinobereka community toimirira kumalocal authority. Ivo vakaenda voga havanzwike.* (We literally carry the poor communities on our back as Dialogue, representing and lobbying for them with the local authorities. Remember if they go on their own, no one listens to them. So, we are the voice of the poor.) We prepare these poor so that they mobilise themselves such that when they speak, they are a force to reckon with and the local authorities can listen to them. Part of the mobilisation involves making sure that they mobilise resources (for example they have a fund called the Gungano Fund) that show to the local authority that given a resource like land, they are in position to develop it. As Dialogue, we assess their progress and put their concerns in a language – technical language – that local authorities can listen. Our idea is that communities should be able to stand on their own. However, they need support and we provide such support hence to them we are a technical partner. We augment their efforts by working with them in areas of fundraising, proposal writing and such like technical areas."[670]

Dialogue has worked with an international partner, the Bill and Melinda Gates Foundation (BMGF) (Box 7.1) on the next page in improving part of the peri-urban settlement in Harare.

669 Interview on 23 May 2013.
670 Interview on 23 May 2013.

Box 7.1: The Contribution of Bill and Melinda Gates Foundation to Improving the Lives of the Urban Poor[671]

Harare began to work in conjunction with the Bill and Melinda Gates Foundation (MBGF) in November 2008. Mayor Muchadeyi Masunda says the link began when he attended the World Urban Forum in China in 2008. After presenting about Harare to 4 000 mayors participating in a round table at the forum, he was approached by an employee of the Bill and Melinda Gates Foundation. Two weeks after this forum, the Mayor participated in an EU development day's symposium in Strasbourg, France where he spoke to an audience of about 2 000 presenting on Harare and Zimbabwe. The same employee of the MBGF re-approached him having liked his presentation. The mayor then participated again in another forum in Barcelona in January 2010. Through dialogue the mayor managed to get US$5 million to use on regenerating high-density areas like Mbare and "… to assist the people in the low end of the market to access funds to build houses for themselves."

Eventually, the foundation got involved in trying to refurbish the 58 blocks of hostels in Mbare by first embarking on enumerations of the squatters. Currently the foundation is working in Dzivarasekwa where, with the blessing of the council is building 486 units which consumes the US$5 million obtained from the foundation. The Mayor points out that, "…Bill and Melinda Gates are very concerned about the relentless migration of people from rural to urban areas to such an extent that by the year 2030, 80 percent of the world's population will be living in urban areas. That concern stems simply from how the cities will cope with that influx of people. That's why they are channelling funds to make sure that cities are able to put the necessary infrastructure in place in terms of housing, water and sanitation. It's a unanimous thing for them to do and we stand ready to benefit from that because our systems as part of all the hardships that we have endured since November 1997 are still the best and better than most countries not only in Africa, but beyond."

The Project Coordinator explains thus:

> "Bill and Melinda Gates Foundation is one of the biggest funders of Slum/Shack Dwellers International (SDI). Our partnership with this foundation began through the link created by the mayor of Harare. They agreed to have a five-year project worth of US$5 million. Initially, we were allocated land kwaTsiga kuMbare and we created a layout of 89 plots. If we had wanted high-rise flats for the area, we would have designed

[671] The Herald "Bill Gates doing a sterling job in Zim." <URL: http://www. Herald .co.zw/index.php?option=com_content&view=article&id=61026:bill-gates-doing -a- sterling – job - in-zim&catid=39:opinion - a-analysis&Itemid=132,> *Accessed on 12 April, 2013.* (22 December 2012).

> for that. The targeted beneficiaries were Mbare residents. But in Mbare, there is Chipangano, a group linked to ZANU-PF. Because we could not take much of its membership as beneficiaries of the scheme, Chipangano made noise about the whole project so we decided to relocate the project to Dzivarasekwa (DZ) Extension. The political squabbles that arose made us to move out in the meantime. The land in DZ had been allocated to us as far back as 2006 because this area had a good number of former Porta Farm residents. Initially we carried out a survey and found out that there were 188 households squatting there. In a second survey, we established 166 households. In a third survey, we found 152 families. To date 150 families have been beneficiaries from the scheme though the layout accommodates 480 plots for housing. You find that our enumerations were showing declining figures of the squatters. This is because each time, some of the households were moving out of the place and benefiting in housing schemes elsewhere, for example in Hatcliffe. The difference between 150 and 480 of the stands have been taken up by members of the Zimbabwe Homeless People`s Federation."[672]

In DZ Extension, Dialogue has brought in a number of affordable solutions to housing the poor including drilling boreholes, introducing a *skyloo* (type of ecological sanitation shortened ecosan) toilets and lobbied Harare City Council to accept incremental housing development and *in situ* upgrading. To this end, the Project Coordinator stresses that,

> "Dialogue works with the community to ensure that they make affordable house plans. The city's duty is to provide infrastructure (including roads' provision, sewer and supervision of the civic works) and in this case, it has to be in the end. On the other hand, it is the federation's duty to provide menial labour on matters like offloading of materials upon their delivery and digging of foundations and other trenches when such are needed. In our negotiations as for land with any local authority, normally we want land that is as close to the source markets of livelihood activities as possible. The land we target is that one which is in close proximity to the central business district, for example in Gweru; we have had 71 plots for housing in Ascot, what we call the Ascot Infill. Such land is not always available as you often find that towns and cities often earmark that for prime development and the land is very expensive hence, the poor cannot afford it. With such a development we

[672] Interview on 23 May 2013.

> then find our projects being pushed to the periphery except where the town may still be small like in Shurugwi."[673]

The words of the Project Coordinator point to the realities in most cities where the poor are pushed to the periphery since the most priced land in most urban centres is central location. Nevertheless, the principle of trying to get the poor as close to their sources of livelihoods and markets is in tandem with the novel realisation b scholars and policymakers that pushing away the poor is in fact costlier in the long run as these groups tend to find their way back into the city. Besides, locating the poor centrally ensures that the principle of diversity that brings in compactness to city is achieved and seems to be more promising than sprawling the city and gentrifying it.

Dialogue established, through its 2009 Epworth Profiling Report, that more than 70% of the Epworth residents are living in squalid conditions and that most residents are settled on un-serviced land without official allocation. The report notes that the settlement is currently faced with water and sanitation challenges, as there is little reticulated water and sewer network notably in Overspill and Chiremba. In addition, the formal planed settlements have the infrastructure to support these services, yet the systems are typically non-functional. Moreover, the water network which was installed in 1992 is still not active and people have resorted to deep well which are not well protected and pose a serious challenge in terms of health. Furthermore, the profiling report notes that Epworth faces sewer challenges as most people have resorted to the use of Blair and pit latrine toilets, which are not well positioned, and conflict with the available deep wells.

The unavailability of electricity in areas like Chiremba and Chinamano has seen people using firewood, sawdust and paraffin as energy sources. However, the ever-growing population has created a strain on the environment the environment Epworth. Whilst the developers are mainly concentration in the development of stands, little has been done concerning environmental protection. This scenario compromises the sustainability of the settlement. The Project Coordinator tells how Dialogue identified the developmental gap:

673 Interview on 23 May 2013.

> "Our work in Epworth began in 1998; we already established savings schemes. In 2008, we thought of having an enumeration in the settlement to get our figures correct in order to convince government of our mandate, philosophy and the route we wanted to establish in helping the urban poor. We realised it was becoming very difficult to get greenfields to initiate sites and services schemes. Upon costing it, we found out that it was even cheaper to get to the people who already held land, negotiate with them and try to upgrade their habitats. With this idea, we approached Epworth and started the profiling, just to get a sense of the place. Our target was all the wards in the settlement, that is, Ward 1 to 7. We also intended to get into detailed enumerations that we then started with ward 7 being the largest. Ward 7 is under a very strong ZANU-PF woman councillor hence it is a ZANU-PF stronghold. At first, we the councillor and her people gave us a hard time. They did not want to cooperate since they had their own plans about the area. when they hit a brick wall, they turned to us. After piloting with Ward 7 we then went to the next stage of producing a layout. I must say the layout differs a great deal with the conventional layout plans. For example, in one area we just designated it as a market corridor. I must point it straight the road that we have moved in Epworth has not been a smooth one. In fact, it has been so rough that we had to overcome a number of obstacles and resistance. For Ward 7, I now realise that the resistance was not just negative. We were drifting in the same direction with the residents only that we had not fully understood each other. When we understood each other, we then flowed. Now, we are in Ward 4 upon invitation to 'repeat' the process that we did in Ward 7. Our intention, though as Dialogue, is not to do everything for Epworth. We believe we have demonstrated how it must be done so that local authority and the community must take over the process. We have not come to replace or supersede the local authority. Our duty has just been to show them the way."[674]

Sustainability and informed stewardship are that which draw actors to a point of agreement. There are numerous players in housing delivery in Zimbabwe including the Government, local authorities, the private sector, cooperatives, and individuals. A variety of skills are needed in housing delivery and these are encapsulated in the professionals and

674 Interview on 23 May 2013.

trades people including engineers, planners, land surveyors, architects, builders, plumbers, carpenters and many others[675].

The 2009 National Housing Convention recommended the re-institutionalisation of the ZIMHABITAT. This is a platform for all actors in housing delivery in the country. It operates outside government. The Deputy Director, DPP states the following:

> "Do you know about ZIMHABITAT? I am a member and I can say I have attended ninety-nine percent of all the meetings it has called for. It is a formation with so many players discussing housing. Sometimes there is dancing and singing during deliberations. ZIMHABITAT derives its agenda from encumbrances that different players have in delivering or getting houses. We have noted that the government cannot hold all the different actors that are into housing. This is because of the diversity. There is need to maximise participation. ZIMHABITAT is a standalone entity, outside government. If you check on what it is doing, you will see that are a number of innovations and initiatives regarding issues of housing and in particular, regarding places like Epworth. Dialogue on Shelter, for example, is talking about upgrading Epworth"[676].

The emergence of ZIMHABITAT can be said to have 'de-mystified' housing delivery so that it is seen as a process done by motley of actors including the poor working in collaboration with the professionals and donors[677]. Collaboration is critical to achieving

---

675 Vakil.A.C, "Housing Co-operatives in Zimbabwe: A contribution to women"s shelter and development," *Journal of Social Development in Africa 9(1),* pp 7-17. (1994); Kamete.A.Y; Mubvami.T, "The contributions of cooperatives to shelter development in Zimbabwe" *UNCHS-Habitat,* Nairobi. <URL: http://www. unhabitat. org/programmes/-housingpolicy/documents/HS618.chm>, *Accessed on 21 September 2008.(*1999);Hall.I, "Partnerships in housing provision; A case study of housing co-operative initiatives in Kwekwe, Bulawayo and Harare, in Municipal Development Program – MDP," undated: *Addressing poverty in the context of decentralisation in Eastern and Southern Africa – Case studies in Malawi, Uganda, Zambia and Zimbabwe: MDP Working Paper 3,* Municipal Development Programme for Sub-Saharan Africa: Harare, pp 31-47. (2001); Toriro.P.," The Urban Housing Question in the Context of Operation Murambatsvina and Operation Garikai/Hlalani Kuhle," *Policy Brief prepared on behalf of the African Institute for Agrarian Studies,* Harare.(2006)\

676 Interview 11 March 2011

677 Franks J.R, Mc Gloin. A, "The Potential of Environmental Co-operatives to Deliver Landscape-scale Environmental and Rural Policy Objectives in the UK. The Rural

sustainability in the face of 'dissenting' voices. At least when actors can agree on working together such is necessary in ensuring that negative impacts to the environment are reduced, that order in land acquisition for urban development is achieved.

The foregoing discourse shows that different actors are 'pushed' by different motives in shaping peri-urban environments. It is evident from the partners' philosophies that most are mutually repellent while others are mutually reinforcing. From these divergent operational objectives, from a management viewpoint, it becomes justified that a mutually reinforcing framework is required in addressing challenges in peri-urban housing and environmental degradation. Formulating such a framework ought to be guided by certain values and ethics of which sustainable development is the undergirding force. Again, what must be its composition and tenets of operation? One scintillating thing from the whole discourse is that synergies, networks and partnerships are primary in building sustainable settlements and programmes. Perhaps, the major challenge is of establishing those, which last. The next chapter will strive to give a summary to this whole study, draw some key lessons, pass conclusions and propose a working model for sustainable peri-urban housing and stewardship.

The concessionary model of local development as shown in this chapter argues that for development of any settlement to take place, the local authority usual gets into contracts and memoranda of various organisations. The local authority is then the fulcrum that determines acceptable processes to be done in the place in the spirit of advancement of public interest. Specifically, this study has demonstrated how the participation of international organisations, for instance, The World Bank, USAID, UNDP, Melinda and Bill Gates Foundation are critical is resolving housing and sanitation challenges. Such partnerships are usually achieved by way of decentralized governance. Nevertheless, such negotiations are quite difficult in formulation given local politics even involving the grassroots. This is found to derail or detour progress. Certain contracts are misunderstood with respect to local private sector

---

Citizen" *Governance, Culture and Wellbeing in the 21st Century*: University of Plymouth, UK. (2006)

negotiations, local authorities normally get involved in transactions that they provide land and the other partners bring in technical and financial resources. The story of Shelter Zimbabwe, largely, explains this move. The civil society groups have also been instrumental in bringing in innovation mechanisms of development, for example Dialogue on Shelter in Epworth has marked in settlement to try to introduce participatory planning tools for upgrading. At first, such efforts were not well received. On the same note, PASA has worked on the same. Such processes need, however to be correctly handled, as political interferences may hinder the expected outcomes or block the planned path for development.

CHAPTER 12
CONCLUSION AND POLICY DIRECTION

It is put across that planners "… can and should take a multi-vocal approach, focusing on the interactions among consensus events, persons of difference, scenarios, and plans."[678] Housing is both an issue of the environment and an issue of community and stakeholders' organisation[679]. These are critical issues in the sustainability concept and debate. This study sought to investigate peri-urban housing, in the framework of regional or place stewardship in Zimbabwe. Use of Ruwa and Epworth has assisted in bringing out issues that pertain to housing and stewardship in peri-urban settings. In its endeavour to historicise the processes of housing and habitat delivery it has indicated the transformations, continuities and discontinuities that have emerged over the years[680]. Specifically, in the coming paragraphs I bring aboard a

---

678 Hopkins.L. ;Zapata.M.A, "Engaging the Future: Forecasts, Scenarios, Plans, and Projects edited," *Journal of Regional Sciencepg3, (*2008)

679 Donaldson.L ;Davis. J.H; "CEO governance and shareholder returns, Agency theory or stewardship theory,". *Paper presented at the annual meeting of the Academy of Management*, Washington, DC. (1989); "Stewardship theory or agency theory, CEO governance and shareholder returns," *Australian Journal of Management 16*: pp 49-64.(1991)

680 CAGOH, "Report on a Study on the Contribution of Urban Housing to National Economic Development in Zimbabwe," *CAGOH,* Harare. (2002);; Toriro.P, "Town Planning in Zimbabwe, History, Challenges and the Urban Renewal Operation Murambatsvina," Chapter 11, Maphosa France, Kraposy Kujinga and Sunungurai D Chingarande (eds.), (2007) "Zimbabwe"s Development Experiences since 1980: Challenges and Prospects for the Future," *OSSREA*, Addis Ababa.(2007); TibaijukaA. K, "Report of the Fact-Finding Mission to Zimbabwe to assess the Scope and Impact of Operation Murambatsvina," *UN Habitat*, Nairobi. (2005); Kamete.A.Y, Urban governance, poverty and urban housing," In O. Musandu-Nyamayaro and T. Mubvami, (Eds.), Urban Governance Outreach Research, pp. 13–27. Harare,

summary of the findings as reflected in the specific research objectives of this study, namely to:

i. Identify and classify stakeholders in housing delivery in the peri-urban zones with the view of explaining policy and practical bearings by each over time.
ii. Explain differential processes and trends, if any, in the transformation and quality of the physical provision of shelter (stocks) in peri-urban settlements.
iii. Relate global and regional efforts in the housing and stewardship debate and practices regarding peri-urban settlements.

Department of Rural and Urban Planning and the Ford Foundation. (1997);"Continuity with change: a review of Zimbabwe" public sector urban low income housing production system," in *Development Southern Africa 15(1) Autumn*: pp13-28(1998); "Government, Building Societies and Civil Society," Exploring the Interface in the Context of Urban Low-income Housing in Zimbabwe, in *African Review on Money Finance and Banking*, Felice Tambussi: Milan: pp 77-98.(1999a);)., "Government, building societies and civil society, exploring the interface in the context of urban low-income housing in Zimbabwe,. *Savings and Development*: pp77–98. http://www.fgda.org/pubblicazioni_schedarivista.php?Id=461, Accessed on 22 April 2008.(1999b); "Restrictive control of urban high-density housing in Zimbabwe, deregulation and challenges for urban design," *Housing, Theory and Society,* 16(3): 136–151. (1999c);)., "Cost recovery in urban high-density housing, a discourse with experiences from Zimbabwe."*Habitat International,* 24(3): 241–60.(2000a); "Examining the Zimbabwean Government"s Drive to House the Urban Poor," *Geographical Journal of Zimbabwe Number 31.* Geographical Association of Zimbabwe: Harare.(2000b); "The quest for affordable urban housing: a study of approaches and results in Harare, Zimbabwe," *Development Southern Africa,* 18(2): 31–44. (2001a); "Governance for sustainability? Balancing social and environmental concerns in Harare," *Chr.Michelsen Institute.* <URL: www.cmi.no.>(2002a); "Governing the Poor in Harare, Zimbabwe: Shifting Perceptions and Changing Responses" *Research Report Series, No. 122. Nordiska Afrikainstitutet*: Uppsala. (2002b); "The rebels within, Urban Zimbabwe in the post-election period. In H. Melber (ed.) Zimbabwe"s presidential elections 2002: evidence, lessons and implications," *Nordic Africa Institute Discussion Paper 14. Uppsala,* The Nordic Africa Institute, pp. 31–48(2002c); "Revisiting the urban housing crisis in Zimbabwe: Some forgotten dimensions?"*Habitat International 30(4):* pp 981-995.(2006);Kamete.A.Y.et.al, "Managing the interface between urban councils and the surrounding rural districts councils: The case of Bulawayo City Council and Umguza Rural District Council,. *Municipal Development Programme for Eastern and Southern* Africa (MDP-ESA): Harare., (2001); Muzvidziwa. V.N, "Informal Settlement Dwellers and Environmental Problems." *UNISWA Research Journal of Agriculture, Science and Technology (Special Volume No. 1)* (2005) pp 25-37.

iv. Propose practical and policy alternatives in tackling peri-urban housing and stewardship matters at different levels of analysis (local and regional).

This summary and discussion of study findings is so organised that, systematically, the three basic aspects to the objectives of the research are outlined, namely the identification and criteria for classifying peri-urban housing stakeholders; housing related processes, trends and effects over time, and, global and regional efforts in the housing and stewardship debate and practices and how these relate to the local context. It is from the discussion and synthesis of the aspects that I then draw some policy implications of peri-urban housing and stewardship in Zimbabwe.

The study has identified and classified a number of stakeholders in the framework of housing and stewardship. Stewardship is best achieved by way of collaborative effort[681]. Housing is very complex so is the peri-urban environment. Stewardship is a process aimed at achieving sustainability by way of their collaboration. In providing a framework for identifying the stakeholders in peri-urban housing and stewardship, it is envisaged that this will help in ensuring that whatever solutions are to be prescribed for this (rather provisional) zone are exerted in keeping with the view that sustainability is achieved by frankness in approach rather than pretending that there are no differential initiatives and responses from different actors. A one-size-fits-all approach to anything is a pretentious way of achieving important results, tantamount to self-deception[682]. The study has revealed, as indicated by especially Chapter 7, that stakeholders in any process also have their stakeholders too. This has a bearing on policy processes and outcomes[683]. The case of Ruwa and Epworth has

---

681 Stoll.L, "Regional Collaboration: A framework for solving complex planning problems." *The Land Tracker 6(2):* pp 1-4. (2006); Hopkins.L. ;Zapata.M.A, "Engaging the Future: Forecasts, Scenarios, Plans, and Projects edited," *Journal of Regional Science, (*2008)8

682 UNHABITAT,"Global report on human settlements 2009, " *Planning sustainable cities*: UNHABITAT, Earthscan (2009);Tibaijuka A.K, "Building Prosperity – Housing and Economic Development Earthscan" London. (2009); Stoll.L, "Regional Collaboration: A framework for solving complex planning problems." *The Land Tracker 6(2):* pp 1-4. (2006)

683 Bourne.L. S, , "The Geography of Housing," *V H Winston and Sons Ltd*, London. (1981);

revealed that there are many players and stakeholders in the housing and habitat sector. At a very local level, the stakeholders can be described according to the prescribed by the criteria I set for their analysis which are: trans-generational status, focus and mode of operation, level of operation, being state or non-state, space use, method of space acquisition, ties to land, period of stay, instruments applied for operations, as well as according to mobility status.

a) Trans-generational status: past, present and future generation

The major stakeholder in stewardship studies is the future generations[684]. Evident in literature and regarding sustainable development is that the present generations are loaning present life and its demands from future generation. Housing, as the major consumer of land and its resources, has resulted in some countries becoming 'urbanised jungles' for example Mexico [685]. By implication, the generations to come in that country will never fully know what rural life is like. They are made to live with the effects of the "urban penalty"[686]. With such a scenario, we are faced with a 'sustainability failure." It is unfortunate that in many developing countries today, that has been the trend so that they now rely on knowledge from museums or tour regions like Africa to see certain, especially, animal species.

---

[684] Cirman.A, "Intergenerational transfers as a response to changes in the housing market" *Paper presented to the ENHR Conference on Sustainable Urban Areas, 25-28 June 2007, Rotterdam.*(2007) <URL: www.enhr2007rotterdam.nl,> 2 August 2007.

[685] Anderson ; Engelsstoft, (2004); Berner. E, "Learning from Informal Markets: Innovative Approaches to Land and Housing Provision." *Development in Practice, 11(2-3):* pp 292-307. (2001); Huby.M, "Social Policy and the Environment," *Open University Press*,Buckingham. (1998); ;Hasse.J ;Lathrop.R, "Land resource impact indicators of urban sprawl," *Applied Geography 23*: pp159–175 (2003);, Houston.F, "Housing America State by State: How Governors Are Leading the Way," in *Housing Facts and Findings 7(1)*: p1.< URL: www.fanniemaefoundation.org/ programs/ hff. html>(2005)

[686] UNCHS, "*The state of the world"s cities 200,"* United Nations Centre for Human Settlements (Habitat), Nairobi(2001); Hood.E, "Dwelling disparities: how poor housing leads to poor health" ,*Environmental May, 2005.* <URL: www.ehponline.org/members/2005/113-5/focus.html,>*Accessed on 22 April 2008* (2005)

The reasons as to why people invest in housing differ from one household to the other[687]. There are those who build to occupy, those to let and those to speculate or to aggrandise on status. From the study, it has emerged that in the colonial days the poor whites were allocated some peri-urban plots but in post-colonial Zimbabwe it is the rich blacks who claim this space[688]. The same was observed by in peri-urban Dar-es-Salaam in which perceptions to peri-urban plot acquisitions changed from being "zones of survival" to being "zones of investments"[689]. In peri-urban Ruwa and Epworth, as well, Harare Metropolitan Province has more than 4,000 farmers who are temporarily making use of the available land until urban development is ushered in. In Magada, Epworth the existence of informal land speculation through 'slumlords' is a critical phenomenon. Those who came earlier tend to hold land in which they build temporary structures in which the homeless from Harare and neighbouring settlements are ready to take. This has brought about informal renting in peri-urban space. Thus, rents paid get into the 'owners' pockets stifling processes of effective development levy collection. The poor are subjected to inadequate housing hence they "pay more" including, in the peri-urban areas, where life is assumed to be cheaper and affordable than in the inner city.

Levels of operation of stakeholders are varied beginning with the private individual's level operation, to a household, then community, cooperative groupings and associations, consortia, government-led operations thus sun-national and national operations, and the regional and global operations. At individual level are usually dreams, aspirations and experiences which may be of homelessness or receiving assistance on housing. At community level, community aspirations and dreams are spelt

---

[687] Mbiba.B ; Ndubiwa.M, "Decent construction and the role of local authorities: the case of Bulawayo city, Zimbabwe,". *Research Report for the Urban and Peri-Urban Research Network (Peri-NET), [S.I.],* <URL: http://eprints.lse.ac.uk/3015/1/Bulawayo_report.pdf>, *Accessed on 22 April 2008.(*2006)

[688] Odero.K, "Local Authorities" Response to Restructuring," *Paper presented at the 39th ISoCaRP Congress 2003*, <URL: www.isocarp.net/Data/case_studies/252.pdf>, *Accessed on 3 May 2008.*(2003)

[689] Briggs; Mwamfupe, "Peri-urban development in an era of Structural Adjustment in Afric," *The City of Dar es Salaam, Tanzania. Urban Studies 37(4),* (2000) pp797-809.

out through community visioning initiatives which sometimes foster community building or even divisions and conflicts[690]. At national level, there are standards and policies which are shaped through stakeholders' input and debate. The processes are better enabled by the state given its powers enshrined in national laws. From regional and global levels are usually sources of concepts and policy agendas. However, some of the concepts are very difficult to practice on the ground given the different contexts and cultural values in different places around the globe. If one looks at why it has taken so long for nations to embrace self-help housing initiatives which were discussed at the Vancouver Housing Conference in 1976, it shows that quite a number of countries were resisting taking this idea on board[691]. It has been argued that housing is a "political hot potato"[692]. As such many governments often use housing as a promissory note to get votes hence remaining in power. For Zimbabwe, after Operation Murambatsvina, the government overcommitted itself to a difficult task of constructing houses for the homeless through Operation Garikayi/Hlalani Kuhle[693]. That was quite myopic given that it had not calculated its capacity. Yet it was a way of demonstrating that at least it 'cared' for its populace – a case of a steward becoming a nanny. In both Ruwa and Epworth, like any other settlement there are traces of the unfinished business of the Operation Garikayi/Hlalani Kuhle houses. The government has since shifted the responsibility to the local authorities.

In being either state on non-state criteria housing and stewardship processes are defined as state-sector-led, private-corporate-led, voluntary-sector-led or community-led. State-led processes usually have a Fordist

---

690 Ziller. A, "The role of planning in community building," *Unpublished Doctor of Philosophy Degree Thesis, Faculty of Architecture*, University of Sydney: Sydney, (2004).

691 Tibaijuka A.K, "Building Prosperity – Housing and Economic Development Earthscan" London. (2009); UNHABITAT,"Global report on human settlements 2009, " *Planning sustainable cities*: UNHABITAT, Earthscan (2009)

692 BourneL.S, "The Geography of Housing," *V H Winston and Sons Ltd*: London. (1981)

693 Mufema. E, "Report of the Operation Garikayi/Hlalani Kule – National Audit with the framework of social accountability, NANGO," Harare.(2008).

appeal in which standardised outputs are delivered[694]. With resources the state tries to achieve much in a short space of time. The private-led processes in housing are usually faster than the state. That the hand of the state as well as that of the voluntary sector in Ruwa is the reason why outputs and outcomes in the general townscape are remarkably appealing. Epworth is typified by community-led processes with the voluntary sector trying as much as it can to assist. An attempt by Practical Action to build a demonstration house for the poor is flawed in that the demonstration house is 'high-pitched' in direct contrast of the 'lowering the ladder' mantra[695]. Perhaps, the actor should have stipulated the time dimensions as to when a family is expected to have accomplished building such a house. The issue of appropriate technology is pivotal in the creation of sustainable habitats in the peri-urban areas[696]. At the same time, sustainability is a meaningful idea if the housing artefacts are to last longer[697]. In most cases, the poor pay more because the materials they use for building are unsustainable. Like Esther's house in the case of Magada, Epworth, the houses will collapse at the point of need, when the user really needs it.

While the four walls and a roof matter for sleeping and cooking needs, space outside the shelter shell has great use value. It can be taxonomised as either productive or reproductive space in which farming and mining or worship and recreational needs are met respectively. The space use can also be viewed as either on-plot or off-plot. Then, there is

---

[694] Noero.J, "Four reasons why housing problem cannot be solved. Buchanan Chris ed." *Planning – Architectural and Planning Review for Southern Africa 135.* (1994) pp 87

[695] Payne.G, Majale. M, "The Urban Housing Manual: Making Regulatory Framework Work for the Poor," Earthscan, London. (2004);Payne.G, "Urban Land Policy Options: Titles or Rights?" *Paper presented at the World Bank Urban Forum Westfields Marriott, Virginia, USA: 03-05 April, 2000.* (2000)<URL:http://www.worldbank.org/html/fpd/urban/forum2000/papers/realestate.pdf> *Accessed on 27 June 2011.*

[696] SWH, "How do we select systems in peri-urban areas?" *Workshop on water and sanitation in peri-urban areas on the 12th of December at 10.00-15.00* (2006)

[697] Dzemydiene. D, "Preface to Sustainable Development Problems in the Issue." *Baltic Journal on Sustainability 14(1)*, (2008) pp 8-10; Mitlin.D,"Sustaining markets or poverty reduction?" *Environment and Urbanisation 14(1)* (2002) pp 173-177.

the consideration of it as either indoor or outdoor. Those who mine and extract sands or concrete pebbles normally are active during the active days of mass constructions and they tend to shift outwards with the shifting of the urban 'boundary." In both Epworth and Ruwa, activities by the minors tended to follow on the residue of past operations by quarry companies. Peri-urban farming is a continuous activity long after settlements are established[698]. Indoor space use is the primary focus of the family or household: whether or not they will let in a lodger, or they allocate rooms to different members of the family or they use the rooms for storage of harvests, for example in the case of Mbuya Todii.

In the method of space acquisition criterion, it is observed that some plots in the peri-urban have been allotted and designated to the holders while others have been invaded by the holders. Those that are designated include those obtained through the market as well as the public processes. By market processes, it means that holders are there by either buying or leasehold. This criterion is linked to the ties holders have to the land (tenure) whether it be ownership or tenancy hence according to the time of stay in place: temporary or 'permanent." The mobility status of the peri-urban dwellers is critical to how they are also defined, as some would seem more mobile than others hence the more permanent settlers could be taken as being in-situ operators. Those with longer tenure in a place are likely to develop their plots with a long-range planning initiative than those who are not sure of their tomorrow in the place in question. Those households that are likely to be evicted from the place of occupancy tend to be sceptical about 'investing' in the area and plot. This is further reinforced by the type and nature of instruments applied in the acquisition, whether legislative provisions were applied or some policy prescriptions define it or it was through some voluntary mechanism of settlement. Ruwa being predominantly formal has followed most of the legislative requirements in the development of modern settlements including planning and subjection to scrutiny of the provisions of the environmental

---

[698] Mushamba et al. "Urban and Peri-Urban Agriculture: Prospects for Food Security and Growth in Eastern and Southern Africa," Report prepared for the Ministers" Conference on August 28-29, 2003, Sheraton Hotel – Harare - Zimbabwe. <URL: http://www.ruaf.org/files/ministers_conference.pdf>, *Accessed on 2 April 2007.(2003)*

impact assessment, whereas in Epworth the settlement has been permitted through policy of tolerance of informal settlements.

The foregoing classification is not conclusive but rather illustrative of how peri-urban dwellers and stakeholders behave in the locations of their habitation. In the next section, I examine the processes, trends and effects of peri-urban housing at local, national, regional and global levels. The classification of stakeholders has very important implications in the planning, governance and stewardship of the peri-urban space[699]. Some of the stakeholders are at local level while others are at the international level. A mixed scanning approach in policy development is very critical in the analysis of how the global-local nexus shapes space (see Table 8.1, for detail).

Housing in the peri-urban settlements is associated with many processes which have different impacts over time. The processes include, *inter alia*:

a) Farming (on-plot and off-plot) to provide the households with additional food for their needs,
b) Mining, especially in the form of quarrying and sand extractions for construction needs of the housing structure,
c) Worship, as religious and spiritual requirement by the family members be it on plot or off-plot or at designated sites,
d) Recreation, as a reproductive activity including sight-seeing, fishing and related activities including those done at schools as part of the extra-curriculum,
e) Tenancy, as a livelihood strategy as families try to eke a living from the rentals earned from letting out space for accommodation or for work and business operations, and,vii). Constructions, as they allow for labour-based survival strategies for bricklayers, building resources miners, painters and related tradespersons.

---

[699] Cortemiglia.A,"Involving informally housed communities in shaping local government policies aimed at poverty alleviation: A South African perspective," *A thesis for the Doctor of Literature and Philosophy in Development Studies, University of South Africa.* (2006).

Table 8.1: Classification of Stakeholders in Peri-urban Housing and Stewardship Implications

Criterion Factor	Typology	Implications
Trans-generational status: past, present and future generations	This mainly households and communities.	Places importance at intra and inter-generational equity. Housing processes from construction to usage must be so planned that some households, communities or generations are not disadvantaged by the behavior of the past or present generation[700]. It is a matter of public and overall generational interest. A governance model helps in bringing actors together to formulate a stewardship model that works for transparency, equity, accountability, trust, and rule of law. The framework has to bring all actors at different levels together.
Focus and mode of operation	Micro-level (households, communities and the local authority) Meso-level (provincial and district) Macro-level (central government ministries,	The micro-level determines the day-to-day operations, events and implementation of plans. This level determines the resultant landscape and architecture in space in terms of the houses built and the environmental improvements or degradation that meet the eye. This is a planning and policy formulation sphere.

[700] Cirman.A, "Intergenerational transfers as a response to changes in the housing market" *Paper presented to the ENHR Conference on Sustainable Urban Areas, 25-28 June 2007, Rotterdam.*(2007) <URL: www.enhr2007rotterdam.nl,> 2 August 2007

	agencies and departments), international bodies and regional bodies	Sometimes it rules through set bye-laws. The national level is a defining sphere in terms of statutory and policy level. Aspirations of the nation are defined. The agencies implement as well as enforce the set standards. At regional and international level are a number of concepts defined. These are trans-boundary but sometimes very difficult to implement or contextualise as the concepts sometimes tend to be vague, too ambitious or rather utopian.
Level of operation	Micro-level (households, communities and the local authority) Meso-level (provincial and district) Macro-level (central government ministries, agencies and departments), international bodies and regional bodies	See above. Yet it must be made clear that implementation and enforceability of standards are largely possible at the micro-level as these are the builders, plot users, polluters, poachers etc. As we move up the ladder it becomes more of rhetoric than actionable. Stewardship is more practicable if it is done by localised people and institutions than by globalised and esoteric institutions that are removed from the realities on the ground. The latter, however, are critical for formulating strategies and casting the picture wider. In reality some mixed scanning approach is required where the bird's eye view of the reality is put together to be in sync

		with the worm's eye view of development. In peri-urban housing planning, such items as the global figures in housing backlog and migration patterns must be so understood so that when land, finance and infrastructure to support the housing process are availed the arithmetical computations balance off.
Either state on non-state:	State actors (central government ministries, departments, agencies, municipalities or local authorities) Non-state actors (NGOs, the private corporate sectors, CBOs, etc.	Overall, the state actors are regulators. Historically they are also providers of housing and environmental goods. In recent years, there has been an increased call that they act more as facilitators and regulators. Due to state failure, the call is a justified one. In their regulation and facilitation, there is need that the instruments they wield are effective and efficient whether in the form of incentives or sanctions (the carrot-and-stick approach). This would make them effective gatekeepers as well as agencies. The action of these is defined by the motifs they hold. It is these motifs that define their effectiveness. If they are to be effective stewards they must balance between profit-making and social corporate responsibility, if they are private corporate; and between advocacy and rationality. There is rationality that

		militates against equity and advocacy that works against rationality. It is the balance or rather the harmonization of rationality and advocacy that creates a more sustainable future. When future generations judge the present generations, this will base on this to define the stewards this generation has been, whether good or bad.
Use of space available	On-plot Off-plot	This applies more at the micro-level picture in which households and members of the community use their plots: for, among other things, gardening, rental accommodation, work-shopping and marketing of different wares. It includes indoor space. This is linked to values, ethics and culture of the space users. This space tends to define the type of people hence stewards of the micro-space in question. Users pay rentals or some levies to show the tenure bracket they belong to, whether ownership (single, block or communal) or leasehold or invasion. This has to do with community public assets in place including the streets, the open spaces, the rivers and streams, the vleis and sacred places. However, some members of the community will privatise some of these

		hence exclude others. The converted spaces are sometimes for farming, manufacturing, vending and recreation. If stewardship is about taking turns, then this purpose will already have been defeated as the rotational facility will have been foiled.
Method of space acquisition	Formal Informal	The formal way is done in cooperation with the institutions and regulations that define areas. Stewardship in this sphere is clear-cut. However, there may be cases of corruption where certain officers in the institutions use their office for private gain. When this happens, this becomes bad stewardship. Some developers have a tendency for hording the space which they acquire formally and waiting until it becomes more profitable to dispose this land and space to desperate home and space seeks. This is speculation. When it happens in informal space then a case of slumlord-ism arises where desperate home-seekers are forced to paying 'the wrong pocket. Desperation by home-seekers has often forced some households to leave big cities into the peri-urban areas so that they invade or illegally occupy land they find. For Epworth, just like Churu Farm

		as noted in this study, it has been the Methodist Church and Reverence Ndabaningi Sithole who invited, on some philanthropic grounds, the people who become occupiers of their farms. The 'beneficiaries' live on the goodwill of the offerer of the space who then occupies the space of a guarantor of their stay. In the case of Epworth, the church had to handover the farms once it found it difficult to manage the growing population and its needs. For Churu farm, the government stopped the process simply because the ruling party may have seen the Reverend (being a politician too) of 'stealing the hearts' of some of their voters. Again, the aspect of the government as the regulator and/or facilitator in the management of peri-urban space comes in.

As noted in this study, all these differential processes have a strong bearing on the quality of the physical provision of shelter (stocks) in peri-urban settlements. For instance, some labour-based techniques in housing provision are offered by unskilled and semi-skilled personnel. They build without putting into cognisance the town planning and architectural requirements such that the products would add to nothing but urban informality in the habitats in question. A whole lot of the processes in shelter delivery in peri-urban settlement that ultimately shape the peri-urban habitats include land acquisition, infrastructure provision (servicing) and building materials' acquisition especially direct extractions in the environment. There is also the observation of mass production versus incremental development of the shelter. Where informal settlement has taken place, regularisation is expected, for instance in Epworth. Livelihood support is a critical process in peri-urban habitats. As already stated, it entails practices of brick moulding, sand poaching, farming, street vending and letting space for accommodation. Other processes include solid waste dumping and the conversions of houses to other uses.

The foregoing processes have happened and continue to happen in different eras which depict critical trends for analysis. In this study, in the context of Africa, trends have been defined according to colonial versus post-colonial policies, ideological pronunciations and resultant nuances by the different governments and political regimes as well as through changing attitudes and tastes by households and families. From this, it has been noted that the key determinants to the quality of housing stocks include: the performance of the economy including pressure exerted by it, income levels of households and families, the overall habitat in terms of how it has been shaped, be it formal or informal, which naturally also depend on the level of application and adherence to set standards, and, aspirations and capacity of the individual investor to build shelter in defined peri-urban settlements just as elsewhere. With these in mind it is further critical to demonstrate how this study has attempted to relate the local experiences to the global and regional efforts in the housing and stewardship debate and practices regarding peri-urban settlements.

This study notes that peri-urbanisation is a growing phenomenon everywhere in the world including in North America[701]. It is observed further that Africa is fast urbanising and the peri-urban settlements in the region are immensely fragile and ever-transitioning[702]. Peri-urban dwellers consist mainly of tribal groups, farmers and city dwellers flowing into this area whose relationship with this environment tend to be uncertain, adverse and sometimes abusive of the resources at their

---

[701] Wissen-Hayek et al. "Measuring and assessing urban sprawl: What are the remaining options for future settlement development in Switzerland for 2030?" – *Applied Spatial Analysis and Policy 4(4)*(2011) pp 249-279.

[702] UNHABITAT, *Global report on human settlements, Planning sustainable cities*: UNHABITAT, Earthscan (2009).

exposure. Still, little remains understood regarding how most peri-urban dwellers move ahead with providing themselves with decent shelter. This is against the background that the state has failed to provide adequate shelter for its citizens. The fulfilment of the 1976 UNCHS Habitat resolution and plea to giving space to self-help housing is manifesting itself in Zimbabwe as in many parts of sub-Saharan Africa, Latin America and Asia[703]. In particular, Zimbabwe is at the crossroads; its urban sector is undergoing wholesale transformation if not complete metamorphosis. Specifically, the housing and habitat sector has shifted from a dominantly state process to the one in the hands of private individuals.

This study has demonstrated that the population dynamics of the peri-urban zone involve two basic users of habitat and housing namely the 'original space occupiers' and in-migrants. The in-migrants or 'new settlers' to the peripheral zone of the peri-urban can further be divided into two. First is the affluent and well-to-do class of people. This group often seeks after 'breathing space' hence move away from the diseconomies of crowdedness, pollution and traffic jams associated with the drudgery of the 'inner city." Second are the urban poor who are after the 'cheap' life in the city outskirts. These usually practise some form of 'mixed economy' in which they seek to maximise on the good that urban life promises them (jobs, markets, the promise for better services and facilities) while tapping on the natural provision of the nearby rural areas including cheap land for gardening and other needs. The house comes in as a place from which households set off to make interactions with the outside world and then come for reproduction and maintenance[704].

Five key lessons hence conclusions can be drawn from this study. Overall, peri-urban stewardship has not been so developed to have a framework that works, particularly in the developing countries where peri-urbanisation is happening at a fast pace hitherto unknown. There are many

---

[703] Zindoga.S, "Need For More Urban Housing In Southern Africa," *Southern African News Features.* (1999)URL: <http://www.sardc.net/Editorial/sanf/1999/10/ 15-10-1999-nf3.htm,> *Accessed on 22 April 2008.*(1999)

[704] Arthurson.K, "Social mix and social interaction: do residents living in different housing tenures mix?"*Paper presented to the ENHR Conference on Sustainable Urban Areas, 25-28 June 2007, Rotterdam.* (2007). URL: <www.enhr2007 rotterdam.nl>, *Accessed on 13 July 2008*

clashes and conflicts at the city borders whose detriments are to the future generations. Housing construction is the major cause of the reality of the ecological footprint. Vernacular practices and materials, including traditional practices and norms, are very rich regarding the concept, philosophy and practice of stewardship. These are defined by local people and conditions which are generally the basis of sustainable practices. From this an understanding of the fundamental factors is derived.

The first key lesson is that peri-urbanisation is a growing phenomenon everywhere, with it being largely the spill-over effect of the population expansion in 'big cities." In light of this, it is noted that it is rentals in the core city that principally push the poor to the periphery. As such, the poor consider peri-urban 'free' and more 'comfortable' in terms of habitability as opposed to those residential areas within the main cities. Yet the same poor, as peri-urban dwellers, do not quite enjoy the houses that they build for themselves or rent in given critical constraints including smallness of rooms and that most of the rooms fail to meet the anthropometric and ergonomic expectations and standards as laid out in approved by-laws. Yet, it must be borne in mind that even if the peri-urban areas may appear cheap to live in, once infrastructure is installed, it must be paid for. This implies having a taxation system befitting purely peri-urban settlements. When this happens, there is betterment of place which, in essence, attracts urban rates of taxation. It is likely that once that happens, by way of gentrification, the poor will be impelled to move away from the improved environments hence creating a vicious cycle of peri-urban settlements that lack in basic infrastructure and services. A case described by Home (2001) of 'eating farmland and building housing' will replicate itself continuously. Moreover, peri-urban development should be examined in the context of metropolitanisation as transpiring with most African major cities today.

Secondly, economic and policy circles are critical in shaping the terrain and approaches to housing delivery. The study has shed some light on how both colonial and post-colonial policies have shaped peri-urban settlement with housing becoming a critical concern as activities in different settlements in the peri-urban areas attract different types of people who must be housed as they pursue their different activities in this zone. In the post-colonial era in Africa, most countries adopted the structural adjustment programmes. These SAPs have had a bearing on how some well-to-do as well as less privileged households have had ties with the peri-urban zones. In Zimbabwe, the fast-track land reform programme has resulted in the development of the so-called 'peri-urban layouts' hence it has ushered in a new dimension in development in which access to land for housing has been achieved to the benefaction of especially the low-income groups.

The third aspect to note is that most of the structures built are so poor that they fail to withstand rains as well as provide the much-needed comfort from the weather elements. Along the same lines, it is observed that housing development in peri-urban Zimbabwe is happening at a very fast pace and that much of it lacks in basic infrastructure given that in recent years incremental development has been hailed as panacea to the housing plight. As such, there are so many stands/plots allocated to households. Yet stands are by no means to be treated as houses as they cannot provide the service that a properly instituted house would provide. The situation is further compounded by the lack of basic supportive infrastructure. Ruwa, though developed to high levels of modern-day housing schemes still lacks in the number of schools that are considered necessary according to the existing town planning standards of one primary school for every 500 stands and one secondary school for every three primary schools. Another major land-use provision of concern due to its scarcity is the provision of burial space.[705]

The fourth key observation and conclusion are that dependency on one's immediate environment for drawing livelihoods is a Constitutional given. In this study, it has emerged that peri-urban dwellers are rational beings capable of developing or sourcing products, which they will market for livelihood enhancement. It has become apparent that most of the poor peri-urban dwellers would not be willing to stay where they stay if realistic prices were in place in terms of fares to and from city centre. Conventional wisdom has it that the poor want to stay close to places with opportunities that they capitalise on. The poor need bigger space to do on-plot farming

---

[705] De Marco.S, "Burlington is running out of cemetery space," *Daily Times Chronicles*. URL: <http://www.woburnonline.com/> (2000).

yet it is prudent and technically ascertained that they must occupy smaller space which they afford. In the long-run, if unchecked, less-cost effective cities are emerging hence the raison d'être for regularisation. But regularisation is costlier relative to sites-and-services schemes. Zimbabwe's cities are sprawling yet no one has tried to measure and understand the ecological footprint happening. Overall activities by the peri-urban dwellers, particularly the poor ones, are damaging to the environment with such theories like the Prisoner's Dilemma and the Tragedy of the Commons being confirmed on the ground. Vandalism of common property and abusage of common resources are rife in the settlements[706]. This shows how the poor operate in ignorance or inconsiderateness of the others let alone future generations. While the Stewardship Theory is loaded with precepts as to how actors can collaborate in determining their common destinies, it says little on the education they each deserve to create the expectable future, let alone shaping the place to sustainable levels.

Lastly, principal stakeholders as defined by the differential levels of operation (micro, meso- and micro-level) are operating in islands hence disjointed efforts. There is a general feeling among the actors that they do not care to what happens in the next office. This implies an urgent need to have offices that operate as one-stop-shops, to manage problems of overlaps, gaps and duplication of effort. Gaps normally leave gray areas where nothing is happening hence creating hollows to stewardship endeavours. this also creates avenues for corruption and mismanagement of different kinds of resources that may avail for housing construction or environmental management.

These noted conclusions and lessons are crucial in formulation of policy alternatives that work. In its essence, stewardship aims at bringing a 'unified model' of addressing common and transcending challenges. Its purpose is to achieve collaboration of key stakeholders through

---

[706] Allen. A, "Environmental planning and management of the peri-urban interface: perspectives on an emerging field." *Environment & Urbanisation* 15(1)(2003) pp. 135-147.

community and place visioning and branding.[707] The study has indicated that there are number of tools and instruments that have been applied over the years in managing peri-urban areas in Zimbabwe (Ndlovu, 2004). Nevertheless, the change in government in 1980 saw enforcement of policies and laws slackening much to the detriment of creating sustainable environments. Most of the institutions dealing with housing and the environment have been noted in this study as weak within as well as in collaborative terms. They are more designed to further parochially, departmental agendas at the expense of having a more holistic approach to issues ravening communities, housing challenges included. In effect, some are quite irrelevant to the agenda of creating affordable and equitable low-income housing. The law, like the Environmental Management Act, cannot be applied in retrospect with the implication that some artefacts are to be there for a long time though their sustainability as structures is questionable.

Stewardship as an issue of 'removing walls' towards progressive thinking and plan implementation, as noted in this study, is greatly compromised along professional, partisan, institutional and other dividing lines. Persistence of this trend means deliberations and practices including participatory planning, participatory budgeting, enforcement of laws with respect to land, housing and the environment of the peri-urban zone will continue in the realm of 'ivory towers' hence fuzziness as critics to the notion of sustainable development have argued[708]. As such, in Zimbabwe, like most developing nations, deliberate stewardship provision of sustainable shelter for peri-urban dwellers collaboration with their facilitators, sponsors and governors to reduce problems of environmental decay so that future generations remain complex. In light of this, it can be noted that there are socio-spatial and political dynamics and ramifications

[707] Franks J.R, Mc Gloin. A, "The Potential of Environmental Co-operatives to Deliver Landscape-scale Environmental and Rural Policy Objectives in the UK. The Rural Citizen" *Governance, Culture and Wellbeing in the 21st Century*: University of Plymouth, UK. (2006); MIT, "Just Jerusalem Competition, Jerusalem 2050," Cambridge,(2007) <http://web.mit.edu.justjerusalem/> *Accessed on 23 August 2007.*

[708] Manjengwa.J.M, "Linking environment and development, easier said than done: learning from the Zimbabwean experience." *Development Southern Africa 24(2):* (2007) pp 225-240.

associated, with not only the understanding but also implementing sustainable practices in housing and peri-urban development in the framework and spirit of stewardship.

Migration to peri-urban settlements is induced by the big cities. In this case Harare has shed off its excess populations into the hinterland Epworth and Ruwa. The migrants purport that life is quite affordable in the periphery than at the centre. Overall, human beings are increasingly becoming *homo urbanus*. Big cities spill over into peri-urban settlements. Once they are in the peri-urban zone, the migrants are usually left with no choice but to depend more on the natural capital: space for peri-urban farming, extractions of rocks, pit sand and river sand, firewood, grass for thatching, to name these few. The different households have different perspectives about their habitats and dwelling conditions. They also have different experiences regarding interaction with the environment and how they engage livelihood coping strategies.

Overall, Ruwa and Epworth cases demonstrate that communities not only depend on their environments but in the process of exploiting resources do harm the environment as well. Some of the ways the environment has been seen to be under assault include: some community members dumping their waste, leaving scars like open pits after moulding bricks and extracting sand, and, destroying floral species as they seek firewood or medicinal value in certain plants. At the same time, it is observed that there are instances in which communities actually 'invest' in the environment by such activities they do like grass cutting, orchard development, and preserving some natural and indigenous trees and shrubs in the area. In certain cases, however, they do it in contradiction with future plans about the place.

A number of policy implications towards the understanding of sustainability can be drawn from this study on peri-urban housing and stewardship in Zimbabwe. These include, among other things:

a) Using remote sensing to measure and monitor urban expansion, which can be assigned as a responsibility of the Department of Physical Planning or Harare Metropolitan Province since they have or should have oversight of broader spatial or regional growth monitoring. This is critical in light of the fact that the same has been applied in North America so that developments are spatially monitored and the means to tame this is put in place. Stewardship is based on the notion that variables must be comprehensible and phenomena be well understood before they can be effectively managed.

b) Setting up an institution responsible for peri-urban stewardship and collaborative planning. Such an institution can be set as a think-tank so that it independently oversees the role played by local authorities and the Department of Physical Planning or Harare Metropolitan Province. Critical with such an instruction is the ability to champion both environmental sustainability and allocation of resources (human and material) required to achieve environmental sustainability. Stewardship without supportive structures demanding transparency, rule of law, accountability and trust which ideally constitute good governance, is meaningless.

c) Governance, in a way, answers concern that planners "can and should take a multi-vocal approach, focusing on the interactions among consensus events, persons of difference, scenarios, and plans."[709] Such a multi-vocal approach is critical for breaking up walls along professional and departmental lines. In another dimension this helps in curbing challenges of policy overlaps and gray areas plus duplication of efforts. It will provide that one-stop-shop for all peri-urban development challenges including housing development and construction, environmental planning and management, livelihoods and management of space including fiscal measures than ensure sustainable development where the respect of the environment, the economy and environment are in a holistic picture. In most cases, as has emerged from this study, there are institutions in place like UDCORP, the DPP and EMA which may not be performing as expected because they have not taken time to re-create themselves. I would propose setting up an Institute of Peri-urban Management and Housing Development which would seek to bring these rather dysfunctional institutions together for the cause of research

---

[709] Hopkins.L. ;Zapata.M.A, "Engaging the Future: Forecasts, Scenarios, Plans, and Projects edited," *Journal of Regional Science,(*2008)

and policy for sustainable development[710]. Such a mechanism will seek to research and do scenario planning taking on board major actors in peri-urban development.

d) The scenario planning process should incorporate the following principal tenets and challenges: design for change, consider governance, incorporate new community designs into local and regional comprehensive plans, phase development; plan for market changes, and connect to common values. These echo the unified model of pluralism which is a fundamental partnership model aspect in which collaborative and inclusive planning are the founding pillars[711]. While putting everything into one picture, the model assets for incremental development as stakeholders, particularly the community 'bite what they can chew' while creating a more sustainable future. What is important though is the picture) put into perspective that,

> "...scenario planning and effective visualisations become both more important and more challenging to achieve when conducting larger and longer-term visioning exercises. Visualisations that provide compelling depictions of activity centres and higher-density, mixed-use neighbourhoods can help to gain public acceptance. Effective mechanisms are also needed to convey to current participants that the planning process is imagining community characteristics and housing and lifestyle preferences for their grandchildren or great-grandchildren many years in the future."[712]

e) Setting up instruments to the degree of environmental damage to the environment so that environmental education is rooted in real time data. The task of environmental education could be a responsibility of environmental think-tanks, universities and civil society organisations including those already active in the peri-urban areas. To be more sustainable the local residents should be actively involved hence the promotion of local initiatives encapsulated in the notion of local

---

710 Benjamin.S, Presenting Two in Contesting Spatialities: Do Everyday Institutional contestations erode the neo-liberal Urban Reforms Agenda? (2008) URL:< http://igs.cla.umn.edu/pdf/BenjaminPaper.pdf>, *Accessed on 21 November 2008. v*

711 Holway.J, "Scenario Planning and the Promise of Open Source Tools." *Land Lines 23(4)*: pp7-13 (2011)

712 Ibid, pg 11

environmental action planning (LEAP). Peri-urban dwellers will appreciate environmental stewardship if they are exposed to the realities of the implications of the behaviour and activities through rigorous advocacy and the raising of awareness. This should cascade down through the schools' curricula so that issues of the ecological footprint are clearly understood. It is prudent that this effort be examined alongside applications in GIS and other remote sensing tools.[713]

f) Educating the citizens on the tax implications of belonging to a city. Such a task could be assigned to the local authorities in conjunction with the Harare Metropolitan Province because they are already involved in the process. Peri-urban settlements are 'pre-urban areas." Having citizens staying in this space without the full knowledge of the urban dynamics including ground taxation and paying for infrastructure, is paralysing to the urban fabric in the long-run. In Africa most peri-urban dwellers must come to terms with city living and its demands. This means, by all means, working against the tide of tribal land ownership or seeking to improve how land is organised, developed and serviced so that in the long run sustainability is ensured. Citizens have a right to the city but rights mean more responsibility coupled by rule of law, transparency, accountability, trust and other governance principles and aspirations.

g) A rights-based approach to development puts stewardship as a critical 'lubricating' factor towards sustaining places, the fragile peri-urban environments included[714]. Rights should not be seen as isolated efforts to draw benefits from a place without acting responsibly[715]. In actual fact, rights are about responsibility, care and accountability. By this definition, rights, stewardship and good governance merge to form one concrete block of a place sustainability framework whose

---

[713] Wilmersdorf.E, "Spatio-Temporal GIS-Design For Real-Time Processes," *Geographia Technica, 2,(2010)*: pp 105 – 115.

[714] Aristizabal N. , Gomez.O.A., "Chapter 6: Are services more important than titles in Bogotá? In PAYNE GEOFFREY (ed.).," *Land, Rights and Innovation – Improving tenure security for the urban poor*, ITDG Publishing: London. (2002); Armitage L., "Customary Land Tenure in Papua New Guinea: Status and Prospects." (2000.) URL< http://dlc.dlib.indiana.edu/archive/00001043/00/armitage.pdf,> *Accessed on 22 April 2008.*,

[715] Flint.J., "The Responsible Tenant: Housing Governance and the Politics of Behaviour," CNR Paper 20. URL: <www.neighbourhoodcentre.org.uk>, (2004.)

raison d'être is of ensuring that even future generations are in a position to receive and enjoy environmental assets (clean water, air and rich lands, infrastructure, to name a few). The present generations have a role to ensure minimised liabilities as they engage in exploitation and use of local resources.

h) *Researching Peri-urban Human Habitats' Phenomena: New Directions*: Studying peri-urban habitats is a multi-pronged task as there are many issues that are linked to housing. This is because housing in itself is a complex phenomenon. When issues are examined along the lines of stewardship, it becomes even more complex. This is because different groups in the peri-urban areas relate differently to the place they live in. This study has adopted different methodological tools to get to the bottom of the realities of peri-urban housing and stewardship. It is suggested that in future, workshops and more focus group discussions be engaged, in the spirit of multi-stakeholder processes to fully understand the issues involved in peri-urban studies, a number of teams, researching on various housing related issues and using different tools, must be constituted and aligned to explore issues of energy, water, sanitation and appropriate technologies, to name but a few. Stewardship is about sustainability and appropriateness of technology. Development must therefore be thoroughly informed by scientific research.

There are a number of areas worth exploring regarding the stewardship and rights wielded by the peri-urban dwellers in Zimbabwe and Africa, in general in the broader concern and framework of sustainable development. These areas include, among other things:

i. Exploring the arrangements for parcelisation of tribal land as cities expand into rural land so that livelihoods are adequately addressed.
ii. Examining the relationships between peri-urban land development, speculation and transfer processes in the legal framework.
iii. Explaining the paradoxes of the 'right-to-the-city," housing rights and land taxation in the framework of social justice and intergenerational equity.
iv. Describing and analysing peri-urban poverty, shelter and services provisioning in light of the 'appropriate technology."

v. Exploring 'researching with them (the peri-urban dwellers)' in light of the vernacular and grassroots approaches to stewardship in environmental sustainability.
vi. Investigating the feasibility of strategic (peri-) urban spatial planning (SUSP) in terms of its meaning and practicability for sustainability putting into consideration the application of community visioning and remote sensing as critical tools in peri-urban stewardship.
vii. Computing and calculating the quantum and extensity environmental degradation (pollution, soil erosion and siltation, etc.) from peri-urban constructions towards arguing with scientific facts hence argumentation in evidence-based policy.
viii. Assessing the possibility of rigorous scenario planning as a tool by which institutions in Zimbabwe can improve policy research and practice.
ix. Examining the political dynamics associated with peri-urbanisation, as peri-urban zones become field associated with discontented social classes including the unemployed youths and the poorly housed.
x. Assessing the trade-offs of establishing a one-stop-shop institution responsible for peri-urban environmental and housing affairs in the country and region.

As noted by this study, these aspects have not been fully explored in literature. In many developing countries, Zimbabwe included, peri-urbanisation is an obtaining reality, much as it is also in Latin America, Asia, Europe and North America. Unless such a review is done issues of social justice, compensation, rights and privileges will continue to be excluded in policy dialogue to the detriment of the poor and minority groups. Moreover, such a deliberate exclusion will create socially, politically and economically less sustainable places whose urban management is a serious challenge in the future of the region.

At present, we continue to experience, 'growth without equity," as well as 'urbanisation without growth'[716]. This means taming poverty and creating cities on a 'liability framework." This is a timebomb, which

---

[716] Kessides.C, *The Urban Transition in Sub-Saharan Africa: Implications for Economic Growth and Poverty Reduction*, The Cities Alliance: Washington D. C. (2006).

may explode any time given the currency of urbanisation[717]. Current and future generations have rights too[718]. In addition, unless, we research with them and perhaps make them realise the great potential for progress and betterment that is in them in producing sustainable habitats, we risk producing 'sickly' habitats that are less of an asset than a liability to future generations.

Perceived and real milestones in constructing sustainable peri-urban habitats in Harare, as elsewhere, are critical in putting into perspective aspects of technology (in terms of methods and materials) while caring for the environment as construction is happening. This implies assessing progress, knowledge, attitudes and practices by the peri-urban dwellers in housing and habitat creating in the outer rings of cities, putting a stewardship framework in place and interrogating the technological arguments in peri-urban housing, sifting between poverty experiences and appropriateness of the technology.

This chapter has successfully summarised the thrust and findings of the research, assisted in the synthesis of the lessons learnt and the formulation of the conclusions. The study has been useful in showing the gaps that still prevail if sustainable development is to be a reality regarding peri-urbanisation and management of the processes linked to housing (see Figure 8.1) on the next page.

---

717 Intsiful, George. W.K, "Housing and urban development initiatives as means towards the alleviation of poverty," in *RICS Foundation Our Common Estate Paper Series*. URL: www.rics-foundation.org(2004)

718 Hogan P.H., "Human Capital and the Theory of Life-Cycle Investing." *American Association of Individual Investors (AAII) Journal*, pp 18-19.(2008) <URL: http://www.hoganfinancial.com/publications/2008-05%20AAII%20Human%20Capital. pdf, Accessed on 22 April 2008.>; High C, Pelling.M AND GUSZTÁV NEMES, Understanding informal institutions: Networks and communities in rural development. (2005) <URL: http://econ.core.hu/doc/konf/ High2005.pdf,> *Accessed on 22 April 2008*; Lurcott R.H , Regional Visioning Public Participation - Best Practices. Report prepared for Sustainable Pittsburgh.(2005) <URL: http://www.sustainablepitts burgh.org/pdf/Regional_Visioning_Jan_05.pdf>, *Accessed on 22 April 2008.*

Figure 8.1: Peri-urban stewardship-sustainability model: Processes, Concepts and Conditions

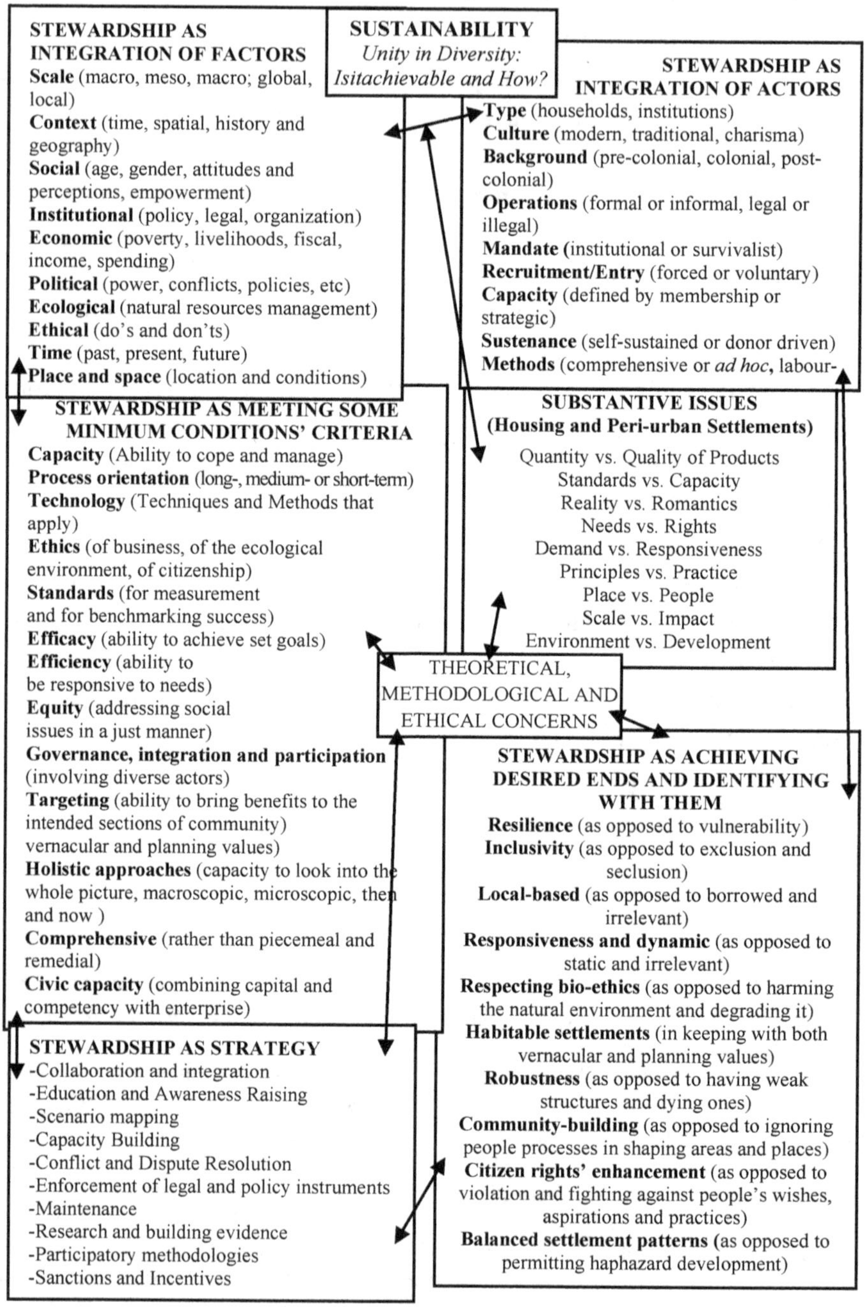

Achieving 'unified pluralism' is a multi-pronged and involving task that would require both resources and capacity to manage the processes, inputs and outputs. It has emerged strongly that both stewardship of a place and housing are in the hands of policy actors and implementers whose intentions, interests and offices often are ever-changing, sometimes enhancing or cancelling past progressive efforts. Both happen in a political, social and economic environment that is sometimes volatile and less stable. Peri-urban stewardship is thus a collaborative effort in which households, communities and pro-place and pro-communities work together to provide habitable space in which both the present and future generations benefit rationally and heeding that transitioning whether spatial or temporal should expand environmental good at the expense of the bad. Both the global and local actors and processes are crucial in achieving this as long as, to a great extent, collaboration, as a networking and connecting tool, is taken aboard.

POSTSCRIPT:
POLICY AND INSTITUTIONAL CHANGES, 2012-2019

Ideally, institutions are socially efficient and are created to provide correct information and guidance on human transactions. These Institutions and policies do not work independently, but are part of overarching systems that govern housing, the environment and the economy. But, as North highlighted , institutions are usually inefficient as human agents have an imperfect and partial knowledge of the political-economic system for which they are created.[719] This paper explores how changes in policy and institutions have affected housing, environment and Peri- urban areas in Zimbabwe from 2012 to 2019. The paper draws from experiences from dollarisation, 2013 harmonised elections, which were won, by ZANU-PF and the aftermath crafted policies, November 2017 coup and the new dispensation era. The United Nations Development Group propounded the theory of change in 2008. The theory explains how a given intervention, or set of interventions, is expected to lead to specific development change, drawing on a causal analysis based on available evidence. A theory of change also helps to identify the underlying assumptions and risks that will be vital to understand and revisit throughout the process to ensure the approach will contribute to the desired change. This chapter is organised as follows: the first part of the study is the theoretical framework. It provides the theoretical framework underpinning the study. The second part of the study is the literature review. It looks at the work in newspaper articles and other publications in relation to the study. The third part of the study sets out the research methodology. It specifies the research methods and techniques used. The

[719] North, D. C.,"Institutions, institutional change and economic performance," *Cambridge University Press*, Cambridge, (1990).

fourth part is concerned with the presentation and analysis of the research findings and trying to evaluate the conceptual issues in light of the research findings. The last part of the chapter is basically concerned with the summary of work, conclusions and recommendations.

This section focuses on the policy instruments, which deals with housing, environment in Zimbabwe from 2012 to 2019. The aim of this section is to explore how changes in policy and institutions have affected housing, environment and Peri- urban areas in Zimbabwe from 2012 to 2019. The literature provides an insight to the reader towards an understanding of the moral premise of policy and institutional changes in Zimbabwe. The review goes further, showing the present gaps in our knowledge about the capabilities of such practices being applied to a Zimbabwean scenario. The first part will provide a brief background of the policies, which were promulgated in Zimbabwe. The second part will explain the laws/statutes as well as national policies, which guides the environment and housing sector. Last but not least a commentary will be provided on the policy instruments in relation to their performance, capacity and priority.

European foreign policy consistency has been the subject of extensive academic debate and a source of concern between European and national policy-makers for almost four decades.[720] The process of moving toward a coherent research policy in Europe has not been a smooth undertaking. Research and innovation policy has become one of the central and most promising areas for regional growth in the European Union (EU).[721] Since 2000 an increasing effort has been put into achieving a more coordinated approach to research policy across the member-states. There are several conceptualizations on how policy learning as a gradual process can lead to institutional transformations. The most widely referenced is Bennett and Howlett's approach explaining policy learning in terms of

---

[720] Nuttall, S. (, "Coherence and Consistency. *In* Hill, C. and Smith, M. (eds.)" *International Relations and the European Union, Oxford*,, Oxford University Press, pp. 91–112. (2005)

[721] Europe 2020."Europe"s growth strategy." Retrieved from <http://ec.europa. eu/europe2020/index_en.htm>. (2015).

who learns what and to what end.[722] The authors differentiate between government learning, lesson-drawing, and social learning, demonstrating how each learning type can lead to organisational change, program change, or paradigm shifts in policies. Radaelli states that the relationship between learning and policy change can break down at several points and the evidence of clear policy change is often limited.[723] Radaelli emphasizes the importance of conflicts of interest, changing power relations, and legitimacy conditions in complex policy processes, making the outcomes unpredictable.

The study of institutional change has become a core research area, not only in organisation theory but also in cognate disciplines such as sociology, economics, and political science.[724] Contrary to earlier portrayals of the institutional perspective as a theory of conformity and stability underpinned by "durable socio-cultural structures," attention has turned to understand how institutional arrangements "are created, transformed, and extinguished". [725]The drive for institutional reform and the creation of 'effective' systems of governance in the global South are central to the current discourse of international development policy. Evans, Khan and Andrews have emphasised the failure of 'monocrop' policy approaches that have sought to impose models of governance, but with little reference to existing institutional environments and power relations.[726] Scholars including Mouzelis, Knudsen, Mahoney and Thelen and Brousseau and Raynaud highlight how institutions are reproduced and adapted through use, with rules being (re) formed incrementally as new practices become accepted and embedded to replace existing institutional

---

[722] Bennett, C. J;; Howlet, M. "The lessons of learning: Reconciling theories of policy learning and policy change";; Policy Sciences, 25(3), 275–294. (1992).

[723] Radaelli, C. M. ,,""Europeanization, policy learning, and new modes of governance," *Journal of Comparative Policy Analysis, 10(3), 239–254.* (2008).

[724] Mahoney, J;; Thelen, K,.., "Explaining institutional change: Ambiguity, agency, and power,," *Cambridge, UK*,,Cambridge University Press.(2009)

[725] Dacin, M. T.,et.al..."Institutional theory and institutional change: Introduction to the special research forum,". *Academy of Management Journal*, 45: 45-56. (2002.)

[726] Khan, m.h. "Governance during social transformations: challenges for Africa,," *New Political Economy* 17(5): 667–75. (2012)

arrangements.[727] Despite the vast study literature on policy and institutional changes there still remains an unfilled knowledge gap on the effectiveness of aggregating existing policy and institutional changes in housing, environment and peri-urban in Zimbabwe.

The history of policy instruments in Zimbabwe is directly related to colonialism. The Government of Zimbabwe pursued housing and environment goals and objectives embedded in international and national frameworks. National policy instruments, which guide housing and environment in Zimbabwe, include statutes/laws and policies. These include the Constitution of Zimbabwe and subsidiary legislation. The current Constitution of Zimbabwe in its Declaration of Rights enshrines socio-economic rights, the so-called second-generation rights, and among them is the right to housing. Constitution of Zimbabwe 2013 adopted housing as a basic human right (Section 28) and freedom from arbitrary eviction (Section 74). [728]

The GoZ guided by its Medium-Term Plan (MTP,) 2011-2015, aimed to transform the economy, reduce poverty, create jobs, maintain economic stability and ensure the positive trend for restoring the economy to its pre-crisis levels. The core priorities of the MTP include: (i) promote private sector, (ii) employment creation and poverty reduction (iii) human development and social security strategy, (iv) infrastructure rehabilitation and development; and (v) cross-cutting issues, such as gender, HIV/AIDS, environment. Under the infrastructure rehabilitation and development pillar, the MTP identified rehabilitation and development of water supply and sanitation as one of the key priority areas for promoting economic growth and reducing poverty.

The National Housing Policy 2012 and the National Housing Delivery Programme 2013 clearly provide a multi-stakeholder framework for human settlement planning, development and management. Lead agencies regarding the provision and management of basic services are local government institutions (Councils). The level of involvement and roles of other actors vary with individual housing projects. Principle 33:5

---

[727] Shand, W. ,"Exploring Institutional change „The contribution of co-production to shaping institutions„" *Working Paper December 2015*. (2015).
[728] Government of Zimbabwe ,Constitution of Zimbabwe 2013. (2013).

and 6 highlights enhanced flexibility and choice regarding spatial planning and environmental codes, alignment of planning, housing and economic policies, design and delivery model diversity, a wide range of permissible building materials and construction models, partnerships, upgrading and renewal processes within the framework of inclusive cities.[729] A follow-on National Housing Delivery Programme II (2014-2018) has been established with a target of 125 000 housing Units (Government of Zimbabwe 2013) but now set at more than 500 000 taking account of expected non-state input with state leverage especially in terms of land access.

The Zimbabwe National Environmental Policy and Strategy 2012 demonstrated the country's willingness to contribute to the preservation of the global climate for the good of present and future generations.[730] It was crafted in response to the need to develop an environmental policy discussed at a national conference that was held as a follow up to United Nations Conference on Environment and Development (UNCED), and response to Agenda 21. Before the NEPS, the sector was under the National Conservation Strategy (NCS) of 1987 which had the aim of promoting the sustainable use of national resources through integrating socio-economic and environmental issues in development programmes, focusing on land degradation and growth, water and energy. [731]The NCS only worked as a framework to guide aspects of environmental and natural resources management before the launch of NEPS in June 2009.

In 2009, Zimbabwe was forced to abandon its currency, which had gone up in an inferno of hyperinflation, and to adopt the US dollar as its principal means of exchange. The enforced dollarisation stabilised the economy and led to an initial 40% rebound in incomes, though these have since flat-lined. With no local currency, money supply became entirely dependent on inflows of US dollars, in effect depriving the authorities of control over monetary policy. In the aftermath of the 2013 harmonised election 'victory," ZANU-PF has had to confront the challenges of

---

[729] Government of Zimbabwe ,National Housing Policy, August 2012. (2012).

[730] Government of Zimbabwe „National climate change response strategy. (2012).

[731] Zimbabwe Economic Policy Analysis and Research Unit , "Strengthening the Zimbabwe National Policy Making Process." (2012)

presiding over a radically transformed political economy, which, while it contributed to electoral success, now poses huge problems for economic progress.[732] In a desperate measure to introduce liquidity, the government introduced bond notes in 2016. These were theoretically backed by hard currency, but have quickly deteriorated in value.

Apart from the economic collapse since the bond note was introduced, 2013 harmonised elections affected the terrain of policymaking and institutions in Zimbabwe. The post-2013 election period has witnessed several significant developments in Zimbabwean politics. While ZANU-PFhas presided over the implosion of the MDC-T, the complete marginalisation of the smaller MDC formation, the largely political irrelevance of the newly formed NCA political party, and the disorientation of the civic movement, the ruling party has also been marred by renewed internal factional struggles and widespread reports of corruption. Moreover, the radical rhetoric that marked ZANU-PF's election campaign has once again given way to a combination of such rhetoric with a new movement towards neo-liberal policies and re-engagement with the West. The "constraints of 'victory' " have become clear as ZANU-PF struggles to find a path through the daunting economic and political challenges that confront it in the new era. The post-2013 election was the uprising of Grace Mugabe bickering, which gave rise to tension between the Lacoste, and G 40. There was no trust in the ZANU-PF camp.

Former President Mugabe has, in terms of Section 100 (200) (c) and (d) of the Constitution, reassigned 10 ministers and made eight new appointments in a Cabinet reshuffle.[733] For the first time in years, the ruling ZANU-PF party and Government portfolios, which used to be under one hand, saw a development that split the portfolios. The affected ministries included Media, Information and Broadcasting Services. The Ministry of Environment was split from the Ministry of Environment, Water and Climate to Ministry of Tourism and Hospitality Industry. The

---

[732] Solidarity Peace Trust, "The End of a Road,, "The 2013 Elections in Zimbabwe." Johannesburg, October 2013."

[733] The ,HeraldUpdated, "Cabinet reshuffled 10 ministers reassigned new portfolios, Eight new appointments, 3 dropped" *Harare*,, Zimpapers.(2017).

former Ministry of Local Government, Public Works and National Housing was shuffled to Ministry of Local Government, Rural Development and National Housing.[734] As a result, the shuffling of the cabinet affected the policy environment, the institutions and decision-making. For example, the Ministry of Local Government, Rural Development and National Housing saw an increase in rural local authorities in developing urban like settlements in peri-urban farms. This saw the increase in land barons' activities in rural local authorities.

Indeed, parastatals as UDCORP have longed been used as part of ZANU-PF's patronage network in the public sector. ZANU-PF unveiled 5 000 residential stands to youths in Norton as part of Government's effort to empower young people. [735]The youths had already been given the residential stand numbers that were officially handed over to them by ZANU-PF. Various policies were introduced which included the following the Zimbabwe Agenda for Sustainable Socio-Economic Transformation (ZIMASSET) recognizes water as a pillar for development. ZIMASSET also encourages the active participation of the private sector and donors in national projects.

The Zimbabwe Agenda for Sustainable Socio-Economic Transformation (ZIMASSET) recognizes housing as a pillar for development.[736] It encourages the active participation of the private sector and donors in national projects. In 2014 the Government of Zimbabwe launched the National Housing Delivery Programme under Zim-Asset across the country's provinces. Under Zim-Asset, Harare province was expected to deliver 105 935 houses by 2018, the Midlands (56 760), Matabeleland North (28 772), Mashonaland West (23 819), Manicaland (21 830), Masvingo (20 269), Mashonaland Central (16 607), Bulawayo (15 100), Matabeleland South (12 500) and 11 776 in Mashonaland East. In a way to try and implement the

---

[734] The HeraldUpdated "Cabinet reshuffled .10 ministers reassigned new portfolios ,, Eight new appointments, 3 dropped,, *Harare,,* Zimpapers(2017).

[735] The Herald "Zanu-PF hands over 5 000 Norton stands" *Harare,,* Zimpapers. (2016).

[736] Government of Zimbabwe "Zimbabwe Agenda for Sustainable Socio-Economic Transformation (ZIM-ASSET),," *Towards and Empowered Society and a Growing Economy,,October 2013 – December 2018.* Zimbabwe (2013).

national housing strategy the then Minister of Local Government Chombo, handed over 45,58 hectares of land to the Infrastructure Development Bank of Zimbabwe (IDBZ) in Marimba suburb to signify the official roll-out of the housing programme in Harare. The Marimba-IDBZ Housing Project has provision for mixed housing development as the layout plan provides for four-storey walk-up flats and medium to high-density housing. The project has 761 housing units, of which 429 are high density, 268 medium density and four flat sites of 16 units each. [737]

In 2016 the Infrastructure Development Bank of Zimbabwe (IDBZ) came up with a draft housing policy detailing guiding sector interventions aimed at easing the housing shortage. IDBZ policy strategy sought to support Government's 2012 National Housing Development Programme target of providing 1,2 million serviced stands, by facilitating the development of at least 5 000 serviced stands annually between 2015 and 2018.[738]The draft policy outlined plans to acquire land for housing development and funding mechanisms for the delivery of affordable units.[739] However, the delivery of housing has been constrained by a number of factors. Structural constraints at the macro and sector levels slowed land delivery, dried up housing finance, made the expansion of trunk services nearly impossible and drained capacity in key institutions. These combined to stall progress in supplying new (housing) units and maintaining existing ones. Investment levels by the state and non-state sectors have been low.

The National Water Policy (NWP) was launched on March 22, 2013 with the overall goal to achieve sustainable utilisation of water resources that in turn will improve: i) Equity in access to freshwater by all Zimbabweans; ii) the efficient use of water among competing users; Provision of affordable and sustainable water and sanitation and hygiene (WASH) services; Environmental protection; v) protection of water sources, including safety of the country's dams and groundwater,

---

[737] The Herald . "Government launches housing scheme,," *Harare,,* Zimpapers. (2014).
[738] The Herald . "IDBZ unveils draft-housing policy,," *Harare,,* Zimpapers. (2016).
[739] The Herald , "IDBZ unveils draft-housing policy,," *Harare,,* Zimpapers. (2016).

Consumer and institutional viability in the sector.[740]This policy underscores that 'given that communities will be responsible for recurrent costs of their sanitation facilities service standard will be reviewed to permit a wide choice among different technologies so as to match the economic capacity of users. Service standards will enable poor communities to improve their levels of servicesas their economic circumstances improve." As part of the operationalization of the NationalWater Policy, there was also a process to develop the National Sanitation and Hygiene strategy to guide all WASH sector makers, managers, practitioners and financiers in achieving the shared vision of sustainable access to safe water, sanitation an hygiene and eliminating open defecation (OD) in Zimbabwe.[741]

The National Climate Policy of November 2017 seeks to create a pathway towards a climate resilient and low carbon development economy in which the people have enough adaptive capacity and continue to develop in harmony with the environment. Upon realisation of the challenges posed by climate, the GoZ embarked on the development of policy and strategic documents to address the unfolding challenges.[742]The objective of the policy was to guide climate change management in the country, enhance national adaptation capacity, scale up mitigation, facilitate domestication of climate-related policies and ensure compliance to the global mechanisms.[743]It provided a framework that calls for multi-stakeholder collaboration, governance systems and a means to integrate and mainstream climate change into different socio-economic sectors.

The tourism sector has been operating without a clear tourism policy. However, given the increasing importance of the tourism sector to economic growth, the need for a comprehensive policy could not be over-emphasised. The Ministry of Tourism and Hospitality Industry came up with a National Tourism Policy to guide the operations of the tourism sector in the country.[744] In line with benchmarking and standardising

[740] Government of Zimbabwe "National water policy, August 2012."(2012).

[741] Government of Zimbabwe "Constitution of Zimbabwe 2013." (2013).

[742] Government of Zimbabwe "National climate policy, November 2017." (2017).

[743] Zimbabwe Climate change Policy, April 2016

[744] Zimbabwe Economic Policy Analysis and Research Unit, *Strengthening the Zimbabwe National Policy Making Process*. (2012)

activities in the tourism industry, the Ministry of Tourism and Hospitality Industry (MoTHI) submitted formal requests for support in aligning the Tourism Act [*Chapter 14:20*] with the Constitution.[745]The project provided technical research support in the review of the Tourism Act [*Chapter 14:20*] for purposes of identifying legislative gaps that are inconsistent with the Constitution and International Conventions and Treaties relating to tourism that the Government of Zimbabwe is a party to.

In 2017 November, Mugabe was dethroned by a coup and Mnangagwa came with his policies, which also affected policy and institutions in Zimbabwe. ZANU-PF promised to empower youths, women, the disabled and the vulnerable through the allocation of farms and residential stands as part of its efforts to ensure indigenous people participate in economic development.[746] Under the indigenisation and economic empowerment policy, the party pledged to "ensuring economic participation by the indigenous people by establishing special economic zones for the local, indigenous investors, prioritise farm land allocation to youth, women, the disabled and vulnerable, prioritise allocation of stands and houses to youth, women, the disabled and vulnerable and avail loans and equipment to SMEs, artisanal miners, farmers and offer skills development and training.[747]

The Government of Zimbabwe through the Ministry of Finance and Economic Development presented to the Parliament of Zimbabwe a 2018 national budget on the 7th of December 2017. Policy measures and interventions of the budget seek to ensure the realisation of the overall objectives of Government economic blueprint, the Zimbabwe Agenda for Sustainable Socio-Economic Transformation (ZIM-ASSET) programs and projects covering the period 2013-2018. The percentage of the national budget allocation on the water was viewed as an expression of the level of commitment to the realisation of the human right to water

---

745 Ministry of Tourism and Hospitality Industry Stakeholder Consultation Report on Alignment of the Tourism Act [*CHAPTER 14:20*] with the Constitution (Southern Region) 18-19 November 2015(2015)

746 The Herald "Farms and stands for women, Youths": ZANU-PF,,*Harare*,, Zimpapers. (2018).

747 2018 ZANU-PF Election Manifesto.

enshrined in Section 77(a) of Constitution Amendment 20, which has been subjected to the limits of resources available.[748]

The trend of events provides a means of exploring Zimbabwe's dramatic upheavals in the light of broader debates, as a result, the pronounced policies. Over the years it is noted that different policies have given birth the following: increased urban expansion and peri urbanisation, increased fragmentation of policy departments and development agencies, violation of planning regulations which led to, corruption, Leapfrog and uncoordinated development, duplicity of institutions and confusion, urban to peri-urban migration and poor service delivery.

Politicshas extreme andfar-reaching implications to coherent urban planning and development of cities. Planners became enmeshed between adhering to planning principles and the government's radical objectives of allocating land for housing. The wilful disregard of planning is evidenced by the lack of planning, infrastructure and basic services in most peri-urban areas, which developed from 2009 to date. The Presidential proclamation (Statutory instrument SI 119/2012 declared the incorporation of Caledonia into Harare Municipality whilst the area falls as part of rural Goromonzi District.[749] Informal processes have provided plots and housing to 23,000-30,000 plots thousands of residents while simultaneously creating an infrastructure dilemma and entrenching patronage systems. After the proclamation by the former President Robert G.Mugabe, the search for residential space in and around Harare has turned into a craze of some sort, with every family striving to get a place they can refer to like theirs. Those who failed to get residential stands in Harare opted for surrounding communal areas like Seke, Domboshava and Goromonzi. Attracting factors include proximity to Harare Central Business District, which allows daily commuting, cheap land and generous portions of space.[750] Urban expansion has

---

[748] Zimbabwe Agenda for Sustainable Socio-Economic Transformation (Zim Asset) *"Towards an Empowered Society and a Growing Economy"* October *2013- December 2018*

[749] Statutory Instrument SI 119/2012

[750] The Herald "Home seekers conned in land deals,," *Harare,,* Zimpapers.(2017).

been encroaching on sensitive wetlands and productive farmlands in the fringe and peri-urban areas. This type of activity led to patches of non-contiguous urban cells, resulting in urban growth characterised as leapfrog development.[751]

However, the rural local authorities' actions are contradictory: providing urban like residential developments, but at the same time failing to provide suitable infrastructure and services to the residents. Thishas strained centre-local relations between the big brother City of Harare and the surrounding rural district councils in terms of service delivery. Most of these rural district councils collect rates and development fees from the beneficiary despite the fact that they are incapacitated to provide infrastructure and services. For example, Zvimba Rural District Council allocated more than 150,000 hectares of land in Nyabira to two developers, Datco Group and Blackdawn Estates.[752] The developers entered into a partnership agreement with Zvimba RDC to develop 5,410 residential stands in Nyabira in two phases. Phase 1 involved developing 3,846 residential stands, with the remaining number of stands totalling 1 664 to be developed under phase two. Mazowe Rural District Council has also developed urban like structures in Mt Pleasant heights Phase 2, where they are depending on City of Harare for services as water.

It is noted from the study that fragmentation of policy departments and development agencies is on an increase. Urban spatial structure is a physical outcome of regulation, planning, and consistent policymaking in a country. It is difficult, if not impossible, to analyse them, particularly with respect to policy changes. The structural-functionalist paradigm considers society as a complex system comprising of interrelated and interdependent parts with each structure performing role function. However, the failure of one structure leads to the dysfunction of the entire system. Sound organisational structures and suitably qualified and well-resourced human resources are crucial for the government and quasi-

[751] Rosni, N.A.et. al,,""Controlling leapfrog sprawl with remote sensing and GIS application for sustainable urban planning,," *International Institute for Applied Systems Analysis and Academy of Sciences Malaysia.* (2018).

[752] The Herald , "Zvimba RDC in Land Scam," *Harare,,* Zimpapers. (2017).

government institutions to deliver high-quality services that meet the customers' needs and expectations.[753]

A plethora of institutions in most sector ministries have contributed to the emergence of more complex problems. Three key elements have been identified; roles are not clear, functions are overlapping, and responsibilities not fully discharged. [754]The inadequacies of the policyare made more severe by the activities of the numerous institutions that conflict, overlap and confuse.[755] There are many institutions that are expected to address the problem but because their roles, functions and responsibilities are conflicting and creating tension make it very difficult for the institutions to address the problem. For example, the creation of the new Ministry of Local Government, Rural Development and National Housing from theformer Ministry of Local Government, Public Works and National Housing brought with it duplicity of institutions and confusion in making and implementing projects. The Environment sector was plucked off from the Ministry of Environment, Water and Climate, which has now been left with Water Resources Development and Climate to the Ministry of Tourism, Environment and Hospitality Industry. This reshuffle provided with its complexity in terms of implementing sector policies in Zimbabwe.[756] These policy statements are often incoherent and serious questions remain about the government's commitment to delivering, as new rules also don't automatically translate into new behaviour.

Due to the lack of clear-cut roles and duties between institutions, this has necessitated the violation of standing rules of planning, corruption and urban development. For example, Housing

---

[753] Heinrich, C.J. „""Outcomes based performance management in the public sector: Implications for government accountability and effectiveness" *Public Administration Review, 62, 712–726.* (2002).

[754]

[755] Wapwera, S., Egbu, C."Planning Authorities: A Review of Roles, Functions and Responsibilities in Jos Metropolis, Nigeria„" *School of the Built Environment, University of Salford, Greater Manchester,* United Kingdom (2013)

[756] The HeraldUpdated, "Cabinet reshuffled „10 ministers reassigned new portfolios, Eight new appointments, 3 dropped" *Harare*„Zimpapers. (2017).

cooperatives have been identified byZimbabwe's National Housing Policy of 2012 as an affordable and socialist strategy to housing delivery and to home ownership.[757]However, a sizeable number of these cooperatives have key distinguishing features such as the use of symbols that either belongs to or are associated with the ruling party (ZANU-PF). [758] Through aligned cooperatives and land barons, the party became a major player in deciding who had access to land for housing. This has exacerbated violation of town planning procedures in land acquisition, allocation and development. It has become difficult for local authorities to deal with land for housing. Housing cooperatives acquire housing stands from corrupt city council officials at very low prices and later sold at inflated prices. [759] The miserable condition of the emerging communities is attributed to poor planning and corruption by officials in the Housing and Community Services Department, as well as among councillors and officials in the urban planning and environmental management committees, where reports abound that corrupt housing cooperative leaders have been allocated land in some reserved open spaces where clinics, schools and shops were meant to be put.[760]

It is alleged that corruption from the rural district councils becameprevalent from the local authority officials.[761] For example, Zvimba Rural District Council (ZRDC) chief executive officer was accused of benefiting from illicit land deals that prejudiced the council of thousands of dollars. Zvimba Rural District Council was embroiled in a land scam after it allegedly allocated more than 150 000 hectares of land in Nyabira to two developers Blackdawn Estates and Nyashanu Butchery and Datco Group.

---

[757] Zimbabwe National Housing Policy 2012

[758] Mutondoro, F.S."Housing Cooperatives, Political Symbols, and Corruption in Urban Land Governance, The Case of Zimbabwe." Available online: <http://kubatana.net/2018/07/06/housing-cooperatives-political-symbols-corruption-urban-land-governance-case-zimbabwe/.>(2018).

[759] Relief web Zimbabwe "s Urban Housing crisis(2013).

[760] Relief web Zimbabwe "s Urban Housing crisis(2013).

[761] The Herald "Zvimba Rural District Council CEO in the dock." *Harare*,, Zimpapers(2018).

Home-seekers were also conned in land deals in Domboshava. In Zimbabwe, it is illegal to sell communal land between private individuals without the approval of a minister.[762] Chapter 3 (iv) of the Communal Lands Act states, "Communal Land shall be vested in the President, who shall permit it to be occupied and used in accordance with this Act."[763] This means that there is no total ownership of communal land, the President is the steward and people can use it but have no legal standing to sell it. However, very few people are informed on this technicality and are being sucked into illegal land sales, losing their hard earned money in the process.

Various issues emerged from the study. The policy network in Zimbabwe has got an uphill terrain where the level of integration amongst stakeholdershas resulted in restrained relationships. It is unfortunate that the understanding and abilities ofpolicy makers remain insufficient. The continuing hostile relationship involving the government and other stakeholders has led to the development of such a state of affairs where there is an absence of consistent information required for the formulation of workable policies. Since policies in Zimbabwe were politically inclined they fail to take into consideration alteration related to proposals from other stakeholders. It is, however ill-fated, that in Zimbabwe the ineffectiveness and individual interest of the political leaders have led to the process of public policy being dominated by one individual. The political leadership remains uncommitted while the imposed ministers on different ministerial positions do not have a vision and most of them do not have the capacity.

Sectoral policies are not complementary in Zimbabwe. In order to ensure that the overall policy environment achieves its intended objectives, there is a need for sectoral policies that are complementary. Policies that share a common objective are key to ensure that the national policy framework generates the desired economic efficiency and welfare gains. [764]Lack of such complementary policies limits the effectiveness of

---

762 The Communal Lands Act

763 The Herald ,,""Home seekers conned in land deals,," *Harare,,* Zimpapers(2017).

764 Zimbabwe Economic Policy Analysis and Research Unit,Strengthening the Zimbabwe National Policy Making Process. (2012)

the enacted policies. There is a challenge related to the way ministries are related to each other.The cabinet is the authority unto itself, and ministers are accountable to it, in addition to being the cabinet members. Policies that are made by fellow cabinet colleagues are made to affect other ministers. This has the challenge that there is a difficulty in supervising other ministers as they all are at the same level. It would have been ideal that the overarching policy organ is above the ministerial level.

The other issue, which emerged from the study, was that most policies, which were made from 2009 to 2018, were not evidence-based. The Policymaking process should be continuous, requiring visualisation to the number of old and new problems such thethatthe best outcomes for the best solution could be attained. Research generally influences policy where policymakers consider the issue to be important thus stimulating a strong desire for research findings or where there is strong advocacy from civil society organisation including the media and business associations on the importance of the research findings.

However, it was a different act from the government of Zimbabwe. These detachments from research do not only become a reason for the failure of a policy, but it also establishes dissonance among other aspects of a similar policy. It is generally accepted that a policy would not meaningfully achieve its intended goals unless it is evidence-based.[765] An evidence-based policy would rely heavily on research, which would see the most viable strategy being adopted. While in other jurisdictions academia and research institutions play a key role in influencing the research agenda, this has not been the case in Zimbabwe. Policy research has tended to be reactive and of an evaluative nature. There has been limited demand from policymakers of research results to inform decision-making.

It has been observed that policy implementation is one of the major problems confronting Zimbabwe. Most of the policies that were made from 2009 to 2018 did not achieve the desired result on the target beneficiaries. This was as a result of the missing basic factors, which are

[765] Court, J"What Political and Institutional Context Issues Matter for Bridging Research and Policy? A Literature Review and Discussion of Data Collection Approaches," *Unpublished Background Paper. (*2005)

very critical to the implementation of public policy.[766] The critical factors, which were missing, include communication, resources, dispositions or attitudes, and bureaucratic structure. The four factors operate simultaneously and they interact with each other to aid or hinder policy implementation. For example, inadequate information can lead to a misunderstanding on the part of the implementers who may be confused as to what exactly is required of them. In effect, implementation instructions that are distorted in transmission, that are vague, or that are inconsistent may cause serious obstacles to policy implementation. Conversely, directives that are too precise may hinder implementation by stifling creativity and adaptability. Such precise directives do not leave room for implementers to exercise discretion and flexibility where and when the need arises.

The study has identified that there are a number of obstacles that need to be addressed to ensure that the policy-making process is improved into one that is evidence-based and inclusive. Firstly, an analysis of some of the existing policies shows that the policies do not have the basic features of a good policy. The policies have some limitations as far as the following are concerned; inclusive and evidence-based. It is noted that there was underutilisation of research and existing knowledge to inform the policy formulation process for some of the policies discussed in the paper. To avoid reinventing the wheel, there is a need to learn from our past experience and the viable policies from other countries. The literature is awash with information, which provides policymakers an the opportunity to learn about what has worked and not worked in other countries and in what context. This will avoid experiments in the policy-making process. The study also highlighted the need for inclusivity throughout the policy-making process. The policies that were reviewed showed varying degrees of stakeholder consultation to ensure ownership of policies and setting the stage for effective implementation of the policies.

Zimbabwe needs to move away from the current incrementalist approach of compromise to policymaking. One option would be to opt for

[766] Zimbabwe Economic Policy Analysis and Research Unit , "Strengthening the Zimbabwe National Policy Making Process." (2012)

the knowledge utilisation approach. The country hosts several research organisations that have over the years undertook a lot of policy research that can easily feed into the policy process for the country. This is even more evident during policy debate, as most of the problems that are affecting the country have solutions that have been suggested to each of them. The policymakers value the outputs of local research institutions and think tanks and use them more to inform the policy making process. This also calls for deliberate efforts to rebuilt capacity of policy research institutions within and outside government. There is need thus for policy making to leverage on the knowledge base resident in the countries and experiences from other countries with similar policy challenges and contexts.

REFERENCES

AARLAND,K ; NORDVIK.V, 'Low-income households and the dynamics of housing demand," *Paper presented to the ENHR Conference on Sustainable Urban Areas, 25-28 June 2007, Rotterdam.* URL: www.enhr2007rotterdam.nl, *Accessed on 2 August 2007*.(2007)

AASCU, 'Stepping Forward As Stewards of Place - A Guide for Leading Public Engagement at State Colleges and Universities," *American Association of State Colleges and Universities*, New York. (2002)

ABRAMS C., 'Man's Struggle for Shelter. Urbanising World,' *the MIT Press, Cambridge* Massachusetts. (1964).

ABRAMS. C, 'Housing in the Year 2000," Chapter 8 in Ewald William R Jr. ed. Environment and Policy: 'The Next Fifty Year's, *Indiana University Press*: Bloomington and Lo(1968);

AECT (Association for Educational Communications and Technology) „"'What Is Descriptive Research? The Handbook of Research for Educational Communications and Technology,' *Association for Educational Communications and Technology*, Bloomington. (2001).

AKROFI. E.O ; WHITTAL.J, 'Land for Peri-urban Infrastructure in Customary Areas: A case study of Kumasi, Ghana. Land for Peri-urban Infrastructure in Customary Areas," *A Case Study of Kumasi, Ghana, FIG Working Week 2011: Bridging the Gap between Cultures, Marrakech, Morocco, 18-22 May 2011* (2011).

ALBEMARLE COUNTY,'Embracing Our Value of Stewardship,' <URL: http: //www.albemarle.org/upload/images/forms_center/departments/budget/ forms/FY09_Budget_Overview.pdf> *Accessed on 27 August 2010.* Pg.4(2008)Pg.4(2008).

ALBERTI.M, 'Advances in Urban Ecology, *Integrating Humans and Ecological Processes in Urban Ecosystems," Springer,* New York., (2009)

AL-DOWSARI. A.,'GIS and Qatar's Physical Development Plan (PDP) Blueprint for the Future." <URL: http://www.gisqatar.org.qa/conf97/ links/g3.html>, *Accessed on 22 April 2008.* (1997).

ALEXANDER C;COX. M;; HALIM A;HAZZARD.E.D;, ILHAN KURAL;SCHUKERT. M,'The grass roots housing process,' <URL: http://www.livingneighborhoods.org/library/grassroots.htm>, *Accessed on 22 April 2008*. (1973).

ALEXANDER.. C,'The Timeless Way of Building," *New York,* Oxford University Press. (1979).

ALEXANDER.;. C;ISHIKAWA. S ;MURRAY. ,S,'A Pattern Language," *New York*, Oxford University Press. (1977).

AL-HUSAINI ABDULRAHMAN H, 'Using GIS in Real Estate Transactions.' <URL: http://www.gisqatar.org.qa/conf97/links/g2.html>, *Accessed on 22 April 2008.* (1997).

ALLEN. A, 'Environmental planning and management of the peri-urban interface: perspectives on an emerging field." *Environment & Urbanisation* 15(1)(2003).

ALSAYED. A. H, 'Housing Management Systems," *Theoretical Approach. Paper presented to the ENHR Conference on Sustainable Urban Areas, 25-28 June 2007*, Rotterdam. <URL: www.enhr2007rotterdam.nl. Accessed on 2 August 2007>.(2007)

AMIRAHMADL H'Toward a Theory of Community Capital, Paper presented at the Sixth Sharjah Urban Planning Symposium," *Sharjah, The United Arab Emirates.* <URL: http://www.caspianassociates.com/towards.doc>, *Accessed on 22 April 2008*. (2003).

ANDERSEN H. T.;.;S.ENGELSTOFT, 'The End of Urbanisation? Transformation of the Urban Concept," *Dela 21*: pp53-67. (2004)

ANSELL. N; VAN BLERK. L, "Where we stayed was very bad…"-migrant children's perspectives on life in informal rented accommodation in two southern African cities. *Environment and Planning 37*: pp423-440. (2004).

ANSTEIN.S.R., 'A Ladder of Citizen Participation." *Journal of American Institute of Planners 35(4)*: pp216-224.(1969).

APTE P.M.'Planning and Development of Peri Urban Areas: Financing and Management of Infrastructure." *Paper submitted at the 56th National Town & Country Planners Congress of ITPI at Kolkata, India, December 2007* <URL: http://www.wikio.com/article/78882466>, *Accessed on 22 April 2008.* (2008),

ARIMAH B. C.'Slums as Expressions of Social Exclusion," *Explaining the Prevalence of Slums in African Countries.* <URL: http://www. oecd. org/dev/pgd/46837274.pdf>, *Accessed on 01 May 2013.* (2010).

ARISTIZABAL. N; GOMEZ.A.O, 'Chapter 6: Are services more important than titles in Bogotá?' In PAYNE GEOFFREY (ed.) (2002)., *Land, Rights and Innovation – Improving tenure security for the urban poor*, ITDG Publishing: London. (2002).

ARMITAGE.L, 'Customary Land Tenure in Papua New Guinea," *Status and Prospects* .<URL : http: // dlc.dlib.indiana.edu / archive / 00001043/00/ armitage.pdf,> *Accessed on 22 April 2008.*(2000).

ARNOTT.R, 'Housing Policy in Developing Countries," *The Importance of the Informal Economy (Working Paper No. 13)*, <URL: http://www.growth commission.org/storage/cgdev/documents/gc-wp-013_web.pdf>, *Accessed on 2 November 2008(*2008).

ARS, 'Regional Stewardship: A commitment to Place,' *Monograph Series. ARS*, California. (2000:4)

ARTHURS. J; BUSENITZ. L. W, 'The Boundaries and Limitations of Agency Theory and Stewardship Theory in the Venture Capitalist/Entrepreneur Relationship," *Entrepreneurship Theory and Practice (Winter)*: pp 145-162. (2003).

ARTHURSON.K, 'Social mix and social interaction: do residents living in different housing tenures mix?," *Paper presented to the ENHR Conference on Sustainable Urban Areas, 25-28 June 2007, Rotterdam.*< URL: www.enhr2007rotterdam.nl>, *Accessed on 13 July 2008*(2007).

ASIAMA.S, 'Land for housing the Urban Poor in Africa' ,Some Policy Options, in Amis P and P Lloyd, *Housing Africa's Urban Poor, Manchester University Press*, UK. (1990).

AUC/ADB/ECA (AFRICAN UNION COMMISSION, AFRICAN DEVELOPMENT BANK AND ECONOMIC COMMISSION FOR AFRICA 'Consultative Workshop 27 to 29 March 2006 on Land Policy In Africa," *A Framework of Action to Secure Land Rights, Enhance Productivity and Secure Livelihoods Issues Paper,* African Union, Addis Ababa(.(2006).,

AURET. D.,'A Decade of Development, Zimbabwe 1980-*1990," Mambo Press*, Gweru. (1990).

AURET.D, 'Urban Housing: A National Crisis?," *Mambo Press: Gweru.* (1995), (1995), AWOTONA. A, 'A review of housing research in West Africa,' *Third World Planning Review 18(1)*: pp45-58. (1996)(1996)

BALAMIR. I,'Chapter 9: Legality and legitimacy of tenure in Turkey." Payne Geoffrey (ed.), 2002, Land, Rights and Innovation – Improving tenure security for the urban poor, *ITDG Publishing*, London. (2002).,

BALCHIN. P.N ; N KIEVE, 'Urban land economics," *Macmillan*, London. (1985).,

BALDWIN E; SHIRLEY T,'Universal Design and Housing in Response to the Human Life Cycle," *PowerPoint Presentation for the Focus on the Future Forum held on April 5 2007.* <URL: http://www.agingking county.org/docs/FutureForum5April07ShirleyTomita.pdf>, *Accessed on 22 April 2008*. (2007).

BALL.M, 'Improving Housing Markets, RICS Leading Edge Series,"<URL: www.rics.org/NR/rdonlyres/6D4B2A3B-A598-4C4B-9868-7B0A18 C 7090A/www.rics.org/NR/rdonlyres/6D4B2A3B-A598-4C4B-9868-7B0 A18C7090A/>, *Accessed on 22 April 2008.(*2003).

BAN. H.; ;OLA AHLQVIST, 'Visualizing the Uncertainty of Urban Ontology Terms," *PowerPoint presentation made at the COST C21: The 1st Towntology Workshop, Geneva*: Swiss Nov. 6-7, 2006. (2006)

BANANA. C., 'Turmoil and Tenacity: Zimbabwe 1890-1990," *The College Press*, Harare. (1989).

BANANA. C. S,'Presidential Speech, Senate Debates, First Session, First Parliament, 1980," *Vol 1, Parliament of Zimbabwe*, Salisbury. (14 May, 1980)

BAROSS P'Land Supply for Low-income Housing: Issues and Approaches," *Regional Development Dialogue 1107(4):* pp24-37(1987).

BARREIRO. P. L.;.;ALBANDOZ. J. P,'Population and sample - Sampling techniques," *Management Mathematics for European Schools. University of Seville*, Seville (Spain).(2001)

BARRY. M;HEINZ. R., 'Data Collection Techniques for Informal Settlement Upgrades in Cape Town, South Africa," *URISA Journal 17(1):* pp43-52(.(2005).,

BAUM, W. C. 'The Project Cycle," *The World Bank,* Washington DC. (1982).

BAUMANN T.'Bridging the Finance Gap in Housing and Infrastructure - Zimbabwe: Financing Options for Community-Based Shelter Initiatives," *Report prepared for Homeless International*(undated).,

Beatley. T, 'Biophilic Cities: Integrating Nature into Urban Design and Planning," *Island Press*, Washington. (2011). H, (2011)BECKER. H,'Photography and Sociology," *Studies in the Anthropology of Visual Communication 1*: pp3-26. (1974).

BÉLANGER. C.,.,"'Analysing an Historical Document,' *L'Encyclopédie de l'histoire du Québec / The Quebec History Encyclopedia.* <URL: http://faculty.marianopolis.edu/c.belanger/quebechistory/Howtoanalyse anhistoricaldocument.html>, *Accessed on 22 April 2008.* (2006).,

BELK. C.L.,'Cohousing Communities: A Sustainable Approach to Housing Development, Unpublished Dissertation,' <URL: http://extension. ucdavis.edu/unit/green_building_and_sustainability/pdf/resources/co_h ousing.pdf>, *Accessed on 22 April 2008.* (2006).

BELLO. H.M;;MALEFANE;S. BABATOPE-OBASA., 'An estimation of water demand function in some peri-urban settlements of Lesotho' *Paper presented at the 11th Annual African Econometrics Society Conference, 5-7th July 2006 UNIDEP Dakar*, Senegal. (2006).

BEN-AMI. D ; RAMP.D, 'Modelling the effect of roads and other disturbances on wildlife populations in the peri-urban environment to facilitate long-term viability," Road Ecology Center eScholarship Repository, John Muir Institute of the Environment, *University of California*, Davis. <URL: http: // repositories.cdlib.org / jmie/roadeco/Ben-Ami2005ahttp: //repositories.cdlib.org/jmie/roadeco/Ben-Ami2005a> *Accessed on 22 April 2008.* (2005)

BENNETT, C. J.; HOWLET, M. 'The lessons of learning: Reconciling theories of policy learning and policy change'; Policy Sciences, 25(3), 275–294. (1992).

BENJAMIN. S, 'Presenting Two in Contesting Spatialities: Do Everyday Institutional contestations erode the neo-liberal Urban Reforms Agenda?' <URL: http://igs.cla.umn.edu/pdf/BenjaminPaper.pdf>, *Accessed on 21 November 2008.*(2008).

BERESFORD W. M. P'The Role of Building Societies in Mobilising Finance for Low Income Housing': *A paper prepared for the Zimbabwe Institute of*

Regional & Urban Planners' Annual School (4-6 July, 1990.). Harare. (1990).

BERNER. E, 'Learning from Informal Markets: Innovative Approaches to Land and Housing Provision." *Development in Practice, 11(2-3):* pp 292-307. (2001).

BERNSTEIN. J. D.,'Land-use Considerations in Urban Environmental Management (Urban Management Programme)," *World Bank*,Washington DC. (1994).

BESC, 'Partnerships for better living: An introductory guide to Habitable Environments Partnerships," *Built Environment Support Group*, Pietermaritzburg. (2003)(2003).

BHP, 'BHP Billiton Sustainability Report." <URL:http://www.bhpbilliton.com/home/investors/reports/Documents/2006SummarySustainabilityReport.pdf. *Accessed on 7 November 2007.(*2006).

BLOCK. C, 'Informal Housing Sector Strategies," *A paper prepared for the Zimbabwe Institute of Regional & Urban Planners' Annual School (4-6 July, 1990)*, Harare. (1990).

BLOMMAERT. J, 'Chronicles of complexity - Ethnography, superdiversity, and linguistic landscapes,' *Tilburg Papers in Culture Studies, Paper 29*, Tilburg University and Ghent University.(2012:7)

BOCH. F;PIOLAT. A,'Note Taking and Learning: A Summary of Research,' *The WAC Journal Vol. 16*: pp 101-113. (2005).

BONGWA. A.,'Land Administration: Hub of Corruption," *Presentation at the Land Management & Informal Settlement Regularisation Course, August 06, 2009 Session IV, IHS, The Netherlands*, Rotterdam. (2009).

BOUDREAUX. K.,'The urbanisation and informality in Africa's housing markets,' *IEA Economic Affairs June 2008:* pp17-24. (2008).,

BOURNE. L. S.,'The Geography of Housing," *V H Winston and Sons Ltd* London.

BOURNE LS, et. al, al,'Contested Ground: The Dynamics of Peri-Urban Growth in the Toronto Region," *Canadian Journal of Regional SciencelRevue canadienne des sciences régionales, XXV 1: 2&3 (Surnmer-Autumn Été-autonme 2003)*: pp251-270.

BRACKEN. I.'Urban Planning Methods: Research and Policy Analysis," *Methuen*, London. (1981).

BRAND. R; GAFFIKIN. F,'Collaborative Planning in an Uncollaborative World," *Planning Theory 6(3):* pp 282-313(.(2007).

BRANOM-ZWICK. J, 'Food vs. Shelter: The Planning DebateJ, 'Food vs. Shelter: The Planning Debate," *Sightline Daily.*<URL:http://daily.sightline.org/daily_score/archive/2006/01/30/food_vs_shelter,> *Accessed on 22 April 2008.* (30 January 2006).

BRENNER.. M. E.,'Interviewing in Educational Research,." J. Green.G. Camilli, & P. Elmore (Eds.*)*, Complementary Methods for Research in Education (pp. 357-370), *American Educational Research Association /Erlbaum*, Washington DC. (2006).

BRIGGS.J ; MWAMFUPE. D, 'Peri-urban development in an era of Structural Adjustment in Afric," *The City of Dar es Salaam, Tanzania. Urban Studies 37(4),* (2000).

BRIGGS. J ;YEBOAH.I, 'Structural Adjustment and the Contemporary Sub-Saharan African City." *Area 33(1):* pp18-26. (2001).

BROOK. R.M;DÁVILA. J.D eds., 'The peri-urban interface: a tale of two cities, School of Agricultural and Forest Sciences," *University of Wales and Development Planning Unit, University College,* London. (2000).

BROOKINGS INSTITUTION, 'The Housing Crisis and Lessons for Monetary Policy," *The Brookings Institution,* Washington, D.C. (2008).

BROWN.A.C, 'Cities for the urban poor in Zimbabwe: urban space as a resource for sustainable development," Westerdoff David and Deborah Eade ed. Development and Cities (A Development in Practice Reader): Essays from Development Practice, *OXFAM GB/UNSRID*, Oxford: pp263-281 (2002)

.BROWN. A.,'Contested Space: Street Trading, public space and livelihoods in developing countries," *Intermediate Technology Publications Ltd,* Warwickshire. (2006).

BRYCESON. F. D; MBARA. T, 'Petrol pumps and Economic Slump: Rural-urban linkages in Zimbabwe's Globalisation Process, *Tijdschrift voor enonomische en sociale geographic. (Journal of Economic and Social Geography) 94(3)*: pp 335-349.(2003).

BRYDEN. J; HART.K, 'Land reform, planning and people: an issue of stewardship' < URL: http: // www.caledonia.org.uk / land/documents / Land%20Reform%20&%20Stewardship.pdf. *Accessed on 27 August 2010.* (2000).

BURGER J, VAN LOON P.P. AND S. BRONKHORST (2007)., Multi-stakeholder planning in an urban decision room. Paper presented to the ENHR Conference on Sustainable Urban Areas, 25-28 June 2007, Rotterdam. Available: www.enhr2007rotterdam.nl, Accessed on 2 August 2007.

BUSCK. A.G;;, SØREN PILGAARD KRISTENSEN, SØREN PRÆSTHOLM, ANETTE REENBERG & JØRGEN.P.,'Land system changes in the context of urbanisation: Examples from the peri-urban area of Greater Copenhagen," in *Danish Journal of Geography 106(2):* pp 21-34. (2006).

BUTCHER. C, 'The Potentials and Possible Roles of Housing Co-operatives in Meeting the Shelter Needs of Low Income Urban Households' *A paper prepared for the Zimbabwe Institute of Regional & Urban Planners' Annual School (4-6 July, 1990):*,Harare. (1990).

BUTCHER. C, 'Urban low-income housing: a case study of the Epworth squatter settlement upgrading programme, Chapter 6 in ZINYAMA L, D TEVERA AND S CUMMING (eds.) 1993' *Harare:* 'The Growth and Problems of the City," *University of Zimbabwe*: Harare. (1993).

BUTCHER. C, 'Low Income Housing in Zimbabwe," *A Case Study of the Epworth Squatter Upgrading Programme -RUP Occasional Paper No 6*, Department of Rural and Urban Planning, University of Zimbabwe: Harare.(1986).

BUTTERWORTH.J et al., 'Peri-Urban Water Conflicts - Supporting dialogue and negotiation," *Technical Paper Series 50*, IRC international Water and Sanitation Centre: Delft, the Netherlands. (2007).

BUXTON. M.;GOODMAN. R;TIEMAN. G.,'Change and Continuity on the urban fringe: an analysis of international trends in peri-urban development," *Presentation made at the World Planning Schools Congress Mexico City, July 2006.* <URL: www.periurban.org.au/ references/ConferMexicoCity2006RobinFinal.ppt>, *Accessed on 5 August, 2010.* (2006).

BYRNE. J; SIPE. N.,'Green and open space planning for urban consolidation – A review of the literature and best practice (Issues Paper 11)," *Urban Research Program, Griffith University: Brisbane.*< URL: www.griffith.edu.au/urp>, *5 August 2010.* (March 2010).

CADMAN. D., 'Property development, 3rd edition.," *Chapman and Hall Publishers*, London (1978).

CAGOH (COMMUNITY ACTION GROUP ON HOUSING)'Report on a Study on the Contribution of Urban Housing to National Economic Development in Zimbabwe," *CAGOH,* Harare. (2002).

CAMINOS. H;R. GEOTHERT 'Urbanisation Premier," *the MIT Press: Cambridge*, Massachusetts. (1978).,

CARE INTERNATIONAL,'Current donor approaches to urban development," <URL: http://www.careinternational.org.uk.> (1999).,

CARTER. S.,'Building Blocks for Strong Communities: Results of Key Informant Interviews," *A research report prepared for Human Resources and Social Development Canada, Imagine Canada and Canadian Policy Research Networks*, Toronto. (2006).

CASLEY. D. J;D. A. LURY'Data Collection in Developing Countries," *English Language Book Society/ Claredon Press*, Oxford. (1981).

CASTELLS. M.,'The Urban Question," *MIT Press: Cambridge*, Massachusetts. (1978).

CATANESE. A.J ;J. C. SYNDER (eds.)'Urban Planning (Second Edition)," *McGraw-Hill Inc,* New York(1988).

CAVAILHÈS. J et al., 'The peri-urban city, why to live between the suburbs and the countryside' *Regional Science and Urban Economics 34(6)*, pp681-703 (2004)

CGAP,'Helping to Improve Donor Effectiveness in Microfinance- Housing Microfinance," *Donor Brief no. 20* (August 2004). <URL: www.cgap.org>, *Accessed on 22 April 2008.* (2004).

CHAERUKA. J ; MUNZWA. K, 'Assessing Regulatory Framework Bottlenecks for Low-cost Housing in Zimbabwe, Final Draft Report," *UNHABITAT and the Government of Zimbabwe*, Harare.(2009)).

CHAKANZA. S.,'Understanding Advocacy. Appendix 4,

HPZ (HOUSING PEOPLE OF ZIMBABWE) (2001).," *Report on the National Stakeholder Validation Workshop held on 24-25 November 2001 at the Management Training Bureau*, Harare. (2001).

CHAKWIZIRA. J.,'Sustainable implementation of urban master plans in Zimbabwe," *Department of Rural & Urban Planning* ,University of Zimbabwe: Harare (Unpublished Master of Philosophy Thesis). (2001).

CHAMBERS R.,'Whose reality counts?: Putting the First Last," *Intermediate Technology Publications*, London. (1997).

CHAPMAN L. S., 'Closing 'thoughts," *The Art of Health Promotion, May/June 2005*: pp 13-14(2005).

CHARMES. E.,'Interactions with Neighbouring Others in French Peri-urban Areas: Barriers and Openness," *Working Paper presented at the Gated Communities Conference: Building Social Division or Safer Communities*, University of Glasgow, 18-19 September 2003(2003).

CHENGA. M. M.,'Provision of Housing in Zimbabwe," Chapter 4 in ZINYAMA L, D TEVERA AND S CUMMING (eds.) (1993)., *Harare:* The Growth and Problems of the City, *University of Zimbabwe*, Harare. (1993).

CHENGA. N, 'Murambatsvina II hovers over Epworth,' The Financial Gazette, <URL:http://www.financialgazette.co.zw/national-report/3011-murambatsvina-ii-hovers-over-epworth.html,> *Accessed on 5 August 2010.* (2010)http://www.financialgazette.co.zw/national-report/3011-murambatsvina-ii-hovers-over-epworth.html,> *Accessed on 5 August 2010.* (2010).

CHEW-GRAHAM CAROLYN A, CARL R MAYA AND MARK S PERRY (2001)., Qualitative research and the problem of judgment: lessons from interviewing fellow professionals. *Family Practice 19(3)*: pp 285-289.

CHIDEME M.,'City of Harare Boundaries Extended," Herald, *Zimpapers*, Harare(13 July 2010).

CHIDEME M.,'Harare water shock," The Herald, *Zimpapers*, Harare. (16 August 2010).

CHIDYAUSIKU. G. G, 'G,'Motion on: Government Policy on Local Government and Housing," *Senate Debates, Parliament of Zimbabwe*,Salisbury. (27 August 1980),

CHIGUDU. A.,'An Assessment of Overcrowdedness and its Effects on Public Health over the Past Decade (1999- 2009)' *A Case of Mbare Residential Area (Ward Three). Unpublished Dissertation, University of Zimbabwe*, Harare. (2009).

CHIKHWENDA.E.J.W, 'Sustainability of Shelter Provision in Malawi's Urban Centers: the Case of Blantyre City," *in Journal of Sustainable Development in Africa 4(1),* pp 25-35. (2002)

CHIKOWORE. E.,'Chapter 1: Harare, past present and future," ZINYAMA L, D TEVERA AND S CUMMING (eds.) (1993)., Harare: The Growth and Problems of the City, *University of Zimbabwe,* Harare. (1993).

CHIKWATI. E.,'Firm accused of stealing water," The Herald, *Zimpapers*:, Harare. (17 August 2010).,

CHIMHANDA.D, The city of Harare, , 'Contentious Development: Urban and Peri-urban Transformations and Livelihoods in Africa." *Report of a Peri-NET Workshop, East and Southern Africa held at Fairview Hotel,* Nairobi, Kenya, 7-9 October 2002.(2002).

CHIPUNGU. L, 'Institutional constraints to land delivery for low-income housing: a case study of Harare, Zimbabwe," in *RICS Foundation Our Common Estate Paper Series*. URL: www.rics-foundation.org, Accessed on 22 April 2008.(2005; 2011)URL: www.rics-foundation.org, Accessed on 22 April 2008.(2005; 2011).

CHIRISA. I., ''Increased Squalor in Urban and Peri-urban Zimbabwe since 2009' Assessing the Rhetoric, Practices and Contradictions of the Government of National Unity, *Southern Peace Review Journal* 2(1): pp118-135(2013c)

CHIRISA. I, 'Prospects for the asset-based community development approach in Epworth and Ruwa, Zimbabwe," A housing and environmental perspective. *African Journal of History and Culture 1(2):* pp028-035. (2009:30).

CHIRISA. I.,Politics in Environmental Stewardship in Zimbabwe,' Reflections on Ruwa and Epworth. *African Journal of History and Culture* 5(1): pp13 – 26, DOI: 10.5897/AJHC11. (2013b).

CHANZA. N ; CHIRISA. I, 'How Will Climate Change Transform African Local Governance?'Assessing the Role of Civic Engagement. *Journal of Public Administration and Policy Research* 1(2): pp 035-046.(2011)).

CHIRISA. I, 'Population Growth and Rapid Urbanisation in Africa: Implications for Sustainability.' *Journal of Sustainable Development in Africa 10(2),(*2008*)* pg.364-391

CHIRISA. I, 'Epworth in Zimbabwe; Inclusivity, Housing and the Stewardship Concept.' *The Built & Human Environment Review 6*: pp 18-29. (2013).

CHIRISA. I;MUNZWA. K.M, 'Collective Collateralisation, Group Democracy and the Urban Marginalised Communities in Zimbabwe," A Case of Tashinga Housing Co-operative in Harare, *Local Governance Development Journal 2(1)*: pp31-46.(2008).

CHIRISA. I, 'Peri-urban Dynamics and regional planning in Africa: Implications for building healthy cities," *Journal of Africa Studies and Development 2 (2)* (2010).

CHOMBO. I, 'Presentation on the Challenges Pertinent to the Provision of Off-Site Infrastructure by Local Authorities," Honourable Minister of Local Government, *Rural And Urban Development on 28 October 2009.*(2009).

CHOY. D.L et al, 'Change and Continuity in Peri-Urban Australia,": *Peri-Urban Futures and Sustainable Development,* <URL: http://periurban.org.au/references/monograph4.pdf.>, *Accessed on 29 April, 2013.* (2008:5).

CHRISTIE. I. et al., *Living spaces: A vision for the future of planning*, The RSPB: Bedfordshire.(2002)

CHROMY. J. R;SAVITRI ABEYASEKERA., 'Chapter 19, Statistical analysis of survey data,' *Household Surveys in Developing and Transition Countries: Design, Implementation and Analysis.* <>http://unstats.un.org/unsd/hhsurveys/finalpublication/ch19fin3.pdf, *Accessed on 22 April 2008.* (2005).

CIRMAN.A, 'Intergenerational transfers as a response to changes in the housing market' *Paper presented to the ENHR Conference on Sustainable Urban Areas, 25-28 June 2007, Rotterdam.*(2007) <URL: www.enhr2007rotterdam.nl,> (2 August 2007)

CIVIC FORUM ON HOUSING ZIMBABWE'Housing in Zimbabwe: Information for Communities and Home-seekers," *Civic Forum on Housing Zimbabwe*,Harare. (1997).

CIVIC FORUM ON HOUSING ZIMBABWE 'Housing Bulletin No. 4," *Civic Forum on Housing Zimbabwe*, Harare. (2001).

CLARK. J.,'Peri-Urban Agglomerations in Southeast Asia - Exurban Change Project White Paper," <URL: http://exurban.osu.edu/papers/periurban_se_aggl.pdf>, *Accessed on 22 April 2008.* (2006).

CLARKE.S; GINSBURG.N.,'The Political Economy of Housing." <URL: http://homepages.warwick.ac.uk/~syrbe/pubs/ClarkeGinsburg.pdf,> *Accessed on 31 March 2013.* (1975).

COHEN. A., 'Urban Unfinished Business,' *Journal of Public Health Policy 10(2)*, <URL: http://www.saniplan.org/UUBartic.htm> (1989).

CORMARCK. I, 'Towards Self-Reliance – Urban Social Development in Zimbabwe," *Mambo Press,* Gweru. (1983).

CORNFORTH.C.J, 'The goveramce of social enterprises: a paradox perspective," *Annals of Public and Cooperative Economics 75(1)*: 11-32. (2004).

CORTEMIGLIA. A., 'Involving informally housed communities in shaping local government policies aimed at poverty alleviation," *A South African perspective, A thesis for the Doctor of Literature and Philosophy in Development Studies*, University of South Africa. (2006).

COURT. J, 'What Political and Institutional Context Issues Matter for Bridging Research and Policy? A Literature Review and Discussion of Data Collection Approaches," *Unpublished Background Paper. (*2005)

COUSINS. B, "The Zimbabwe Crisis in its Wider Context: The Politics of Land, Democracy and Development in Southern Africa," Amanda Hammar, and Brian Raftopoulos, (Eds.) *Zimbabwe's Unfinished Business - Rethinking Land, State and Nation in the Context of Crisis, Weaver Press*, Harare (2003).

CRANE. J.L'Huts and houses in the tropics,' in *Unaslyva 3(3)*. <URL: http://www.fao.org/docrep/x5350e/x5350e04.htm>, *Accessed on 22 April 2008.* (undated).

CRESWELL J. W;A. TASHAKKORI, 'Developing Publishable Mixed Methods Manuscripts," *Journal of Mixed Methods Research 1(1)*: pp 107-111(2007).

CRESWELL JOHN W, WILLIAM E. HANSON, VICKI L. CLARK PLANO AND ALEJANDRO MORALES 'Qualitative Research Designs : Selection and Implementation," *The Counseling Psychologist 35*: pp 236-264. (2007).

CRESWELL, J.W 'Qualitative enquiry and research design: choosing among 5 approaches," *2nd ed. Sage publications*, California (2007a).

CRESWELL, J.W.'Research design: qualitative, quantitative and mixed methods approaches," *3rd ed. Sage publications*, California(2005).

CRESWELL, JOHN W. (2007b)., 'Research design: A qualitative, quantitative, and mixed method approaches (2nd edition')*, Sage,Thousand Oaks*, CA.

CROOK ADH 'Fiscal austerity, affordable housing and the planning system: betterment and hypothecation,''*Town Planning Review 69(4)*, *Liverpool University Press*, Liverpool, pp iii-vii. (1998).

CROSS E G, 'The economics of ecosystems management. Ritchken J (ed.)," *The Rhodesian Science News 9(1)*: pp 21-22. (1975).

CSO (CENTRAL STATISTICAL OFFICE) (2002)., 'Zimbabwe Population Census 2002 – Enumerator Manual," *CSO*, Harare.

CSO (CENTRAL STATISTICS OFFICE OF Zimbabwe) '*Demographic and Healthy Survey," Government Printers*, Harare. (2003).

CUDS, 'Housing Microfinance Initiatives – Synthesis And Regional Summary: Asia, Latin America and Sub-Saharan Africa with Selected Case Studies," *Center for Urban Development Studies, Harvard University Graduate School of Design*, Development Alternatives Inc. (Dai), Maryland(2000).

CULLINGWORTH, J'The Political Culture of Planning: American Land-use Planning in Comparative Perspective," *Routledge,* London. (1993).

CUMMING.S.D, 'Post-colonial urban residential change in Harare," a case study. Chapter 13, ZINYAMA L, D TEVERA AND S CUMMING (eds.) 1993: *Harare: The Growth and Problems of the City*, University of Zimbabwe: Harare. (1993).

CUNNINGHAM.G ;MATHIE. A, 'Asset-Based Community Development-An Overview Coady International Institute." <URL: http://www. synergos. org,>*Accessed on 22 April 2008*. (2002).

CURLEY. A.M, 'Theories of Urban Poverty and Implications for Public Housing Policy," *Journal of Sociology and Social Welfare 32(2)*: pp. 97-119. (2005).

DARLOW C 'Valuation and development appraisal: 2nd edition," *The Estate Gazette Limited*,London. (1988).

DACIN, M. T.,et.al, 'Institutional theory and institutional change: Introduction to the special research forum," *Academy of Management Journal*, 45: 45-56. (2002.))

DAVIDSON. F;PAYNE.G, 'Urban Projects Manual – a guide to preparing upgrading and new development projects accessible to low income groups," *Liverpool University Press*, Liverpool. (1983).

DAVIDSON. M.,'Estimating the costs to society of poor housing," *Paper presented to the ENHR Conference on Sustainable Urban Areas, 25-28 June 2007*, Rotterdam. <URL: www.enhr2007rotterdam.nl>, *Accessed on 2 August 2007*. (2007).

DAVIES D. H.,'From Rhodesia to Zimbabwe: The Geographer and the Road Ahead." *Area, 10(4)*: pp. 286-288 (1978).

DAVILA. J. D. et al. 'A Review of Policies and Strategies Affecting the Peri-Urban Interface (Draft for discussion), Development Planning Unit," *University College London*, London. <URL: http://www.ucl.ac.uk /dpu/pui,> *Accessed on 22 April 2008* (1999).

DAVIS J.H et al. 'Toward a stewardship theory of management," *Academy of Management Review* 22: pp20-47. (1997).

DAVISON.C, 'An evaluation of existing residential layout design approaches in Zimbabwe and suggestions for alternative approaches," *Urban Forum 13(4):* pp187-204(2002).

DAY.B, 'The Quality of Sprawl' *Tom Mckenna Memorial Lecture*, pp2 <URL:http://www.greataustraliandream.net.au >*Accessed on 6 March 2007*.(2005)

DE KORT.A.I, 'Designing a Strategic Plan Development Approach for Integrated Area Development Projects' *Published PHD Thesis, University of Twente*, The Netherlands. (2009:9)

DE MARCO.S, 'Burlington is running out of cemetery space," *Daily Times Chronicles*. URL: <http://www.woburnonline.com/> (2000).

DE SHERBININ. A;MARTINE.G,'Urban Population Development and Environment Dynamics,' *Committee for International Cooperation in National Research in Demography*, Paris.<URL:http://www.cicred.org/ Eng/Publications/pdf/Policypapers/PP3.pdf, *Accessed on 22 April 2008*.(2007).

DE VALK. P, 'An Analysis of Planning Policy in Zimbabwe (Unpublished Paper)," *Department of Rural and Urban Planning, University of Zimbabwe*, Harare. (1986:5-6)

DE VRIES.J.R, 'Trust as a central concept in planning research and practice," *Paper presented at the 23rd Congress of the Association of European Schools of Planning, 15th – 18th July 2009*, Liverpool, UK (2009),

DEBORAH, POTTS, D., 'Viewpoint: What do we know about urbanization in sub-Saharan Africa and does it matter?" *International Development Planning Review, 34 (1):* pp. v-xxi.(2012).

DENG F. FREDERIC AND YOUQIN HUANG'Uneven land reform and urban sprawl in China: the case of Beijing, in Progress in Planning 61, pp 211–236," <URL: http://www.albany.edu/~yhuang/Deng&Huang_ UnevenLandReformAndUrbanSprawlBeijing.pdf>, *Accessed on 22 April 2008*. (2004).

DENT. J., 'Civic capacity and community response to government action, Endangered Species Act and state law in the Methow and Walla Walla in the Pacific Northwest," *International Journal of Public Administration 31(3)*: pp262-276.(2008:270).

DEVELOPMENT WORKS'Spatial Planning, Land Development and Land-use Management in a Context of HIV and AIDS," *the South African Cities Network.* <URL: http://www.sarpn.org.za/documents/d0001724/ Land _HIVAIDS_Oct2005.pdf>, *Accessed on 22 April 2008*. (October 2005).

DHV CONSULTING ENGINEERS 'A Methodology for Slum Improvement Studies: Methodology for studies aimed at the improvement of housing conditions in large cities in the third world," *Amersfoort,* the Netherlands. (1975).

DIRWAI.D, 'Demographic Study of a holding camp: The case of Hatcliffe Extension, Zimbabwe." *Unpublished MSc thesis, Centre for Population Studies, University of Zimbabwe*: Harare. (2000).

DIXON. D et al. 'Stewardship of the Great Lakes environment, A review of literature," *HDRU Publication No. 95-5, Dept. of Natural Resour., N.Y.S. Coll. Agric. and Life Sci.*, Cornell Univ., Ithaca, N.Y.(1995).

DONALDSON.L ;DAVIS. J.H; 'CEO governance and shareholder returns, Agency theory or stewardship theory." *Paper presented at the annual meeting of the Academy of Management*, Washington, DC. (1989).

DONALDSON L AND JH DAVIS., 'Stewardship theory or agency theory, CEO governance and shareholder returns," *Australian Journal of Management 16*: pp 49-64.(1991).

DOUGLAS.I, 'Peri-urban ecosystems and societies: Transitional zones and contrasting values. McGregor, D., Simon, D. and Thompson, D. (eds) *The Peri-Urban Interface*, Earthscan, London,'pg 18-27.(2006)

DOWALL D. E; CLARKE. G.,'Urban Management and Land - A Framework for Reforming Urban Land Policies in Developing Countries (Policy Paper)," *The International Bank for Reconstruction and Development/The World Bank*, Washington, D.C. (1996).

DRECHSEL P, C QUANSAH, ;F PENNING DE VRIES.,'Rural-urban interactions - Stimulation of urban and peri-urban agriculture in West Africa: characteristics, challenges, and need for action," Available:< http://www.idrc.ca/> (1999).

DU TOIT F, 'Musha: The Shona Concept of Home: Aspects of Zimbabwe Architecture Monograph 1," *Zimbabwe Publishing House*, Harare. (1981).

DUANY. A. et al.. 'Suburban Nation, " *The Rise of Sprawl and the Decline of the American Dream,* North Point Press: New York. (2003).

DUBE.C, 'Housing coops frustrated over land," *Zimbabwe Independent*. <URL: http://www.thezimbabweindependent.com/business/14311.html>, *Accessed on 22 April 2008.*(2004).

DZEMYDIENE. D, 'Preface to Sustainable Development Problems in the Issue." *Baltic Journal on Sustainability 14(1)*, (2008).

EARLEY., MA.,'Lessons Learned from Students' Research Experiences, " *Journal of Research Practice 3(1)*: pp 1-7. (2007).

ECOSANRES, 'Adapting Planning Tools to the Peri-Urban Setting - A Combination of Existing Tools," <URL: www.ecosanres.org,> *Accessed on 2 June 2010.* (2010:1).

EDUSA.S; SIMON. D, 'Land-use and land allocation in Kumasi peri-urban villages, in McGregor Duncan and James Quashie-Sam eds. CEDAR /IRNR Paper 9 <URL:http://www.gg.rhul.ac.uk/kumasi/ Project_ Related_Papers/Cedar_IRNR/Paper_9_9tmlhttp://www.gg.rhul.ac.uk/kumasi/Project_Related_Papers/Cedar_IRNR/Paper_9_9tml>, *Accessed on 13 October 2011.*(2001).

EDWARDS. M. M, 'Community Guide to Development Impact Analysis,' Wisconsin Land-use Research Program, Program on Agricultural Technology Studies, *University of Wisconsin–Madison*, Madison. <URL: www.cherry.gatech.edu/6602/2002-archive/PUBP6602-2002.pdf >(2000)

EL-HEFNAWI AYMAN IBRAHIM KAMEL,"Protecting" agricultural land from urbanisation or "Managing" the conflict between informal urban growth while meeting the demands of the communities," (Lessons learnt from the Egyptian policy reforms). <URL: http://www.worldbank.org/urban/urscd/papers/elhefnawi.pdf>, *Accessed on 22 April 2008*. (Undated).

EMA (ENVIRONMENTAL MANAGEMENT AGENCY) 'Local Environmental Action Planning Manual' *Environmental Management Agency/UNDP*, Harare. (2007).

ENGELS. F, 'The Housing Question. Karl Marx and Frederick Engels," *Selected Works in Two Volumes*, Lawrence and Wishart Ltd: London.(1887).

EPAESSC, 'Everyday Choices: Opportunities for Environmental Stewardship (Technical Report)," <URL: http://www.epa.gov/innovation/pdf/techrpt .pdf>, *Accessed on27 August 2010*. (2005:9).

EPWORTH, "*Minutes of the Land and Environmental Management Committee," Meeting Number 19,10 July 2010)*

EPWORTH, 'Minutes of the Land and Environmental Management Committee," Meeting Number 107(13 July 2005).

EPWORTH, 'Minutes of the Land and Environmental Management Committee," Meeting Number 2(13 November 2008).

EPWORTH, 'Local Board Progress Report, ELB, Epworth."

EPWORTH, 'Local Board Proposed Development Report, ELB, Epworth."(1987b).

EPWORTH, 'Epworth Local Board Development Proposals," ELB, Epworth ,(2002:8).

EPWORTH, 'Local Board Treasury Report on Debtors Databank," *ELB*, Epworth.(2007).

EPWORTH, 'Minutes of the Land and Environmental Management Committee," Meeting Number 125(25 July 2007).

EPWORTH, 'Minutes of the Land and Environmental Management Committee," Meeting Number 103 (3 November 2004).

EPWORTH, "*Minutes of the Land and Environmental Management Committee," Meeting Number 12,(4* November 2009).

EPWORTH, "Minutes of the Land and Environmental Management Committee," Meeting Number 111,9 March 2006).

ESPEY. M et al ., 'Living on the edge, Residential Property Values in the Urban Rural Interface," *Journal of Agricultural and Applied Economics (December 2007),* pp 19-34.(2007).

ESSLEMONT DON, SUSAN PETERSEN AND K S SELVAKUMAR, 'Telephone Directories as Sampling Frames," *Marketing Bulletin,* 1992(3): pp. 38-45(1992).

EUROPE 2020, 'Europe's growth strategy' Retrieved from <http://ec.europa.eu/europe2020/index_en.htm> (2015).

EYRE L ALAN, 'Quasi-Urban Melange Settlement, Cases from St. Catherine and St. James," Jamaica. *Geographical Review 69(1),* pp 95-100(1979).

FALZON MARK-ANTHONY, 'Introduction , Multi-sited Ethnography: Theory, Praxis and Locality in Contemporary Research," *Ashgate*, London. (2009).

FANNIE MAE FOUNDATION.,.,"'Downtown Housing as an Urban Redevelopment Tool: Hype or Hope?," In *Housing Policy Debate 10(2)*: pp 477-505. (1999).

FERGUSON.B, 'Process, Policy, and Public-Private Partnerships in Housing in Developing Countries, What Can the United States Learn?," <URL: http://www.huduser.org/Publications/pdf/brd/07Ferguson.pdf>, *Accessed on 22 April 2008.*(2007).

FERNANDES. E, 'Chapter 12: Combining tenure policies, urban planning and city management in Brazil, in PAYNE GEOFFREY (ed.), 2000," Land, Rights and Innovation – Improving tenure security for the urban poor, *ITDG Publishing*, London (2002).

FISHMAN.R. A; GECHTER. K. I, 'Smart Growth: An Overview and Issues.' *Paper prepared for American College of Real Estate Lawyers Conference, March 18-21, 2004, Orlando*, Florida (2004); Stoian, 2003

FLINT.J., 'The Responsible Tenant: Housing Governance and the Politics of Behaviour," CNR Paper 20. URL: <www.neighbourhoodcentre.org.uk>, (2004.).

FLYVBJERG BENT'Making Social Science Matter: Why Social Inquiry Fails and How it Can Succeed Again (Edition 1'*), Cambridge University Press*, Cambridge. (2001).

FOSTER. K.'The electoral register as a sampling frame," *SMB 33(7)*: pp 1-7 (1993).

FOSTER, KATHRYN A '*Regionalism on purpose' ,Cambridge, MA*,Lincoln Institute of Land Policy. (2001).

FOTHERGILL SK, S MON AND M PERRY 'Property and Industrial development," *Hutchison*, London(1987).

FOURIE CLARISSA 'Reviewing conventional land administration approaches and proposing new alternatives: peri-urban customary tenure and land readjustment." <URL: http://www.fig.net/commission7/pretoria_2002/papers/SYM_LR_PRETORIA_PAPER_FOURIE.pdf>, *Accessed on 22 April 2008*. (2002).

FRANCESCHI PAUL 'Le plan dialectique: pour une alternative au paradigm.(The dialectic plan: an alternative to the paradigm)," *Semiotica 146(1-4)*: pp. 353-367). (2003).

FRANKS J.R, MC GLOIN. A, 'The Potential of Environmental Co-operatives to Deliver Landscape-scale Environmental and Rural Policy Objectives in the UK. The Rural Citizen' *Governance, Culture and Wellbeing in the 21st Century*: University of Plymouth, UK. (2006).

GALLENT N.;KWANG SIK KIM 'The changing housing role of mixed-use development in Seoul," in *Town Planning Review 69(4), Liverpool University Press*,Liverpool, pp 425-440. (1998).

GANDIDZANWA.P, 'Attitudes and practices towards water supply and sanitation facilities: the case study of the Epworth upgrading programme,' *Unpublished M.Sc. thesis, University of Zimbabwe*, Harare. (2003)

GAPPERT. G.,'The future of urban environments: implications for the business community," *Business Horizons.Business Horizons*. Available:< http://findarticles.com> (1993).

GARAU PIETRO, ELLIOTT D. SCLAR,;GABRIELLA Y. CAROLINI'A Home in the City: Urban Millennium Project Report on Improving the Lives of Slum Dwellers." *Global Urban Development Magazine 2(1), Global Urban Development (GUD:* London. <URL: http://www.globalurban.org>, *Accessed on 22 April 2008.* (2006).

GARDNER. D.; RUST. K.,'Access to Housing Finance in Africa: Exploring the Issues – Zambia,' *Report of a scoping study commissioned by FinMark Trust.* Available: www.finmark.org.za. (May 2007).,

GBADEYAN ROTIMI A 'Private Sector's Contributions to the Development of the Nigerian Housing Market,"*Current Research Journal of Social Sciences 3(2):* pp.104-113. (2011).

GEHAN.R; GEHANI. R, 'Mary Parker Follett's Constructive Conflict: A "Psychological Foundation of Business Administration" for Innovative Enterprises," *International Journal of Public Administration 30(4)*: pp387-404.(2007).

GIENOW-HECHT J.CE 'Cultural Transfer. Chapter 16 in Hogan Michael and Thomas G Paterson (eds.)," Explaining the History of American Foreign Relations (Second edition), *Cambridge University Press*, Cambridge, pp. 257-278(2004).

GILBERT. A, 'Forms and Effectiveness of Community Participation in Squatter Settlements," *Regional Development Dialogue 8(4)*: pp 56-85; (1987)., 'Land and Shelter in Mega-Cities," Some Critical Issues, in Fuchs Roland J., Ellen Brennan. Joseph Chaimie. Fu-chen Lo, and Juha Uitto (eds.), 'Mega-City Growth and the Future," *United Nations University*, Tokyo.(1994).

GILBERT. A ,WARD.P.M, 'Land for the rich and land for the poor," Gugler J (ed.)., 'The Urbanisation of the Third World," *Oxford University Press*, London. (1990).

GIRARDET.H., 'Creating Sustainable Cities (Schumacher Briefings 2,": *Greenbooks for the Schumacher Society*:,Bristol. (1999).

GIRAUT FRÉDÉRIC ;BRIJ MAHARAJ 'Contested terrains: Cities and hinterlands in post-apartheid boundary delimitations," *GeoJournal 57(1-2) :* pp 39-51(2002).

GITTINGER PRICE J., 'Economic Analysis for Agricultural Projects," *John Hopkins University Press,* Baltimore and London, Revised edition,(1982).

GLASS J. E, 'Visceral Verstehen," *Electronic Journal of Sociology 2005*: pp 1-15. (2005).

Glennon.M ; Kretser.K, 'Impacts to wildlife from low density, exurban Development -Information and Considerations for the Adirondack Park," *Adirondack Communities & Conservation Program - Technical Paper No. 3. Available:* <http://www.wcs.org/adirondacks.(2005).

GOETGELUK R,;TOM DE JONG.'What about the spatial dimension of subsidiarity in housing policy?," *Paper presented to the ENHR Conference on Sustainable Urban Areas, 25-28 June 2007, Rotterdam.* Available:< www.enhr2007rotterdam.nl>, *Accessed 2 August 2007.* (2007).

GOLDBERG R. M.,'How Our Worldviews Shape Our Practice,." *Conflict Resolution Quarterly26 (4)*: pp. 405-431. (2009).

GORDON. P ; RICHARDSON.H.W, 'Are compact cities a desirable planning goal?'*Journal of the American Planning Association 63(1)*: pp95-117 (1997)

GOSLING S. D.; SIMINE V.; SANJAY S.; OLIVER P. J.,'Should We Trust Web-Based Studies? A Comparative Analysis of Six Preconceptions about Internet Questionnaire," *American Psychologist 59(2)*: pp 93–104. (2004).

GOUGH.K; YANKSON, 'Land Markets in African Cities, The Case of Peri-urban Accra, Ghana," *Urban Studies* 37(13): 2485 – 2500 (2000).

GOUGH.K, 'From Bamboo to Bricks: Self-Help Housing and the Building Materials Industry in Urban Colombia," PhD thesis, University College London. (1992).

GOVERNMENT OF MAHARASHTRA., '(Draft State) Housing Policy," *Housing Department* Mumbai (2007).

GOVERNMENT OF SWAZILAND 'The Draft Peri-urban Growth Policy."., Available: <www.ecs.co.sz/periurban/pup_periurban_policy.htm>(1997).,

GoZ (GOVERNMENT OF ZIMBABWE)/ UNDP 'Zimbabwe Millennium Development Goals – 2004 Progress Report,' *UNDP*, Harare. (2004).

GOVERNMENT OF ZIMBABWE/ UNHABITAT.,'Towards an Integrated Approach to Sustainable and Affordable Social Amenities Delivery in Zimbabwe.,' *Proceedings Report for the National Housing Convention held from the 26th to the 30th of October 2009 at Elephant Hills Hotel, Victoria Falls, Zimbabwe,* Government of Zimbabwe/ UNHABITAT, Harare. (2009).,

GoZ, 'Transitional National Development Plan 1982/83 -1984/85," *Vol 1, Government Printer*, Harare.(14 May 1980:116)).

GOZ.'First Five-Year National Development Plan 1986-1990," *Vol 1, Government Printer*, Harare. (1986).

GoZ. 'Development and Building Control – Control, Applications, Permits, And Enforcement: Building Plan Appraisal and Regulations," *Government Printers*, Harare. (1990).

GOVERNMENT OF ZIMBABWE 'Zimbabwe Agenda for Sustainable Socio-Economic Transformation (ZIM-ASSET)," *Towards and Empowered Society and a Growing Economy,October 2013 – December 2018*. Zimbabwe (2013).

GoZ., Constitution of Zimbabwe 2013. (2013).

GoZ., National Housing Policy, August 2012. (2012).

GoZ., National climate change response strategy. (2012).

GoZ. 'National water policy, August 2012."(2012).

GoZ. 'Constitution of Zimbabwe 2013.' (2013).

GoZ. 'National climate policy, November 2017." (2017).

GoZ., 'Report on Development of Human Settlements in Zimbabwe," *Government Printers*, Harare. (1991a).

GoZ., Second Five Year National Development Plan 1991 – 1995, *Government Printers*, Harare(1991b).

GoZ 'Land Acquisition Act (Amendment No 3)," *Government Printers*, Harare. (1992a).

GoZ'Report of the Commission of Inquiry into Appropriate Agricultural Land Tenure System, chaired by Professor Mandivamba Rukuni," *Government Printers.*,Harare. (1992b).

GoZ 'Regional, Town and Country Planning Act: Chapter 29:12," *Government Printers,* Harare (1996).

GoZ'Draft National Housing Policy for Zimbabwe," Government Printers: Harare. (1999).

GoZ., 'Study and Review of the Current Minimum High-density Housing Standards," *Government Printers*,Harare. (2001).

GoZ 'Environmental Management Act," *Government Printers,* Harare. (2004).

GoZ'National Environmental Policy and Strategies, Ministry of Environment and Natural Resources Management' Harare. (2005).

GoZ/UNHABITAT, 'Proceedings of the National Symposium convened by the Ministry of National Housing and Social Amenities under the theme ,"*Towards an Integrated Approach to Sustainable Housing and Social Amenities Delivery in Zimbabwe' on 28 May 2009*, Mendel Training Centre, Harare.(2009)

GoZ/World Bank, Proceedings Report of the Workshop held under the theme, 'Infrastructure Recovery and Development in Zimbabwe: Current Needs, Medium Term Solutions and Long-Term Vision," on Wednesday 25th November 2009, Wild Geese lodge.(2009).

GRANT. J, 'Encouraging mixed use in practice. Paper prepared for, International Planning Symposium on *Incentives, Regulations, and Plans –The Role of States and Nation-States in Smart Growth Planning,'* National Centre for Smart Growth Research and Education, University of Maryland, Habiforum Foundation, The Netherlands, Maryland Department of Planning, September 30 – October 1, 2004: Available:< http://www.smartgrowth.umd.edu>(2004).

GRANT.M. R, 'Rental Shelter as a Coping Mechanism in Gweru, Zimbabwe," *PHD Thesis, Queen's University*, Ontario, Canada.(1991)

GREEN. C, 'An Analysis of the Use Of Limited Real Rights in Tax Planning.' *Unpublished MBA Thesis, Faculty of Business and Economic Sciences,* Nelson Mandela Metropolitan University. <URL:http://dspace.nmmu.ac.za:8080/jspui/bitstream/10948/809/1/Consolidated%20thesis%20document%20_V3_%203_.pdf,> *Accessed on 01 May 2013.* (2008)

GREENE. M.;.;EDUARDO. R., 'Incremental construction: a strategy to facilitate access to housing," *Environment and Urbanisation 20(1), International Institute of Environment and Development (IIED,)* ,London, pp89-108. (2008).

GUBRIUM. J. F. ;HOLSTEIN. J. A., EDS. 'Handbook of interview research: context & method," *Sage* Thousand Oaks, CA. (2002).

GULYANI.S; CONNORS.G., 'Urban upgrading in Africa: a summary of rapid assessments in ten countries," *World Bank,* Washington DC. URL: http://www.worldbank.org/urban/upgrading/docs/afr-assess/countrysummary.pdf>, *Accessed on 22 April 2008.(*2002)).

GUMBO.T, 'Eccentric housing finance sources by the urban poor in Zimbabwe: case of Cowdray Park low-income self help housing scheme in Bulawayo," *Economia. Seria Management 13(1)*: pp 89-104. (2010)

GURNEY.E.T, 'Definition and Standards in Housing," National Housing Convention Report (Public Private Partnership) Victoria Falls Nov. 1997, National Housing Convention: pp 50-56 (1997:54)

GWAGWA. N. N., 'Women as 'home-makers and men as 'heads' of households: Who is responsible for housing improvements," Chapter 4 in Sithole-Fundire S.A. Zhou, A. Larsson & A. Schlyter, 1995: Gender Research on Urbanisation, Planning and Everyday Life, *Zimbabwe Women's Resource Centre Network*, Harare.(1995).

HABITAT PLATFORM, 'Treasures in your neighbourhood: International exchange at neighbourhood level." *VNG Uitgeverij: The Hague.*(2002).

HÂKANSSON. M.;LJUNGBLAD. S; HOLMQUIST. L. E.,'Capturing the Invisible: Designing Context-Aware Photography," <URL: www.sics.se/fal/projects/photo/DUX_hakansson.pdf>, *Accessed on 22 April 2008.* (2003).

HALL.N, 'Partnerships in housing provision; A case study of housing co-operative initiatives in Kwekwe, Bulawayo and Harare, in Municipal Development Program – MDP," undated: *Addressing poverty in the context of decentralisation in Eastern and Southern Africa – Case studies in Malawi, Uganda, Zambia and Zimbabwe: MDP Working Paper 3,* Municipal Development Programme for Sub-Saharan Africa: Harare, pp 31-47. (2001).

HANSEN. T,'Housing standards and health, welfare, policy and planning." *Paper presented to the ENHR Conference on Sustainable Urban Areas, 25-28 June 2007, Rotterdam,* <URL www.enhr2007rotterdam.nl, Accessed on 2 August 2007.> (2007).

HARARE, Harare Combination Master Plan: Written Statement, Department of Works, Harare (1989:3).

HARARE, Harare Combination Master Plan, Study Report And Written Statement, Department of Works, Harare (1992).

HARARE 'Local Development Plan No 31, Southern Incorporated Areas," *Unpublished Report, Department of Works,* Harare. *(1999).*

HARARE'Gletwyn Farm Local Development Plan: Draft Report of Study and Written Statements," *Unpublished Report*(2000).

HARARE , 'Saturday Retreat Local Development Plan No. 50; Report of Study and Written Statement," *Unpublished Report, Department of Works,* Harare(2002).

HARDEN. C.D, WOOLF. A ;ROSEBERRY. J.,'Influence of exurban development on hunting opportunity, hunter distribution, and harvest efficiency of white-tailed deer," *in Wildlife Society Bulletin 33(1), Wildlife Society,*Washington, DC pp233-242 (2005).

HARDOY J ;D SATTERTHWAITE 'Shelter: Need and Response,' *John Wiley,* Chichester. (1981).

HARDOY et al., 'The Poor Die Young: Housing and Health in Third World Cities," *Earthscan Publications Ltd*: London.(1990).

HARDOY. J ; SATTERTWAITE. D., 'Squatter Citizen: Life in the Urban Third World," *Earthscan Publications*, London.(1995).

HARISALO.R; MIETTINEN.E. 'Trust Capital – The third force of entrepreneurship," *University of Tampere, Department of Administrative Science*: Tampere.(1997), .

HARRISON C.,'Tip Sheet on Survey Sampling, Coverage and Non-response," *Programme on Survey Research*, Harvard University. (2006).

HARRISS.. J.,'Urban Poverty and Urban Poverty Alleviation," *Cities 9(3)*: pp 186-94. (1989).

HARVEY. D, 'Urban Land Economics. The Economics of Real property," *Basing stoke*, Macmillan(1991)

HASSAN. A, 'The unplanned revolution – Observations on the processes of socio-economic change in Pakistan," *Oxford University Press*, Oxford. (2008: 195-6)

HASSE.J ;LATHROP.R, 'Land resource impact indicators of urban sprawl," *Applied Geography 23*: pp159–175 (2003).

HEATH. T. et al., 'Impact of climate change on peri-urban areas in Lusaka," *Report prepared by Cranfield University, Water Supply for the Urban Poor (WSUP),* London.(2010).

HECHT. B. L.,'Housing-Led Economic Development: Managing Housing Assets for Economic Development of Residents," <URL: http://www.nhi.org/online/issues/89/housingecodev.html>, *Accessed on 22 April 2008.* (1996).

HEINRICH, C.J, 'Outcomes based performance management in the public sector: Implications for government accountability and effectiveness' *Public Administration Review, 62, 712–726.* (2002).

HERALD., 'Projects benefit over 280 villagers," The Herald, Zimpapers, Harare,(16 August 2010b).

HERALD., 'Gvt gets tough on veld fires," 'Gvt gets tough on veld fires," The Herald, Zimpapers, Harare(16 August 2010a).

HERALD ., 'Use Powers to save Environment, Chiefs Urged,"The Herald, Zimpapers, Harare.(17 2010).

HERALD., 'Sewage catastrophe looms, EMA," The Herald, Zimpapers, Harare(18 August 2010).

HERALD., 'Shurugwi Town Council owed US$120 000,' The Herald, Zimpapers, Harare.(19 August 2010a)

HERALD., 'Wood poaching rife in Hwange West," The Herald, Zimpapers,Harare.(19 August 2010b).

HERALD'Epworth residents defaulting: Local board," The Herald, Zimpapers, Harare. (20 October, 2010).

HERALD., 'Veld fires destroy National Parks estates: Chadenga," The Herald, Zimpapers, Harare.(20 September 2010).

HERALD.,'Bill Gates doing a sterling job in Zim." <URL: http://www.herald.co.zw/index.php?option = com_content&view=article&id=61026:bill-gates – doing – a – sterling – job - in-zim&catid = 39:opinion-a-analysis&Itemid=132,> *Accessed on 12 April, 2013.* (22 December 2012).

HERALD.,'Ministry sets new standards for urban housing developments," Zimpapers, Harare. (22 February 2005)

HERALD., 'EMA drags city council to court," The Herald, Zimpapers, Harare. (24 August 2010)

HERALD., 'Tobacco Firms Urged to Plant Trees," The Herald, Zimpapers, Harare. (8 February 2010)

HERALD., '200 000ha destroyed by veld fires — EMA," The Herald, Zimpapers, Harare.(8 September 2010)

HERALD., 'Integrate food systems in urban expansion, town planners told," *Zimpapers,* Harare. (November 11, 2010).

HERALD, 'Shopping Complex for Ruwa," Zimpapers, Harare.(2008)2008)

HERALD., 'Harare's Expansion Inevitable' <URL: http://allafrica.com/stories/ 201007280723 . htmlhttp://allafrica.com / stories/201007280723.html>, *Accessed on 2 April 2012.(*28 July 2010)

HERALD, 'Clinic wards now classrooms," The Herald, Zimpapers: Harare(.(30 September 2010).

HERITAGE. J.,'Goffman, Garfinkel and Conversation Analysis," Chapter 4, M. Wetherall, S. Taylor and S.J. Yates eds., Discourse Theory and Practice, S*age*, London. (2001).

HERNANDEZ.. F.; KELLETT.. P.;ALLEN, L.K., 'Rethinking the Informal City: Critical HEURKENS. E, 'Changing Public and Private Roles in Urban Area Development in The Netherlands." *Paper prepared for the 4th International Conference of the International Forum on Urbanism (IFoU) , 2009, Amsterdam/Delft under the theme "The New Urban Question – Urbanism beyond Neo-Liberalism": pp 1263 – 1272*. (2009: 1268)

HIGH. C et al. 'Understanding informal institutions," Networks and communities in rural development. <URL: http://econ.core.hu/ doc/konf/High2005.pdf>, *Accessed on 22 April 2008.* (2005).

HIGHLANDS. D., 'What's Indigenous? An Essay on Building' in Turan, M. (ed.) 'Vernacular Architecture: Paradigms of Environmental Response," *Aldershot, Avebury*, 31-62.

HMP, 'Harare Metropolitan Provincial Development Plan 2011," *Government of Zimbabwe*, Harare (2011:4)

HODKINSON .P. H, 'The return of the housing question' *Ephemera - Theory & Politics in Organization 12(4)*: pp. 427 (2012)

HOGAN P.H., 'Human Capital and the Theory of Life-Cycle Investing." *American Association of Individual Investors (AAII) Journal*, pp 18-19.(2008) <URL: http://www.hoganfinancial.com/publications/2008-05%20AAII%20Human%20Capital.pdf, Accessed on 22 April 2008.>

HOGREWE. W.et. al,'The Unique Challenges of Improving Peri-Urban Sanitation,' *WASH Technical Report No. 86., Report prepared for the Office of Health, Bureau for Research and Development*, U.S. Agency for International Development, under WASH Task No. 339, U.S. Agency for International Development: Washington, DCpg.9(1993)

HOLDEN.E., 'Ecological footprints and sustainable urban form."*Journal of Housing and the Built Environment 19*: pp91–109 (2004).

HOLWAY.J, 'Scenario Planning and the Promise of Open Source Tools,; *Land Lines 23(4)*: pp7-13 (2011)

HOME.R, 'Eating farmland, growing houses': *Peri-urban settlements and customary land tenure in Botswana, Southern Africa,* <URL:http://www.naerus.net/web/sat/workshops/2001/papers/home.pdf>(2001)'Negotiating security of tenure for peri-urban settlement: traveller gypsies and the planning system in the United Kingdom," in *Habitat International 26(3):* pp 335-346. (2002).

HONADLE. G.;J. VANSANT., 'Implementation for Sustainability," Lessons from Integrated Rural Development, *Kumarian Press*, Connecticut. (1985).

HOOD E.,'Dwelling disparities: how poor housing leads to poor health," *Environmental May, 2005*. <URL: www.ehponline.org/members/2005/113-5/focus.html>, *Accessed on 22 April 2008.* (2005).

HORENZ.J.W.G, 'An approach to regional planning." *Zimbabwe Science News 13(11):* pp261-264. (1976).

HOUSTON. P.,'Re-valuing the Fringe: Some Findings on the Value of Agricultural Production in Australia's Peri-Urban Regions," *Geographical Research 43(2):* pp 209 – 223(2005).

HOUSTON.F, 'Housing America State by State: How Governors Are Leading the Way," in *Housing Facts and Findings 7(1)*: p1.< URL: www.fanniemaefoundation.org/programs/hff.html>(2005).

HOWLETT. M;RAMESH.R, 'Studying Public Policy: Policy Cycles and Policy Subsystems and Political Organisations," *Princeton University Press*, Princeton. (1995)(1995).

HPZ , 'Community Action Group on Housing: Advocating for improved low-income housing." *Report on the National Stakeholder Validation Workshop, 24-25 November 2001 at the Management Training Bureau, HPZ:* Harare.(2001).

HUBY.M, 'Social Policy and the Environment," *Open University Press*,Buckingham. (1998).

HUCHZERMEYER M., 'The new instrument for upgrading informal settlements in South Africa: Contributions and Constraints," *UCT Press*, Cape Town. (2006).

HUTCHINS W. J., 'On the Problem of 'Aboutness' In Document Analysis," *Journal of Informatics* 1(1) April1977: pp.17-35. (1977).

HYDE RICHARD ed'Bioclimatic Housing Innovative Designs for Warm Climates," *Earthscan,* London. (2008).

IANNACCHIONE V;MORTON. K; MCMICHAEL.K,CUNNINGHAM. D, CAJKA. J; CHROMY.J.,'Comparing the Coverage of a Household Sampling Frame Based on Mailing Addresses to a Frame Based on Field Enumeration," <URL: http://www.amstat.org/sections/srms/proceedings/y2007/Files/JSM2007-000675.pdf>, *Accessed on 13 July 2011.* (2007).

IAQUINTA. D; DRESCHER.W,"Peri-urban Typology Defined, Defining Peri-urban: Understanding Rural-Urban Linkages and Their Connection to Institutional Contexts." *Paper presented at the Tenth World Congress, IRSA,* Rio: August 1, 2000.(2000)

ICG,'Zimbabwe's Operation Murambatsvina, The Tipping Point?' *Crisis Group Africa Report N 97, ICG.* (2005:1).

IDRC, 'Catastrophe or New Society? A Latin American World Model, International Development Research Centre," Ottawa. *Catastrophe or*

New Society? A Latin American World Model, International Development Research Centre: Ottawa. (1976).

IFVERSEN. J..''Text, Discourse, Concept: Approaches to Textual Analysis," *KONTUR 7 (2003)*: pp 60 -69. (2003).

INTSIFUL, GEORGE. W.K, 'Housing and urban development initiatives as means towards the alleviation of poverty," in *RICS Foundation Our Common Estate Paper Series*. <URL: www.rics-foundation.org >(2004).

IRURAH.D, 'Urbanisation and Housing Challenges: Cities in Africa Conference.' *Parallel sessions on urban land management – Rapporteur's Report;* December 8, 2003. (2003).

JACK. C., 'Unjust waters: climate change, flooding and the urban poor in Africa," *Environment and Urbanisation 20(1)*: pp187-206. (2008).

JACOBS. J.,'The death and life of great American cities – The failure of town *planning," Penguin Books*, New York. (1965).,

JACOBS. K ;MANZI.T, 'Evaluating the Social Constructionist Paradigm in Housing Research." *Housing, Theory and Society 17*: pp.35–42.(2000:36).

JENKINS. P,'African Cities: Competing claims on urban land," *News for the Nordic Africa Institute no. 3*: Nordic Africa Institute: Uppsala.(2006).

JOHNSON.A.J, 'Mary Parker Follett: Laying the Foundations for Spirituality in the Workplace," *International Journal of Public Administration 30(4)*: pp425-440. (2007).

JOHNSON.J.H,'Urbanisation (Second Edition)," *Thomas Nelson and Sons Ltd*, South Melbourne. (1990. R. B.; A. J. ONWUEGBUZIE., 'Mixed Methods Research: A Research Paradigm Whose Time Has Come'), *Educational Researcher 33(7)*: pp. 14–26(2004).

JORDAN.J. D., 'Local Government in Zimbabwe,' *Mambo Press*, Gweru.(1984); JORGEN. A, 'Meanings and perceptions of the built environment in peri-urban areas of Maputo, Mozambique," *African Perspectives 2009, The African Inner City*(2009).

KADZERE M.,'Woodlots - Alternative Source of Curing Tobacco," The Herald, *Zimpapers*, Harare. (1 April 2010).

KAHN.M.E, 'The Environmental Impact of Suburbanisation," *Journal of Policy Analysis and Management 19(4)*, pp569-586.(2000).

KAITILLA. S.,'The Upgrading of Squatter Settlements in Tanzania: The Role of Security of Land Tenure and the Provision of Amenities in Housing Improvement," in *Journal of Asian and African Studies, XXVI (3-4):* pp 220-236. (1991).

KALIMBA. I.; MARIUS DE LANGEN., 'Infrastructure Provision as Part of Slum Upgrading: The Case of Kigali, Rwanda,' *Paper presented to the ENHR Conference on Sustainable Urban Areas, 25-28 June 2007*, Rotterdam. <URL: www.enhr2007rotterdam.nl>, *Accessed on 14 August 2007*. (2007).

KALIPENI.E, 'Contained Urban Growth in Post-Independence Malawi,' *East African Geographical Review 19(2),* pp. 49-66.(1997).

KAMETE. A.Y,'Continuity with change: a review of Zimbabwe' public sector urban low income housing production system," in *Development Southern Africa 15(1) Autumn*: pp13-28(1998).

KAMETE. A,Y, 'Governance for sustainability? Balancing social and environmental concerns in Harare,' *Chr.Michelsen Institute.* <URL: www.cmi.no>(2002).

KAMETE AMIN Y., 'Governing the Poor in Harare, Zimbabwe: Shifting Perceptions and Changing Responses' *Research Report Series, No. 122. Nordiska Afrikainstitutet*: Uppsala. (2002b).

KAMETE AMIN Y., 'Revisiting the urban housing crisis in Zimbabwe: Some forgotten dimensions?'*Habitat International 30(4):* pp 981-995.(2006).

KAMETE.A.Y, Urban governance, poverty and urban housing," In O. Musandu-Nyamayaro and T. Mubvami, (Eds.), Urban Governance Outreach Research, pp. 13–27. Harare, *Department of Rural and Urban Planning and the Ford Foundation.* (1997).

KAMETE.A.Y,'Government, Building Societies and Civil Society," Exploring the Interface in the Context of Urban Low-income Housing in Zimbabwe, in *African Review on Money Finance and Banking*, Felice Tambussi: Milan: pp 77-98. (1999).

KAMETE AY., 'Government, building societies and civil society, exploring the interface in the context of urban low-income housing in Zimbabwe. *Savings and Development*: pp77–98. http://www.fgda.org/pubblicazioni_schedarivista.php?Id=461, Accessed on 22 April 2008. (1999b).

KAMETE.A.Y, 'Restrictive control of urban high-density housing in Zimbabwe, deregulation and challenges for urban design," *Housing, Theory and Society,* 16(3): 136–151. (1999c).

KAMETE. A. Y., 'Cost recovery in urban high-density housing, a discourse with experiences from Zimbabwe."*Habitat International,* 24(3): 241–60.(2000a).

KAMETE. A. Y., 'Examining the Zimbabwean Government's Drive to House the Urban Poor," *Geographical Journal of Zimbabwe Number 31.* Geographical Association of Zimbabwe: Harare.(2000b)

KAMETE. A.Y., 'The quest for affordable urban housing: a study of approaches and results in Harare, Zimbabwe," *Development Southern Africa*, 18(2): 31–44. (2001a).

KAMETE A. Y.,.,"'USAID's private sector housing programme in urban Zimbabwe: examining the terrain from the terraces," *Environment and Urbanisation,* 12 (1): 125–35. (2001b).

KAMETE. A. Y., 'Civil society, housing and urban governance, the case of urban housing cooperatives in Zimbabwe." In A. Tostensen, I. Tvedten and M. Vaa (Eds.), *Associational Life in African Cities: Popular responses to the urban crisis*, pp. 162–179. Uppsala: The Nordic Africa Institute.(2001c)

KAMETE. A.Y., The rebels within, Urban Zimbabwe in the post-election period. In H. Melber (ed.) Zimbabwe's presidential elections 2002: evidence, lessons and implications," *Nordic Africa Institute Discussion Paper 14. Uppsala*, The Nordic Africa Institute, pp. 31–48(2002c)

KAMETE. A. Y, et.al, 'Managing the interface between urban councils and the surrounding rural districts councils' *The case of Bulawayo City Council and Umguza Rural District Council.* Municipal Development Programme for Eastern and Southern Africa (MDP-ESA): Harare.(2001).

KAO. R, 'Stewardship-based economics," *World Scientific Publishing Co.* (2007).

KASHAWO.L, 'Let's save our environment from veld fire,' The Sunday Mail, Zimpapers,Harare. (22 August 2010.)

KATZ, BRUCE; BRADLEY. J.,'Divided We Sprawl, *Atlantic Monthly* 284(6) (December 1999), pp26-42." <URL: www.theatlantic.com/issues>, *Accessed on 2 September 2008*. (1999).

KAWONGA.A. J.C, 'Access to land for low-income housing in Malawi: The case of Zomba Municipality, in Municipal Development Program – MDP, undated," *Addressing poverty in the context of decentralisation in Eastern and Southern Africa – Case studies in Malawi, Uganda, Zambia and Zimbabwe: MDP Working Paper 3,* Municipal Development Programme for Sub-Saharan Africa: Harare, pp 65-81.(1996);

KAZEROONI E., A., 'Fundamentals of Clinical Research for Radiologists - Population and Sample," *American Journal of Radiology (AJR) 177*: pp 993-1000. (2001).

KEELEY, J.; SCOONES. I,'Understanding Environmental Policy Processes' *A Review- IDS working Paper 89*. IDS: Brighton(1999).

KELLETT. P, 'Contemporary Vernaculars: Informal housing processes and vernacular theory." *Journal of the International Society for the Study of Vernacular Settlements - ISVS e-journal 2(1)*: pp 1-12.,(2011)

KELLETT. P., 'Constructing Home: Production and Consumption of Popular Housing in Northern Colombia," PhD thesis, University of Newcastle upon Tyne. (1995).

KELLETT, P., 'The Construction of Home in the Informal City," in F. Hernández, M. Millington, and I. Borden (eds.), Transculturation: Cities, Space and Architecture in Latin America. *Amsterdam and New York*, Rodopi, pp 22-42(2005).

KELLET. P ; NAPPIER. M., 'Squatter Architecture: a Critical Examination of Vernacular Theory and Spontaneous Settlement with Reference to South America and South Africa," *Traditional Dwellings and Settlements Review 6(2) May 1995*: pp 7-24. (1995).

KEMENY. J.,'Housing and Social Theory," *Routledge*, London. (1992).

KESSIDES.C, 'The Urban Transition in Sub-Saharan Africa: Implications for Economic Growth and Poverty Reduction," *The Cities Alliance*, Washington D. C. (2006).

KHAN. F.; THURMAN. S.,'Setting the Stage: Current Housing Policy and Debate in South Africa, Isandla Institute." <URL: www.isandla.org.za/papers/20. Housing Policy in SA (2001).pdf>, *Accessed on 22 April 2008*. (2001).

KHAN, M.H. 'Governance during social transformations: challenges for Africa," *New Political Economy* 17(5): 667–75. (2012).

KHORSHIDI HADI A. ;M. SOLTANOLKOTTABI., 'Hegelian Philosophy and System Dynamics." <URL: http: // www.systemdynamics . org/ conferences/2010/proceed/papers/P1146.pdf>, *accessed on 25 May 2013*. (2010).

KINYUNGU.N.A, , 'The city of Nairobi, Kenya, 'Contentious Development: Urban and Peri-urban Transformations and Livelihoods in Africa." *Report of a Peri-NET Workshop, East and Southern Africa held at Fairview Hotel,* Nairobi, Kenya, 7-9 October 2002.(2002).

KISEMBO. C, 'Appropriate Technology Options for Managing Drainage Flows From Low-Cost Peri Urban Settlements In South Africa," *Unpublished Masters of Science Thesis, Faculty of Engineering and the Built Environment, University of Witwatersrand*, Johannesburg.(2004).

KNUTH. L, 'Legal and institutional aspects of urban, peri-urban forestry and greening," *A working paper for discussion, FAO Legal Papers Online #48*. <URL: http://www.fao.org/legal/prs-ol/paper-e.htm,> *Accessed on 22 April 2008*. (2005).

KNUTSSON.P. , 'The Sustainable Livelihoods Approach: A Framework for Knowledge Integration Assessment." *Human Ecology Review 13(1):* pp90-99.(2006)

KOMBE.W.J, 'Land-use dynamics in peri-urban areas and their implications on the urban growth and form: the case of Dar es Salaam, Tanzania." *Habitat International 29(1)*: pp 113-135 (2005).

KOMBE W.J ;V. KREIBACH'Informal land management in Tanzania," *Spring Research Series no. 40*. (2000).

KOVATS.R; AKHTAR.S, 'Climate, climate change and human health in Asian cities," *Environment and Urbanisation 20(1):* pp165-176.(2008).

KRETZMANN. J.P, 'Building Communities from the Inside Out.". <URL: http://www.thecommunityconnection.org/CC_aboutpubs/14_Bldg_Co mms_InsideOut.doc>, *Accessed on 22 April 2008,* (1995).

KUHN T. S.,'The Structure of Scientific Revolutions (Second Edition," *International Encyclopedia of Unified Science 2(2),The University Of Chicago Press*, Chicago(1962).

KUMAR A.,'Housing Report - Rural mud house with pitched roof," *World Housing Encyclopedia*. <URL: http://www.world-housing.net/ where port1view.php?id=100056>, *Accessed on 22 April 2008*. (2002).

KUMAR K.,'Conducting Key Informant Interviews in Developing Countries A.I.D. Program Design and Evaluation Methodology Report No. 13," *Center for Development Information and Evaluation, A.I.D., Agency for International Development*, Washington DC. (1989).

KUNDU. A., 'Chapter 8: Tenure security, housing investment and environmental improvement: the cases of Delhi and Ahmedabad, India. Payne Geoffrey (ed.), 2002: 'Land, Rights and Innovation – Improving tenure security for the urban poor," *ITDG Publishing*, London.(2002).

KURIAKOSE.B, 'An alternative approach to housing Tsunami reconstruction project by SIFFS'< www.preventionweb.net>, *Accessed on 22 April 2008.*(2006).

KVALE S.,'The qualitative research interview: A phenomenological and a hermeneutical mode of understanding," *Journal of Phenomenological Psychology 14*: pp 171-196. (1983).

LALEYE.O.M ; AYENI. V, 'Two Issues for Contemporary Africa: Political Boundaries and Traditional Rulers," *International Journal of Politics, Culture, and Society 6(4)*: pp 555-571 (2005).

LANDIS J. D.;HEATHER H.,'The Future of Infill Housing in California: Opportunities, Potential, Feasibility and Demand, Volume One: Study Overview," *California Business, Transportation, and Housing Agency*(2005).

LANNAS. J; TURPIE.J. K, 'Valuing the Provisioning Services of Wetlands, Contrasting a Rural Wetland in Lesotho with a Peri-Urban Wetland in South Africa," *Ecology and Society 14(2)*: 18. <[Online] URL: http://www.ecologyandsociety.org/vol14/iss2/art18/>, *Accessed on 2 October 2010*. (2009:22);

LARSSON. A; SCHYLTER.A, 'Changing gender and housing conflicts," Chapter 14 in Sithole-Fundire S.A. Zhou, A. Larsson & A. Schlyter (1995)., *'Gender Research on Urbanisation, Planning and Everyday Life,"* Zimbabwe Women's Resource Centre Network: Harare. (1995).

LAWRENCE. R. J, 'Housing and health: Beyond Disciplinary Confinement," *Journal of Urban Health 83(3):* pp540-549(2006).

LE CORBUSIER 'Vers Une Architecture (Towards a New Architecture)," *NDLecorbu29*, Paris. (1923).

LENSSEN.N ; ROODMAN.M. D, 'Making better buildings," Brown LR, Flavin, C, French, H, Postel, S and Starke, L, eds. State of the World 1995, Earthscan: London.(1995).

LERISE. F. S.,'Case Method and Narratology in Practice: Studying and Reporting on Resources Management in Rural Tanzania (Draft Manuscript)," *Ardhi University*, Dar es Salaam. (2009).

LIGHT.I, 'Immigration and Ethnic Economies in Giant Cities, in Crowley, John (ed.)' *International Social Science Journal Issue 181*, Blackwell Publishing/UNESCO: Paris. (2004).

LOCATELLI. F; NUGENT. P., 'African Cities. Competing Claims on Urban Spaces," *Brill,* Leiden. (2009).

LODHI A. Y., 'African Settlements in India' *Nordic Journal of African Studies 1(1): pp83–86(1992).*

LOPEZ-MARRERO. T ; TSCHAKERT.P, 'From theory to practice: building more resilient communities in flood prone," *Environment and Urbanisation 23(1):* pp229-249.(2005)

LUPALA. A, 'The peri-urban poor as land development managers, in *id21': Insights 41*.(2011:6)

LURCCORT.R, 'Regional Visioning Public Participation - Best Practices," *Report prepared for Sustainable Pittsburgh.*< URL: http://www.sustainablepittsburgh.org/pdf/Regional_Visioning_Jan_05. pdfURL: *Accessed on 22 April 2008.* (2005).

MABALA R., 'Youth and "the hood" – livelihoods and neighbourhoods,' *Environment and Urbanisation 23(1)*: pp 157-181. (2011).

MACWAN'GI M.,'Social and physical conditions of nannies in high cost residential areas of Lusaka, Zambia," Chapter 12 in Sithole-Fundire S.A. Zhou, A. Larsson & A. Schlyter, 1995: Gender Research on Urbanisation, Planning and Everyday Life, *Zimbabwe Women's Resource Centre Network*, Harare. (1995).

MADAYI.Z, 'Land Transactions and Rent Appropriation in Peri-Urban Areas of Dar es Salaam. PowerPoint presentation for the NORAD Fellowship Network Conference held in Kampala 25th – 27th February," <URL:http://siu.no/vev.nsf/d48a0ecf27ae054dc1256f630063e8d7/708a7443a9fa2900c125700e003d93bd/$FILE/Workshop%20A%20PRESENTATION%20ON%20LAND%20TRANSACTIONS%20IN%20PERI-URBAN.ppt>, *Accessed on 22 April 2008.* (2005).

MAFICO. C.J,C, 'Urban low-income housing in Zimbabwe," *Averbury:Aldershot.(* 1991).

MAGATU. G,'Sites and Services for Low Income Housing," in *Review of Rural & Urban Planning in Southern and Eastern Africa 1/1991*. pp. 35-56. (1991).

MAGIGI. W ; MAJANI.B.B.K, 'Housing themselves in Informal Settlements: A Challenge to Community Growth Processes, Land Vulnerability and Poverty Reduction in Tanzania," *Paper presented at the 5th FIG Regional Conference, Accra, Ghana*, March 8-11, 2006 (2006);

MAHONEY, J; THELEN, K., 'Explaining institutional change: Ambiguity, agency, and power," *Cambridge, UK*, Cambridge University Press. (2009)

MALIZIA.E.E, 'City and Regional Planning: A Primer for Public Health Officials," *The Art of Health Promotion*, May/June 2005: pp 1-12.(2005).

MALPASS P. ;A. MURIE, 'Housing Policy and Practice (Section Edition," *MacMillan Education Ltd,* London. (1987).

MALPEZZI. S, 'Economic Analysis Of Housing Markets in Developing and Transition Economies," Chapter 44 Mill E.S and P. Cheshire eds. 'Handbook of Regional and Urban Economics," *Elsevier Science B.*

V(1999).S.; J. SA-AADU,'What have African housing policies wrought?," *In Real Estate Economics, Vol. 24*, <URL: http://www.questia.com/googleScholar.qst>, *Accessed on 22 April 2008.* (1996).

MANDAZA, I., ed,'Zimbabwe: The Political Economy of Transition 1980-1986," *Jongwe Press,* Harare. (1987).

MANJENGWA. J. M.,.,"'Linking environment and development, easier said than done: learning from the Zimbabwean experience," *Development Southern Africa 24(2):* pp 225-240. (2007).

MAPEDZA.E, 'Forestry policy in colonial and postcolonial Zimbabwe: continuity and change," *Journal of Historical Geography 33(4)*:pp 833-851 (2007).

MAPHOSA. F. et al. 'Zimbabwe's Development Experiences since 1980: Challenges and Prospects for the Future," OSSREA, Addis Ababa

TORRES HAROLDO DA GAMA (2008)., Social and Environmental Aspects of Peri-Urban Growth in Latin American Megacities. *Paper presented at the United Nations Expert Group Meeting on Population Distribution, Urbanisation, Internal Migration and Development, Population Division, Department of Economic and Social Affairs, United Nations Secretariat*, New York, 21-23 January 2008(2007).

MAPIRA.J, 'An Historical Perspective of the Problem of Housing and Some Attempted Solutions in the City of Mutare (1890-2002)." *Zambezia* XXXI (i/ii), *University of Zimbabwe,* Harare, pp 80-103 (2004)

MARONGWE.N, 'The Fast Track Resettlement and Urban Development Nexus: the case for Harare,' Paper Presented at the Symposium on Delivering Land and securing Rural Livelihoods: Post Independence Land Reform and Resettlement in Zimbabwe, Mont Clair, Nyanga, 26-28 March 2003. <URL: http://www.sarpn.org.za/documents/d00006 17/P624-nelson.pdf>, *Accessed on 22 April 2008.*(2003).

MARONGWE. N, 'Conflicts Over Land And Other Natural Resources In Zimbabwe," *ZERO Publications*, Harare. (2002).

MARSHALL. F, 'What does peri-urban sustainability mean in the context of Delhi?' <URL: http://stepscentre-thecrossing.blogspot.com/2008/12/what-does-peri-urban-sustainability.html*Accessed on 2April 2009.*(4 December 2008); 4 December 2008).

MARSHALL.F et al. '*On the Edge of Sustainability:* Perspectives on Peri-urban Dynamics," STEPS Working Paper 35, STEPS, Centre Brighton. (2009).

MARX.C ; CHARLTON.S, 'Urban Slums Reports: The case of Durban, South Africa," *Unpublished Report*. (2003)

MASSER. I, 'Managing our future," An *International Journal of Applied Earth Observation and Geo-information 3(4)*,(2000).

MATETE-LIEB T.,'Basotho Women's Role in Urban Housing: The Case of Maseru," Chapter 5 in Sithole-Fundire S.A. Zhou, A. Larsson & A. Schlyter, 1995, Gender Research on Urbanisation, Planning and

Everyday Life, *Zimbabwe Women's Resource Centre Network*, Harare(1995)..

MATOVU.G, 'Upgrading Urban Low-Income Settlements in Africa," *Constraints, Potentials and Policy Options. Paper presented at the Regional Roundtable on Upgrading Low-Income Settlements, Johannesburg, South Africa: October 3-5 2000.*< URL: http://www.worldbank.org/urban/upgrading/afrnd/docs/mdp_low_income_upgrading_paper_2000_final_doc.pdf, >*Accessed on 22 April 2008.(*2000).

MATTINGLY C.; LAWLOR. M,'Learning from Stories: Narrative Interviewing in Cross-cultural Research, . *Scandinavian Journal of Occupational Therapy 7(1)*: pp 1-14. (2000).

MBIBA.B, 'Urban Agriculture in Zimbabwe," *Avebury*, Aldershot.(1995).

MBIBA. B, 'Contentious development: peri-urban studies in sub-Saharan Africa,' in *Progress in Development Studies 2(2),* pp113-131 (2002).

MBIBA.B., 'Zimbabwe's Global Citizens in 'Harare North': Some preliminary observations," Palmberg Mai and Ranka Primorac eds., *Skinning The Skunk – Facing Zimbabwean Futures, Discussion Paper 30, Nordiska Afrikainstitutet*: pp 26-38.(2005).

MBIBA.B ; NDUBIWA.M, 'Decent construction and the role of local authorities: the case of Bulawayo city, Zimbabwe." *Research Report for the Urban and Peri-Urban Research Network (Peri-NET), [S.I.],* <URL: http://eprints.lse.ac.uk/3015/1/Bulawayo_report.pdf>, *Accessed on 22 April 2008.(*2006).

MBIRIRI P.,'Zones in Transition and the Pressure of Land Subdivision on Boarder Regions,": *The present criteria for decision making. Paper presented at the Zimbabwe Institute of Regional and Urban Planners (ZIRUP) Annual School*, August 1999. (1999).

MCAUSLAN. P.,'Chapter 2: Tenure and the law: the legality of illegality and the illegality of legality, in PAYNE GEOFFREY (ed.), 2002," *Land, Rights and Innovation – Improving tenure security for the urban poor, ITDG Publishing*, London. (2002).

MCAUSLIN. P.,'Urban land and shelter for the poor,' Earthscan: London. (1985).

MCCANN. P, 'Urban and regional economics," *Oxford University Press* Oxford.(2001).

MCELFISH J.M, 'Commentary: Ten Things Wrong with Sprawl," <URL: http://www.emagazine.com/view/?3641,> *Accessed on 22 April 2008.* (2008); http://www.emagazine.com/view/?3641,> *Accessed on 22 April 2008.* (2008).

MCIVOR. C., 'Do Not Look Down On Us,," Child Researchers Investigate Informal Settlements in Zimbabwe," *PLA Notes (2001), Issue 42*, pp 34–38. (2001).

MCKINNEY.M. et al. Working across Boundaries: A Framework for Regional Collaboration, in LeRoyer Ann ed. *Land Lines 16(3),* Lincoln Institute of Land Policy: Cambridge (USA).(2004)

MCLEOD. R.,'Costs associated with accessing legal shelter for low-income groups in new urban developments." *Paper prepared for Geoffrey Payne and Associates for the Regulatory Frameworks for Affordable Shelter project, May 2001.* (2001).

MENDS. T.M ; DE MEIJERE.J, 'A Study of the Institution of the Customary Land Tenure System in the Supply of Property Rights for Urban - An Example of Accra, Ghana," *Paper presented at the 5th FIG Regional Conference, Accra, Ghana: March 8-11, 2006.* <URL: www.fig.net/pub/accra/papers/ts03/ts03_01_mends_demeijere.pdf,> *Accessed on 22 April 2008.* (2006).

MENRAM (MINISTRY OF ENVIRONMENT AND NATURAL RESOURCE MANAGEMENT)., 'Zimbabwe's Fourth National Report to the Convention on Biological Diversity.' *MENRAM*, Harare. (2010).

MERRILL SAM'Environmental finance for affordable housing," *in Communities & Banging (Spring 2007).* <URL: www.bos.frb.org/ commdev/c&b/index.htm>.> pp 22-23, *Accessed on 22 April 2008.* (2007).

MHASHU F. C.,'Minister's Welcome Remarks. Proceedings of the National Symposium convened by the Ministry of National Housing and Social Amenities at Mendel Training Centre," *Harare, 28 May 2009.* (2009).

MHLAHLO.S.R, 'The impact of housing policy on housing problems in Gweru before and after independence' *The Dyke – The Journal of Midlands State University 1(1):* 107-115.(2004)).

MILBOURNE.P.,'Housing conflict and domestic property classes in rural Wales," *Environment and Planning A* 29(1), pp43–62. (1997).

MILLETT. K., DELE OLOWU ;CAMEROON. R.,'Local Governance and Poverty Reduction in Africa," *Joint Africa Institute*. (2006).

Ministry of Tourism and Hospitality Industry Stakeholder Consultation Report on Alignment of the Tourism Act [*CHAPTER 14:20*] with the Constitution (Southern Region) 18-19 November 2015(2015)

MIT, 'Just Jerusalem Competition, Jerusalem 2050," Cambridge,(2007) <http://web.mit.edu.justjerusalem/http://web.mit.edu.justjerusalem/> *Accessed on 23 August 2007.*

MITLIN D.,'Finance for housing, livelihoods and basic services.' *Environment and Urbanisation 20(1):* pp3-12. (2008).

MITLIN. D., 'Sustaining markets or poverty reduction?," *Environment and Urbanisation 14(1):* pp 173-177.(2002).

MLALAZI. A, 'Residential Development: Public and Private Sector Involvement: Some Preliminary Thoughts," *Paper presented at the ZIRUP Annual School*, Harare. (1990).

MLALAZI. E, 'Employment of Planning Graduate and Gaps:7-8 October 2010, Harare: Perspectives from the Department Of Physical Planning," *Paper presented an the Workshop On Strengthening Planning Education In Zimbabwe,* 5th October 2010 (Ref: B/2/3)9(2010).

MNHSA.,'Terms of Reference (ToRs) for the Zimbabwe Housing and Social Amenities Needs Survey," *Government of Zimbabwe*, Harare. (2009b).

MNHSA, 'An Abridged Version of the Second National Housing Convention Held from 26 to 30 October 2009," *Government of Zimbabwe*, Harare.(2009c)MNHSA, 'The Ministry's Organisational Structure - Head Office," *Government of Zimbabwe,* Harare.(2009e)

MNHSA, 'The Ministry's Organisational Structure - Provinces and Districts," *Government of Zimbabwe*, Harare.(2009f).,'A Questionnaire for the Evaluation of the 2004-2008 National Housing Delivery Programme (NDHP)," *Government of Zimbabwe* Harare. (2009g).

MNHSA, 'The Ministry of National Housing and Social Amenities Annual Report for 2009," *Government of Zimbabwe*, Harare.(2009h:2).

MNHSA, 'The Ministry's MNHSA (Ministry of National Housing and Social Amenities) (2010),Integrated Performance Agreement for the Year 2010," *Government of Zimbabwe* Harare.(2010a),

MNHSA'The Ministry of National Housing and Social Amenities Annual Report for 2010," *Government of Zimbabwe*,Harare. (2010b).

MNHSA (Ministry of National Housing and Social Amenities) '2010 to 2014 Strategic Plan," *Government of Zimbabwe*, Harare. (December 2009a).

MOBILE LIVES FORUM, 'Sustainbale mobilities in peri-urban areas," *Which lifestyles in the alter-urbain, suburban rural/citta diffusa/ Zwischenstadt? Brochure for The 2nd International Meeting of Mobile Lives Forum on January the 24th and 25th,* 2013 at the Maison Rouge, Paris 12pg 1, (2012).

MONAGHAN. J.,'People and Theory," <URL: http://ife.ens-lyon.fr/publications/edition-electronique/cerme6/plenary-02-monaghan.pdf>, *accessed on 30 April 2013*(2009).

MORRELL. K.,'Using Documentary Data,' <URL: http://www.kevinmorrell.org.uk/Analysing%20Text%20and%20Documents.pdf>, *Accessed on 13 May 2008. (2004).*

MORRIS EARL W ;WINTER M., 'Housing, Family and Society," *John Wiley and Sons,* New York. (1978).

MOUGEOT L. J.A.'Urban Agriculture: Definition, Presence, Potentials and Risks, and Policy Challenges, Cities Feeding People Series Report 31, International Development Research Centre (IDRC)." <URL: http://idl-bnc.idrc.ca/dspace/bitstream/10625/26429/12/117785.pdf.> *Accessed on 01 May 32013*(2000).

MOUKHTAR M. M..""Transformation of Vernacular Housing Pattern in Peri-urban Abuja due to Informal Urbanism, 1976-2006," *Universiti Teknologic Malaysia Institutional Repository.* (2007).

MOUTON. J.'How to succeed in your Master's and Doctoral Studies – A South African Guide and Resource Book (13th Impession*)," Van Schaik Publishers*, Pretoria.(2009).

MPCNH (MINSTRY OF PUBLIC CONSTRUCTION AND NATIONAL HOUSING)., 'The Public Sector Involvement in Housing," *A paper prepared for the Zimbabwe Institute of Regional & Urban Planners' Annual School (4-6 July, 1990,),* Harare. (1990).

MPOFU.B, 'Perpetual 'Outcasts'? Squatters in peri-urban Bulawayo, Zimbabwe," *Afrika Focus 25(2)*: pp.61(2012:61).

MUBVAMI.T; KAMETE.A.Y, 'The contributions of cooperatives to shelter development in Zimbabwe' *UNCHS-Habitat*, Nairobi. <URL: http://www.unhabitat.org/ programmes/-housingpolicy/documents/HS6 18.chm. *Accessed on 21 September 2008.(*1999).

MUBVAMI.T ; MUSANDU-NYAMAYARO.O, 'Procedural Impediments to the Low-income Housing Land Delivery in Cities of Zimbabwe," *Department of Rural and Urban Planning. University of Zimbabwe*, Harare. (1993)).

MUBVAMI TAKAWIRA,'Urban poverty, housing and municipal governance in Zimbabwe, Municipal Development Program – in MDP, undated," *Addressing poverty in the context of decentralisation in Eastern and Southern Africa – Case studies in Malawi, Uganda, Zambia and Zimbabwe, MDP Working Paper 3,* Municipal Development Programme for Sub-Saharan Africa, Harare, pp 13 – 29. (2001).

MUFEMA. E, 'Report of the Operation Garikayi/Hlalani Kule – National Audit with the framework of social accountability, NANGO," Harare.(2008).

MUGOVA, A; O.MUSANDU-NYAMAYARO'Housing urban people in Zimbabwe – A handbook of housing application procedures and building processes," *Intermediate Technology Zimbabwe*, Harare. (1998).

MUKAMURI.B, 'Indigenous knowledge, perceptions and management of climate change in South Central Zimbabwe." *Presentation in the Earth in Transition (EIT) Proceedings for the Society for Ecological Restoration International, Zaragosa, Spain on September 12, 2005,* <URL: http://www.ser.org/iprn/proceedings.asp>, *Accessed on 13 October 2011.*(2005)

MUKUKA.L, 'Factors affecting delivery of social and infrastructure services in municipalities – A case study of housing, water supply and sanitation in Bwacha Compound, Kabwe, in Municipal Development Program – MDP, undated," *Addressing poverty in the context of decentralisation in Eastern and Southern Africa – Case studies in Malawi, Uganda, Zambia and Zimbabwe: MDP Working Paper 3,* Municipal Development Programme for Sub-Saharan Africa,Harare, pp 105-128.(2001).

MULENGA. M, et al. 'Building Links for Improved Sanitation in Poor Urban Settlements," *Recommendations from Research in Southern Africa, Institute of Irrigation and Development Studies*, Southampton. (2004).

MULLER.G, 'What is a Process? Embedded Systems Institute," *Eindhoven, The Netherlands,* <URL: http://www.gaudisite.nl/WhatIsAProcess Paper.pdf>, *Accessed on 27 June 2011*.pg.1(2008)

MULWA.F.M, 'Participatory Monitoring and Evaluation of Community Projects," *Paulines Publications Africa*, Nairobi.(2008).

MUN˜IZ. I.;GALINDO. A,'Urban form and the ecological footprint of commuting - The case of Barcelona," *Ecological Economics XX*: pp1-16. (2005).

MUNHENGA. C, 'Board Fines Firm for Dumping Chemicals," The Herald, Zimpapers, Harare. (2011).

MUNYORO. D. C.,'Speech by the Permanent Secretary (MNHSA). Proceedings of the National Symposium convened by the Ministry of National Housing and Social Amenities at Mendel Training Centre," Harare, 28 May 2009. (2009).

MUNZWA. K.M, 'Housing development project financing in Zimbabwe with special focus on housing co-operatives' in Brown A and C Davidson eds. Responsive design and plan implementation, *Department of City and Regional Planning, Cardiff University*, Cardiff. (1999).

MUNZWA. K.M et al., 'Participatory Budgeting and Participatory Planning," Defining the theoretical and practical emphases in the two approaches, in *Local Governance Development Journal 1(2)*: pp 45-72.(2007).

MURERWA. H, 'Speech by The Minister of Lands and Rural Resettlement, Hon. H. M. Murerwa (MP) On Land Delivery For Housing," *Housing Convention Victoria Falls 26 – 30 October 2009* (2009).

MUROWE.S; CHIRISA.I, 'Sally Mugabe Heights: The tale of an incidental Zimbabwean peri-urban housing scheme seeking legitimation," *Zambezia XXXIII (i/ii)*: pp71-89.(2006).

MURRAY.S, 'Managing forest influences in urban and peri-urban areas." <URL:http://www.fao.org/docrep/w0312E/w0312e08.htm,> *Accessed on 27 June 2011.(*2008)

MUSANDU-NYAMAYARO.O, 'Housing Design Standards for Urban Low-income People," *Third World Review 15(4),* Liverpool University Press (1993)

MUSANDU-NYAMAYARO.. O, 'Legal Audit, Key Finding and Recommendations, Appendix5, HPZ (HOUSING PEOPLE OF ZIMBABWE) (2001).

MUSEKIWA.A, 'Low-income housing development in Harare: a historical perspective," Chapter 5 in ZINYAMA L, D TEVERA AND S CUMMING (eds.) 1993: *Harare: The Growth and Problems of the City, University of Zimbabwe,* Harare. (1993).

MUSHAMBA. S et al. 'Urban and Peri-Urban Agriculture: Prospects for Food Security and Growth in Eastern and Southern Africa," Report prepared for the Ministers' Conference on August 28-29, 2003, Sheraton Hotel – Harare - Zimbabwe. <URL: http: // www.ruaf.org/files/ ministers _conference.pdf>, *Accessed on 2 April 2007.(2003.).*

MUSHAWEVATO. P., 'Utilise idle land: Karimanzira," The Sunday Mail (November 14, 2010), *Zimpapers*,Harare (2010).

MUTANDWA. E.;N.SIGAUKE ;C. P. MUGANIWA 'Urban Women's Participation in the Construction Industry, An Analysis of Experiences from Zimbabwe," *Journal of International Women's Studies 9 (3):* pp 256-268. (2008).

MUTANGA. B, 'Housing Shortages because of Legislation, Policy and Attitude," *National Housing Convention Report (Public Private Partnership) Victoria Falls Nov. 1997,* National Housing Convention (1997).

MUTEKEDE. L.;SIGAUKE. N.,'Low income housing finance – post-independence experiences, prospects and policy implications for Zimbabwe," *Paper presented to the ENHR Conference on Sustainable Urban Areas, 25-28 June 2007, Rotterdam,* <URL: www.enhr2007rotterdam.nl>, *Accessed on 22 June 2009*. (2007).

MUTIZWA-MANGIZA N. D.,'Urban informal transport policy: the case of emergency taxis in Harare," Chapter 9 in ZINYAMA L, D TEVERA AND S CUMMING (eds.) 1993: Harare: The Growth and Problems of the City, *University of Zimbabwe,* Harare. (1993).

MUTIZWA-MANGIZA, N. D.'Post-Independence urban low-income shelter policies in Zimbabwe: A preliminary appraisal of affordability," in S. D. Romaya and G. H. Franklin (eds.), Shelter, Services and the Urban Poor ,*Cardiff, University of Wales Institute of Science and yTechnology,* pp 81-98(1985).

MUTIZWA-MANGIZA, N. D.;MARCIANO, M., 'Building Brigades and Urban Low-cost Shelter Provision in Zimbabwe: A Preliminary Evaluation,*London, International Centre for Technical Research, Paper presented at an International Conference on Urban Shelter in Developing Countries, mimeo..* (1987).

MUTIZWA-MANGIZA, N.D., 'Experience with the project approach to shelter delivery for the poor in Zimbabwe," *United Nations Centre for Human Settlements (Habitat,*), Nairobi. (1990).,

MUTONDORO, F.S. 'Housing Cooperatives, Political Symbols, and Corruption in Urban Land Governance, The Case of Zimbabwe.' Available online: <http://kubatana.net/2018/07/06/housing-cooperatives-political-symbols-corruption-urban-land-governance-case-zimbabwe/.>(2018).

MUTUTU.R, 'The Role of Housing People in Promoting Self-Help Shelter in Epworth, Upgrading Initiatives in Epworth," Brown A and C Davidson eds. 'Responsive design and plan implementation," *Department of City and Regional Planning, Cardiff University:*,Cardiff. (1999).

MUZIAMBA. M, The City of Lusaka, Zambia, 'Contentious Development: Urban and Peri-urban Transformations and Livelihoods in Africa." *Report of a Peri-NET Workshop, East and Southern Africa held at Fairview Hotel,* Nairobi, Kenya, 7-9 October 2002.(2002).

MUZONDO. I. V.;.;, BARRY. M;; D.DEWAR. ; J.WHITTAL., 'Land Conflicts in Informal Settlements," Wallacedene in Cape Town, South Africa. *Paper presented at the FIG Working Week 2004 Athens, Greece: May 22-27, 2004*(2004).

MUZVIDZIWA.V.N; ZAMBERIA.A.N, Chapter 1: Urbanisation and Development an introduction in MUZVIDZIWA VICTOR N AND AGOSTINO M ZAMBERIA (eds),'Urbanisation and Development in Swaziland," *JAN Publishing Centre*, Manzini.(2006).

MUZVIDZIWA. V.N, 'Informal Settlement Dwellers and Environmental Problems.' *UNISWA Research Journal of Agriculture, Science and Technology (Special Volume No. 1)*(2005).

MUZVIDZIWA.V.N; ZAMBERIA.A.N, 'Urbanisation and Development in Swaziland," *JAN Publishing Centre*, Manzini.(2006).

MWANAMAKONDO.B.Y, 'The state of resettlement areas in Zambia," *A paper presented at the Swedish Cooperative Centre (SCC) at the Chrismar Hotel, 27-28 February 2007*, Lusaka.pg3. (2007).

MWAURA. J.,'Integrated Urban Housing Development - Nachu Housing Credit Scheme: Huruma Informal Settlement," *Working Paper 3, DFID/ITDG.* <URL: http://www.itdg.org/docs/shelter/iuhd_wp3_nachu_housing_huruma.pdf>, *Accessed on 2 April 2007.* (2000).

MWESIGWA.D, 'Water and Sanitation in peri-urban settlements," *Paper presented at the 21st WEDC Conference with the theme:* Sustainability of Water and Sanitation Systems, held in Kampala: Uganda.(1995).

MYERS.G.A, 'Peri-Urban Land Reform, Political-Economic Reform, and Urban Political Ecology in Zanzibar." *Urban Geography*, 29 (3), pp. 264–288. <URL:http://spot.colorado.edu/~hunterlm/EnvSocReadings/ Wk3MoreTheory/MyersPoliticalEcologyZanzibar.pdf*Accessed on 2 April 2008*.(2008).

MYERS.G.A, 'Social Construction of Peri-Urban Places and Alternative Planning in Zanzibar," *African Affairs 109* (437): pp575-595.(2010).

NABUTOLA.W, 'Affordable Housing – Some Experiences from Kenya,' *Paper presented at the FIG Working Week 2004, Athens, Greece*, (May 22-27, 2004).

NATURAL HERITAGE TRUST (Australia.,)'Barriers and Enablers for Peri-Urban NRM (Peri-Urban Incentive Scheme)' (undated).

NDLOVU.S, 'Peri-urban transformation in Zimbabwe: A review of peri-urban subdivision policy and strategy with reference to Harare, 1950-2001," *Unpublished Dissertation: Department of Rural of Urban Planning, University of Zimbabwe*, Harare.(2004).

NEEDHAM. B.; ROELOF VERHAGE'Housing and Land in Israel and The Netherlands: a comparison of policies and their consequences for access to housing." *Town Planning Review 69(4), Liverpool University Press*, Liverpool, pp 397-424. (1998).

NEEFJES KOOS 'Environments and Livelihoods for Sustainability," *OXFAM GB*, London. (2000).

NELSON ARTHUR C;T.W SANCHNEZ., 'Ex-urban and suburban households: a departure for the traditional location theory?," *Journal of Housing Research 8(2)*: pp249-276(1997).

NENNO MARY K AND PAUL BROPHY eds. 'Housing and Local Government,' *International City Management Association,* Washington. (1983).

NEW BRUNSWICK.,'Private land stewardship: a guide for landowners," *New Brunswick,* Canada(undated).

NEW ZEALAND DIGITAL LIBRARY PROJECT .,.,"'Zimbabwe: Low-income housing pilot projects." <URL: http://www.greenstone.org/greenstone3/nzdl;jsessionid>, *Accessed on 4 April 2007. (undated).*

NGUYEN M. I, 'Analysing the encroachment process of informal settlements in the periurban of Ho Chi Minh City, Vietnam," *unpublished Master's thesis*, Lund University: Lund(2006).

NHEMA. F, 'Foreword. GoZ, National Environmental Policy and Strategies," *Ministry of Environment and Natural Resources Management*: Harare. (2005).

NHEMA. F, 'Speech By The Minister Of Environment And Natural Resources Management Hon. Francis Nhema (MP) At The National Housing Convention at Victoria Falls, 28 October 2009." (2009).

NKAMBWE.M, 'Problems of Data Acquisition and Information Management for Planning Peri-Urban Settlements in Botswana." *The International Archives of the Photogrammetry, Remote Sensing and Spatial Information Sciences, Vol. XXXIV, Part 6/W6*: pp 144-146. (2006).

NKWAE. B, 'Conceptual Framework for Modelling and Analysing Peri-urban Land Problems in Southern Africa. Ph.D. dissertation," *Department of Geodesy and Geomatics Engineering, Technical Report No. 235, University of New Brunswick, Fredericton, New Brunswick*, Canada, 363 pp.(2006:108) .

NNKYA.T. J, 'Why planning does not work? Land-use planning and residents rights in Tanzania," *Mkuki na Nyota Publishers*: Dar es Salaam. (2008);

NORTH, D. C., 'Institutions, institutional change and economic performance," *Cambridge University Press*, Cambridge, (1990).

NOERO.J, 'Four reasons why housing problem cannot be solved. Buchanan Chris ed." *Planning – Architectural and Planning Review for Southern Africa 135*. (1994).

NOVICEVIC. M.M et al. 'Communities of Creative Practice, Follett's Seminal Conceptualisation," *International Journal of Public Administration 30(4):* pp367-385(2007).

NSAMA.N, 'Gender Dimensions of Land Customary Inheritance under Customary Tenure in Zambia," Paper presented at the Shaping the Change XXIII FIG Congress, Munich, Germany, October 8-13, 2006. <URL: http://www.fig.net/pub/fig2006/papers/ps07/ps07_04_nsama_ 0731.pdf,> *Accessed on 27 June 2011.*(2006).

NSIAH-GYABAAH KWASI., 'Urbanisation Processes – Environmental and Health effects in Africa," *Panel Contribution to the PERN Cyberseminar on Urban Spatial Expansion*(undated).,

NUTTALL, S. 'Coherence and Consistency. *In* Hill, C. and Smith, M. (eds.)' *International Relations and the European Union, Oxford,* Oxford University Press, pp. 91–112. (2005)

NUWAGABA A.,Kampala City Uganda. Presentation in Peri-NET (Urban and Peri-urban Research Network) (2002)., 'Contentious Development: Urban and Peri-urban Transformations and Livelihoods in Africa," *Report of a Peri-NET Workshop, East and Southern Africa held at Fairview Hotel, Nairobi, Kenya, 7-9 October 2002*. (2002).

NYAMVURA T,BROWN.A, 'Epworth – an informal, unplanned and squatter settlement, Upgrading Initiatives in Epworth.' Brown A and C Davidson eds. *Responsive design and plan implementation*, Department of City and Regional Planning, Cardiff University: Cardiff. (1999.).

O'DONNELL.P.M, 'Preservation of the Spirit of Place," <URL:http://www.international.icomos.org/quebec2008/cd/toindex/77_pdf/77-hFCw-13.pdf.*Accessed on 27 June 2011.pg8.* (2008).

OAKLEY A.,'Paradigm wars: some thoughts on a personal and public trajectory," *International Journal of Social Research Methodology 2(3)*: pp 247 – 254. (1999).

ODERO.K, 'Local Authorities' Response to Restructuring," *Paper presented at the 39th ISoCaRP Congress 2003*, <URL: www.isocarp.net/Data/case_studies/252.pdfwww.isocarp.net/Data/case_studies/252.pdf>, *Accessed on 3 May 2008.*(2003).

ODUNUGA. O.V.,'Exploring spatial growth pattern of informal settlements through Agent based simulation," *Unpublished MSc Thesis, Utrecht University, Delft University of Technology, Wageningen University and the International Institute for Geo-Information Science*, The Netherlands. (2009).

OKPALA.D, N. MUTIZWA.,MOISSEV. I.,'I.,'Financing Urban Housing, United Nations Global Report on Human Settlements,' *Global Urban Development 2 (1): pp19-32..* (2006).

OLTHOF. W.,'Financial Aspects of Project Appraisal: RUP Teaching Paper No. 5," *Department of Rural and Urban Planning*, University of Zimbabwe.(1990).

OLTHOF. W.,'Urban Management in Southern and Eastern Africa – Proceedings of the 1991 Meeting held in Lilongwe," *Malawi, 7-10 October 1991.* (1991).

OPDENAKKER. R.,'Advantages and Disadvantages of Four Interview Techniques in Qualitative Research," *Forum Qualitative Sozialforschung /Forum: Qualitative Social Research* 7(4): <http://nbn-resolving.de/urn:nbn:de:0114-fqs0604118http://nbn-resolving.de/urn:nbn:de:0114-fqs0604118>, *Accessed on 24 June 2012.* (2006).

ORAM.N, 'Towns in Africa," *Oxford University Press*: London,(1965); OSCE,'*Report on Informal Settlements in Bosnia and Herzegovina,* OSCE." <URL: www.oscebih.org/documents/1467-eng.pdf >- Bosnia and Herzegovina, *Accessed on 27 June 2011.* (*Undated).*

OZAKI. R,URŠIC.M, 'What makes 'urban' urban and 'suburban' suburban? Urbanity and patterns of consumption in everyday life," *Paper presented at the Sociology of Consumption Research Network, the ESA 2005 Conference, Toruń, Poland, 9-12 September 2005.* <URL: http://www.sifo.no/files/Ozaki_Ursic.pdf,> *Accessed on 27 June 2011.* (2005).

PALYS T.,'Purposive Sampling , Given Lisa M (ed.).," *The Sage Encyclopedia of Qualitative Research Methods Vol.2,* pp.697-698. (2008).

PARKIN. S;COOMBER. R.,'Value in the Visual: On Public Injecting, Visual Methods and their Potential for Informing Policy (and Change)," *Methodological Innovations Online 4(2)*: pp 21-36(2009).

PARNELL.S PEITERSE.E, The 'Right to the City': Institutional Imperatives of a Developmental State,' *International Journal of Urban and Regional Research 34(1)*: pp.146–62. (2010:150).

PARR, J et al. 'The practice of stewardship," *Developing leadership for regional action. Denver,* CO: Alliance for Regional Stewardship: March. (2002)

PASTEUR. K, 'Tools for Sustainable Livelihoods: Policy Analysis," *Institute of Development Studies*, Brighton(2001).

PASTORIZA.D; ARINO.A, 'When Agents Become Stewards: Introducing Learning in the Stewardship Theory." <URL: http://www.iese.edu/en/files/6_40618.pdfhttp://www.iese.edu/en/files/6_40618.pdf,> *Accessed on 21 June 2008.(*2008)

PATEL D.H.; R.J. ADAMS.., (1981)., '*Chirambahuyo: A Case Study in Low Income Housing," Mambo Press,* Gweru.

PATEL. D.'Some Issues of Urbanisation and Development in Zimbabwe," *Journal of Social Development in Africa 3(2)* :pp17-31(1988).

PATEL. S, BURRA. S; D'CRUZ. C.,"'Slum/Shack Dwellers International (SDI) – foundations to treetops,," *Environment and Urbanisation 13(2):* pp 45-59.(2001).

PAYNE.G, MAJALE. M, 'The Urban Housing Manual: Making Regulatory Framework Work for the Poor," Earthscan, London. (2004).

PAYNE.G, 'Urban Land Policy Options: Titles or Rights?' *Paper presented at the World Bank Urban Forum Westfields Marriott, Virginia, USA: 03-05 April, 2000.* (2000) < URL: http:// www.worldbank.org / html/ fpd/urban/forum2000/papers/realestate.pdf*Accessed on 27 June 2011.*(2000).

PAYNE.G.,.,"'Lowering the ladder: regulatory frameworks for sustainable development,' *Development in Practice 2(2&3).* <URL: http://tom_bowen.members.beeb.net/>, *Accessed on 27 June 2011.* (2002).

PAYNE G.K., 'Urban Housing in the Third World, Leonard Hill," London. (1977).

PECK A.J.A, 'Agora," *Kingstons Limited*, Salisbury (Rhodesia). (1970).

PERI-NET, 'Contentious Development: Urban and Peri-urban Transformations and Livelihoods in Africa. Report of a Peri-NET Workshop," *East and Southern Africa held at Fairview Hotel*, Nairobi, Kenya, 7-9 October 2002. (2002).

PHELPS. N.A.,'On the edge of something big: edge-city economic development in Croydon, South London," *Town Planning Review 69(4)*: pp 441-465. (1998).

POPPER. K.,'The Poverty of Historicism,"*Routledge*, London.(1961).

POTTS. D, 'Restoring Order'? Operation Murambatsvina and the Urban Crisis in Zimbabwe. *Journal of Southern African Studies 32 (2)* : pp 273 - 291 (2006).

POWERS ANDREW AND PEER ASSOCIATES'PEEC Research Brief #2 – Stewardship Behaviour," Place-based Education Evaluation Collaborative (PEEC).' <URL: http://www.peecworks.org/PEEC/PEEC_Reports/0344F22E007EA7AB.1/PEEC%202009%20Stewardship%20Brief.pdf>, *Accessed on 27 June 2011*. (January 2009).

PRACTICAL ACTION, 'Terms of Reference for Promoting Examples of Participatory Local Empowerment Urban Planning (PEOPLE-UP)," *Practical Action*, Harare.(2011).

PU-GEC (Peri-urbanisation and Global Environmental Change) (2009)., Peri-urban Area, URL: <http://web.ntpu.edu.tw/~shuli/PUGEC_02Peri-urban.htm,> *Accessed on 27 June 2011*.pg 1(2009).

RADAELLI, C. M. ,'Europeanization, policy learning, and new modes of governance,' *Journal of Comparative Policy Analysis, 10(3), 239–254.* (2008).

RADEMACHER. A, 'When is Housing an Environmental Problem Reforming Informality in Kathmandu," *Current Anthropology 50(4)*, pp 513-533 (2009).RAKODI C.,'Housing finance for lower income urban households in Zimbabwe,' *Housing Studies 10(2):* pp199 – 227(1995a).

RAKODI. C.,'Self-help housing in Harare and Gweru. RUP Occasional Paper No 36," *Department of Rural and Urban Planning, University of Zimbabwe*,Harare. (1995b).

RAKODI.C, 'Land for Housing in African Cities: Are Informal Delivery Systems Institutionally Robust and Pro-Poor?," In *Global Urban Development Magazine 3(1)*, Global Urban Development (GUD): London. <URL: http://www.globalurban.org,> *Accessed on 27 June 2011*. (2007).

RAKODI. C;MANGIZA N.,'Housing Policy, Production and Consumption: A case study of Harare," *Department of Rural and Urban Planning, University of Zimbabwe,* Harare. (1989).

RAPOSO.I, 'Urban planning and management instruments and institutions versus socio spatial cohesion in Maputo and Luanda: resettlement or upgrading and rehabilitation of the informal peri-urban areas (land and housing issues)," '*Informality and Access to Services in Cities of Africa' Workshop in Johannesburg, School of Architecture and Planning at Wits University, South Africa,* 3-4 July 2008. (2008:3). ,2008:3).

RAY. K.,'The Challenge of Infrastructure for the Urban Poor," <URL: http://www.water2001.de/outcome/workinggroupa/6Ray.ppt>, *Accessed on 12 June 2010*. (2001).

Relief web Zimbabwe 's Urban Housing crisis(2013).

RINGELHEIM. J; DONAHUE. A.;HEDLUND. E;RUBIN. A., 'Oral History Interview Guidelines," *United States Holocaust Memorial Museum*, Washington DC. (2007).

RIVERA. R.L.K.,'Culture, gender, transport: contentious planning issues," in *Transport and Communications Bulletin for Asia and the Pacific No 26.* <URL: http://www.unescap.org/ttdw/Publications / TPTS_pubs/ bulletin76/chapter1.pdf>, *Accessed on 27 June 2011.* (2007).

RLB, 'Ruwa at a Glimpse, Report prepared to support the application of Ruwa for a Town Status (Unpublished)," Ruwa (2007).

ROGERSON. C. M.,'Globalization or informalization? African urban economies in the 1990s. Chapter 10," *Urban Challenge in Africa: Growth and Management of its Large Cities*, UNU. <URL: http://www.greenstone.org/greenstone3/nzdl>, *Accessed on 22 June 2008.* (1997).

ROHREGGER.B, 'Shifting boundaries of support, Renegotiating distance and proximity in trans-local support relations in an urban fringe area in Lilongwe City," Malawi. *Ethnic and Racial Studies, 29(6)*: pp 1153-1168. (2006:1155).

ROSNI, N.A.et. al, 'Controlling leapfrog sprawl with remote sensing and GIS application for sustainable urban planning," *International Institute for Applied Systems Analysis and Academy of Sciences Malaysia.* (2018).

ROTH. A, 'After the bubble, ghost towns across America," *The Wall Street Journal*, <URL: http:// www.galesburg.com / business / x223022858/ After-the-bubble-ghost-towns-across-America>(2008).

ROUX. N, 'Migration and Urbanisation, Towards a 10-Year Review of the Population Policy Implementation in South Africa (1998-2008)," *Department of Social Development*, Pretoria. (2009:13).

ROWNTREE. K. M et al. 'Changing Patterns of Erosion In A Peri-urban Catchment, Maseru, Lesotho, Sediment and Stream Water Quality in a Changing Environment," *Trends and Explanation (Proceedings of the Vienna Symposium, August 1991) IAHS Publ. no. 203, 1991.* (1991).

RTC,RUWA, 'Ruwa Town Council at a Glimpse as at June 2010," Ruwa. (2010).

RUBIN. M, 'Inner-city redevelopment programmes and its impact on housing and evictions. Presentation made at Refresher Course on Urbanising Africa," *the city centre revisited at Witwatersrand University, Johannesburg: 16-27 August 2010* (2010:1).

RUBY. J, 'When is a Suburb not a suburb? When it is Oak Park," *A Paper presented at the 2002 American Anthropological Association Meetings: A Work in Progress, Circulated from comments, criticisms and suggestions*, Accessed on 27 June 2011.(2002)

RUTURI S.,'Measures of Expanding and Improving the Supply of Housing Finance in Zimbabwe," *University of Derby, School of Business* (Unpublished Dissertation). (2000).

RUWA., 'Study Report. Department of Physical Planning,' Harare(1991).

RUWA, 'Ruwa Local Development – Addendum to the 1991 Study Report. Department of Physical Planning' Harare pg 2 (1997).

RWADZI. M. S.,.,"'The Problem of Housing Affordability, and its Economic and Social Effect on the City of Gweru, Zimbabwe," in *Eastern Africa Social Science Research Review 21(2)*, Michigan State University Press, pp. 39-52(2005).

SALTMAN ; FERROUSSIER-DAVIS, 'The concept of stewardship in health policy," *Bulletin of the World Health Organisation, 2000*, 78 (6): pp 732-739. (2000).

SANYAL.B;MUKHIJA.V.M, 'Institutional Pluralism and Housing Delivery - A Case of Unforeseen Conflicts in Mumbai, India."< URL: http:// archidev.org/IMG/pdf/Sanyal.pdf>, *Accessed on 5 April, 2013.* (2000).

SARAH. P., 'Doing Visual Ethnography Images, Media and Representation in Research," *Sage Publications*,London. (2001).

SASAKI H.;SUZUKI; K.IGARASHI; B.TAMBATAMBA;MULENGA. P.,'Spatial Analysis of Risk Factor of Cholera Outbreak for 2003–2004 in a Peri-urban Area of Lusaka, Zambia," *American Journal of Tropical Medicine and Hygiene 79(3),* pp. 414-421. (2008).

SATTERTHWAITE.D;TACOLI. C, 'The role of small and intermediate urban centres in regional and rural development," Paper prepared for the workshop, *Integrating Rural Development and Small Urban Centres: An Evolving Framework for Effective Regional and Local Economic Development,* March 18-19, 2003: Washington DC, World Bank/IFC Headquarters.< URL: http: / /www.worldbank.org/urban / urbanrural seminar/papers/satterthwaite-tacoli.pdf>, *Accessed on 27 June 2011.* (2003).

SAVORY.A, 'Holistic Resource Management," *Gilmour Publishing*. Harare, (1988).

SCANLAN C. L., 'The Role of Statistical Analysis in Research," <URL: http://www.umdnj.edu/idsweb>, *Accessed on 22 May 2009.* (2001).

SCHILDERMAN. T, 'Putting people at the centre of reconstruction." Chapter 1 in Lyons Michal and Theo Schilderman with Camillo Boano eds. 'Building Back Better - Delivering people-centred housing reconstruction at scale," *Practical Action Publishing Ltd/ Schumacher Centre for Technology and Development*, Warwickshire, <URL: www.practicalactionpublishing.org>, *Accessed on 27 June 2011. (*2010),

SCHLYTER A., 'Multi-Habitation: Urban Housing and Everyday Life in Chitungwiza, Zimbabwe – Research Report No 123," *Nordiska Africainstitutet,*Uppsala. (2003*).*

SCHLYTER, A.,'Housing Policy in Zambia: retrospect and prospect," *Habitat International,* 22(3), pp259 – 271. (1998).

SCHNUG.E. et al. 'Organic farming – stewardship for food security, food quality, environment and nature conservation," in Aspects of Applied Biology *79*: pp 57-62.(2006).

SCHWARZ. N., 'Cognition and communication: Judgmental biases, research methods and the logic of conversation," *Hillsdale, NJ*, Erlbaum.(1996).

SCHYLTER A.,'Approaches to women and housing in development policy," Chapter 2 in Sithole-Fundire S.A. Zhou, A. Larsson & A. Schlyter, 1995: Gender Research on Urbanisation, Planning and Everyday Life, *Zimbabwe Women's Resource Centre Network,* Harare. (1995).

SCHYLTER. A;ZHOU. A.,'Gender Research on Urbanisation, Planning, Housing and Everyday Life, Chapter 1 in Sithole-Fundire S.A. Zhou, A. Larsson & A. Schlyter, 1995," *Gender Research on Urbanisation, Planning and Everyday Life*, Zimbabwe Women's Resource Centre Network: Harare. (1995).

SEEMANN. K;MARINOVA. D, 'Understanding Connectivity of Settlements: Implications of the Power Curve," *Paper presented at the 18th World IMACS / MODSIM Congress, Cairns*, Australia 13-17 July 2009. <URL: http://mssanz.org.au/modsim09, 27 June 2011>. (2009).

SEIDMAN I., 'Chapter 6, Technique isn't everything.' *Interviewing as Qualitative Research Teachers 3 edition, College Press*, London. (2005).

SENE El HADJI 'Urban and peri-urban forests in sub-Saharan Africa," *The Sahel.* <URL: http://www.fao.org/docrep/u9300e/u9300e09.htm, 25 June 2009>. (undated).

SERT O.;P.SEEDHOUSE., 'Introduction: Conversation Analysis iIn Applied Linguistics," *Novitas-ROYAL (Research on Youth and Language) 5 (1)*: pp1-14(2011).

SEYAMA.S.S, 'Chapter 8: Urban Planning and Development, Problems and Prospects for the Future, in Muzvidziwa Victor N and Agostino M Zamberia (eds.)' *Urbanisation and Development in Swaziland,* Department of Sociology, University of Swaziland, JAN Publishing Centre Ltd (JANPC): Manzini. (2006).

SHABA L.,'Gender Analysis of the Low-income Housing Framework of Zimbabwe. Appendix 6,

HPZ (HOUSING PEOPLE OF ZIMBABWE) (2001).," *Report on the National Stakeholder Validation Workshop held on 24-25 November 2001 at the Management Training Bureau*, Harare. (2001).

SHAH. F, 'Local Financing for Rural and Peri-Urban Water Supply and Sanitation." <URL: www.protos.be/protosh2o/copy _ of _ Links-metbestanden/LocalFinRurPeriUrbWATSAN.pdf.*24 June 2011.(*2007).

SHAND, W.SHAND, W. 'Exploring Institutional change, The contribution of co-production to shaping institutions," *Working Paper December 2015.* (2015).

SHEKDAR.D.; ADUSUMILLI. U.,'Regulatory guidelines for affordable shelter – the Indian case study," *Navi*,Mumbai India(2003).

SHILDO.G, 'Housing Policy in Developing Countries," *Routledge*, London. (1990).

SHINN. C. W, 'Theory, Research and Practice," *Administrative Theory and Praxis 21*: 103-119. (1999).

SHIPLEY. R;NEWKIRK. R, Vision and visioning in planning: what do these terms really mean? *Environment and Planning: Planning and Design 2*: pp 573-579(1999).

SIETCHIPING. R, 'Prospective Slum Policies: Conceptualization and Implementation of a Proposed Informal Settlement Growth Model," *Paper presented at the Third Urban Research Symposium on "Land Development, Urban Policy and Poverty Reduction," 4-6 April 2005, Brasilia, Df, Brazil:* <URL:http://citeseerx.ist.psu.edu/viewdoc/download?doi=10.1.1.124.6877&rep=rep1&type=pdf (2005).

SIGAUKE.N, 'Improving Urban Livelihoods: Epworth Sustainable Livelihoods Benchmark Study," <URL: http://practicalaction.org/docs/region_southern_africa/Epworth_Benchmark_Study.pdf, *Accessed on 27 June 2011*.(2002:20); 'Knowledge and Information Systems (KIS) In Epworth - ITDG Southern Africa Report.,"< URL: http:// practical action.org/docs/region_southern_africa/kis.pdf, 27 June 2011.>(2002b).

SIHLONGONYANE.F, the city of Manzini, 'Contentious Development: Urban and Peri-urban Transformations and Livelihoods in Africa." *Report of a Peri-NET Workshop, East and Southern Africa held at Fairview Hotel,* Nairobi, Kenya, 7-9 October 2002.(2002).

SIMON.D, 'Urban Environments: Issues on the Peri-Urban Fringe," *Annual Review of Environment and Resources 33*: 167-185. (2008).

SITHOLE-FUNDIRE S.A.; ZHOU, A.; LARSSON ; A. SCHLYTER'Gender Research on Urbanisation, Planning and Everyday Life," *Zimbabwe Women's Resource Centre Network*, Harare. (1995).

SITHOLE-FUNDIRE SYLIVIA A.,'Gender issues amongst Dombotombo lodgers: A case study approach," Chapter 8 in Sithole-Fundire S.A. Zhou, A. Larsson & A. Schlyter, 1995: Gender Research on Urbanisation, Planning and Everyday Life,*Zimbabwe Women's Resource Centre Network*, Harare. (1995).

SIU KIN WAI M.,'Culture and Design: A New Burial Concept in a Densely Populated Metropolitan Area," *Design Issues 21(2)*: pp79-89(2005).

SIYENI. Y. M.,M.,'Expanding Water Service Delivery through Partnership between Water Utility and Small Scale Water Providers in Lusaka, Zambia," *A Case of Lusaka's Peri-Urban Areas. University essay from Linköpings universitet/Tema vatten i natur och samhälle,*< URL: http://www.essays.se/essay/4d116540c8/>, *Accessed on 14 August 2010. (2008).,*

SMALL J;WITHERICK.M, 'A Modern Dictionary of Geography,*' Third Edition, Arnold*: London.pg 23(1986).

SMITH.K, 'Stewardship of Land and Resources,' *The Housing Journal (2005)*: pp10-11. (2005).

SMITH.M, 'A Guide to Housing," *Housing Centre Trust*, London. (1981).

SNOXELL. S, 'Formalisation of Urban Markets and Street Trading – Research Project. Presentation in Peri-NET (Urban and Peri-urban Research Network) (2002).," Contentious Development: Urban and Peri-urban

Transformations and Livelihoods in Africa. *Report of a Peri-NET Workshop, East and Southern Africa held at Fairview Hotel, Nairobi, Kenya, 7-9 October 2002.* (2002).

SOLIDARITY PEACE TRUST, 'The End of a Road, 'The 2013 Elections in Zimbabwe.' *Johannesburg*, October 2013.'

SOLO.T.V, 'Financial exclusion in Latin America – or the social costs of not banking the poor," *Environment and Urbanisation 20(1)*: pp89-108.(2008).

SOLOMON L.,'Dead Space,' *National Post,* <URL: http://www.urban-renaissance.org/urbanren/index.cfm?DSP=content&ContentID=12717> , *Accessed on 13 June 2008*. (26 March 2005).

SONTAG S.,'On Photography.' Farrar, Straus and Girroux, New York. (1977).

SPALING,H ; WOOD,J, 'Greed, need or creed? Farmland ethics in rural-urban fringe,' *Land-use Policy 15(2)*:pp105-118.(1998).

SAVORY.A, 'Holistic Resource Management," *Gilmour Publishing*. Harare, (1988)Harare, (1988).

SPT, "Meltdown," 'Murambatsvina one year on,"s <URL: http://www.zimbabwesituation.com/meltdown.pdf,> *Accessed on 22 July 2009.(*2006).,2006).

STANDLEY. T.,'GIS Implementation in Developing Countries - A United Nations Perspective." <URL: http://www.gisqatar.org.qa/conf97/links/m3.html>, *Accessed on 24 July 2008*.(1997).

Statutory Instrument SI 119/2012

STASOLLA. M;GAMBA. P.,.,"'Exploiting Spatial Patterns for Informal Settlement Detection in Arid Environments Using Optical Spaceborne Data. Stilla U et al (Eds) PIA07.., *International Archives of Photogrammetry, Remote Sensing and Spatial Information Sciences, 36 (3/W49A)*: pp 31-36. (2007).

STEGGELL.C. D et al., 'The role of theory in the study of housing." *Housing and Society 28(1&2)*: pp.87-100.(1)., 'Exploring theories of human behaviour in housing research," . *Housing and Society 30(1)*: pp.3-32 (2003).

STEIN. A ;VANCE.I, 'The role of housing finance in addressing the needs of the urban poor: Lessons from Central America," *Environment and Urbanisation 20(1)*: pp13-30. (2008).

STOIAN. D.,'Making the best of two worlds: rural and peri-urban livelihood options sustained by non-timber forest products from the Bolivian Amazon,' *Paper presented at the Conference "Rural Livelihoods, Forests and Biodiversity," held in Bonn, Germany, on May 19-23, 2003.* <URL: http://www.catie.ac.cr/bancomedios/documentos%20 pdf/BONN_2003_Paper_Stoian.pdf>, *Accessed on 21 December 2008*(2003).

STOLL. L.,'Regional Collaboration: A framework for solving complex planning problems.' *The Land Tracker 6(2):* pp 1-4. (2006).

STREN.R.E, 'An Urban Problematique: The Challenge of Urbanisation for Development Assistance," *Centre for Urban and Community Studies*, Toronto. (1992).

STURGES J.E.;K.J. HANRAHAN 'Comparing telephone and face-to-face qualitative interviewing: a research note' *Qualitative Research* 4(1): pp 107-118. (2004).

SUKUMAR. G, 'Institutional potential of housing cooperatives for low-income households: The case of India," in *Habitat International 25(2)*: pp 147-174(2001).

SUNDAY MAIL.,'Serviced residential stands now lucrative investment," Harare. (29 June, 2003).

SVENDSEN. L, 'Cultivating Resilience, Urban Stewardship as a Means to Improving Health and Well-being Campbell, Lindsay; Wiesen, Anne, eds," . *Restorative commons: creating health and well-being through urban landscapes. Gen. Tech Rep. NRS-P-39.* U.S. Department of Agriculture, Forest Service, Northern Research Station: pp58-87.(2009).

SVENDSEN.E; CAMPBELL.L, 'Urban Ecological Stewardship, Understanding the Structure, Function and Network of Community-based Urban Land Management," *City and the Environment1 (1)*: pp 1-31. (2008).

SVERDLIK. F, 'Ill-health and poverty: a literature review on health in informal settlements," *Environment and Urbanisation 23(1)*: pp 123-155. (2011).

SWH, 'How do we select systems in peri-urban areas?' *Workshop on water and sanitation in peri-urban areas on the 12th of December at 10.00-15.00* (2006).

TABB.W.K, 'Marxism, Crisis Theory and the Crisis of the Early 21st Century.," <URL: http://www.networkideas.org/featart/mar2011/William_Tabb.pdf,> *Accessed on 31 March 2013.*(2011).

TACOLI. C, 'Changing rural-urban interactions in sub-Saharan Africa and their impact on livelihoods," a summary, *Working Paper Series on Rural-Urban Interactions and Livelihood Strategies (Working Paper 7), International Institute for Environment and Development (IIED)*, London.(2002).

TAWODZERA G.; L.ZANAMWE;J.CRUSH.,"The State of Food Insecurity in Harare, Zimbabwe." *Urban Food Security Series No. 13. Queen's University and AFSUN*, Kingston and Cape Town. (2012).

TAYLOR.J, 'Declining Life Support Systems: An NGO Response." *WESSA, Wildlife and Environment Society of South Africa – A Celebration of 85 Years of Caring for the Earth:* pp18-20. (2011).

TAYLOR P J,'Political Geography, World Economy, Nation State and Locality," *Longman*, Essex(1985).,

TEDDLIE C.;FEN YU., 'Mixed Methods Sampling - A Typology with Examples," *Journal of Mixed Methods Research 1(1)*: pp77-100.(2007).

TEN HAVE, P.'Conversation Analysis versus Other Approaches to Discourse. Review Essay: Robin Wooffitt (2005). Conversation Analysis and

Discourse Analysis,"A Comparative and Critical Introduction [32 paragraphs]. *Forum Qualitative Sozialforschung / Forum: Qualitative Social Research. 7(2), Art.* <http://nbn-resolving.de/urn:nbn:de:0114-fqs060239*3*, <http://nbn-resolving.de/urn:nbn:de:0114-fqs060239>, *Accessed on 12 October 2008*. (2005).

TEVERA. D.S;CHIKANDA. A, 'Urban Poverty, Livelihood Strategies and Policy Responses in Harare, Zimbabwe, The Case of Ward Three in Mbare High-density Suburb," *Geographical Journal of Zimbabwe Number 31, Geographical Association of Zimbabwe*, Harare.(2000).

TEVERA.D.S ;CHIMHOWU.A.O, 'Urban Growth, Poverty and Backyard Shanties in Harare, Zimbabwe," in *Geographical Journal of Zimbabwe Number 31, Geographical Association of Zimbabwe*. Harare.(1998).

THE BUSINESS DIARY, 'PPP key to development of Ruwa," p42. (December 2010).

THE HERALD UPDATED, 'Cabinet reshuffled 10 ministers reassigned new portfolios , Eight new appointments, 3 dropped' *Harare*, Zimpapers.(2017).

The Herald 'Zanu-PF hands over 5 000 Norton stands' *Harare,* Zimpapers. (2016).

THE HERALD, 'Government launches housing scheme," *Harare*, Zimpapers. (2014).

THE HERALD,'IDBZ unveils draft-housing policy," *Harare*, Zimpapers. (2016).

THE HERALD 'Farms and stands for women, Youths': ZANU-PF,*Harare*, Zimpapers. (2018).

THE HERALD, 'Zvimba RDC in Land Scam,' *Harare*, Zimpapers. (2017).

The Herald 'Zvimba Rural District Council CEO in the dock." *Harare*, Zimpapers(2018).

THE HERALD 'Home seekers conned in land deals," *Harare*, Zimpapers.(2017).

The Communal Lands Act

THEOBALD. D.M, 'Landscape patterns of exurban growth in the USA from 1980 to 2020." *Ecology and Society* 10(1): 32. <URL: http://www.ecologyandsociety.org/vol10/iss1/art32/,>, *Accessed on 27 July 2008* (2005)

THOMAS. D., 'Architecture and the urban environment – a vision for the new age," *Architectural Press: London* (2002).

THOMAS.S, 'Urbanisation as a driver of change," *The Arup Journal 1/2008*: pp58-66.(2008).

THORNTON.A, 'Beyond the Metropolis: Small Town Case Studies of Urban and Peri-urban Agriculture in South Africa." *Urban Forum 19(3)*: pp 243-262. (2008)

TIBAIJUKA A.K, 'Building Prosperity – Housing and Economic Development Earthscan' London. (2009); UNHABITAT,'Global report on human settlements 2009," *Planning sustainable cities*: UNHABITAT, Earthscan (2009).

TIBAIJUKAA. K, 'Report of the Fact-Finding Mission to Zimbabwe to assess the Scope and Impact of Operation Murambatsvina," *UN Habitat*, Nairobi. (2005).

THE TIMES NEWSPAPER, 'Housing land runs out." <URL: www.thetimes.co.za/www.thetimes.co.za/, Accessed on 23 July 2008.> (2008)TOFFLER. A, 'The Future Shock," *Pan Books Limited*, London.(1970).

TORIRO.P, 'Town Planning in Zimbabwe, History, Challenges and the Urban Renewal Operation Murambatsvina," Chapter 11, Maphosa France, Kraposy Kujinga and Sunungurai D Chingarande (eds.), (2007) 'Zimbabwe's Development Experiences since 1980: Challenges and Prospects for the Future," *OSSREA*, Addis Ababa.(2007).

TORIRO.P., 'The Urban Housing Question in the Context of Operation Murambatsvina and Operation Garikai/Hlalani Kuhle," *Policy Brief prepared on behalf of the African Institute for Agrarian Studies*, Harare.(2006).

TORRES.H. et.al., São Paulo Peri-Urban Dynamics: Some Social Causes and Environmental Consequences (2008:3).

TRODIN. R, 'Statement by the International Co-operative Alliance' <URL:http:// www.un.org/Conference/habitat/eng-stat/7/ica7.txt http:// www.un.org/Conference/habitat/eng-stat/7/ica7.txt>, *Accessed on 23 July 2008* (2007:1),

TURNER. A. G, 'Sampling frames and master samples,' <URL: unstats.un.org/unsd/demographic/meetings/egm/Sampling.../no_3.pdf>, *Accessed on 12 March 2013.* (1976)UMP (URBAN MANAGEMENT PROGRAMME)'Streetchildren and gangs in African cities – guidelines for local authorities (UMP Working Paper Series 18," *UNCHS (Habitat,),* Nairobi. (2000).

UNCHS.,'Financing cities for sustainable development – with reference to East Africa," *UNCHS,* Nairobi. (1997).

UNCHS (HABITAT)'An Urbanising World: Global Report on Human Settlements," *Oxford University Press,* United Kingdom. (1996).

UNCHS, 'Proceedings of the International Conference on Urban Poverty, 9 – 13 November 1997," *Florence, Italy. UNCHS*, Nairobi. (1998).

UNCHS, '*The state of the world's cities 2001,"* United Nations Centre for Human Settlements (Habitat), Nairobi(2001).

UNDP, 'Human Development Report 2007/2008 – Fighting climate change: human solidarity in a divided world,' *Palgrave Macmillan*: New York.(2007).

UNFPA, 'State of World Population 2007."*Unleashing the Potential of Urban Growth.* UNFPA: New York. (2007).

UNHABITAT 'Informal settlements upgrading- The demanding for capacity building in six pilot cities," *UNHCS,* Nairobi. (1999).

UNHABITAT., 'The Challenge of the Slums: Global Report on Human Settlements," *UNHABITAT*, Nairobi. (2003).

UNHABITAT ., 'Financing urban shelter: global report on human settlements," *UNHABITAT*, Nairobi. (2005).

UNHABITAT.,'United Nations Human Settlements Programme, Annual Report," *UNHABITAT*, Nairobi. (2005).

UNHABITAT.,'Situation Analysis of Informal Settlements in Addis Ababa, Cities without Slums Sub-Regional Programme for Eastern and Southern Africa," *Addis Ababa Slum Upgrading Programme, United Nations Human Settlements Programme (UNHABITAT,)*, Nairobi. <URL: www.unhabitat.org>(2007a).

UNHABITAT 'What are slums and why do they exist? (Secretary General's visit to Kibera, Nairobi 30-31 January,2007)'<URL: http://www. unhabitat.org/downloads/docs/Press_SG_visit_Kibera07/SG%2013.pdf >, *Accessed on 22 April 2008.* (2007b).

UNHABITAT, '*The state of African cities 2008: A framework for addressing urban challenges in Africa,"* UNHABITAT: Nairobi.(2008).

UNHABITAT, 'Global report on human settlements 2009*, " Planning sustainable cities*: UNHABITAT, Earthscan (2009).

UNHABITAT.,'Solid Waste Management in the World's Cities – Water and Sanitation in the World's Cities 2010," *Earthscan*, London. (2010).

VAKIL A. C,'Housing Co-operatives in Zimbabwe: A contribution to women's shelter and development," *Journal of Social Development in Africa 9(1),* pp 7-17. (1994).

VENTEGODT SØREN, JOAV MERRICK.; NIELS JØRGEN ANDERSEN.,'Measurement of Quality of Life V: How to Use the SEQOL, QOL5, QOL1, and Other Global and Generic Questionnaires for Research," *The Scientific World Journal (2003):* pp 1002-1014. (2003).

VESTBRO. D. U.,.,"'House types to combat urban sprawl in African cities, in Volvo Environment Prize Seminar, 12 November 2004," on Environmental Aspects of Urbanisation. (2004).

VUKOVIC. H, 'Concepts of quality urban environment and sustainability," in Brown Alison and Celia Davison, eds. Responsive Design and Plan Implementation in Zimbabwe, *Workshop Proceedings 29 March to 1st of April 1999, Department of Rural and Urban Planning, University of Zimbabwe and Department of City and Regional Planning*, Cardiff University (1999).

WACKERNAGEL.M ;WILLIAM.R, 'Our Ecological Footprint,," *New Society Publishers*, Gabriola Island, BC.(1996).

Walt. G, 'Health Policy – an introduction to process and power," *Zed Books. London.*(1994).

WAMPLER B.,'Participatory Budgeting in Brazil: Contestation, Cooperation and Accountability," *Pennsylvania University Press*,Pennsylvania. (2007).,

WAPWERA, S., EGBU, C. 'Planning Authorities: A Review of Roles, Functions and Responsibilities in Jos Metropolis, Nigeria," *School of the Built*

Environment, University of Salford, Greater Manchester, United Kingdom (2013).

WARD.P. M; PETERS.P. A, 'Self-help housing and informal homesteading in peri-urban America: Settlement identification using digital imagery and GIS,." *Habitat InternationalHabitat International 31(231(2)*, pp205-218 (2007:16).

WEBSTER. D, 'On the Edge: Shaping the Future of Peri-urban East Asia," *Asia/Pacific Research Center*, <URL: http://APARC.stanford.edu>, *Accessed on 22 April 2008*.pg 6(2002)

WEICHER J. C.,'Urban housing programs: what is the question?," *Cato Journal, 2(2),* pp 411-436(1982).

WEINER. D ; HARRIS.T, 'Community-integrated GIS for Land Reform in South Africa," *URISA Journal 15*: pp 62-73. (2003).

WEKWETE.K.H, 'The case for an Urban Development Corporation in Zimbabwe – a preliminary assessment," *Department of Rural and Urban Planning, University of Zimbabwe*, Harare. (1987).

WEKWETE.K.H., 'Rural Growth Points in Zimbabwe – prospects for the future,' *Journal of Social Development in Africa 3(2)*: pp 45-57. (1988).

WEKWETE.K.H, 'New Directions for Urban Development and Management in Zimbabwe in Rapidly Urbanising Countries," The Case of Zimbabwe. *Habitat International 16(2)* pp53-63(1992).

WEKWETE.K. H., 'Urbanisation,*Southern and Eastern Africa*, Avebury, Belmont. (1994).

WEKWETE K. H.,'CO RAMBANEPASI (eds.) '*Planning Urban Economies in Southern and Eastern Africa," Avebury,* Belmont. (1994).

WHITEA.L, 'Who speaks for future generations?," *Business for Social Responsibility* (BSR),< URL: www.bsr.org>(2007)www.bsr.org> (2007).

WHITELAW.G., 'The Role of Environmental Movement Organisations in Land-use Planning, : Case Studies of the Niagara Escarpment and Oak Ridges Moraine Processes." *Unpublished PhD Thesis: Waterloo University*, Ontario.(2007).

WILKINSON, P.,'Housing policy in South Africa," *Habitat International, 22(3)*: pp 215 – 229. (1998).

WILLIAMS.B.L;MAGSUMBOL.M.S, 'Perceptions toward Stewardship among Residents Living Near U.S. Department of Energy Nuclear Facilities." *Environment, Development and Sustainability:* pp 49-78. (2006).

WILLIAMS. C.C.; ROUND. J, 'Re-theorising the Nature of Informal Employment: Some Lessons from Ukraine," in *International Sociology 23(3):* pp367-388 (2008).

WILLIAM. M.,'Interpretivism and Generalisation,' *Sociology 34(2)*: pp 209-224(2000).

WILMERSDORF.E, 'Spatio-Temporal GIS-Design For Real-Time Processes," *Geographia Technica, 2*,(2010).

WISSEN-HAYEK et al. 'Measuring and assessing urban sprawl: What are the remaining options for future settlement development in Switzerland for

2030?' – *Applied Spatial Analysis and Policy 4(4)*(2011) pp 249-279.(AOKI. P.M., 2011)'Conversation Analysis and the User Experience,' <URL: http://arxiv.org/ftp/cs/papers/0405/0405109.pdf>(2003).

WOOLCOCK. G;GLEESON. B.,'Child-Friendly Cities: Critically Exploring the Evidence Base of a Resurgent Agenda," *Urban Research Program,* Griffith University. (undated).

WORLD BANK, 'Voices of the Poor: Can anyone hear us?," *Oxford University Press*: New York. (2000:51)

WORLD BANK, 'In Search Of Land and Housing in the New South Africa," *The Case of Ethembalethu* <URL: www.worldbank.org/southafrica> (2004).

WORLD BANK , Brazil: 'Toward a More Inclusive and Participatory Budget in Porto Allegre Volume 1: Main Report," *World Bank*, Washington DC., (2008).

WROE. M;DONEY. M. (eds.)., '*Developments 42*, Department for International Development (DFID)," <URL: www.developments.org.uk>, *Accessed on 15 November 2008*. (2008).

WVI (WORLD VISION INTERNATIONAL) 'Participatory Processes in the Community, WVI Evaluation Department Module," *World Vision International*(2002).

YEBOAH. I.E, 'Housing the Urban Poor in Twenty-First Century Sub-Saharan Africa," Policy Mismatch and a Way Forward for Ghana, in *GeoJournal 62(1-2)*: pp 147-161 (2005).

YINGER. J, 'Housing and Commuting,' *The Theory of Urban Residential Structure*, an e-book(2005)',"(1994).

YOUNG C.,'True Stewardship," *Brownfields: AG News for America.* <URL: www.brownfieldagnews.com/>, *Accessed on 4 August 2007*. (2007).

ZANU-PF (ZIMBABWE AFRICAN NATIONAL UNION (PATRIOTIC FRONT)) 'Rebuilding Zimbabwe: Achievements, Problems and Prospects – at 5 years of independence," *Jongwe Press*, Harare. (1985),

ZILLER. A, 'The role of planning in community building," *Unpublished Doctor of Philosophy Degree Thesis, Faculty of Architecture*, University of Sydney: Sydney, (2004).

ZIMBABWE ECONOMIC POLICY ANALYSIS AND RESEARCH UNIT , 'Strengthening the Zimbabwe National Policy Making Process." (2012)

Zimbabwe National Housing Policy 2012

Zimbabwe Economic Policy Analysis and Research Unit, *Strengthening the Zimbabwe National Policy Making Process*. (2012)

Zimbabwe Agenda for Sustainable Socio-Economic Transformation (Zim Asset) *"Towards an Empowered Society and a Growing Economy"* October *2013- December 2018*

Zimbabwe Climate change Policy, April 2016

ZIMSTAT, 'Census 2012 – Preliminary Report," *ZIMSTAT*, Harare. (2012).

ZINDOGA.S, 'Need For More Urban Housing In Southern Africa," *Southern African News Features.* (1999)URL: <http://www.sardc.net/Editorial/

sanf / 1999 /10/15-10-1999nf3.htmhttp://www.sardc.net/Editorial/sanf/ 1999/10/15-10-1999-nf3.htm,> *Accessed on 22 April 2008*.(1999).

ZINGONI. E et al., 'Effects of a semi-formal urban settlement on groundwater quality: Epworth (Zimbabwe)," Case study and groundwater quality zoning. *Physics and Chemistry of the Earth, Parts A/B/C 30 (11-16),* pp 680-688 (2005).

ZINS CHAIM .,'Conceptual Approaches for Defining Data, Information, and Knowledge,' *Journal of the American Society for Information Science and Technology 58(4)*: pp 479-493. (2007).

ZINYAMA L, D TEVERA.; S. CUMMING (eds.) 1993, Harare, 'The Growth and Problems of the City," *University of Zimbabwe,* Harare. (1993).

ZORICH. D.M, 'Defining stewardship in the digital age, in First Monday 12(7)' <URL : http://firstmonday.org/issues/issue_7 / zorich/index.htmlhttp:// firstmonday.org/issues/issue_7/zorich/index.html>, *Accessed on 2 August 2007.* (2007).

2018 ZANU-PF Election Manifesto.

www.ingramcontent.com/pod-product-compliance
Lightning Source LLC
LaVergne TN
LVHW010533300926
849162LV00016B/1873/J
* 9 7 8 1 6 8 0 5 3 1 9 7 8 *